W9-DJK-114

The King James Bible after 400 Years

2011 marks the 400th anniversary of the King James version of the Bible. No other book has been as vital to the development of English writing or indeed to the English language itself. This major collection of essays is the most complete one-volume exploration of the King James Bible and its influence to date. The chapters are written by leading scholars from a range of disciplines, who examine the creation of the King James Bible as a work of translation and as a linguistic and literary accomplishment. They consider how it differed from the Bible versions which preceded it, and assess its broad cultural impact and precise literary influence over the centuries of writing which followed, in English and American literature, until today. The story will fascinate readers who approach the King James Bible from the perspectives of literary, linguistic, religious, or cultural history.

Hannibal Hamlin is Associate Professor of English at The Ohio State University. He is the author of *Psalm Culture and Early Modern English Literature* (Cambridge, 2004), the co-editor of *The Sidney Psalter: The Psalms of Sir Philip and Mary Sidney* (2009), and has written numerous articles and reviews on Shakespeare, Donne, Milton, and Renaissance literature.

Norman W. Jones is Associate Professor of English at The Ohio State University. He is the author of *Gay and Lesbian Historical Fiction: Sexual Mystery and Post-Secular Narrative* (2007), and has had essays and reviews published in *American Literature, Modern Fiction Studies,* and *Christianity & Literature.*

The King James Bible after 400 Years

Literary, Linguistic, and Cultural Influences

EDITED BY

Hannibal Hamlin
and
Norman W. Jones

CABRINI COLLEGE LIBRARY
610 KING OF PRUSSIA ROAD
RADNOR, PA 19087

CAMBRIDGE
UNIVERSITY PRESS

653083446

CAMBRIDGE UNIVERSITY PRESS
Cambridge, New York, Melbourne, Madrid, Cape Town, Singapore,
São Paulo, Delhi, Tokyo, Mexico City

Cambridge University Press
The Edinburgh Building, Cambridge CB2 8RU, UK

Published in the United States of America by Cambridge University Press, New York

www.cambridge.org
Information on this title: www.cambridge.org/9780521768276

© Cambridge University Press 2010

This publication is in copyright. Subject to statutory exception
and to the provisions of relevant collective licensing agreements,
no reproduction of any part may take place without the written
permission of Cambridge University Press.

First published 2010
3rd Printing 2011

Printed in the United States of America

A catalogue record for this publication is available from the British Library

Library of Congress Cataloguing in Publication data
The King James Bible after four hundred years : literary, linguistic, and cultural influences /
edited by Hannibal Hamlin, Norman W. Jones.
     p.   cm.
Includes bibliographical references and indexes.
ISBN 978-0-521-76827-6
1. Bible. English. Authorized–History.   2. Bible. English. Authorized–Influence.
I. Hamlin, Hannibal.   II. Jones, Norman W.
BS186.K56   2010
220.5′2038–dc22
2010034943

ISBN 978-0-521-76827-6 Hardback

Cambridge University Press has no responsibility for the persistence or
accuracy of URLs for external or third-party internet websites referred to in
this publication, and does not guarantee that any content on such websites is,
or will remain, accurate or appropriate.

Contents

Figures

Illustrations

Contributors

Robert Alter, Class of 1937 Professor of Hebrew and Comparative Literature, University of California, Berkeley. Author of *The World of Biblical Literature* (1992), *Canon and Creativity: Modern Writing and the Authority of Scripture* (2000), and *Pen of Iron: American Prose and the King James Bible* (2010); translator of and commentator on *The David Story* (2000), *The Five Books of Moses* (2004), and *The Book of Psalms* (2007); co-editor of *The Literary Guide to the Bible* (1990).

Katherine Clay Bassard, Professor of English, Virginia Commonwealth University. Author of *Spiritual Interrogations: Culture, Gender and Community in Early African American Women's Writing* (1999) and *Transforming Scriptures: African American Women Writers and the Bible* (2010).

Paul C. Gutjahr, Associate Professor of English and Adjunct Associate Professor of American Studies and Religious Studies, Indiana University. Author of *An American Bible: A History of the Good Book in the United States, 1777–1880* (1999) and *Charles Hodge: Guardian of American Orthodoxy* (2011); editor of *American Popular Literature of the Nineteenth Century* (2001).

Hannibal Hamlin, Associate Professor of English, The Ohio State University. Author of *Psalm Culture and Early Modern English Literature* (2004); co-editor of *The Sidney Psalter: The Psalms of Sir Philip and Mary Sidney* (2009); editor of the journal *Reformation*.

Norman W. Jones, Associate Professor of English, The Ohio State University. Author of *Gay and Lesbian Historical Fiction: Sexual Mystery and Post-Secular Narrative* (2007).

Gergely Juhász, Assistant Professor at Lessius University College and an Affiliated Researcher at the K.U. Leuven, also teaches at the Kairos Program of Rolduc Roman Catholic Seminary (Diocese of Roermond, Netherlands). Author of articles on New Testament exegesis, eschatological expectations

in the Bible, biblical anthropology, reformation theology, biblical translations, ecumenical perspectives (especially Anglican–Roman Catholic relations), and translation studies.

John N. King, Distinguished University Professor of English and Religious
Studies, The Ohio State University. Author of *English Reformation
Literature: The Tudor Origins of the Protestant Tradition* (1982), *Tudor
Royal Iconography: Literature and Art in an Age of Religious Crisis* (1989),
Spenser's Poetry and the Reformation Tradition (1990), *Milton and Religious
Controversy: Satire and Polemic in* Paradise Lost (2000), and *Foxe's* Book of
Martyrs *and Early Modern Print Culture* (2006).

Adam Potkay, William R. Kenan, Jr., Professor of the Humanities and
English, The College of William and Mary. Author of *The Story of Joy from
the Bible to Late Romanticism* (2007), *The Passion for Happiness: Samuel
Johnson and David Hume* (2000), and *The Fate of Eloquence in the Age
of Hume* (1994); co-editor of *Black Atlantic Writers of the Eighteenth
Century: Living the New Exodus in England and the Americas.*

Aaron T. Pratt, Ph.D. student at Yale University, M.A. in English, The Ohio
State University, 2010. Research focuses on sixteenth- and seventeenth-
century polemical literature, especially works by John Bale and Gerrard
Winstanley; biblical exegesis; and the history of the English book trade.

Stephen Prickett, Regius Professor Emeritus of English Language and
Literature, University of Glasgow, and Honorary Professor, University
of Kent at Canterbury. Author of *Words and the Word: Language, Poetics
and Biblical Interpretation* (1986), *Origins of Narrative: The Romantic
Appropriation of the Bible* (1996); co-author of *The Bible* for Cambridge
University Press's Landmarks of World Literature Series (1991); editor of
Reading the Text: Biblical Criticism and Literary Theory (1991), co-editor
of *The King James Bible* for Oxford World's Classics (1997), and co-editor
of *The Bible and Literature: A Reader* (1999).

Isabel Rivers, Professor of Eighteenth-Century English Literature
and Culture, Queen Mary, University of London and Co-Director, Dr.
Williams's Centre for Dissenting Studies. Author of *Reason, Grace, and
Sentiment: A Study of the Language of Religion and Ethics in England,
1660–1780*, 2 vols. (1991–2000); editor of *Books and their Readers*

in Eighteenth-Century England, 2 vols. (1982 and 2001); co-editor of *Dissenting Praise: Religious Dissent and the Hymn in England and Wales* (2011).

Jason P. Rosenblatt, Professor of English, Georgetown University. Author of *Torah and Law in* Paradise Lost (1994) and *Renaissance England's Chief Rabbi: John Selden* (2006); co-editor of *Not in Heaven: Coherence and Complexity in Biblical Narrative* (1991) and editor of *Milton's Selected Poetry and Prose* (Norton Critical Edition, 2010).

R. S. Sugirtharajah, Professor of Biblical Hermeneutics, University of Birmingham. Author of *The Bible and the Third World: Precolonial, Colonial and Postcolonial Encounters* (2001), *Postcolonial Criticism and Biblical Interpretation* (2002), *Postcolonial Reconfigurations: An Alternative Way of Reading the Bible and Doing Theology* (2003), *The Bible and Empire: Postcolonial Explorations* (2005), and *Troublesome Texts: The Bible in Colonial and Contemporary Culture* (2008); editor of *Voices from the Margins: Interpreting the Bible from the Third World* (1991, 1995, 2006).

Heather Walton, Head of Theology and Religious Studies and Director of the Center for Literature, Theology, and the Arts, University of Glasgow. Author of *Literature, Theology and Feminism* (2007) and *Imagining Theology: Women, Writing and God* (2007); co-author of *Theological Reflections: Methods* (2005); editor of *Literature and Theology: New Interdisciplinary Spaces* (2010).

Michael Wheeler, Visiting Professor of English, University of Southampton, founding Director of the Ruskin Programme at Lancaster University. Author of *The Art of Allusion in Victorian Fiction* (1979), *English Fiction of the Victorian Period, 1830–1890* (1985), *Death and the Future Life in Victorian Literature and Theology* (1990), *Ruskin's God* (1999), and *The Old Enemies: Catholic and Protestant in Nineteenth-Century English Culture* (2006).

James Wood, Professor of the Practice of Literary Criticism, Harvard University. Author of *The Broken Estate: Essays in Literature and Belief* (1999), *The Book Against God* (2003), *The Irresponsible Self: On Laughter and the Novel* (2004), and *How Fiction Works* (2008).

Acknowledgments

The editors would like to thank their Ohio State colleague Richard Dutton, who first drew attention to the upcoming 400th anniversary of the King James Bible. We reap what he sowed. David Daniell and David Norton were highly supportive of this project from its inception; the influence of their work can be seen throughout the book. At Cambridge University Press, Sarah Stanton and Rebecca Jones shepherded the project and patiently assisted at many points. Anna Oxbury copyedited the volume with expert care. Hannibal Hamlin is grateful, as always, for the keen editorial eye and organizational sense of Cori Martin. Norman Jones greatly appreciates the support and encouragement of Heidi Jones.

Introduction

The King James Bible and its reception history

HANNIBAL HAMLIN AND NORMAN W. JONES

The story of the King James Bible (KJB) – or the Authorized Version (AV) – is, as its multiple names suggest, not one but many stories. To begin with, its creation entailed many different stories. It was the work not of one translator but of several groups or "companies" of translators[1] whose charge was not to produce their own original translation but rather to cull from and revise the work of earlier English translations of the Bible. The end result was the product of a collective effort not only of the various individuals who made up each company of translators, and the different companies (each assigned to particular sections of the Bible), but also the amalgamated efforts of prior English translators dating back over roughly a hundred years before the 1611 KJB was first published. In addition, this transhistorical translation story itself originated in the court of James I, which involved a still more complex tale about the intimate relationship between politics and religion in Jacobean England.

Yet these are just the beginning of a vastly more complicated and multi-faceted story – indeed, a collection of interrelated stories – of how, over the course of the past four centuries, the KJB became the most popular and influential translation of the Bible among English-speaking peoples. Indeed, it became the single most influential book in the English language and arguably the greatest work ever produced by a committee. This larger story – the reception history of the KJB – is a story that comprises not only different individuals but also different peoples, countries, and historical eras. It is a story so complex that it is best told not by one voice but by many. That is why we created *The King James Bible after 400 Years*. Bringing together leading scholars from a wide range of different fields of study relating to the KJB and its influence, this book offers new insights intended to spark new kinds of conversations about the many different roles the KJB has played since 1611.

Yet even a volume that provides as many different perspectives as this one attempts to do must necessarily leave parts of the story untold. Indeed, this inevitable incompleteness forms part of an implicit argument that runs throughout the various chapters in this book, uniting them in their very heterogeneity: the story of the KJB is large, multifaceted, and multiform. Nevertheless, *The King James Bible after 400 Years* is the most complete one-volume exploration of the story of the KJB and its influence to date, and it is designed as an introduction to some of the different fields of study currently contributing to the ongoing development of our understanding of the KJB and its reception history. Each chapter exemplifies a broader field of study in relation to the KJB, such as literary history, women's studies, the history of the book, translation studies, African American studies, postcolonial studies, and the history of Christianity.

Of course, the extraordinary range of the KJB's influence over the past four centuries extends far beyond the confines of scholarly research and debate. As such, *The King James Bible after 400 Years* addresses not only scholars but a wider audience, as well. This introduction is designed particularly for the non-specialist – and it is worth noting that no one person is a specialist in all of the many fields explored in this volume. The introduction offers an overview of the KJB and its reception history, as well as some underlying theoretical issues, that will help frame the ensuing chapters in terms of their larger contexts.

The specialist and non-specialist alike will also find useful resources for further exploration in the chronologies and bibliography with which this book concludes, as well as in the footnotes that accompany each chapter. The bibliography focuses on major works relating to the KJB; the footnotes offer a more varied range of sources relating to each chapter's specific topic. All of these resources emphasize how large and complex the story of the KJB is and that it cannot be contained, let alone exhausted, in a single volume – even one that speaks in as many different voices as this one does. *The King James Bible after 400 Years* is thus meant to spark further exploration, to invite more voices to join in the telling of this story.

The background and creation of the KJB

The story of the KJB and its Reformation predecessors has been told many times, for both scholarly and popular readers. Although there were some earlier translations of individual books, the history of the English Bible properly begins with John Wyclif in the late fourteenth century. Wyclif and his anti-establishment followers, the Lollards, aimed to make the Bible available to ordinary Christians in a language they understood. The large number of manuscript copies that survive testify to the success of this movement, despite the official legislation against all Bible translation in the 1409 Constitutions of Archbishop Arundel. In the Reformation period, William Tyndale sought to follow the model of Martin Luther and produce a scholarly translation of the Bible into English from the original languages (as opposed to translating from the Latin Vulgate). Tyndale's goal, like Wyclif's, had a political component; Tyndale shared the dream of Erasmus that "the husbandman might sing parts of [the Bible] at his plow, that the weaver may warble them at his shuttle, that the traveler may with their narratives beguile the weariness of the way."[2] Bible translation was still illegal and heretical in England, however, so Tyndale was forced to work abroad. Before his death, and in the face of considerable obstacles, he managed to finish translations of the New Testament (Cologne 1525, Worms 1526, Antwerp 1534), the Pentateuch (Antwerp 1530), Jonah (Antwerp 1531), and the historical books from Joshua to 2 Chronicles (unpublished at his death). Tyndale was strangled as a heretic in 1536 and his body was burned (as Wyclif's had been in 1428, his body exhumed for that purpose forty-four years after his death). Bible translation was serious business.

The obvious proof of the quality of Tyndale's translations, both in their accuracy to the Hebrew and Greek originals and in the strength of their prose style, is the retention of so much of his language in subsequent translations. According to David Katz, in the portions of the KJB that Tyndale translated the text remains about 90 percent "verbatim Tyndale";[3] this is a liberal estimate, and such tallies are bound to vary (as Gergely Juhász argues in ch. 4), but it is clear to anyone who reads Tyndale's translations alongside later ones that he established a model which was followed remarkably closely until the twentieth century. Simply put, he got a lot of it right, and what wasn't broken, later scholars saw no need to fix.

The first complete English Bible (Antwerp 1535) was the work of Miles Coverdale and was translated not from the original languages but from Latin and German. Despite his lack of expertise in Hebrew, Coverdale also influenced subsequent English Bibles, especially in the poetical books, like the Psalms, which Tyndale hadn't translated. For whatever reason, Coverdale had a knack for capturing, at secondhand, the distinctive parallelistic patterns that define ancient Hebrew poetry. Subsequently, in 1537, the "Matthew" Bible was published (again in Antwerp), which, despite its ascription to one "Thomas Matthew," was actually the work of John Rogers, who took all of Tyndale's translations, including those unpublished at his death, filled in the rest of the Bible with Coverdale's 1535 text, and introduced some revisions of his own. By this time, Henry VIII, with the prodding of Thomas Cranmer and Thomas Cromwell, had come round to reconsidering his position on the idea of a vernacular Bible, and he thus commissioned an official new translation from Miles Coverdale. The Great Bible, so called for its massive size, was published in London in 1539, and reflected Coverdale's thorough revision of Rogers's "Matthew" text. The Great Bible was officially authorized (as the KJB, despite its alternative popular title, never actually was), and it was required to be used and made available to the public in all churches. Henry's 1541 proclamation decreed that, "in al and synguler paryshe churches, there shuld be provided by a certen day nowe expired, at the costes of the curates and paryshioners, Bybles conteynynge the olde and newe Testament, in the Englyshe tounge, to be fyxed and set up openlye in every of the sayd paryshe churches."[4] To encourage the sale of the Great Bible, Henry also fixed its cost at ten shillings, unbound. The translation had a relatively short life, however, since Queen Mary banned the English Bible between 1553 and 1558, and new translations became available early in the reign of Elizabeth I. Nevertheless, Coverdale's Great Bible Psalms became perhaps the best known Psalms version over the next half millennium, since they were eventually incorporated into the English Book of Common Prayer. It is these Psalms, for instance, that (along with the metrical versions of Philip and Mary Sidney) shaped the poems of George Herbert, and they have been heard since the Restoration (1660) by millions of English-speaking Christians set to the harmonies of Anglican chant.[5]

During the reign of Mary, English Protestant exiles in Geneva were busy translating the Bible. The Geneva of John Calvin and Theodore Beza was a hotbed of Bible translation and printing, producing important editions and translations in French (Pierre Robert Olivétan, revised, among others), Italian, Spanish, and Latin (a re-edited Vulgate as well as the "Protestant Vulgate" by Immanuel Tremellius and Franciscus Junius) as well as English. Though the KJB is the most famous translation-by-committee in English, the Geneva was the first, and the scholarship of its committee members was impressive. Supervised by William Whittingham, who completed an

Oxford MA and further studies on the continent, the known members of the team (no complete list survives) included Anthony Gilby (Cambridge MA and noted linguist), Christopher Goodman (Lady Margaret Professor of Divinity at Christ Church, Oxford), Thomas Sampson (Cambridge MA and Dean of Chichester), and Miles Coverdale, at this point the grand old man of English Bible translation. Other contributors may have included the Scots firebrand John Knox and John Bodley, father of Thomas, the founder of the Bodleian Library. The title page of the 1560 Geneva Bible announced that it was "translated according to the Ebrue and Greke, and conferred with the best translations in diverse languages." It represented the state of the art of English (and continental) biblical scholarship, and was recognized as such. It also represented the state of the art in Bible printing, introducing into English important innovations of the Genevan translators and printers. For instance, the Geneva was the first Bible set in Roman type as opposed to the traditional Black Letter, which corresponded with Genevan Bibles in other languages. More significantly, following French models, the Geneva was the first complete English Bible to include both chapter and verse divisions; without it, English Bible readers could never have referred to the idiomatic "chapter and verse." The Geneva title page also advertized that it included "moste profitable annotations upon all the hard places, and other things of great importance." This was a Bible designed for the general reader, the original of the many "Study Bibles" currently on the market. As the preface (perhaps by Whittingham) explained these annotations, "I have endeavored so to profit all therby, that both the learned and others might be holpen."[6] Given that the Geneva Bible was also printed in inexpensive quarto or smaller editions, it is no wonder that it became the English Bible of choice for the next century.

The Bishops' Bible of 1568 was the work of another team of translators, under the direction of Archbishop Matthew Parker. Despite its popularity, the Geneva Bible was never officially adopted by either the Church or the Crown; its Genevan Protestantism was too radical for the *via media* of the English Church establishment. The Bishops', conceived as a revision of the authorized Great Bible, was an attempt to produce an English Bible more under the control of the Church authorities, a large proportion of whom had never been comfortable with the idea of an English Bible at all. The Bishops' Bible was physically impressive, printed in a massive folio with beautiful engraved illustrations. It was the Bible read in English churches between 1568 and the appearance of the KJB in 1611.[7] It was never popular, however, and was continuously out-sold, and out-read, by the Geneva. Furthermore, it was to the Geneva Bible that writers like Spenser, Marlowe, and Shakespeare alluded most often, though words and phrases from the Bishops' also appear, presumably lodged in their ears after hearing them in church, which everyone was required to attend by law.[8] The last major Bible translation before the KJB in 1611 was the Rheims New Testament, published in 1582, the work of English Catholic scholars in exile in France. Recognizing that the movement to vernacular Bible translation was irresistible, English Roman Catholics decided to make available an English translation that still essentially reflected the Latin Vulgate sanctioned by Rome. They therefore translated not from Greek and Hebrew but from the Vulgate, a decision defended at length in the preface by the translator Gregory Martin. Although the Rheims was one of the many translations consulted by the KJB teams, and may have had some small influence, it had little impact outside the English Catholic community.[9]

Bible translation has clearly always been controversial. Wyclif's remains were burned for Englishing the Bible, Tyndale died for it, the Coverdale, Matthew, Geneva, and Rheims translations were made in foreign countries by religious exiles, and printed abroad. Even the officially sanctioned Great and Bishops' Bibles arose out of conflict, the first an attempt by the King to wrest control of the vernacular Bible from the influence of Tyndale, the second an attempt by conservative bishops to supplant the too-radically Protestant Geneva Bible. The KJB also began in controversy. The 1604 Hampton Court conference was convened in an attempt to negotiate the future of the English Church between those who wanted it to continue in the direction of reform (the "Puritan" side), and those who resisted more radical reform and advocated a "higher" Church. In the midst of hot debate, John Reynolds, the Puritan President of Corpus Christi, Oxford, suggested a new English translation of the Bible. Although Reynolds's motive seems to have been a dislike of the official Bishops' Bible, King James I, who accepted the suggestion, had in mind instead his own dislike of the Geneva, some of whose marginal notes he found politically, theologically, and personally offensive. Out of Hampton Court developed the largest-scale Bible translation project yet seen in England.

Despite the peculiar popular legend that the translation of the KJB is shrouded in mystery, it isn't. We know a great deal about it. There were six companies of translators, a total of about fifty scholars (the numbers vary slightly, since a few members died or dropped out over the years, and others replaced them): two at Westminster, two at Oxford, and two at Cambridge, all under the general supervision of Lancelot Andrewes, Dean of Westminster and chaplain to the Chapel Royal. The scholars involved were the most learned men in the country, expert in ancient languages. Some, like Andrewes himself, were also brilliant writers, though, as David Norton has pointed out, the translators seem to have been little concerned with literary style.[10] They were primarily concerned, rather, with accuracy, as most Bible translators had been before them. The KJB translators recognized the achievements of scholars from Tyndale on. Thus, as "The Translators to the Reader" declared,

wee never thought from the beginning, that we should neede to make a new Translation, nor yet to make of a bad one a good one, (for then the imputation of Sixtus had bene true in some sort, that our people had bene fed with gall of Dragons in stead of wine, with whey in stead of milke:) but to make a good one better, or out of many good ones, one principall good one, not justly to be excepted against.[11]

This statement of intent is also an accurate description of the result, which is not "new," for the most part, but a compilation and recension of the best of Tyndale, Coverdale, Geneva, Bishops', and even Rheims, with revisions by the translators according to the latest scholarly standards and their own critical judgment.

Despite modern "AVolatry" – Norton's coinage for the near-worship of the KJB (or AV) from the nineteenth century on – the KJB was not particularly well received in 1611 or for some decades thereafter. The Bishops' Bible, Reynolds would have been happy to know, did disappear, being last printed in 1602. But the Geneva was more popular than ever. The KJB was the Bible now read in English churches, but there was widespread grumbling, from all corners, about both its scholarship and its style. Ambrose Ussher, brother of the more famous James, Bishop of Armagh (famous for calculating biblically the chronology of the world, and also the number of extra sheep required to feed the carnivores on Noah's ark), criticized the KJB as a rushed job, scholarly fast-food, in which "the cook hasted you out a reasonable sudden meal."[12] Those criticizing the KJB style also included the polymath John Selden, the poet Samuel Butler, and the

scientist Robert Boyle, among many others.[13] Even as "high" a churchman
as William Laud continued to use the Geneva Bible long after 1611, and,
ironically, the KJB translators themselves quote from the Geneva, rather
than their own translation, in the KJB preface.[14] The new Bible was not a
runaway success.

The last regular printing of the Geneva Bible was in 1644, and by the
Restoration of Charles II in 1660 the KJB was securely established as the
Bible of the English Church and people. This establishment involved many
different forces, some intentional, some accidental. None was probably
more important than the printing trade (see ch. 3 on Bible printing by
John King and Aaron Pratt). Although printing the KJB bankrupted its
first printer, Robert Barker, there was money to be made from the English
Bible, and the privilege of printing it, a royal monopoly, was highly sought
after. Although the monopoly broke down along with the monarchy itself
in the 1640s, English (mainly London) printers continued to prefer the
KJB to the Geneva, perhaps because so many editions of the Geneva continued to be printed across the channel. Although one might think that
the Puritan Commonwealth would have been committed to the Bible most
associated with English Puritans (the Geneva), even Oliver Cromwell now
favored the KJB (printed by John Field, first Printer to Parliament and then
"one of His Hignes [i.e., Cromwell's] printers"), as did the Quaker printer
Giles Calvert, a small KJB being the only Bible he ever printed.[15] The independent (non-Stationers' Company) Finsbury printer William Bentley
printed five editions of the KJB, in octavo and duodecimo, between 1646
and 1648. He was shut down by Field and Henry Hills, who accused him
of printing "Popish-Books" but were likely just enforcing their monopoly.[16]
Even before the end of the Commonwealth, no one was printing anything
but the KJB, and its domination of the English Bible market was assured
for the next 250 years.

Translation

As Paul Gutjahr shows (see ch. 7 below), there are many different atti-
tudes and approaches to translation, whether of the Bible or other works.
One common distinction in current translation theory, originating in the
work of Eugene Nida, is between "functional" and "formal" equivalence.
Nida, whose work inspired *Good News for Modern Man* and the *Good*

News Bible, favored the "functional," urging Bible translators to translate, as Gutjahr puts it, "thought-for-thought, rather than word-for-word." The goal of such an approach is accessibility, rendering the original text into language a modern reader can easily understand. Nida made his argument with reference to the Prophets in an early essay:

for most persons in the Western world, presenting the prophetic utterances of the Old Testament in poetic form, as the closest formal equivalence, often results in serious lack of appreciation for the urgency of the prophet's message, which was put into poetic form in order to enhance its impact and to make the form more readily remembered. Such poetic forms are often interpreted by persons in the Western world as implying a lack of urgency, because poetic forms have become associated with communications which are over-estheticized and hence not relevant to the practical events of men's daily lives.[17]

Whatever one may think of such generalizations about poetry and readers in the "Western world," this approach to translation, which aims to convey the message of the Bible rather than its specific words (and conceives this as possible), is responsible for the *Good News* translation of Isaiah 40:1–3:

"Comfort my people," says our God. "Comfort them! Encourage the people of Jerusalem. Tell them they have suffered long enough and their sins are now forgiven. I have punished them in full for all their sins." A voice cries out, "Prepare in the wilderness a road for the LORD! Clear the way in the desert for our God!"[18]

The message is clear, whether more urgent or not, and Isaiah's poetry has been converted into prose.

The KJB translators, and indeed all English Bible translators between Wyclif and the KJB, aimed instead for a "formally equivalent" translation. In the KJB preface, the translators declared, "wee have not tyed our selves to an uniformitie of phrasing, or to an identitie of words," posing facetiously, "Is the kingdome of God become words and syllables?" Yet, by any modern standard they stayed scrupulously close to the Hebrew and Greek originals. Indeed, the translators go on to say, "we desire that the Scripture may speake like it selfe, as in the language of *Canaan*, that it may bee understood even of the very vulgar."[19] Letting the Scripture "speake like it selfe" meant adapting the English language to the requirements of the original non-English text. Gerald Hammond has described in detail the Hebraic English of the KJB and its precursors.[20] For example, the unusually paratactic style of the KJB, stringing together clause after clause with only the semantically neutral coordinating conjunction, "and," follows Hebrew practice, in which subordinating pronouns are rarely used. Hebrew also has no genitive or possessive construction equivalent to the English's, and the many instances in the KJB of "noun + of + noun" constructions reflects this ("the face of the deep" in Gen. 1:2, for instance, rather than "the deep's face"). A variety of other grammatical and syntactical peculiarities result from the translators' efforts to find formal equivalents for the Hebrew. Even vocabulary is sometimes Hebraicized, as in the famous case of "biblical knowledge." In Genesis 4:1, readers of the KJB (and Geneva, though not Tyndale) are told that "Adam knew his wife," which makes no sense according to any recorded usage of "know" in English. The New International Version ("Adam lay with his wife") or especially the New Living Translation ("Adam had sexual relations with his wife") make the meaning much clearer for English readers.[21] What is lost in these later versions, though, is the Hebrew wordplay that links the first postlapsarian sex with the "knowledge" of the forbidden fruit (Gen. 2:17) and also Adam and Eve's subsequent "knowing" that they are naked (3:7). Robert Alter pursues such matters in greater detail in chapter 2.

The "formalistic" approach of the KJB translators was not without critics even in the seventeenth century. John Selden, for instance, himself a brilliant Hebraist, criticized the KJB translators for rendering the Bible "into English words rather than into English phrases," which resulted, he claimed, in mockery from the common reader ("Lord what gear do they make of it!").[22] Over time, of course, what at first seemed awkward Hebraisms became naturalized into English, though such language was still recognizable as specifically biblical. This is one of the ways in which the KJB influenced literature in English, when writers, deliberately or not, imitated biblical prose style (for more on this, see the chapters by Stephen Prickett, Michael Wheeler, and James Wood). When George Wither wrote prophecies of England's fall, for instance, he adopted a suitably biblical style:

> harke ye *People*: harken you, I pray,
> That were preserv'd with me to see this day;

And listen you that shall be brought upon
This *Stage* of action, when our *Scaene* is done:
Come harken all; and let no soule refraine
To heare; nor let it heare my words in vaine.
For, from the Slaughter-house of *Death*, and from
The habitations of the *Dead* I come.[23]

The rhythms, syntax, and diction of the KJB style are also easy to recognize in Christopher Smart's *Jubilate Agno* ("Let Joshua praise God with an Unicorn – the swiftness of the Lord, and the strength of the Lord, and the spear of the Lord mighty in battle") and William Blake's *Jerusalem* ("And Rahab Babylon the Great hath destroyed Jerusalem / Bath stood upon the Severn with Merlin & Bladud & Arthur/ The Cup of Rahab in his hand: her Poisons Twenty-seven fold"), both of which might in today's prosodic terminology be called prose-poems (for more on Blake, see Adam Potkay, ch. 10).[24] Even a twentieth-century American novelist can use this style, however, when it suits his purposes:

In those days, I was the one who came down from Nazareth to be baptized by John in the River Jordan. And the Gospel of Mark would declare that on my immersion, the heavens opened and I saw "a spirit like a dove descending." A mighty voice said: "You are my beloved Son in whom I am well pleased." Then the Spirit drove me into the wilderness, and I was there for forty days and was tempted by Satan.

This is Norman Mailer, at the opening of *The Gospel According to the Son*.[25] Even in the twenty-first century, what readers recognize as a "biblical style" is essentially that of the Hebraic, formally equivalent KJB translation.

Allusion

From 1611, the KJB was the Bible heard in English churches, and from the mid 1640s, it was the only current one in bookshops. Copies of earlier translations continued to circulate, of course, but seventeenth-century biblical culture – and the culture was pervasively biblical – became increasingly KJB-centric.[26] This was naturally reflected in works of English literature, which had always been steeped in the Bible since its origins in the Anglo-Saxon period. This was most obvious in biblical paraphrases or adaptations, like the recounting of the Crucifixion in *The Dream of the Rood*, the countless Psalm paraphrases from Alfred the Great to Sir Philip and Mary Sidney, Countess of Pembroke, or the metrical versions of biblical books like Christopher Tye's *Acts of the Apostles*, Michael Drayton's *Harmony of the Church* (including *The Song of Solomon*), John Donne's *Lamentations of Jeremiah*, and George Sandys's *Job* and *Ecclesiastes*. But the Bible was also present in more complex ways in non-biblical works through the use of allusion: by means of verbal references or parallels writers pointed the reader to biblical phrases, episodes, or characters which resonated with, or against, their own writing, in ways which (ideally) produced a greater depth or complexity of meaning.[27] Chaucer's *Miller's Tale*, for instance, alludes in hilarious and parodic ways to the story of Noah's Flood, popularized through medieval mystery plays. Spenser's *Faerie Queene* is also extremely dense with biblical allusions, especially in its first book about Redcrosse Knight, the Knight of Holiness, who sets out to rescue Adam and Eve from a dragon and on the way battles a creature called "Errour," half serpent, half woman. The plays of Marlowe and Shakespeare continually allude to the Bible, as when Barabas in *The Jew of Malta* compares himself (absurdly) to Job, or when we are encouraged to compare Orlando in *As You Like It* to the prodigal son through allusions to the gospel parable. As stated above, Spenser, Marlowe, and Shakespeare allude mostly to the Geneva Bible, occasionally the Bishops'; when writers began alluding primarily to the KJB, a cultural shift had taken place.

The first major English writers who allude predominantly to the KJB are John Milton and John Bunyan, in works written after the Restoration of the monarchy (see the chapters by Jason Rosenblatt and Hannibal Hamlin). Bunyan knew the Geneva Bible too, as well as the metrical Psalms of Sternhold and Hopkins and others, and Milton also knew the Bible in Hebrew, Greek, Latin, and other languages. But in *Pilgrim's Progress* and *Paradise Lost*, when Bunyan and Milton allude to the Bible, it is the language of the KJB we most frequently hear. One mark of the KJB's dominance over other translations at this point is its use by writers like these, who had little sympathy with King James and his Church. Thus, even for non-conformists, radicals, and dissenters, the KJB had become *the* English Bible.

For the next three centuries, the overwhelming majority of biblical allusions in English literature are to the KJB. The early American poet Ann

Bradstreet, for instance, alludes to lines from the Song of Solomon in her poem to her husband:

> My love is such that rivers cannot quench,
> Nor aught but love from thee, give recompense.[28]

The same biblical verse (as well as the following one, Song of Sol. 8:8, "We have a little sister, and she hath no breasts") is alluded to in "Sheba" by contemporary Canadian poet Jay Macpherson:

> I have a little sister far undersea,
> The winds and the waters bring her words to me:
> "True love is a durable fire the floods shall not drown."
> The bird sings burning and on her branch sinks down.[29]

Isaac Watts's eighteenth-century hymn, "Crucifixion to the World by the Cross of Christ," alludes to the Gospels of Matthew and John:

> See from his head, his hands, his feet,
> Sorrow and love flow mingled down;
> Did e'er such love and sorrow meet?
> Or thorns compose so rich a crown?[30]

The flowing down of sorrow and love alludes to, and transfigures, the blood and water that spring from the crucified Jesus's pierced side in John 19:34. The striking adjective "mingled," on the other hand, while it might seem appropriate to John's account, actually alludes to a different telling of the Crucifixion (Matt. 27:34), in which the soldiers give Jesus "vinegar to drink mingled with gall." The contemporary British poet Geoffrey Hill seems also to blend allusions to the different fluids of Matthew 27:34 and John 19:34 (perhaps remembering Watts) in "Canticle for Good Friday":

> A clamping, cold-figured day
> Thomas (not transfigured) stamped, crouched.
> Watched
> Smelt vinegar and blood.[31]

Prose writers allude to the KJB just as often as do poets. Charlotte Brontë's *Jane Eyre*, for instance, is continually alluding to the Bible. At Jane's "bitter hour," when she has discovered Rochester is already married to Bertha, she recites (unidentified) Psalm 69:1–2: "the waters came into my soul; I sank in deep mire: I felt no standing; I came into deep waters; the floods overflowed me."[32] In the Canadian author Margaret Laurence's *The Stone Angel*, Hagar Shipley, who is named after the handmaid of Abraham's wife Sarah (Gen. 13), recounts the story of her long life. As she is dying in a home for the elderly, her son visits and holds her hand tightly. "Now it seems to me he is truly Jacob," she says, "gripping with all his strength, and bargaining. I will not let thee go, except thou bless me."[33] The allusion is to Jacob wrestling the angel (or God) in Genesis 32:24–32. A subtler allusion is made as Hagar dies, calling for a nurse, "I'm – thirsty." When the nurse arrives, Hagar says, "I wrest from her the glass, full of water to be had for the taking."[34] It is when an angel shows the biblical Hagar a "well of water" in the desert (Gen. 21:19) that she and her son Ishmael are saved from thirst and preserved.

In a looser sense, but one in tune with the word's etymology from the Latin *transferre* ("to carry across"), paraphrases, adaptations, and allusions are also "translations," importing the Bible, carrying it across, from its original languages and cultures into English and the many English-speaking cultures across the world.

Wrestling with angels: Questioning the authority of the Authorized Version

The KJB has long held the ironic distinction of being the English translation of the Bible most emphatically associated with the monarchy and the established church – thus having a strongly traditional, even conservative pedigree – while also being a translation favored by dissenters and radicals such as Milton and Bunyan, as noted above. This irony in the reception history of the KJB has grown only more pronounced over the course of its four hundred years, becoming more complicated and multifaceted as the forms of resistance, resignification, and outright subversion of the KJB have grown increasingly various and have taken place in so many different cultural contexts. Indeed, this irony is one of the key themes shared by many of the chapters in this volume, despite their many differences.

As Isabel Rivers illustrates in chapter 5, the Bible pervaded eighteenth- and nineteenth-century literatures and cultures in Great Britain and what became the United States as well as in many other colonies. During these two centuries, one of the most dramatic changes in the Bible's reception history occurred as a result of the advent of the Higher Criticism, which implicitly undermined the authority of the Bible as a sacred text by analyzing it in the same way historians analyzed any other historical document. Developed especially in Germany, the Higher Criticism aimed to distinguish the mythological from the historically verifiable. This method of biblical interpretation did not exert a strong influence in Great Britain until well into the nineteenth century. Yet, as Michael Wheeler explains in his chapter on John Ruskin, Victorian culture witnessed a growing sense of disjunction between the aesthetic beauty of the KJB as literature and its religious authority, which was coming under increasing scrutiny and doubt as the Higher Criticism questioned the reliability of the text by subjecting the Bible to literary and historical critique.

This resulted in a tension between the KJB as literature – in which light it was widely regarded as having striking aesthetic power – and its increasingly besieged authority as a religious text.[35] Indeed, the idea of the KJB "as literature" often implicitly relegates the Bible to the status of historical document rather than sacred scripture, in keeping with the general thrust of the Higher Criticism. As Stephen Prickett contends in *The Origins of Narrative*, however, the reception of the English Bible "as literature" arguably predates the widespread influence of the Higher Criticism and instead owes as much or more to the rise of the novel as a popular mainstay of English literature.[36] As readers grew accustomed to narrative conventions associated with the novel, they increasingly interpreted the KJB much as they would interpret a novel, reading especially for the psychological dramas experienced by the characters (one could argue that this shift was Miltonic as well as novelistic). While it is important to remember that sermons were far more popular than novels among eighteenth-century English readers, nevertheless there was a growing tendency to read the KJB "as literature" not so much in the sense of reading it as a historical artifact to be analyzed on the basis of archeological and historical evidence but rather as a collection of narrative prose, poetry, and epistles to be read in the same way fictional versions of these literary forms were read – even though the Bible was widely considered to be nonfiction. This meant focusing not, for example, on the medieval practice of interpreting the fourfold levels of meaning in holy scripture but rather on narrative plot and character (which arguably accords with how the texts were originally composed, as Alter and others contend).

While the Higher Criticism certainly expanded the variety of ways in which readers and writers inspired by the aesthetic qualities of the KJB might also wrestle with or even subvert its religious authority – or interpret the KJB in ways that implicitly or explicitly criticized certain religious and political institutions associated with it – such uses of the KJB by dissenters and radicals predated the Higher Criticism. In addition to the seventeenth-century dissenters discussed above, one finds iconoclastic and even radical uses of the KJB in the writings of William Blake, William Wordsworth, and Percy Shelley, as Adam Potkay details (ch. 10). These writers fashioned such uses of the KJB in terms not of historicist critique but rather of religious, artistic, and political ideals. Likewise one finds similarly motivated uses of the KJB as an ironic vehicle for criticizing authority in the work of Jonathan Swift, Laurence Sterne, Charles Dickens, and Thomas Hardy, among others. There are of course substantial differences among the above writers in terms of their religious and political beliefs, artistic commitments, and cultural contexts. Their uses of the KJB are also quite different in many respects; yet they all at times invoke the Authorized Version as an ironic counter to various institutions and claims associated with its authority.

Herman Melville is another such writer: in *Moby-Dick*, as Alter argues, Melville subverts the authority of social hierarchies in part by subverting literary decorum, mingling "high and low, modern and archaic" in his writing style, "with a strong biblical thread running through the pattern."[37] To this implicit social and political critique, Melville joins a historicist critique of the Bible even as he frames that critique in biblical terms; he is "at once profoundly biblical and paradoxically anti-biblical."[38] Thus he uses the figure of Leviathan in *Moby-Dick* to undermine biblical chronology with a vaster sense of geologic time: "Who can show a pedigree like Leviathan? Ahab's harpoon had shed older blood than Pharaoh's. Methusaleh seems a schoolboy. I look round to shake hands with Shem. I am horror-struck at this antemosaic, unsourced existence of the unspeakable horrors of the whale, which, having been before all time, must needs exist after all humane ages are over."[39] Despite Mikhail Bakhtin's assertion that biblical texts are so authoritatively canonical or univocal as to be antithetical to what he considered the uncanonical multivocality of novels,[40] Melville is part of a rich and long tradition of iconoclastic interpretations and resignifications of biblical formal and thematic elements in novels – indeed, a tradition so varied as to include, in the twentieth century, novelists as different from one another as William Faulkner, Ernest Hemingway, and James Baldwin.

In writing *Leaves of Grass*, Walt Whitman famously intended to create a "new American Bible" that would be exuberantly and democratically anti-hierarchical, anti-authoritarian; yet it drew on the Authorized Version for its fundamental form. Whitman's free verse was inspired so strongly by the KJB, especially the Psalms, that H. T. Kirby-Smith describes it as "biblical-anaphoric free verse."[41] The parallelism of the Psalms is evident in the otherwise seemingly unstructured "Song of Myself, 6," each line divisible in half, echoing or expanding on itself:

> A child said *What is the grass?* fetching it to me with full hands;
> How could I answer the child? I do not know what it is any more than he.
> I guess it must be the flag of my disposition, out of hopeful green stuff woven.
> Or I guess it is the handkerchief of the Lord,
> A scented gift and remembrancer designedly dropped.[42]

Compare these lines with the opening of Psalm 98:

> O sing unto the Lord a new song; for he hath done marvellous things: his right hand, and his holy arm, hath gotten him the victory.
> The Lord hath made known his salvation: his righteousness hath he openly shown in the sight of the heathen. …
> Make a joyful noise unto the Lord, all the earth: make a loud noise, and rejoice, and sing praise.

Whitman, in turn, was the major precursor for later generations of poets writing in free verse. A century after Whitman's "Song of Myself, 6," the free verse of Allen Ginsberg's *Howl* is similarly informed by Whitman's adaptation of biblical form:

> I saw the best minds of my generation destroyed by madness, starving hysterical naked,
> dragging themselves through the negro streets at dawn looking for an angry fix,

> angelheaded hipsters burning for the ancient heavenly connection
>   to the starry dynamo in the machinery of night,
> who poverty and tatters and hollow-eyed and high sat up smoking
>   in the supernatural darkness of cold-water flats floating across
>   the tops of cities contemplating jazz
> who bared their brains to Heaven under the El and saw Mohammedan
>   angels staggering on tenement roofs illuminated.[43]

In addition to the parallelism, the syntactical inversion "noun + adjective" is a Hebraicism, as Hammond points out: "tenement roofs illuminated" thus echoes Whitman's "remembrancer designedly dropped."[44]

The enumerative structure of free verse lines such as Whitman's and Ginsberg's, and their frequent use of parallelism (typically echoing or extending the thought expressed in the first half of the line in its second half), has the uncanny effect of making Christopher Smart's *Jubilate Agno* – which, as a kind of housecat Psalm, no doubt seemed like madness in the mid eighteenth century when it was composed – now, and ever since it was first published in 1939, look so prescient in relation to Whitman, Ginsberg, and modern poetry more broadly as to be in some sense prophetic:[45]

> For I will consider my Cat Jeoffry.
> For he is the servant of the Living God, duly and daily serving him.
> For at the first glance of the glory of God in the East he worships in
>   his way.
> For is this done by wreathing his body seven times round with
>   elegant quickness.
> For then he leaps up to catch the musk, which is the blessing of God
>   upon his prayer.[46]

It would be the work of another book to offer a detailed discussion of the many nineteenth- and twentieth-century poets who, like Whitman and Ginsberg, formally or thematically draw on the KJB while also engaging in iconoclastic resignifications of its authority (often rejecting that authority completely while nevertheless finding themselves repeatedly drawn back to its aesthetic beauty and power, as in the case of Wallace Stevens[47]).

In tracing various ways in which the KJB has been used both on behalf of institutionalized authorities and on behalf of those opposed to such authorities, it is important to remember that the kinds of authority attributed to the KJB are complex, varying substantially according to context. The cultural position held by the KJB during much of the past four hundred years as *the* English Bible has contributed to its being often associated with oppressive claims to both religious and political authority on behalf of various governments, institutions, and social groups in order to marginalize others. The language of the KJB has been deployed in the name of sexism, racism, imperialist colonization, anti-Semitism and other forms of religious bigotry, and homophobia. As Katherine Bassard, R. S. Sugirtharajah, and Heather Walton illuminate in their respective chapters, for some who have experienced the KJB in such contexts, the text also lends itself to counter-readings and resignifications – to being re-appropriated from those who would use it as a tool of oppression.[48] Yet for some, the text is beyond the point of recuperation.

Even for many Christians, over the course of the past half century the KJB has ceased to speak with the authority it once did: new discoveries of ancient texts and other advances in understanding the Hebrew, Aramaic, and Greek originals, along with demands for Bibles that speak in more contemporary language, have rendered the KJB obsolete for many, as Paul Gutjahr explains (ch. 7). Indeed, in creating *The King James Bible after 400 Years*, we have more than once been led to wonder whether we weren't creating a kind of elegy for the KJB at the end of its four hundred years.

Yet it seems equally if not more likely that, as it enters its fifth century, the KJB is experiencing a resurrection of sorts. The very existence of books such as this one, representing the work of current scholars at every stage of their professional careers, is symptomatic of a larger resurgence of interest in religious culture and history among scholars and the broader public alike. We seem to be in the midst of a turn to religion in literary studies, which necessarily entails various reexaminations of the KJB and its influence, which not long ago had become generally under-appreciated and had regularly gone completely unrecognized by many scholars whose biblical literacy was, on average, waning as much as that of the broader public's, relative to prior generations of readers.

One of the things scholars are "discovering" is that the KJB has been with us all along, even if we have not always been aware of it. Some might have predicted the complete dethroning of the KJB in the twentieth century as a result not only of historicist critiques of its authenticity but also as a result of its increasingly archaic language (which was at least slightly archaic even in 1611 when it was first published), as well as the general decline of biblical literacy. On the contrary, the KJB has in many instances acquired a different but still powerful sense of authority, one Norman Jones terms a ghostly presence (ch. 13). Witness the frequent role of the KJB in horror films, where it often has only a tenuous relationship to traditional Christian teaching and theology but nonetheless has a vague but effective kind of oracular power.[49] Often, this power is indeed so vague that the KJB can be played, as it were, by a Hollywood look-alike. Thus in *Pulp Fiction*, the oracular "Bible" passage quoted by Jules – which is portrayed as being powerful enough to help inspire his conversion (to what is unclear) and rejection of his job as a hitman – is only KJB-esque but not actually from the KJB:

The path of the righteous man is beset on all sides by the iniquities of the selfish and the tyranny of evil men. Blessed is he who, in the name of charity and good will, shepherds the weak through the valley of darkness, for he is truly his brother's keeper and the finder of lost children. And I will strike down upon thee with great vengeance and furious anger those who attempt to poison and destroy my brothers. And you will know my name is the Lord when I lay my vengeance upon you.[50]

As exemplified by *Pulp Fiction*, collage is one of the indicatively modern and postmodern art forms. To the extent that the KJB, in the twentieth and twenty-first centuries, increasingly lends itself to being read as collage – a translation of translations, created by committee, for which there exists no autograph first edition of the original Hebrew, Aramaic, and Greek texts, and which (in Christian traditions) centers on a figure (Jesus) who, like Socrates, never wrote anything down, and which offers four rather different stories of his life, not to mention the vast complexities of the sources and compilation of the Old Testament – in all this, the KJB ironically seems to remain quite relevant. Indeed, in Tony Kushner's *Angels in America*, which is one of the most highly acclaimed dramas of the past few decades and is a postmodern work that thoroughly embraces collage, we find the KJB used in a way similar to its incantatory role in *Pulp Fiction* (though this time the KJB is played by the actual KJB). As Kushner creates a new version of the biblical story of Jacob wrestling with an angel, it is not enough for Prior simply to wrestle the angel; he feels his actions require textual support, "scriptural precedent." The text he turns to is the KJB, which he quotes as a kind of spell: "I will not let thee go except thou bless me!"[51] The spell works for Prior, helping him to attain his blessing from the angel. In a larger sense, this invocation of the KJB works for Kushner's play, as well, resonating productively with its rich collage of fragmentary allusions to various religious and literary texts.

Again, the story of the KJB is large: it contains multitudes (to borrow a phrase from Whitman) and refuses to be contained in a single, unified narrative. Even so, one of the most influential and enduring strands of that story is the way in which the KJB seems to "work" most powerfully – and has kept working again and again over the course of its four hundred years, often in new and surprising ways – when contested.

NOTES

1 As the product of a large group of translators, the creation of the KJB stands in contrast to such Bible translations as Jerome's Latin Vulgate in the fourth century, Martin Luther's German Bible in the sixteenth century, the first complete English translation of the Bible by John Wyclif and his associates in the fourteenth century, and William Tyndale's highly influential, though incomplete, English translation in the sixteenth century. Of course, translation of sacred scriptures by large groups of scholars dates back at least to the third-century BCE Septuagint translation of Hebrew scriptures into Greek, said to have been translated by seventy scholars. Several sixteenth-century English Bibles – e.g., the Geneva Bible and the Bishops' Bible – were also translated by large groups, and this method of translation has become standard for most complete Bible translations undertaken in English since the KJB.

2 Erasmus's *Paraclesis*, the preface to his Greek New Testament, cited (in English) in David Daniell, *The Bible in English: Its History and Influence* (New Haven, CT and London: Yale University Press, 2003), 117. Tyndale refers his readers to this work in the preface to his own *Obedience of a Christian Man* (1528).

3 David Katz, *God's Last Words* (New Haven, CT and London: Yale University Press, 2004), 38.

4 *Records of the English Bible*, ed. Alfred W. Pollard (London, New York, and Toronto: Oxford University Press, 1911), 262.

5 See Nicholas Temperley, *Music of the English Parish Church*, 2 vols. (Cambridge: Cambridge University Press, 1979). Among the composers of these chants over the centuries are Henry Purcell, John Goss, Samuel Wesley, Henry Walford Davies, Hubert H. Parry, Edward Bairstow, and Charles Villiers Stanford, as well as many others.

6 *Records*, ed. Pollard, 277.

7 This at least is the story usually told. It was supposed to be the Bible used in English worship, but no study has yet determined to what extent it actually was used. Presumably for at least some time after 1568, some churches continued to use the Great Bible, given the enormous cost of the Bishops'. How many used the Geneva, before or after 1568, is unknown. Whittingham, for instance, became Dean of Durham on returning to England. He got into trouble in 1563 for celebrating communion without cope or surplice. Might he not also have used his own Bible translation?

8 See Naseeb Shaheen, *Biblical References in* The Faerie Queene (Memphis: Memphis State University Press, 1976), and *Biblical References in Shakespeare's Plays* (Newark, NJ: University of Delaware Press, 1999).

9 It also generated a famous controversy and publication war between Gregory Martin and the Protestant polemicist William Fulke. See Daniell, *The Bible in English*, 358–68. On the translation and its influence, see Gerald Hammond, *The Making of the English Bible* (Manchester: Carcanet, 1982), 158–73.

10 David Norton, *A History of the English Bible as Literature* (Cambridge: Cambridge University Press, 2000), 56–75.

11 *Records*, ed. Pollard, 369.

12 Cited in Norton, *A History* (2000), 94.

13 *Ibid.*, 107–14.

14 *Ibid.*, 103–4.

15 See Henry R. Plomer, *A Dictionary of the Booksellers and Printers Who Were at Work in England, Scotland and Ireland from 1641 to 1667* (London: Printed for the Bibliographical Society by Blades, East & Blades, 1907), and Ariel Hessayon, "Giles Calvert," *Oxford Dictionary of National Biography*.

16 See William Bentley, *The Case of William Bentley, Printer at Finsbury near London, touching his Right to the Printing of Bibles and Psalms* (1656) and *A Short Answer To a Pamphlet, Entitled, The Case of William Bentley, Printer* [etc.] (1656). Bentley did print two editions of the Royalist *Eikon Basilike* in 1649, but it is not clear which of his publications qualify as "Popish-Books."

17 Eugene A. Nida, "Science of Translation," *Language* 45.3 (1969): 483–98; 494.

18 Citation from the online text at *Bibletools* (http://bibletools.org).

19 *Records*, ed. Pollard, 374, 376.

20 Hammond, *The Making of the English Bible*.

21 Texts online at *Biblos.com* (http://bible.cc).

22 Cited in Norton, *A History* (2000), 108.

23 George Wither, *Britains Remembrancer* ([London?], 1628), 16.

24 *Jubilate Agno*, Fragment A, line 26, in Christopher Smart, *Selected Poems*, ed. Karina Williamson and Marcus Walsh (Harmondsworth: Penguin, 1990), 43;

Jerusalem, plate 75, in William Blake, *The Complete Poems*, ed. Alicia Ostriker (Harmondsworth: Penguin, 1977), 795.

25 *The Gospel According to the Son* (New York: Ballantine, 1997), 1.

26 On the remarkable extent to which seventeenth-century English culture was biblically determined, see Christopher Hill, *The English Bible and the Seventeenth-Century Revolution* (Harmondsworth: Penguin, 1993), and Katz, *God's Last Words*, ch. 2, among many other works.

27 On allusion, see John Hollander, *The Figure of Echo: A Mode of Allusion in Milton and After* (Berkeley: University of California Press, 1991) and Christopher Ricks, *Allusion to the Poets* (Oxford and New York: Oxford University Press, 2002).

28 "To my Dear and Loving Husband," in *The New Oxford Book of Christian Verse*, ed. Donald Davie (Oxford: Oxford University Press, 1981), 102. The allusion is to Song of Solomon 8:7.

29 Jay Macpherson, *Poems Twice Told* (Toronto: Oxford University Press, 1981), 19.

30 Watts, in Davie, ed., *The New Oxford Book of Christian Verse*, 146.

31 *Chapters into Verse: Poetry in English Inspired by the Bible*, ed. Robert Atwan and Laurence Wieder (Oxford: Oxford University Press, 1993), vol. 2, 197.

32 *Jane Eyre* (Harmondsworth: Penguin, 1966), 324. Ps. 69:1–2 reads "Save me, O God, for the waters are come in unto my soul. I sink in deep mire, where there is no standing." Brontë has the KJB in mind here, since the Prayer Book version is distinctly different. See Catherine Brown Tkacz, "The Bible in *Jane Eyre*," *Christianity and Literature* 44.1 (1994): 3–27.

33 *The Stone Angel* (Toronto: McClelland and Stewart, 1968), 304.

34 *Ibid.*, 308.

35 Regarding the rise of the perception of the KJB as a work of aesthetic power and beauty, see Norton, *A History* (2000), ch. 11.

36 Stephen Prickett, *Origins of Narrative: The Romantic Appropriation of the Bible* (Cambridge: Cambridge University Press, 1996), especially ch. 3. See also Prickett, "Eighteenth Century and Romantic: Introduction," in *The Blackwell Companion to the Bible in English Literature*, ed. Rebecca Lemon, Emma Mason, Jonathan Roberts, and Christopher Rowland (Malden, MA: Blackwell, 2009), 313–28.

37 Robert Alter, *Pen of Iron: American Prose and the King James Bible* (Princeton: Princeton University Press, 2010), 74, 76.

38 *Ibid.*, 72.

39 Herman Melville, *Moby-Dick*, quoted in Alter, *Pen of Iron*, 73.

40 Mikhail Bakhtin, *The Dialogic Imagination: Four Essays*, trans. Caryl Emerson and Michael Holquist (Austin: University of Texas Press, 2004), ch. 1.

41 H. T. Kirby-Smith, *The Origins of Free Verse* (Ann Arbor: University of Michigan Press, 1996), 43.

42 Walt Whitman, "Song of Myself, 6," lines 1–5, in *The Norton Anthology of Poetry*, 3rd edn., ed. Alexander Allison, Herbert Barrows, Caesar Blake, Arthur Carr, Arthur Eastman, and Hubert English (New York: W. W. Norton, 1970), 760–1.

43 Allen Ginsberg, *Howl*, lines 1–5, in in *The Norton Anthology of Poetry*, 3rd edn., 1273.

44 Hammond, *The Making of the English Bible*, 45.

45 For an extended analysis of this poem in relation to the KJB, see Jeanne Murray Walker, "'Jubilate Agno' as Psalm," *Studies in English Literature* 20.3 (1980): 449–59.

46 *Jubilate Agno*, Fragment B, lines 1–5, in Smart, *Selected Poems*, 105.

47 See Eleanor Cook, "Wallace Stevens and the King James Bible," *Essays in Criticism* 41.3 (1991): 240–52.

48 For a discussion of biblical themes and allusions in gay and lesbian literature, see Raymond-Jean Frontain, ed., *Reclaiming the Sacred: The Bible in Gay and Lesbian Culture* (Binghamton, NY: Hayworth Press, 1997, 1st edn., and 2003, 2nd edn.); see also Norman W. Jones, *Gay and Lesbian Historical Fiction: Sexual Mystery and Post-Secular Narrative* (New York: Palgrave Macmillan, 2007).

49 See Mary Ann Beavis, "'Angels Carrying Savage Weapons': Uses of the Bible in Contemporary Horror Films," *Journal of Religion and Film* 7.2 (2003). See also Adele Reinhartz, "Scripture on the Silver Screen," *Journal of Religion and Film* 3.1 (1999).

50 In *Pulp Fiction*, Jules, who speaks these lines, attributes them to Ezekiel 25:17, though they are only partially related to this verse in the KJB. The lines are adapted from the 1973 film, *Karate Kiba*, released in the US in 1976 as *Chiba the Bodyguard*.

51 Tony Kushner, *Angels in America* (New York: Theatre Communications Group, 1995), 250–1. The KJB quotation is from Gen. 32:26.

PART I

The Language of the King James Bible

1 | Language within language
The King James steamroller
STEPHEN PRICKETT

The language of the King James Bible (KJB) has not been lacking in admirers. From T. B. Macaulay (1828)[1] onwards, praise has come thick and fast. For Richard Chenevix Trench, writing thirty years later,

all is clear, correct, lucid, happy, awaking continual admiration by the rhythmic beauty of the periods, the instinctive art with which the style rises and falls with the subject, the skilful surmounting of the difficulties the most real, the diligence with which almost all which was happiest in preceding translations has been retained and embodied in the present; the constant solemnity and seriousness which, by some nameless skill, is made to rest on all.[2]

For George Saintsbury it (with Shakespeare) represents "the perfection of English, the complete expression of the literary capacities of the language" (1887).[3] For others it is "a wonder before which I can only stand humble and aghast" (Arthur Quiller-Couch, 1916);[4] "probably the most beautiful piece of writing in all the literature of the world" (H. L. Mencken, 1930),[5] its style is "characterized not merely by homely vigour and pithiness of phrase, but also by a singular nobility of diction and by a rhythmic quality ... unrivalled in its beauty (John Livingstone Lowes, 1936);[6] in short, it is "a miracle and a landmark" (H. Wheeler Robinson, 1940).[7]

But before we are totally drowned in this flood of superlatives, we need to notice two very interesting facts. The first is that this cascade of delight really dates only from the beginning of the nineteenth century. As David Norton has shown, if we go back to the first two hundred years of the KJB the evidence suggests both that the new version was not at first seen as in any way distinctive, nor was it greatly admired stylistically.[8] Indeed, there is a paradox here, in that this crescendo of praise has roots in a reaction against earlier eighteenth-century criticism suggesting that the language of the KJB was "harsh," "uncouth," and "obsolete."[9] The second is that this praise, when it comes, is presented as exclusively aesthetic. Though there was, as so often, a political agenda not far below the surface,[10] it coincides quite uncannily with the rise of the idea of "literature" as a quality over and above any ostensible content – a move located by the *OED* as occuring in the last decades of the eighteenth century.[11] It takes no account of either perceived "religious" content, or of the faithfulness of the translation itself – and, as we shall see, these two factors are both more relevant to each other, and to the apparently unrelated question of the felicity of its style, than might appear at first sight. Indeed, my thesis here is that the literary style of the KJB – "the King James steamroller" as it is sometimes called – is as much a product of its theology as its aesthetics.

The majestic cadences of this Bible have become so familiar to us as "Church English" that only those with the most scholarly cast of mind may stop to consider either its origins or its peculiar skill in rendering the Hebrew, Aramaic, and Koine Greek of the original texts into a single, dignified, linguistic system. Yet there are real mysteries about both its sources and the phenomenon of its actual creation. For Saintsbury, "it is curious that such an unmatched result should have been the result of labours thus combined, and not, as far as is known, controlled by any one guiding spirit … no known translator under James has left anything which at all equals in strictly literary merit the Authorized Version."[12] Quiller-Couch is no less puzzled "that a committee of forty-seven should have captured a rhythm so personal, so constant, that our Bible has the voice of one author speaking through its many mouths."[13] Nearly forty years later Mary Ellen Chase, while increasing the number of translators, is equally baffled by the stylistic consequences: "Perhaps the greatest of literary mysteries lies in the unanswered question of how fifty-four translators managed to infuse their work with a unity of effect which seems the result of one inspired imagination. The mystery will never be solved."[14]

By the time we reach Gustavus Paine in 1959, a second mystery begins to intrude – just *how many* translators were there behind this enigmatically uniform translation? "How did this come to be?" muses Paine:

How explain that sixty or more men, none a genius, none even as great a writer as Marlowe or Ben Jonson, together produced writing to be compared with (and confused with) the words of Shakespeare?[15]

But the problem of the rising number of translators (doubtless all in buckram suits) is as nothing to the problem posed by their collective prose style.

Paine continues: "to know that the Bible words were beyond the choosing of the best of them, we have only to look at their individual writing." Here names can be named, though hardly to their credit, especially if they are placed in comparison with Marlowe or Shakespeare:

Because he was the final critic who looked for flaws and smoothed out the whole translation, there is perhaps more of Dr. Miles Smith in the King James version than of any other man. Some critics said that his own style was heavy, involved, rough.

Thomas Bilson, Bishop of Winchester, with Miles Smith, at the end revised all that the rest had done. We may well ask how his style fitted him to burnish the whole final draft, but if we use this criterion we may ask in vain. Bishop Bilson was for the most part a dull writer.[16]

Again, this is a theme that has been repeatedly taken up by subsequent critics. Charles C. Butterworth comments that, "In their general effect, the six sections of the 1611 Bible show a remarkable uniformity of style, considering that in the English backgrounds of each there were differences not only between the sections, but also within each section."[17] By 1982, Olga Opfell reintroduces the word "miracle" into the critical vocabulary, this time not applied to the prose style, but to its uniformity and ubiquity as a piece of group-think.[18]

A recurring theme in such material is the comparison with the translators' contemporaries in what is generally believed to be one of the great ages of English prose. Bilson and Smith, it is agreed, were not in the same class as Jonson, Marlowe, or Shakespeare – a view that had sufficient orthodoxy to be repeated as a modern comparison by Kenneth Grayston, one of the translators of the New English Bible, who surrenders even before the first shot is fired in this particular battle of the Ancients and Moderns:

The New English Bible does not compare with the Authorized Version, certainly not in language and style: this is not a period of great writers equal to Spenser, Sidney, Hooker, Marlowe and Shakespeare. Modern English, it seems to me, is slack instead of taut, verbose and not concise, infested with this month's cliché, no longer the language of a proud and energetic English people, but an international means of communication.[19]

On this list, we notice, Jonson has now been dropped in favor of Spenser, Sidney, and Hooker, but the invocation of the Elizabethan and Jacobean greats is delivered in much the same spirit. There is an oddity about both invocations however. Christopher Marlowe *died* in 1593 – almost two decades before the publication of the new Bible. Grayston's list is even odder: Sir Philip Sidney died in 1586; Edmund Spenser in 1599; Richard Hooker in 1600. In other words, none of these prose heroes got even within a decade of the King James Bible of 1611. The sole figure to have even been alive and active in all these lists is William Shakespeare. And this is where the story gets interesting.

But before we turn to the ritual invocation of Shakespeare, however, we need to look at what would now be called the committee's "terms of reference" laid down at the start of the enterprise in 1603. Among the fourteen rules of procedure laid down were the following:

1 The ordinary Bible read in the church, commonly called the Bishops' Bible, to be followed, and as little altered as the original will permit.
2 The names of the prophets and the holy writers, with other names in the text, to be retained as near as may be, accordingly as they are vulgarly used.
3 The old ecclesiastical words to be kept, viz. as the word *church* not to be translated *congregation* &c.
4 When any word hath divers significations, that to be kept which hath been most commonly used by the most eminent fathers, being agreeable to the propriety of the place and the analogy of faith …
14 These translations to be used, when they agree better with the text than the Bishops' Bible, viz. Tindal's, Matthew's, Coverdale's, Whitchurch, Geneva.[20]

In other words, this was to be a deeply conservative text. But such conservatism goes well beyond the above-mentioned brief of simply retaining where possible the original phraseology. William Tyndale's perfectly scholarly translation of the Latin *ecclesia* as "congregation" rather than "church" was political dynamite, in that it implicitly handed over organizational control from the clergy to the rank-and-file in the pew – which, of course, was precisely what Tyndale had intended with his direct and forceful contemporary vernacular. In contrast, this translation was to be deliberately archaic, latinized, and conservative.

One result of this may be seen in the disarming of the Christmas angels who appeared to the shepherds in Luke 2:13. The Bishops' Bible – the authorized template for the new translation – actually follows Tyndale at this point: "And suddenly there was with the Angel a multitude of heavenly soldiers, praising God, and saying … " The Greek here is quite explicit: *stratias ouraniou*. In the plural form, *stratia*, this would mean "soldiers" – members of a land army as distinct from a navy; in the singular, as here in Luke, the most literal translation would simply be "army." The associations of the word not merely with the men, but with the actual weapons of war can be seen from elsewhere in the New Testament, when Paul, in 2 Corinthians 10:4, uses it again, this time metaphorically, to mean "the weapons of warfare" ("for the weapons of our warfare are not carnal").[21] Jerome's Latin Vulgate here follows the Greek very closely with *multitudo militiae caelistis*: in English, "a multitude of the heavenly army." The first break in these serried military ranks seems to be in Luther's great German translation of 1534, where the passage appears as *die Menge der himmlischen Heerscharen* – that final word *Heerscharen* corresponding almost exactly to the English "hosts." Whether or not it owes anything directly to Luther, the systematic disarming of these massed ranks of Heaven by the KJB is quite remarkable. In the Bodleian Library copy of the Bishops' Bible used by the translators we can see by successive annotations that Tyndale's literal "heavenly soldiers" was first marked as needing revision, then altered to "heavenly army," and then finally changed again to the well-known "heavenly host."[22]

It is not difficult to see why the translators might have preferred the more disciplined-sounding "army" to Tyndale's loose collectivity of "soldiers," and why, on further reflection, both contemporary military words were eventually excised in favor of the altogether more archaic and distanced word "host" – with its convenient echoes of 1 Kings 22:19 ("I saw the LORD sitting on his throne, and all the host of heaven standing by him …"). At a time when religion and politics were not merely inseparably mixed but would, within a generation, spill into civil war, all suggestions of heavenly soldiers (whether or not organized as an army) were clearly unacceptable – and probably with good reason, for Tyndale's blunt translation was indeed prophetic of later Puritan rhetoric. On the other hand, "heavenly host," like so many phrases of the KJB, has passed into the language, effectively playing down the immediate military connotations without scholarly falsification. Too close an association with that other heavenly army, Elisha's "horses and chariots of fire" (2 Kings 6:17), has been quietly circumvented.

Moreover the English word "host" – an archaism by the seventeenth century – already had a lengthy and loaded history. Though the *OED* distinguishes four primary meanings of the word "host" in English, all ultimately seem to derive from the Latin roots *hostem/hospitem* which in one form meant "stranger" as "foreigner" and therefore "enemy," and in the other, "stranger" as "foreigner" and therefore "guest" or "one who receives guests." Thus the Latin *hostis*, meaning "stranger" as "enemy" came, by extension, to include large numbers, and therefore "an army" of enemies. But, via the Old French *hoste*, it also acquired the opposite meaning of one who entertains strangers in his house. The route to the disarming of the Nativity angels can be traced in the successive meanings listed in the *OED*: beginning with "an armed company or multitude of men" (1290) we pass to its peaceful opposite, "a great company; a multitude" (1440), and then, quite specifically, to its "biblical and derived" usage, "the host, or hosts of heaven (Heb. *ts'ba hashsha-mayim*) applied to (a) the multitude of angels that attend upon God, and (b) the sun, moon, and stars" (1382). In Old Testament times, angels were, of course, *armed* – and any King James translator wanting to defend his choice of words needed only to cite 1 Kings 22:19 or 2 Kings 6:17 to make his point. But as we have seen, even in Greek New Testament angels were still unequivocally military. It was, paradoxically, the use of the more archaic word, with its Old Testament associations, rather than the contemporary military term, that allowed the subseqent elision of the *OED*'s third meaning (the "hosts of heaven") from being a kind of adjunct of its first meaning (military), to that of its second (a multitude). This peaceful takeover was, of course, cemented by the parallel use of the word as the "host" in the Eucharist – reflecting Christ as host at the Last Supper. What all these meanings suggested – or (aided by poets such as Herbert) came to suggest – was an idea of strangeness as "difference," whether distanced by the past, or by metaphysics: an outcome entirely appropriate for angels.

But if the initial motives here were demonstrably political, the outcome was nevertheless theological. Just over a hundred years later, a biblical commentary reminds us of the polyvalency of all scripture: explaining that according to St. Gregory, the shepherds were types of "the true pastors of the Church"; the angels denoting the appearance of our Savior; while their light signified the divine light in the world. The moral or tropological meaning is that "we should also imitate the Shepherds by glorifying God for the wonderful things he hath made known to us."[23] We are reminded that these are not peculiar way-out interpretations, but a normal part of the seventeenth-century reading process. For the whole of the seventeenth century and much of the eighteenth, every event in the Bible had at least a fourfold meaning, and the language of the KJB was chosen with this in mind.

But whether or not we hail the result as a miracle, there is nothing very mysterious about the *process* by which the style of the KJB was created. It did not arise from nowhere, but (for all the vilification of him) drew heavily on Tyndale, not to mention Coverdale, the Geneva Bible, and the others. A natural conservatism in the face of a very rapidly changing language would probably have given the new translation an archaic feel anyway, but the instructions to follow, where possible, the Bishops' Bible, and a clear political agenda merely reinforced this tendency. Moreover, given that it was the creation of a large committee, with so many checks and balances, it is hardly surprising that the result was a massive uniformity, "the King James steamroller," which flattened differences between Hebrew, Aramaic, and Koine Greek into a single dignified amalgam.

This came to be, in effect, not so much a linguistic subset as a new and enduring idiolect within English – a "Church English" that was, in its own way, to be almost as influential as the "Church Latin" created by Jerome's Vulgate. But this "idiolect" was not so much a personal as a collective language, originally, of course, intended to be read aloud (much as actors might speak their lines – another, unsurprising, link with the theater) rather than for private study and perhaps not at all for spontaneous conversation – often high-flown and poetic, related to everyday speech but also at one remove from it. Such separate linguistic subsets are not infrequent: what makes the language of the KJB so impressive is that it was, as we are informed on the first page, "appointed to be read in Churches" at a time when Church attendence was still compulsory.

There is, in fact, nothing unusual about conducting religious ceremonies and services in a separate linguistic subset, or even a separate language. Hebrew was not, after all, the language of the Jews in first-century Palestine. Jesus would have spoken Aramaic (the language of the Persian Empire) in ordinary life, and worshipped in the Synagogue in Hebrew. There is also strong evidence, from his use of the Septuagint, that he knew Greek – and to judge from his reported conversation with Pilate, probably

Latin as well. To confuse matters still further, the New Testament is written in Koine Greek, the then patois of the Levantine trading community, and very different from the Greek of the Septuagint. Until after the middle of the twentieth century, the Roman Catholic Church read from Jerome's Vulgate and conducted all its Masses in Latin, even though that had ceased to be the language of anywhere in Europe fifteen hundred years before. The Qur'an is written in seventh-century Arabic, not now the language of any Muslim country. Indeed, it has been striking how all of the three great world religions claiming written descent from Abraham – Judaism, Christianity, and Islam – have traditionally conducted their worship in a language different from that of their worshippers' common speech. On this scale, the language of the KJB is historically *unusual* not in its difference, but in its closeness to the English language as a whole.

From Tyndale and Luther onwards the separation of religious language from ordinary speech has been a subject of vigorous debate and condemnation. The attacks on Tyndale – and his eventual judicial execution – make it clear that translation was actually regarded by the ecclesiastical authorities (not to mention the king, Henry VIII) as a form of blasphemy.[24] For many traditionalists, religion was never meant to be in the vulgar tongue. For the more radical translators, on the other hand, it always *had been* in the vulgar tongue. Here is Tyndale in his own defense:

They will say that it [the Bible] cannot be translated into our tongue, it is so rude. It is not so rude as they are false liars. For the Greek tongue agreeth more with the English than with the Latin. And the properties of the Hebrew tongue agreeth a thousand times more with the English than with the Latin. The manner of speaking is both one, so that in a thousand places thou needest not but to translate it into the English word for word when thou must seek a compass in the Latin & yet shall have much work to translate it well-favouredly, so that it have the same grace and sweetness, sense and pure understanding with it in the Latin as it hath in the Hebrew. A thousand parts better may it be translated into the English than into the Latin.[25]

Interestingly – but not implausibly – this is a claim that has been made by a number of later European translators for their own particular languages – including, to my knowledge, Czech, French, Italian, Hungarian, and Romanian. The key to this, of course, is the question of word order. Classical and Church Latin alike rely on a highly structured order of words, commonly with the verb at the end of the sentence, unlike most modern European languages which have much more flexible constructions. Much of the peculiar structure of the KJB results from the confluence of Hebrew parallelism – the repetition of parallel phrases that lies at the heart of Hebrew poetry – with Latinate constructions.

Thus in Psalm 104 – whose origins may well go back to Ahkenaton's Hymn to the Sun – each parallel phrase begins with the material object and is followed by the appropriate verbal epithet:

He causeth the grass to grow for the cattle, and herb for the service of man: that he may bring forth food out of the earth; and wine that maketh glad the heart of man, and oil to make his face to shine, and bread which strengtheneth man's heart. The trees of the LORD are full of sap; the cedars of Lebanon, which he hath planted; where the birds make their nests; as for the stork, the fir trees are her house. The high hills are a refuge for the wild goats; and the rocks for the conies. He appointed the moon for seasons; the sun knoweth his going down. Thou makest darkness, and it is night: wherein all the beasts of the forest do creep forth … (vv. 14–20)

Comparison with a modern, deliberately colloquial translation such as the *Good News Bible* highlights the difference at once.

Although such linguistic, theological and political conservatism can go a long way to explain the tenor of the translation and even the careful choice of words, none serves to account for the overall style – and this is where our various commentators start drawing comparisons with those whom they consider the great stylists of the age (who were, as we have seen, all inconveniently dead except for the omnipresent Shakespeare). Though it was to gather strength in the nineteenth century, this link has roots that go back at least as early as 1725, when John Sharp, Archbishop of York, is reported to have said that the Bible and Shakespeare had made him archbishop.[26] But for a more recent connection, on the grounds that it takes one to know one, we turn to another great English prose stylist: Rudyard Kipling. First published in 1932 in the *Strand Magazine*, "Proofs of Holy Writ" was his last short story, and appeared too late to be included in *Limits and Renewals*, his last volume of collected stories. In it, Shakespeare, now in retirement at New Place in Stratford, is drinking with his old friend and rival Ben Jonson when a messenger arrives with a sheaf of proofs from Miles Smith in Oxford. Smith has been working on the prophetic books from Isaiah to

Malachi, and is now consulting his literary advisor about the finer points of style. With the aid of Ben's superior Latin the two run through a series of emendations of the Bishops' and Geneva Bibles to give the final KJB readings. Perhaps the most striking is that of Ezekiel 27:25, where the KJB (actually translating fairly literally) gives "The ships of Tarshish did sing of thee in thy market." Just how striking is this phrase, however, can be seen from modern translations.

Lightfoot's Revised Version of 1885 clearly finds this too obscure, and explains that "The ships of Tarshish were caravans for thy merchandise." This has been retained by the New English Bible and its successor, the Revised English Bible. The *Good News Bible* finds even this a bit exotic and, flat-footed as ever, comes up with: "Your merchandise was carried in fleets of the largest cargo ships …"

In contrast, Kipling's Shakespeare finds the original irresistible, waxing lyrical in conflating Tarshish with his contemporary London:

But, Ben, ye should have heard my Ezekiel making mock of fallen Tyrus in his twenty-seventh chapter. Miles sent me the whole, for, he said, some small touches. I took it to the bank – four o'clock of a summer morn; stretched out in one of our wherries – and watched London, Port and Town, up and down the river, waking all arrayed to heap more evident excess. Ay! "A merchant for the peoples of many isles" … "The ships of Tarshish did sing of thee in thy markets"? Yes! I saw all Tyre before me neighing her pride against lifted heaven … But what will they let stand of mine at long last? Which?

I'll never know."[27]

We will indeed probably never know if Kipling's hunch was correct, and that Shakespeare acted as leaven in the lump of the translators' work. Though improbable, it is certainly not impossible. Moreover, we should note in passing that Kipling has an eerie track-record of knowing things he had no business to know.[28] In *Puck of Pook's Hill* (1906) he introduces a well into the wall of Pevensey Castle that was not in fact discovered until 1935. Similarly, he was accused of willful inaccuracy in placing the Seventh Cohort of the Thirtieth Legion on Hadrian's Wall when records clearly showed it had been no further north than York at the period. In his own memoirs, published in 1937, he notes that:

I quartered the Seventh Cohort of the Thirtieth (Ulpia Victrix) Legion on the Wall, and asserted that there Roman troops used arrows against the

Picts ... Years after the tale was told, a digging party on the Wall sent me some heavy four-sided, Roman-made "killing arrows" found in situ and – most marvellously – a rubbing of a memorial tablet to the Seventh Cohort of the Thirtieth Legion![29]

Whether or not the language of the KJB really was enlivened by Shakespeare's touch, Kipling is surely right that much of its language has the richness and density of a Shakespeare play. But whereas much of Shakespeare's verbal brilliance comes from innovation and invention of new words, much of the KJB's depends on selective resuscitation. In the First Epistle of Timothy, for instance, Tyndale's choice of the word "erred" is replaced by the curiously modern-sounding "swerved."[30] In fact, of course, the word is Anglo-Saxon, connoting rapid uncontrolled movement, and, like so many in the early seventeenth century, carried both a physical and a metaphorical meaning – as in Othello's grotesquely evocative description of Desdemona as a "bed-swerver." The fact that none of the major twentieth-century translations has chosen to keep the word, replacing it with a variety of other less vigorous metaphors of semi-intentional motion ("falling short" [New English Bible], "gone off" [Jerusalem], "wandered away" [New International Bible], "deviated" [New American Bible, New Revised Standard Bible]) suggests the degree to which the original action has been largely smothered by an induced ambiguity between intention and accident.

But the greater story, that told by the Bible from Genesis to Revelation, from the beginning to the end of Creation, demanded an even more separated and elevated style – and on a grander scale than even Milton himself could sustain. If the scaffolding had been laid down by the original rules – many from King James himself – and much of the actual content taken from earlier translations, it is enlivened by the kind of brilliant gemlike metaphor, such as that of the ships of Tarshish, which reminds us how infinitely more lively, and even witty, the KJB can be in comparison with its modern successors.[31]

In Tyndale's New Testament, John 8:46 is rendered as "Which of you can rebuke me of sin?" Instead of following this perfectly intelligible reading, the KJB has the more obscure and archaic "Which of you convinceth me of sin?" The Greek word in question, *elengcho*, is translated at different points in the KJB by no fewer than six English words: "convince," "convict," "tell one's fault," "reprove," "discover," and (as Tyndale has it here) "rebuke."

Why then the change? The answer seems to lie with the history of that word "convince." Though the *OED* offers only one current meaning of the word, it also lists seven obsolete senses – all of which were current in the early seventeenth century. Lady Macbeth, for instance, says of Duncan's chamberlains

> Will I with wine and wassail so convince
> That memory, the warder of the brain,
> Shall be a fume, and the receipt of reason
> A limbeck only;   (1.7.64–7)

Shakespeare glossaries explain that "convince" here means "overpower," but other meanings of the word, such as "to prove a person guilty … especially by judicial procedure," or "to disprove, refute," or "to demonstrate or prove absurdity" all suggest how her mind is racing ahead to visualize how they might be overpowered, their protestations swept aside and refuted as absurd, and finally be convicted. Similarly in the KJB's careful substitution of "convince" for "rebuke" we may catch just a hint that Jesus is challenging the whole network of semi-judicial accusations flung against him as absurd – without, of course, losing sight of the fact that one day soon these will indeed overpower him and bring him to the ultimate absurdity of the cross.[32]

What is interesting is the relationship between this polyvalent, stylized, artificial, and poetic form of English and the rapidly evolving colloquial language of the streets. What we have seen over the last 400 years is not – as one might reasonably expect – a steadily growing gap between the already-conservative diction of the KJB and the colloquial English of successive centuries, but rather that the KJB has exerted a steady gravitational pull on the ordinary speech, not to mention poetry, of future English. Time and again we find quotations or references from the KJB being incorporated back into the language, preventing the ordinary speech from losing touch completely with Church English around which it orbits. Most of us have heard the story of the NEB translators who decided to find the modern equivalent of "fatted calf" by enquiring at Smithfield [Meat] Market in London – only to be told that the phrase was "fatted calf" because it was in the Bible! Similarly, as Norton has pointed out, the word "ponder" was rescued from archaic oblivion by a single usage: "and Mary kept all these things, and pondered them in her heart."[33] It is arguable, indeed, that this gravitational tension between the Scriptures and common speech over the past 400 years has immensely enriched the English language and its aesthetic resources. But it is precisely that gravitational pull between formal Church English and current colloquial speech that has been the object of the greatest unease among modern translators, who seem unanimous in trying to eliminate that gap and keep up with all the latest linguistic turns.

This may, or may not, make the contents of the Bible more "immediate" for the public such translators hope to reach, but the perceived greater remoteness of the KJB turns out in many ways to encompass a more accurate and even theologically more subtle translation than most modern versions. While our knowledge of the biblical languages has increased substantially in the last 400 years, sensitivity to language seems to have decreased. Whether or not Grayston was correct in his gloomy forebodings about English, one only has to look at specific cases to see the differences between the KJB and recent translations.

Most modern translations have stayed with the "heavenly hosts" of Luke 2, but the *Good News Bible*, true to its evangelical roots, has chosen to return to Tyndale, circumventing militarism by metaphor: "a great army of heaven's angels." Not so Elijah and the Still Small Voice of 1 Kings, 19.[34]

And, behold, the Lord passed by, and a great and strong wind rent the mountains, and brake in pieces the rocks before the Lord; but the Lord was not in the wind: and after the wind an earthquake; but the Lord was not in the earthquake: and after the earthquake a fire; but the Lord was not in the fire: and after the fire a still small voice. (vv. 11–12)

A literal translation of the Hebrew for what the prophet hears would be "a voice of thin silence." Bearing in mind that in Elizabethan English "small" could still mean "thin" (as in "small beer," or Wyatt's "her arms long and small") this is a remarkably accurate translation. In so far as it is obscure or ambiguous, these are obscurities and ambiguities in the original. Something very odd had clearly happened to Elijah.

Modern English translations, however, seem to be unanimous in *rejecting* any such ambiguity or oddity. In the *Good News Bible* what Elijah hears is no more than "the soft whisper of a voice." But the New English Bible isn't sure whether it is a voice at all, and has "a low murmuring sound," while the Catholic Jerusalem Bible outdoes the nascent naturalism of its

Protestant rivals by calling it "the sound of a gentle breeze" – which is a fair translation of the Vulgate's "Et post ignem sibilis aurae tenuis" ("and after the fire, a thin whistling sound of the air"), but does little to address the original Hebrew. More recently the New Revised Standard Version has "a voice of sheer silence" – which at least tries to capture the oxymoron of the Hebrew, though it is not quite clear what "sheer" means in this context.

What is clear is that the modern translators are deeply unwilling to allow ambiguity. Indeed, the *Good News Bible* is quite specific on this point, assuring the reader that

The primary concern of the translators has been to provide a faithful translation of the Hebrew, Aramaic, and Greek texts. Their first task was to understand correctly the meaning of the original … every effort has been made to use language that is natural, clear, simple, and unambiguous.

At first glance this sounds confident and businesslike; then doubts begin to intrude. Would Augustine, Dante, Herbert, Wesley, Coleridge, or Newman have thought that the depths of human spiritual experience could be set out in language that was natural, clear, simple, and unambiguous? Contrast this with John Bois, who was both a translator of the KJB and also a member of the final revision committee for parts of the New Testament. "We have not thought," he wrote, "that the indefinite sense ought to be defined."[35] A modern mental set, it seems, cannot tolerate a blurring of the boundaries between an "inner" visionary experience, and an "outer" naturalistic one. Apparently it has to be one or the other: to float between the two is to leave translators uneasy, even if it keeps poets happy.

Yet such a distinction is as foreign to the KJB as it is to the Hebrew world-picture. Classical Hebrew had no word (and therefore no concept of) "nature" in our sense. The normal progression of the seasons was seen as being as much the result of God's direct action as the whirlwind that, we are told, whisked Elijah to Heaven.[36] As a result, there could be no concept of the "miraculous" either. The relationship between humanity and environment was fundamentally different. Yet it is clear that there was an essential discontinuity between the cyclical world of "primal participation" as expressed in the cult of Baal, and the world of meaningful change, and therefore of History, into which Yahweh was perceived as bringing his people. Yahweh is not a fire God (like Baal), nor one of winds and earthquakes, yet from whom, if not from him, did these come? To use those modern categories in which – it is true – we are culturally conditioned to think, are we to understand this as a "miracle" – linking it for instance with the parallel story of Moses and the burning bush (Exod. 3:1–4:17) which supposedly happened in the same spot, or are we to understand it as a "vision" (like Isaiah's vision of the Lord in the temple, when he, too, is purged by fire)? Can we, perhaps, dispense with the supernatural altogether, and join the modern translators in understanding it as soft whispers in the night, or the wind on the heath? The Hebrew holds us poised at every level between different kinds of event that cannot, and *must* not, be told in any other way without destroying the meaning – just as Kierkegaard discovered in *Fear and Trembling* that the story of Abraham and Isaac could not be re-interpreted and re-told. The whole thrust of this story seems to be to deny *and* simultaneously affirm certain connections. Thus Yahweh *is*, and *is not*, a God of natural phenomena (a paradox more familiar as "immanence" and "transcendence"); revelation is both "miraculous" and "natural"; and God is concerned both with the individual *and* the shaping of history.

One could go on: the passage is a rich and fascinating one which has attracted much commentary through the ages, but another problem is beginning to intrude. Whereas the KJB's rendering meets these Kierkegaardian criteria, the modern translators, and the Bible Society, apparently confident of knowing "the correct meaning of the original" text, have shown very little interest in any *literal* meaning of the text, or the problems inherent in it, and have instead chosen quite blatantly interpretative paraphrases to suit what they must believe are modern sensibilities.

If we began with the unlovely metaphor of a steamroller, flattening diverse languages and styles into a single medium; we continued with an appropriately contemporary seventeenth-century image of gravitational attraction; we conclude with Kierkegaardian literalism as an existential commitment to truth. Indeed, *Fear and Trembling* might be an excellent place to begin to understand a poetic theology virtually unknown today. If the KJB began with politics, it was driven by a kind of literalism which sought not to simplify but to convey the original texts in all their full complexity – creating in the process a huge range of poetic phrases that have enriched both our language and our theology. Poetry, as we know, is an immensely compressed, immensely allusive and imaginative use of language, taking us to, and even beyond, the very boundaries of thought. It is less often observed – sadly, even by theologians themselves – that these are the very qualities that are, or should be, central to their own discipline.

If I seem here to have come full circle, back to the aesthetic praise heaped upon the KJB over the past two centuries, it is to make a sometimes overlooked point: that aesthetics is not an end in itself. In Northrop Frye's brilliant analogy, aesthetics is a psychopomp, a conductor of souls of the dead to where it cannot follow. Having guided Dante through Hell and Purgatory, Virgil finally disappears at the very moment when the poet actually encounters Beatrice, the divine vision and object of his desire. Art can point the way to where it cannot follow. In the end, what is most remarkable about the KJB is not any inherent beauty of its prose style, or originality of its imagery, but its essential *modesty* – its translucency even – that points beyond the poetry to what, in its own inimitable way, that poetry is all about.

NOTES

1 "The English Bible – a book which, if everything else in our language should perish, would alone suffice to show the whole extent of its beauty and power." T. B. Macaulay, "On John Dryden," (1828) *The Life and Works of Lord Macaulay Complete*, 10 vols. (London: Longman, 1903), vol. 5, 101.

2 *On the Authorized Version of the New Testament*, (1858, 2nd edn. London: Parker, 1859), 6.

3 George Saintsbury, *History of Elizabethan Literature* (London: Macmillan, 1901), 218.

4 Sir Arthur Quiller-Couch, *On the Art of Writing* (Cambridge: Cambridge University Press, 1916), 134.

5 H. L. Mencken, *Treatise on the Gods* (New York: Vintage Books, 1930), 188.

6 John Livingston Lowes, *Essays in Appreciation* (Port Washington, NY: Kennikat Press, 1967), 4.

7 H. Wheeler Robinson, *The Bible in Its Ancient and English Versions* (Oxford: Clarendon Press, 1940).

8 David Norton, *A History of the English Bible as Literature* (Cambridge: Cambridge University Press, 2000), ch. 5.

9 David Norton, *A History of the Bible as Literature* (2 vols., Cambridge: Cambridge University Press, 1993), vol. 2, 73–85.

10 Henning Graf Reventlow, *The Authority of the Bible and the Rise of the Modern World*, trans. John Bowden (London: SCM Press, 1984), 329.

11 See Stephen Prickett, *Origins of Narrative: The Romantic Appropriation of the Bible* (Cambridge: Cambridge University Press, 1996), ch. 2.

12 Saintsbury, *History of Elizabethan Literature*, 215.

13 Quiller-Couch, *On the Art of Writing*, 134.

14 Mary Ellen Chase, *The Bible and the Common Reader* (New York: Macmillan, 1952), 23.

15 Gustavus S. Paine, *The Learned Men* (New York: Thomas Y. Crowell, 1959), 167.

16 *Ibid.*, 50.

17 Charles C. Butterworth, *The Literary Lineage of the King James Bible* (Philadelphia: University of Pennsylvania Press, 1941), 232.

18 "It is a miracle and a mystery, since group writing seldom achieves great heights. Individual writings of the committeemen show no trace of the magnificent style ..." Olga S. Opfell, *The King James Bible Translators*, (Jefferson, NC: McFarland, 1982).

19 Kenneth Grayston, "Confessions of a Biblical Translator," *New Universities Quarterly*, 33.3 (1979): 288.

20 See Norman Sykes, "The Authorized Version of 1611," *The Bible Today* (London: Eyre & Spottiswode, 1955), 141–3.

21 I owe this translation and the subsequent illustration to Professor David Jasper.

22 See Edward Craney Jacobs, "King James's Translators: the Bishops' Bible New Testament Revised," *The Library*, ser. 6, 14.2 (1992): 105.

23 *The History of the Old and New Testament Extracted from the Sacred Scriptures, the Holy Fathers, and Other Ecclesiastical Writers* ... 4th impression, 1712, NT, 17.

24 See David Lawton, *Blasphemy* (Philadelphia: University of Pennsylvania Press, 1993).

25 See David Daniell, *Tyndale's New Testament* (New Haven, CT: Yale University Press), 1989, xxii. Such claims are common among European translators. Norton cites Augustinus Steuchus's statement that Hebrew poetry "is similar to the Italian rather than to the Latin"; and Le Clerc that the genius of Hebrew in its poetic form is "conformable to that of the French tongue" (*A History* [1993], vol. 1, 278–9).

26 Gilbert Burnet, *History of My Own Time* (London: Printed for the Company of Booksellers, 1725), vol. 3, 100.

27 Rudyard Kipling, "Proofs of Holy Writ," *The Complete Works in Prose and Verse of Rudyard Kipling*, Sussex edn. (Macmillan, 1937–9), vol. 30, 354.

28 See Prickett, *Victorian Fantasy*, 2nd edn. (Waco: Baylor University Press, 2005), 210–13.

29 Rudyard Kipling, *Something of Myself for my Friends Known and Unknown* (London: Macmillan, 1964), 189.

30 1 Timothy 1:6. See Ward Allen, "The Meaning of δστσζησατεξ at 1 Timothy 1:6," *Bulletin of the Institute for Reformation Biblical Studies*, 2.1 (1991): 15–18.

31 For an extensive list of these verbal gems that have passed into the language, see Norton, *A History* (1993), vol. 2, 80–5.

32 I am indebted to Ward Allen for this example.

33 Luke 2:19.

34 See Prickett, *Words and the Word: Language, Poetics and Biblical Interpretation* (Cambridge: Cambridge University Press, 1986), ch. 1.

35 Cited by Ward Allen (ed.), *Translating for King James* (London: Allen Lane/the Penguin Press, 1970), 89.

36 See H. Wheeler Robinson, *Inspiration and Revelation in the Old Testament* (Oxford: Oxford University Press, 1962), 34.

2 | The glories and the glitches of the King James Bible

Ecclesiastes as test-case

ROBERT ALTER

Four centuries on, the King James Bible (KJB) still stands as one of the towering achievements of style in the English language. Subsequent translations of the Bible have only highlighted the grandeur of the 1611 version. The Revised Standard Version in its various recensions, though relatively more correct and less archaic, is a flattening and dilution of the seventeenth-century translation. The sundry English versions done by the scholarly-ecclesiastical committees of the different denominations in the second half of the twentieth century are for the most part stylistically inept and often embarrassing in their mixture of disparate linguistic registers and in their misguided efforts to make the syntax and diction of the ancient texts sound up-to-date. The power of the KJB is vividly registered in the multiple ways it has affected the shape of literary English from the seventeenth century to the present – in England, early on, in George Herbert, Bunyon, Blake, and others; in America, where the legacy of the KJB eventually became more pervasive, in the poetry of Emily Dickinson and Whitman, in the prose style of Melville, Hemingway, Faulkner, and all the way to Marilynne Robinson and Cormac McCarthy in the present literary moment.

And yet, the justified admiration for the KJB ought not to entail an idolatrous attitude toward it. To begin with, we need to remember that the 1611 translation, the product of different sub-committees assigned different groups of books, is not all of one piece, and even within any single book, the translators often performed considerably better in some passages than in others. There is also the uncomfortable fact of inaccuracy, which I shall mention only briefly. Biblical Hebrew is much better understood today than it was in Christian Hebraist circles at the beginning of the seventeenth century. (Hebrew exegetes of the Middle Ages and the Early Modern Period were on the whole much more sure-footed with the language, though there were inevitable gaps in their knowledge, perhaps especially in regard to rare terms.) Consequently, one repeatedly encounters small misconstructions of idioms, syntax, and lexical values in the 1611 version, and there are more than a few real howlers. Let me offer just three instances. In Genesis 15, at the awesome moment of the covenant between God and Abraham over the cloven animal parts, it is said of Abraham, "and, lo, a horror of great darkness fell upon him." The actual meaning of the Hebrew is "a great dark horror [or dread] fell upon him." Because the Hebrew feminine adjective *hasheikhah*, "dark," is formally identical with the noun that means "darkness," the seventeenth-century translators confused the syntax and made Abraham our forefather afraid of the dark (in fact, it is twilight when this event occurs in the narrative). In Job's initial death-wish poem, we read, "Let them curse it that curse the day, who are ready to raise up their mourning" (3:8). Although Job is fixated on death, he is not in the least thinking of mourning here. The 1611 translators misconstrued *livyatan*, Leviathan, for a homonym that means "their mourning" (though they ignored the fact that the purported possessive suffix of this homonym is, incongruously, feminine). Through this mistake, they deleted from the poem a powerful mythological invocation of the primordial sea-monster who will reappear at the culminating moment of the Voice from the Whirlwind. Finally, in 2 Samuel 18, the second messenger sent by Joab to announce to David the victory over Absalom is called "Cushi," but the Hebrew is a gentilic designation, not a proper name – that is, "Cushite," which probably means Ethiopian. The inadvertent comic effect of this mistake is especially keen for speakers of modern Hebrew: *cushi*, once the term for "Negro," is now felt to be derogatory, and it formerly enjoyed some currency as a name for black-haired dogs.

Misconstructions of this sort reflect the limitations of knowledge of the era, and we need not dwell on them further. My concern here, precisely because the King James Bible exhibits so many stylistic splendors, is to what extent it is an apt stylistic equivalent of the original. The 1611 translators made many sound choices of stylistic policy, which by and large have been jettisoned by the sundry modern English versions to their palpable detriment. Because the translators convened by King James believed that the Bible was inspired by God word for word, their representation of the original is on the whole quite literal. Hebrew idioms are often treated literally, and as a result of the prestige that the translation acquired, some of these have become English idioms (for example, "found favor in his eyes"). With the great model of Tyndale before them, the 1611 translators favored – though not invariably – a homespun English diction that conveyed a good deal of the eloquent plainness and concreteness of the Hebrew prose. (Tyndale, we should recall, spoke of an underlying affinity between Hebrew and English.) The KJB also generally follows the syntactic contours of the Hebrew, reproducing the predominant parataxis that is the vehicle of some of its most important literary effects, especially in the narrative prose. Parataxis is not a native form of expression in English prose, but after the King James Bible it exerted an attraction for some prose writers that it would not have done otherwise, as the signal instances of Melville and Hemingway, in other respects poles apart stylistically, illustrate.

Much of the literary power of the ancient Hebrew texts derives from their terrific compactness of formulation. This quality often cannot be readily conveyed in English because English is an analytic language and biblical Hebrew is a synthetic language – that is, a language that packs objects of verbs and possessive pronouns into suffixes, indicates the pronominal subjects of verbs simply by the conjugated forms, and so forth. As a result, what can be said in three or four words in Hebrew often takes eight or ten in English. There are, moreover, very few polysyllabic words in biblical Hebrew, and consequently both the poetry and the prose exhibit a strong rhythmic compactness that is an essential element of their expressive force. Sometimes the KJB handles this challenge very well and sometimes very badly, though it does not appear that compactness was a conscious stylistic aim of the 1611 translators. It is fair to say that the eloquence they often attained was more Jacobean than biblical, more orotund and expansive, exhibiting a certain relish for piling on syllables and words. Their rendering of Psalms, for example, which is in many instances quite fine, is closer to the sprawling free-verse line of Whitman (who of course was directly influenced by the King James Psalms) than to the rhythmic concision of the Hebrew. Here is a verse from Job (3:11) in which the King James Bible nicely renders the concision of the Hebrew in the first half of the line and then stumbles badly in the second half of the line: "Why died I not from the womb? *why* did I *not* give up the ghost when I came out of the belly?" The first half of the line is rhythmically right and could scarcely be better as a rendering of the four Hebrew words, *lamah lo' meireḥem 'amut*. In the second half of the line, we are given fifteen English words for three in the

Hebrew, *mibeten yats'ati ve'egvah*. (My own version, still not as compact as the Hebrew, cuts this down to "from the belly come out, breathe my last.") For translators who exhibit such great literary sensitivity elsewhere, this sprawling arhythmic half-line suggests that neither concision nor rhythm was an aspect of the Hebrew they considered essential to convey, though they sometimes intuitively reproduced those qualities. This particular example is symptomatic of the translation as a whole: it is often wonderfully eloquent, as everyone tends to remember, but there are more places than we are accustomed to recognize in which awkwardness occurs, in which the translation gets caught in an unnecessary tangle of words.

I would like to concentrate on Ecclesiastes as an exemplary instance of the strengths and the shortcomings of the KJB precisely because by and large it is one of the most admirable achievements of the 1611 translators. Most attentive English readers remember, for good reason, the haunting cadences of the great prose-poem about the futility of all things that begins the book and the solemn insistence of the first of the book's two formal poems, "A time to be born and a time to die," in the third chapter. Let me quote five verses from the opening prose-poem:

What profit hath a man of all his labour which he taketh under the sun? *One* generation passeth away, and *another* generation cometh: but the earth abideth for ever. The sun also ariseth, and the sun goeth down, and hasteth to his place where he arose. The wind goeth toward the south, and turneth about unto the north; it whirleth about continually, and the wind returneth again according to his circuits. All the rivers run into the sea; yet the sea *is* not full; unto the place from whence the rivers come, thither they return again. (1:3–7)

This splendid English rendering could not easily be surpassed. Its stylistic power derives directly from its ability to create faithful equivalents for the most prominent features of the Hebrew. Unlike the sundry modern translators, who seem to focus narrowly on lexical values and semantics, the seventeenth-century committee of scholars was clearly listening to the solemn music of the Hebrew. The clauses, almost exclusively paratactic after the first sentence, are beautifully weighted, with pauses at just the right points, to create cadences quite like those of the Hebrew, deploying a diction that strongly favors the Anglo-Saxon component of English. (One exception, "circuits," probably worked better in the seventeenth century than it does now, when the word has accrued a variety of alien associations, though perhaps in any case "rounds" might have been a better choice.) The polysyllabic "generations" is the only English equivalent for the monosyllabic Hebrew *dor*, but otherwise the King James translators nicely manage to use compact English words that hew to the rhythmic contours of the Hebrew. Elegant synonymity, which has held a disastrous attraction for modern translators of the Bible, is scrupulously avoided, as one can see especially in the ordinary verbs, many of them pointedly repeated, that are used here: go, come, arise, run, turn, return. The Hebrew, it should be said, manifests even more repetition, a practice idiomatically natural in the biblical language but also in keeping with this book's vision of reality as an endless cycle of repetition. Thus, "all his labour which he taketh [an odd verb to use here] under the sun" is in the Hebrew "all his labour which he laboureth under the sun," and instead of "All the rivers run into the sea," the Hebrew uses, once again, the verb "to go." The virtues in evidence in the translation of this opening passage recur throughout the book. Time after time, the translators resist the temptation to embellish the language of Ecclesiastes or to transpose it into an alien rhetoric in an effort to make it more indigenously English. Consider the lovely monosyllabic directness of "All go unto one place; all are of the dust, and all turn to dust again" (3:20); and note the apt diction of "*It is* better to go to the house of mourning, than to the house of feasting: for that *is* the end of all men; and the living will lay *it* to his heart" (7:2). The last phrase here is a small indication of the sure sense of appropriate English idiom generally exhibited by the King James translators. The literal meaning of the Hebrew is "give to his heart," and "lay it to his heart" gets both the meaning and the linguistic register exactly right.

The indisputable power of the treatment of Ecclesiastes in the King James Bible obliges one to qualify an often made assertion about the reason for the overall success of the 1611 translation. Wondering how it was possible for a committee – or more precisely, a team of committees – to produce a work of genius, many observers have claimed that it was because the various committees abundantly cribbed from a single translator of genius, William Tyndale. There may be a measure of truth in this explanation, but no Tyndale translation exists for Ecclesiastes, so there could be no borrowing in this case. Tyndale established a precedent in the handling of diction and syntax that no doubt pointed the way for his successors in the next century, but the instance of Ecclesiastes is evidence that, even working as a committee, they had their own splendid sense of language.

In light of all this, it is hardly surprising that the 1611 rendering of Ecclesiastes has imposed itself on the imagination of many later writers in English. Hemingway's *The Sun Also Rises* is an instructive case in point. He not only took his title from Ecclesiastes but used as an epigraph the entire passage from chapter 1 that I have quoted here. This makes it an unusually long epigraph, and Hemingway surely could have announced his theme of the futility of all things by citing one or two verses instead of five. Perhaps he was in part drawn to more extensive quotation because the prominent parataxis of the prose established a kind of ground for his own paratactic style, though at the same time he would of course have avoided the incantatory character of the language used in Ecclesiastes. But I suspect that, beyond all other considerations, he ended up with this hundred-word epigraph because of the mesmerizing power of the passage in the KJB: it works, like the original, by emphatic incremental repetition, and once you begin quoting it, you don't want to stop.

There is an affinity between Hemingway's cultivation of plain diction and the language of the KJB, but the 1611 version of Ecclesiastes could exert a strong magnetism even upon a writer at the stylistic antipodes from it, as is the case with Faulkner. Throughout his novels, the words he loved the most are recondite and gorgeously polysyllabic, and his characteristic syntax is hypotactic and elaborately convoluted. Yet Thomas Sutpen, the protagonist of what is probably Faulkner's greatest novel, *Absalom, Absalom!*, though he speaks a self-consciously high-falutin language, several times echoes in his own bombastic style the disillusioned vision of Ecclesiastes; and the explosive revelation he experiences that there is a leisure class waited upon hand and foot by the subjected is couched in the following terms: "it meant more than all the human puny mortals under the sun that might lie in hammocks all afternoon with their shoes off."[1] The Ecclesiastean phrase, "under the sun," recurs perhaps half a dozen times in the novel, always in thematically freighted contexts, echoing the biblical perception, impressed by the force of this foundational English rendering, that nothing changes, nothing meaningful is accomplished, "and *there is* no new *thing* under the sun" (1:9).

The King James Ecclesiastes, then, still strongly resonant after four centuries, invites a degree of awe for its stylistic achievement, but that should not preclude a critical perspective, for the 1611 translation of this as of other books of the Bible is far from a perfect thing. Let me begin with the famous phrase that stands at the head of the book and is many times repeated: "Vanity of vanities, saith the Preacher, vanity of vanities; all *is* vanity" (1:2). This phrase is soon joined in the text with another reiterated thematic phrase, "behold, all *is* vanity and vexation of spirit" (1:14). Now, an English reader is likely to notice that both these phrases as Latinate abstractions diverge from the plain diction evident elsewhere which faithfully represents the stylistic cast of the Hebrew. But inaccuracy as well as a shift in register is involved here. "Vanity of vanities," as I shall explain, is somewhat misleading about the Hebrew, and "vexation of spirit" is altogether wrong. The King James translators were obviously drawn to the former translation choice by the *vanitas* of the Vulgate. The Hebrew does in fact imply something like futility or emptiness, but it suggests more than that precisely because it is not an abstraction – abstractions are relatively rare in biblical Hebrew – but a concrete metaphor. The Hebrew *hevel* means "breath," or more precisely, "exhaled breath." A few occurrences in other biblical texts open the possibility that it may have been a lexicalized metaphor in biblical usage, though in rabbinic Hebrew it explicitly denotes the physical entity of breath. My own translation is "mere breath," and for the superlative form *havel havalim*, "merest breath." As mere breath, it lacks substance, is evanescent, elusive, scarcely perceptible. The metaphor thus conveys this whole package of overlapping attributes, not just *vanitas*, and representing it as a single abstraction dilutes the richness of what is said. "Vexation of spirit" is still more problematic. For whatever reasons, the 1611 translators exhibit a special fondness for the term "vexation," and not merely in Ecclesiastes, using it as the English equivalent for several different Hebrew words. My guess is that in this case they arrived at "vexation" because they misconstrued the Hebrew *re'ut* as deriving from *ra'*, "evil" or "harm." It may be true that humankind in Ecclesiastes is subject to many vexations, but those are not indicated by this particular term. *Re'ut* in fact derives from the verbal stem *r-'-h*, which means to shepherd (or, in the Song of Solomon, by metonymic extension, to graze, which is what the shepherded flocks do). *Ruah*, the Hebrew term translated in this phrase as "spirit," does sometimes mean that, but as with equivalent terms in many other languages, it also means "breath" or "wind" (as in 1:6, quoted above), and you have to look at the context to decide which of these three senses is most likely. The bracketing with *hevel*, "breath," argues against construing the term as "spirit." The most probable meaning of *re'ut ruah* is "herding the wind," a preeminently futile activity because you can't pen in the wind or crack a whip over it, and as we are reminded in 1:6, the wind turns round and round, from one point of the compass to its opposite. "Vexation of spirit," like much else in the KJB, may have become proverbial, but it replaces a vivid and original metaphor in the Hebrew that much better expresses the sense of the futility of human endeavor which is central to this book.

The strength of the 1611 translation is in large part a consequence, as I have noted, of its reproducing the concreteness of the Hebrew, but, as with "vanity" and "vexation," it occasionally interposes an abstraction – characteristically, a Latinate word – where there is nothing like it in the original. Thus in 1:16 we read, "yea, my heart had great experience of wisdom and knowledge." What the Hebrew says is simply "my heart has seen much wisdom and knowledge," for Ecclesiastes imagines the undertaking of philosophic investigation on which he is embarked in virtually bodily terms – turning around to every side, looking, seeing. The introduction of "experience" is not altogether wrong in representing the intention of the statement, but it does what modern translations do repeatedly and what the KJB does only rarely, which is to make the translation an explanation of the original. Another translation choice that does much the same thing is "In the day of prosperity be joyful, but in the day of adversity consider" (7:14). The very sound of the two tetrasyllabic Latinate abstractions is a dissonance in the chain of plain words in which they appear. What the Hebrew actually says is, "On the day of good enjoy [literally "be in"] the good, and on the day of evil, see." One may grant that "good" could be extended to mean "good things" or even "good luck," but "prosperity" and "adversity" constitute an interpretative gloss on the primary vocabulary of the original, a move that is almost always a tactical error in translation, and they also eliminate the strong repetition of "good" (repetition is at the heart of biblical rhetoric) and the neat antithesis with "evil."

In a few cases, the recourse to an abstraction appears to reflect a struggle to understand the Hebrew. There are a good many Hebrew phrases and even whole clauses in Ecclesiastes that are not readily intelligible, and given that the most philologically keen modern scholars have not had much success with these knotty junctures, one can hardly fault the King James translators for failing to make good sense of them. At other points, however, the text is only slightly crabbed or gnomic, and in these instances the falling back on a misleading abstraction is regrettable. At the very end of the seventh chapter, we encounter: "Lo, this only have I found, that God hath made man upright; but they have sought out many inventions." The appearance here of "inventions" is a little puzzling. The Hebrew *hishbonot* means "reckonings." It is of a piece with the book-keeping or mercantile vocabulary that Ecclesiastes uses again and again. At times, the King James translators seem to grasp this usage, as in their apt rendering of the phrase that appears at the beginning of the book, "What profit hath a man of all his labour." The Hebrew noun here, *yitron*, might be very literally rendered as "surplus" or "plus," and "profit" is exactly right in meaning and feeling as an English equivalent. When the translators chose "inventions," what they had in mind was obviously not the sort of thing one sends to the patent office but something like "devisings," a meaning that can be indicated by this Hebrew verbal stem. That rather general notion, however, does not do justice to the bottom-line calculation that Ecclesiastes is excoriating here. God had made man upright, or honest, but driven by the profit motive, human beings have contrived many figures to juggle and may readily be led astray from their native disposition to honesty.

Another problem with the KJB is that it does not always respect the commitment of the Hebrew to reiterate the same thematic key-words – a formal device that Ecclesiastes shares with biblical narrative and that Franz Rosenzweig and Martin Buber described as *Leitwortstil*, literally, leading-word style. An English term that the seventeenth-century translators seem particularly fond of is "travail." It is a fine old word for duress or suffering, and to our ears in the twenty-first century it has a nice literary ring. What is unfortunate is that it stands in for two different Hebrew words in this brief text and a few others elsewhere in the Bible. In 2:26 we read, "to the sinner he giveth travail, to gather and to heap up." The two infinitives that follow the noun here may themselves suggest that it is not quite the right word. The Hebrew *'inyan* is one of Ecclesiastes' lexical innovations, or perhaps merely a reflection of a development in Late Biblical Hebrew, and it is used repeatedly. The term is part of the mercantile vocabulary of the book, and it means something close to "business." What the verse under consideration is saying is that God gives the sinner a lot of business with which to occupy himself, gathering and heaping up possessions that in the end will only pass on to someone better than himself. Similarly, in 1:13, where one encounters in the translation "sore travail hath God given to the sons of man to be exercised therewith," the Hebrew noun is again 'inyan, and the proper sense is "an evil business God has given to the sons of men to busy themselves with." Three chapters on, we come across "Again, I considered all travail, and every right work, that for this a man is envied of his neighbor" (4:4). The subordinate clause that comes after "travail" is a clear indication that it is a wrong translation choice because a man's travail would surely not be something for others to envy. In this instance, the Hebrew noun is 'amal, which is properly translated in 1:3 as "labour." How did the translators arrive at "travail" here? This same Hebrew term can mean either "labor"/"toil" or, as repeatedly in Job, "misery"/"travail." It never has the latter meaning in Ecclesiastes. Again and again, this skeptical Late Biblical writer asserts that man toils but gets nothing from his toil, or worse, excites the envy of others for what he temporarily profits from his labor (the Hebrew 'amal means both toil and, by extension, the consequences of toil). In fact, Ecclesiastes links 'amal and 'inyan as related terms for onerous activity – labor and business or busy-ness – that in the end leads to nothing. Thus, in 4:8, the translation has: "For whom do I labour, and bereave my soul of good? This is also vanity, yea, it *is* a sore travail." The Hebrew term represented by "labour" is in this instance the verbal form of 'amal; "travail" should again be "business," 'inyan, which is much like labor. Etymologically, of course, "travail" is also associated with labor by way of the French *travaille* from which it derives, but even in the seventeenth century, the pain linked with labor was the leading edge of the word, so its use here loses the sense of strenuous workaday effort conveyed by the two different Hebrew words for which it is made the English equivalent in the translation.

Perhaps the least noticed, or the least remembered, feature of the King James Bible is that there are moments when, for all its justly celebrated eloquence, it sounds altogether awkward. I raise this criticism with a degree of humility learned from my own experience as a translator of the Bible: no one is infallible, and there are times when in the sheer concentration on getting right in English what you perceive the original to be saying, you may produce an unlovely sentence without quite realizing it. Stylistic pratfalls of this sort are scattered through all the books of the King James Bible, and there are a few instances in Ecclesiastes. I will pass in silence over those cases that appear to be a consequence of floundering to get at the meaning of a difficult crux in the original, but let me cite just two examples where the Hebrew is perfectly clear in order to indicate that this translation, abounding though it is in stylistic felicities, is far from flawless in regard to style.

One of the injunctions to diligence, which actually sounds more like Proverbs than like Ecclesiastes, reads as follows: "By much slothfulness the building decayeth; and through idleness of the hands the house droppeth through" (10:18). There is one real error here, which has the effect of obscuring a vivid image in the Hebrew. The verb "decayeth" reflects a confusion on the part of the translators of *yimaq*, which does mean to decay, and *yimakh*, the word that appears in the text, which means to go down low or to sag. The plain sense of the verse is: "Through sloth the roof-beam sags, and through slack hands the house leaks." The slightly off-target translation choices in the first half of the verse eliminate the sagging beam entirely, while the wording for the second half of the line is likely to leave a reader in a state of confusion. Perhaps "droppeth through" in the seventeenth century could be a way of referring to a leaky roof, but it certainly sounds awkward, and it leaves some ambiguity as to whether the biblical writer is speaking of rain leaking into the house or the house collapsing.

My second example does not involve any misconstruction of the Hebrew, but the wording is likely to make the reader struggle with the verse – the seventeenth-century reader, I would guess, as well as the present-day one: "There is a vanity which is done upon the earth; that there be just *men*, unto whom it happeneth according to the work of the wicked; again, there be wicked *men*, to whom it happeneth according to the work of the righteous: I said that this also is vanity" (8:14). It is obvious that "work" here means "acts," a sense of the word for which the *Oxford English Dictionary* cites the Geneva Bible as the earliest instance, and which is certainly put into play repeatedly in the KJB. Even so, the formulation is cumbersome and at least a little opaque. The problem here is the translators' attachment to the literal configuration of the Hebrew, a practice that elsewhere, as I have noted, yields stylistic strengths. The single Hebrew word *kema'aseh* does mean "according to the work," but in the original it is a very common, compact, and fluent idiom, whereas this English equivalent is anything but fluent as a way of representing "for what is done by" (the verbal stem of this noun means "to do"). The sensible way to get this idiom across in English is to abandon the reproduction of the Hebrew noun-form to which the 1611 translators were committed and also to get rid of the awkward "according to" to indicate the Hebrew particle *ke*. I would propose the following for this verse: "There are righteous to whom it befalls as though they did wickedly, and there are wicked to whom it befalls as though they did righteously."

In all this, I do not mean to carp but merely to suggest that, in the midst of the celebration of the glories of the KJB, it is also well to keep in mind that there are more than a few moments when the seventeenth-century translators stumbled. Their achievement is nevertheless remarkable, and at its best deeply moving, manifesting some of the finest literary English written in this century of extraordinary literature. Consider their rendering of the great somber poem on mortality and the decay of the body that begins the last chapter of the book:

Remember now thy Creator in the days of thy youth, while the evil days come not, nor the years draw nigh, when thou shalt say, I have no pleasure in them; While the sun, or the light, or the moon, or the stars, be not darkened, nor the clouds return after the rain: In the day when the keepers of the house shall tremble, and the strong men shall bow themselves, and the grinders cease because they are few, and those that look out of the windows be darkened, And the doors shall be shut in the streets, when the sound of the grinding is low, and he shall rise up at the voice of the bird, and all the daughters of musick shall be brought low; Also *when* they shall be afraid of *that which is* high, and fears *shall be* in the way, and the almond tree shall flourish, and the grasshopper shall be a burden, and desire shall fail: because man goeth to his long home, and the mourners go about the streets: Or ever the silver cord be loosed, or the golden bowl be broken, or the pitcher be broken at the fountain, or the wheel broken at the cistern. Then shall the dust return to the earth as it was: and the spirit shall return unto God who gave it. (12:1–7)

There are obscurities in the original of this haunting poem that are not managed well by the King James translators, but this scarcely matters in regard to the literary power of the English text they have produced. Most modern scholars, for example, think that the word rendered as "desire" actually refers to a plant, the caper-fruit, but the failing of desire – a beautiful phrase – is very much in keeping with the mood of the poem. That mystifying "the grasshopper shall be a burden" is probably also a mistake because the Hebrew *hagav* here in all likelihood indicates not a grasshopper, as it usually does elsewhere, but the locust tree, so the clause would then mean "and the locust tree is laden." The equally mystifying "wheel broken at the cistern" is actually "the jug smashed at the pit," and the reference is to an ancient practice, confirmed by archaeology, of smashing earthern vessels at the gravesite in a ritual of mourning.

But what powerfully overrides all inaccuracies of this sort is the solemn music of the language. Note how consistently the translation hews to the dignified simplicity of diction of the Hebrew, deploying an abundance of monosyllabic words and favoring the Anglo-Saxon component of the language – "Then shall the dust return to the earth as it was." In this passage, there is no intrusion of terms such as "experience," "prosperity," "adversity," "vexation." The translators appear to have understood the text as rhythmic prose, whereas the Hebrew uses formal lines of parallelistic verse, but the admirable effect in English is a long series of stately cadences that perfectly reinforce the poem's somber evocation of mortality. And there is a felicity of phrasing that reflects one of the great strengths of the King James Bible, as in "Or ever the silver cord be loosed, or the golden bowl be broken." "Loosed" is as fine a rendering as one could imagine of the slightly obscure Hebrew *yeiraḥeq*, which appears to mean "be distanced" or "go away" (though many now emend it to a similar-sounding verb that means "to be snapped"). Even more remarkable, I think, is "because man goeth to his long home." The literal sense of the noun phrase at the end of the clause is "everlasting home" or "eternal home." The translators' choice of "long home" is brilliant both because it enters into the spirit of how the biblical writers conceive great temporal duration – not anything as ponderous as "eternity" but rather something that goes on and on – and because its stark understatement and its very compactness are so much in keeping with the stylistic tenor of the Hebrew.

It is true, as I have tried to show through these examples, that the King James Bible sometimes misleads English readers in nuance and even in egregious substance about the meaning of the original, sometimes obscures significant figurative language in the original, occasionally violates its own general principle of eloquently plain language, and from time to time is unaccountably awkward or needlessly obscure. But as the rendering of the concluding poem in Ecclesiastes on mortality vividly demonstrates, the translation overall is one of the great literary creations in English of the seventeenth century. As such, it achieved two culturally momentous ends. As this version of the Bible was rapidly adopted not merely by ecclesiastical authority but also by the reading public as canon-ical, it significantly intervened in the evolution of literary English: a whole lexicon, a different kind of diction, and a way of ordering words syntactic-ally became an available resource for writers of both poetry and prose. At the same time, the King James translators realized much of the aim they had consciously in mind: their work made the experience of the Bible – its poetic peaks and the powerful reticence of its terse narratives – accessible to readers in a language that was at one and the same time indigenously English and a faithful sounding-box for the cadences and the tonalities of the original. After four centuries, we clearly need more than the KJB to get the Bible right in English, but we still cannot get along without it. As Edmund Wilson, who devoted a good deal of thought to the role of the Bible in our culture, once observed, we have been living with it all our lives.

NOTE

1 William Faulkner, *Absalom, Absalom!* (New York: Vintage, 1990), 192.

PART II

The History of the King James Bible

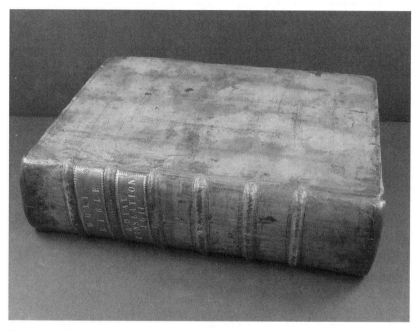

Illustration 1   The King James Bible, 1611 edition.

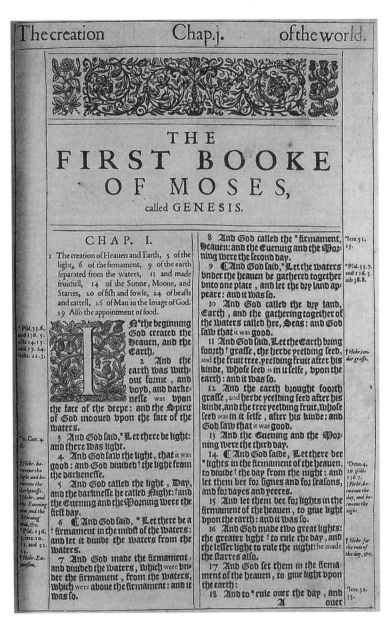

THE
FIRST BOOKE
OF MOSES,
called GENESIS.

CHAP. I.

1 The creation of Heauen and Earth, 5 of the light, 6 of the firmament, 9 of the earth separated from the waters, 11 and made fruitfull, 14 of the Sunne, Moone, and Starres, 20 of fish and fowle, 24 of beasts and cattell, 26 of Man in the Image of God. 29 Also the appointment of food.

* Psal.33.6.
and 136. 5.
act 14.15.
and 17. 24.
hebr. 11.3.

N the beginning God created the heauen, and the Earth.

2 And the earth was without forme, and voyd, and darkenesse was vpon the face of the deepe: and the Spirit of God mooued vpon the face of the waters.

* 2.Cor.4. 6.

3 And God said, * Let there be light: and there was light.

4 And God saw the light, that it was good : and God diuided † the light from the darkenesse.

† Hebr. be-
tweene the
light and be-
tweene the
darkenesse.
‡ Hebr. and
the Euening
was, and the
Morning
* Psal. 136.
† Iere.10.
12. and 51.
15.
† Hebr. Ex-
pansion.

5 And God called the light, Day, and the darknesse he called Night: †and the Euening and the Morning were the first day.

6 ¶ And God said, * Let there be a † firmament in the midst of the waters: and let it diuide the waters from the waters.

7 And God made the firmament, and diuided the waters, which were vnder the firmament, from the waters, which were aboue the firmament: and it was so.

8 And God called the * firmament, Heauen: and the Euening and the Morning were the second day.

* Iere.51. 15.

9 ¶ And God said, * Let the waters vnder the heauen be gathered together vnto one place, and let the dry land appeare: and it was so.

* Psal.33.7.
and 136.5.
iob 38.8.

10 And God called the dry land, Earth, and the gathering together of the waters called hee, Seas: and God saw that it was good.

11 And God said, Let the Earth bring foorth † grasse, the herbe yeelding seed, and the fruit tree, yeelding fruit after his kinde, whose seed is in it selfe, vpon the earth: and it was so.

† Hebr.ten-
der grasse.

12 And the earth brought foorth grasse, and herbe yeelding seed after his kinde, and the tree yeelding fruit, whose seed was in it selfe, after his kinde: and God saw that it was good.

13 And the Euening and the Morning were the third day.

14 ¶ And God saide, Let there bee * lights in the firmament of the heauen, to diuide † the day from the night: and let them bee for signes and for seasons, and for dayes and yeeres.

* Deut.4,
19. psal.
136.7.
† Hebr. be-
tweene the
day, and be-
tweene the
night.

15 And let them bee for lights in the firmament of the heauen, to giue light vpon the earth: and it was so.

16 And God made two great lights: the greater light † to rule the day, and the lesser light to rule the night: he made the starres also.

† Hebr. for
the rule of
the day, &c.

17 And God set them in the firmament of the heauen, to giue light vpon the earth:

18 And to * rule ouer the day, and ouer

* Iere.31. 35.

A

Illustration 2   The King James Bible, 1611 edition: Genesis 1.

3 | The materiality of English printed Bibles from the Tyndale New Testament to the King James Bible

JOHN N. KING AND AARON T. PRATT

The story of the printing of the early modern English Bible has often been told, typically from the vantage points of religious, literary, political, or publication history.[1] Nonetheless, older studies have devoted little attention to issues of present concern within the field of the History of the Book, a discipline that has emerged during the last three decades under the influence of scholars such as Robert Darnton, D. F. McKenzie, Roger Chartier, and many more. This vital, albeit heterogeneous, field of inquiry moves beyond long-standing investigation of the physical processes involved in the production of printed books and intentions of translators, editors, printers, and publishers to consider newly posed questions related to reading practices, the reception of books, the manner in which the material form of books effects the production of meaning, and manifold ways in which books entered into the social, devotional, and cultural lives of individual readers.

The present essay devotes particular attention to the materiality and artifactuality of English Bibles as a means of cultivating discrete readerships and promoting the authority of translations ranging from translations by William Tyndale, which were originally produced surreptitiously by continental printers, to the King James Bible, which the King's Printer published in London in 1611. Although our focus is on books in print, we must acknowledge that they succeed a preexisting manuscript tradition dominated by the Wycliffite translation. Matters under consideration involve the size of books, the number of sheets of paper required for their production, typography, book format, illustration, and, to a lesser degree, the inclusion of paratext such as prefaces and marginal notes. This investigation ranges from small-format books whose efficient use of paper made them affordable even to humbler consumers, to the largest English folio Bibles of this era.

The study of book format, for example, enhances our understanding of reading practices because octavos and books in smaller formats lent themselves to private reading, both orthodox and heterodox, in the form of bound pocket-sized copies or quired sheets of unbound paper capable of easy concealment. By way of contrast, the massive first folio of the King James Bible (KJB) required a sturdy binding suitable for reading from pulpits in churches, institutional libraries, or the homes of well-to-do readers. The formats of some books under investigation afford insight into the reading practices of notable historical figures, including Anne Boleyn, John Bradford (the Marian martyr), and Elizabeth I. Biblical reading offered succor to all of them when they were at risk of beheading or being burnt alive. For example, Foxe's *Book of Martyrs* reports that when Lady Elizabeth entered into the Tower of London for imprisonment during the reign of her half-sister, Mary I, she alluded to the Parable of Two Houses (Matt. 7:24–7) when she "called to her gentlewoman for her Book, desiring God not to suffer her to build her foundation upon the sands but upon the rock, whereby all blasts of blustering weather should have no power against her." It seems likely that this text refers to a readily portable quarto Bible or octavo New Testament.[2]

Printed Bible translations in English underwent gradual transformation from dissident documents, the reading or ownership of which warranted the death penalty, to a series of official versions (Great Bible, Bishops' Bible, and KJB), whose reading in English parish churches was mandated by government order. The complicated publication history that predated production of the KJB encompassed numerous Bible versions in many different translations, formats, and typographical styles. As we move beyond the seventeenth century, though, this new version established a hegemony that extended through the twentieth century – not only in England, but throughout the English-speaking world. In light of the fact that hundreds of editions of scriptural texts predated the KJB of 1611, this essay considers their materiality in a highly selective manner that addresses only complete New Testaments and complete Bibles, with or without Apocrypha. Excluded from consideration are printings of particular books or subsections, most notably the *Whole Book of Psalms*, a metrical psalter that went into hundreds of editions throughout the sixteenth and seventeenth centuries.[3] The vast amount of material under study necessitates that we focus primarily on first editions of different versions; broad surveys of trends in format, typography, and so forth; and selected editions or copies that highlight emerging norms or particular departures from the norms of the Bible marketplace. Important findings in this chapter relate to the ways in which Bible publishers responded – or failed to respond – to the gradual transition from black-letter to roman type that was then occurring more generally in the English book trade; to ways in which printers supplied consumer demand for large pulpit folios suitable for use in churches in addition to affordable small-format New Testaments for private consumption, a trend that began with the editions of the Coverdale version; to the domination of the Bible market by three markedly different versions of the Geneva Bible (four including the single 1557 edition of the Whittingham New Testament) during the decades prior to the publication of the King James Bible; and to an increasing tendency for publishers to produce New Testaments in very small formats suitable for binding together with staple books such as the *Whole Book of Psalms* in order to satisfy the demand of some readers for highly portable compendia to read during church services or private devotions. Though scholars have frequently attended to early modern Bible translations, the ways in which Bibles circulated as *books* – as objects of commerce and consumption – has remained insufficiently understood. While a comprehensive study would require far more than the space allotted here, it is the aim of this chapter to begin mending this critical gap.

William Tyndale struggled against adversity in order to publish the New Testament translation for which he is deservedly famous. Frustrated by the opposition of Cuthbert Tunstall, Bishop of London, he moved to Cologne where production of his forbidden translation began at the printing house of Peter Quentell in 1525.[4] In accordance with the model of Lutheran New Testaments, compositors imposed type in small-quarto format. The use of black letter was unsurprising, because it still represented the typographical standard in vernacular books designed for readers in England, the Low Countries, and northern Europe in general. Indeed, it remained standard in New Testaments and Bibles printed in London for several generations, long after it fell out of use in the Low Countries. When local authorities suppressed publication, Tyndale and his assistant, William Roy, migrated to Worms, carrying newly printed sheets from the disrupted printing run.[5] They became waste paper, however, because the printer, presumably Peter Schoeffer, undertook a wholly new edition in octavo format.[6] With leaves roughly half the size of those in the interrupted Cologne edition, which survives in a single fragmentary copy,[7] this edition established a more or less standard format and size for many years to come. Its small format not only made for a more readily concealed text, but when combined with the printer's choice of long primer type (10-point[8]), it perhaps also made for a more affordable one. Size could have an immediate bearing on the price of books, because the cost of paper was the chief determinant of the price of books during the hand-press era. By utilizing both small format and small type, a printer could significantly reduce the number of sheets that a text required.[9] The Worms octavo, for example, comprised only 43.5 sheets, whereas the first complete quarto of Tyndale's translation (with a comparable amount of paratextual material) comprised 69.[10] Prohibited books of this size lent themselves to smuggling in the form of unbound sheets concealed in barrels, among unbound sheets of permissible books, and other secret places.

We do not know when Tyndale arrived in Antwerp, but the city's printers, most notably Merten de Keyser (or Caesar or l'Empereur), published his books on a regular basis from 1528 until not long before the translator's execution in 1535. (This Brabantine port remained the epicenter for publication of books by English Protestant exiles until 1546, when promulgation of the Index of Prohibited Books banned evangelical publication.) Nonetheless, Catherine van Ruremund's publication of George Joye's emendations to the Tyndale translation in August 1534[11] predated Tyndale's own promised revision,[12] published by de Keyser in November of the same year.[13] In his revision, Tyndale attacked Joye for his unauthorized alteration of his translation. In particular, Joye had substituted "the lyfe after this" (or similar) for Tyndale's "resurrection" in twenty-two places, which Tyndale rightly saw as evidence of Joye's belief that the soul did not die (or lie dormant) after one's death and before the Second Coming – a position at odds with Tyndale's own.[14] Widow Ruremund's employment of sixteenmo format for the Joye revision and its reprint a year later[15] offered a pronounced contrast to Tyndale's octavos. These smaller editions were printed in brevier type (8-point), whose alternative name of *petit texte* is quite apposite. Very small type sizes made strenuous demands on the eyesight of readers who were forced to resort to the use of magnifying glasses or spectacles, whose lenses fell short of modern standards for the correction of refractive deficiency. Even readers with relatively sharp eyesight might have been forced to squint to read a New Testament whose bulk, including binding, approximated that of two decks of cards. Despite such difficulties, however, Bibles and other books using such small type seem to have become increasingly popular throughout the sixteenth and seventeenth centuries. The only known copy of the first edition of Joye's revision is a diminutive book that would fit very neatly in the palm of a rather small hand.[16]

If we exclude the Cologne fragment from consideration, it may be appropriate to suspect that the employment of octavo and sixteenmo format for the first nine editions of the English New Testament (*c.* 1525–35) and their successors was motivated at least to a considerable degree by consumer demand for affordable and/or readily concealed books. Nevertheless, examination of a copy of the 1534 Tyndale New Testament once owned by Anne Boleyn provides an instructive exception to this rule of thumb.[17] We know nothing about the commissioning of this volume other than the fact that it predated her fall from favor and decapitation in spring 1536. The use of vellum rather than paper marks it as a deluxe object. At this time, printing on vellum was typically found in books commissioned by royalty, aristocrats, or very well-to-do individuals or by recipients of or suitors for reward from aristocratic patrons or wealthy individuals. Vellum copies typically cost between three and eight times the price of copies on rag paper.[18] Their tendency to be rubricated and illuminated drove up the cost even further. Even though the Anne Boleyn copy is printed in octavo format, its folios are thick, difficult to turn, and impossible to hold in place without manual effort or weights. Despite the small format of this book, it is difficult to read in the absence of a lectern or prie-dieu. The decoration of this book accords with the exalted status of its owner. The royal arms are painted over de Keyser's title-page border. Red rulings are drawn on the pages, woodcuts at the beginning of books and some initial capitals are painted, and initial capitals are rubricated. More than double the thickness of copies of the same edition that are printed on paper,[19] it is as thick a book as someone with a very large hand can hold by the spine. Tyndale's involvement in the production of this book is minimized by the painting over of his name on the title page and absence of the translator's general prologue, but prologues to particular books are signed with his initials. Copy-specific features demonstrate how a humble and relatively affordable book underwent transformation into a precious possession designed for private reading by a queen consort with evangelical sympathies, whose ownership was clearly evident in red lettering on the book's gilded edges: "ANNA REGINA ANGLI." With luxury features of the sort present in Anne Boleyn's copy, even a book printed in a small format could be appropriate to the prestige of a reader at the apex of the social order – that is, until the next turn of Fortune's Wheel.[20]

Ten extant editions of the New Testament were printed during the decade following the publication of Tyndale's Worms New Testament, all of them abroad. A notable shift took place in 1536, when a London printer, possibly Thomas Godfray, employed folio format in the first extant New Testament printed in England.[21] Its large leaves required more than twice the number of sheets of paper used in the production of previous New Testaments. The ostentatiousness of this expensive book and its production in a format disproportionate to the length of the text represented a material manifestation of the fact that the English Bible was no longer a forbidden book. Its publication took place during a brief interval (c. 1535–41) when about twenty-nine extant English New Testament and thirteen extant English Bible editions were printed in England and abroad.

This surge in the publication of Bibles and New Testaments took place during the heyday of Thomas Cromwell, the chief minister of Henry VIII who implemented the Royal Supremacy over the Church of England and, as the king's vicegerent for religious affairs, promoted publication of the English Bible. At a time when Cromwell consolidated absolute power on behalf of the king, the first complete English Bible was printed abroad, in all likelihood by Merten de Keyser in Antwerp.[22] Compiled by Miles Coverdale, it constituted a revision and completion of the translation project begun by Tyndale. The materiality of this large and expensive folio offered a sharp contrast to the humility of copies of Tyndale's prohibited translation and Joye's revision of the New Testament. The Coverdale Bible (1535) was not formally authorized, but it was read with impunity and presumably circulated under Cromwell's patronage.[23] Like the use of black letter, the inclusion of abundant woodcuts was unexceptional in Bibles produced on the continent of Europe. A bold depiction of Henry VIII on the title page, designed by Hans Holbein the Younger in the manner of a traditional dedication portrait, glorifies the king's replacement of the pope as head of the Church of England. Coverdale's preface praises this shift in ecclesiastical polity.[24] James Nicolson published a separate issue of this book in Southwark, which includes eight preliminary leaves (including a newly set title page) printed using an English black-letter typeface unlike what was used for the rest of the Bible.[25] These new sheets may have conveyed the initial impression that the entire edition had been printed in England. Published by Nicolson and in fact wholly printed in England, the second Coverdale edition (1537) contains a title-page border built out of the woodcuts used in both issues of the first edition.[26] Although we do not know who transported these blocks across the English Channel, Miles Coverdale or someone close to him is a likely candidate. Because importation of foreign blocks was rare, their presence in England may attest to the high value that the importer placed on constructing an appealing title page.

The Coverdale Bible established a firm precedent for the use of folio format in succeeding Bibles published during Henry VIII's reign and the early years of Edward VI. With the exception of a single quarto Coverdale edition in 1537,[27] all complete Bibles through 1549 were printed in folio. The legibility of english type (13.5-point, also known as Augustyn), furthermore rendered this book and other folios printed with larger types suitable for reading from lecterns by clerics during church services. Combining translations by Tyndale and Coverdale, the first royally licensed version of the English Bible appeared in print in 1537. Its ascription to Thomas Matthew is commonly taken to refer to the names of a disciple of Christ and an evangelist in order to form a pseudonym for John Rogers, a one-time associate of Tyndale, who edited the essentially Tyndalean translation.[28] Pseudonymy made good sense if we recall that Tyndale and two of his associates – Rogers, and, according to tradition, Roy – were executed because of their evangelical beliefs and activities. It is uncertain whether Coverdale was an actual associate of Tyndale, but it is worthy of note that he alone lived into old age. Failing to gain traction even though it furnished what became the primary basis for later versions,[29] the Matthew translation and its revisions by Richard Taverner and Edmund Becke were published in only nine among close to two hundred Bible and New Testament editions produced prior to the King James Bible.[30]

Generally known as the Great Bible, first published in 1539, the only English Bible ever officially authorized by a monarch constituted Miles Coverdale's revision of the Matthew version.[31] At the same time that it enshrined the work of Tyndale, Rogers, and Coverdale, it eclipsed the three earlier versions. Published in 1539 under the patronage of Thomas Cromwell, it derives its name from the directive in the Second Royal

Injunctions of Henry VIII (1538) that clerics procure "one boke of the hole byble of the largyest volume in Englyshe" for placement in parish churches where their "parishoners may moste commodiously resorte to the same and reade it."[32] At a time when the high price of these Bibles restricted the ability of ordinary readers to acquire copies, this order mandated the provision of chained copies for public "reading or hearing."[33] The royal auspices of the Great Bible are clearly apparent in its elaborate title-page border, modeled on the Holbein compartment in the Coverdale Bible, which portrays Henry VIII transmitting this book to Cromwell and Thomas Cranmer, Archbishop of Canterbury, who then transmit it downward through stratified clerical and social ranks.[34] In publishing the second edition of the Great Bible in 1540,[35] the King's Printer, Thomas Berthelet, creates a visual impression that it is an heir of the Coverdale Bible by constructing the title-page borders for the Old and New Testaments out of woodcuts identical to those employed on the title page of the 1535 Bible. In this case, texts set within apertures in the wooden blocks are in Latin rather than English. Close to the time of the fall and execution of Cromwell, Cranmer contributed to the alteration of the material form of this Bible through provision of a preface to what became either the second or third edition.[36] It gave rise to the alternative name of the Cranmer Bible (1540).[37] The earlier version is sometimes called the Cromwell Bible.

The eight editions of the Great Bible published between 1539 and 1541, all but one of which were produced by Richard Grafton and/or Edward Whitchurch, provided a capstone for an extended run of New Testaments and Bibles. The last six years of the reign of Henry VIII then witnessed the publication of only three New Testaments including one Tyndale version printed abroad and two domestic editions of the Great Bible. This dramatic shrinkage coincided with the conservative reaction against religious reform that culminated in the Act for the Advancement of True Religion (1543), which forbade Bible reading by laborers and non-genteel women. We need only recall the fate of Anne Askew, who encountered clerical disapproval for reading the Bible within Lincoln Minster, for evidence that such reading could be a very dangerous activity. She was burnt at the stake as a heretic on July 16, 1546, little more than six months before the death of King Henry.

Everything changed at the accession of nine-year-old Edward VI (1547–53), during whose minority Archbishop Cranmer and powerful lords who governed in the king's name implemented a militantly Protestant program of religious reform. The Royal Injunctions of July 31, 1547 led the way when they "auctorized and licensed" English subjects to read and interpret the Bible.[38] A thread that ran through the publication of thirty-one Bibles and New Testaments that crowded bookstalls in London and the hinterland was adherence to the dictum in *Paraclesis*, one of three prefaces to Erasmus's Latin-Greek New Testament (1516), that even lowly individuals should read and interpret the Scriptures for themselves. Flaunting of a New Testament appears to have constituted an ostentatious display of piety – or hypocrisy – during the evangelical moment of King Edward's reign. This semiotic indeterminacy is notable in *Lusty Juventus*, a moral interlude composed by a preacher named Richard Weaver (fl. 1547–53). When Hypocrisy spots the New Testament borne by Juventus, a personification of Youth, the Vice exclaims "Let me see your portas, gentle Sir John" (i.e., show me your portable breviary, priest). Juventus's rejoinder – "No, it is not a book for you to look on / You ought not to jest with God's testament" – is ambiguous because the Vice objectifies the fraudulent piety of a youth who has yet to experience "true" religious conversion.[39]

Although the present enumeration of editions excludes Erasmus's 1548 *Paraphrases upon the New Testament*, this embodiment of principles inculcated in *Paraclesis* greatly expanded accessibility of the New Testament through its inclusion of the whole of the Great Bible version. Nonetheless, this large folio disseminated scriptural text in a radically different material form. Consuming more than 500 sheets of paper between its two "tomes," it would have been more costly to produce than complete Bibles already in print. In employing roman type for passages of biblical text, Edward Whitchurch's editions of the *Paraphrases* are also anomalous in their departure from the use of black letter for setting scripture.[40] Composed in rather small pica type (12-point), the roman passages are dwarfed by the prolix black-letter text of Erasmus's ensuing commentary. Its setting in large english type, also used in the Coverdale Bible, commands the attention of readers. Printers commonly employed contrasting typefaces and sizes in order to emphasize differentiation between texts and commentaries, translations, or marginal notes.[41]

During the reign of Edward VI, ordinary people experienced unprecedented access to the English Bible, access that had been denied to unfortunate individuals such as Anne Askew only a short time before. The Royal

Injunctions ordered every parish church to acquire the first "tome" of *Paraphrases*, which contains the Gospels, as a companion to the complete text of the Great Bible. Nicholas Udall edited it under the patronage of Catherine Parr, the widow of Henry VIII. Not all parishes complied with this order, of course, but Archbishop Cranmer and the Protestant lords who governed England intended to permit open access to chained copies of both the Great Bible and Erasmus's *Paraphrases* in parish churches. Clergymen were ordered to "diligently studye the same, conferringe the one with the other."[42] In compliance with government orders that permitted him to commandeer the workers and equipment of other printers, Whitchurch published five separate editions on January 31, 1548.[43] Miles Coverdale edited the second "tome," also published by Whitchurch on August 16, 1549, under the patronage of the Duchesses of Somerset[44] and Suffolk. It contains the remainder of the New Testament.[45]

Distinctive features of the reign of Edward VI include spikes in the number of extant New Testament (twenty during six and one-half years versus thirty-six during the previous twenty-two years) and Bible editions (ten during four years versus thirteen over the previous twelve years). Publication of two New Testaments in Worcester highlights a notable departure from centralization of the book trade in London under Henry VIII. John Oswen's printing of these books during service as King's Printer for Wales and the Marches accorded with the government's unprecedented effort to disseminate reformist books in the hinterland.[46]

Diversification in the formats for biblical translations would presumably have allowed for proliferation of both public and private ownership and reading by a demographically stratified readership. In a departure from the prevailing use of folio format in Henrician Bibles, about half of Edwardian Bibles were gathered as relatively inexpensive quartos or, in the case of one uniquely affordable Bible printed in six separate parts, octavo format. As opposed to one duodecimo New Testament and four sixteen-mos, the relatively large number of six New Testaments in quarto format may have catered to demand from more well-to-do individuals for a more readily usable format than folio. Sixteenmos made significant demands on the eyesight of readers because they were set in minute type. For example, compositors employed minion type (7-point) for Jugge's 1548 sixteenmo.[47] The cognate French name for this type, *mignonne* ("dainty" or "tiny") is appropriate. The prevalence of woodcut illustration and universality of black-letter typography remains unexceptional, because they then represented standard components of English Bibles.

Other printers broke into the market for publication of New Testaments and Bibles that Grafton and Whitchurch had dominated during the last years of Henry VIII. Printing for a variety of English publishers, a Dutch immigrant named Stephen Mierdman drew upon production practices that he had acquired in partnership with his brother-in-law, Mattias Crom, a printer in Antwerp who specialized in the production of Bibles.[48] Mierdman printed five New Testaments for Richard Jugge, the latter four of which contained his own revision of the Tyndale version. Jugge would dominate this market sector during the next two decades. Other than a single octavo, his Edwardian imprints included two quartos and two sixteenmos, including one that Mierdman printed prior to his departure from Antwerp.[49] Continuing in a tradition established by the Coverdale and Great Bibles, Jugge commissioned a woodcut portrait of Edward VI that Mierdman built into the title pages of his octavo and quarto editions.

John Day entered into the Bible trade when he relied on Mierdman to produce a folio Bible – the Matthew version edited by Edmund Becke – that Day published in 1549 in partnership with William Seres.[50] As a young printer-publisher new to the London book trade, Day seems unlikely to have had any opportunity to acquire the expertise necessary to produce this large and complicated book on his own. It may have been due to his involvement in the production of his first folio Bible that Day acquired the experience requisite to print and publish a second folio Bible in 1551, Becke's revision of the Taverner Old Testament and Tyndale's New Testament, on his own. With support from powerful patrons, Day controlled capital sufficient to fund the large number of sheets of paper required for producing folio Bibles in addition to a plethora of inexpensive books and pamphlets in small formats with low sheet counts during the explosion in the number of editions published that took place under Edward VI.[51] In so doing he established a career-long practice of making lucrative short-term profits by catering to demand for cheap and ephemeral books at the same time that he tied up capital during the lengthy production and long-term sale of costly folios.

His catering to a demographically stratified vernacular readership was evidently motivated by both entrepreneurship and Protestant ideology. Day's publication of the Bible in large and small formats indicates that he cultivated a mixed clientele that ranged from poor to well-to-do readers. Like any shrewd businessman, he wished to maximize income by expanding his market and utilizing his presses most efficiently through concurrent printing in larger and smaller formats, but we have no reason to doubt his claim to ideological motivation for publishing scripture "in which all men ought to delight and exercise themselves both day and night, to the amendment of their own lives and to the edifying of their neighbours."[52] The success of his marketing strategy is notable in his 1551 folio Bible, which combines Taverner's revision of the Matthew Bible (for the Old Testament and Apocrypha) with Tyndale's New Testament.[53] Day was able to publish this folio on his own, unlike the group of seven booksellers who shared both investment and risk by entering into a consortium to publish a competing folio Bible of the Matthew version during the same year. The printer, Nicholas Hill, incorporated variant title pages or colophons that identify the sale of these books at the premises of William Bonham, Richard Kele, Thomas Petyt, Robert Toy, Abraham Veale, John Walley, and John Wight. Unlike Day, who commissioned a new border for his 1551 Bible, one that incorporated his printer's device, the consortium's edition pays homage to the Coverdale Bible by reusing its woodcuts in the construction of its own title page border.[54] Becke's acknowledgment that high book prices reduce Bible circulation because ordinary people have been discouraged by "the price of late time … from buying of the same" helps to explain the caution of this syndicate at the same time that it emphasizes Day's relative freedom from financial constraint.[55]

Day and Seres articulated particular concern for less well-off readers in their innovative project of publishing the Bible in six separate octavo editions, including the Apocrypha (1549–51).[56] Two parts were published in 1549, three in 1550, and one in 1551. If copies of all editions remain extant, these parts were not printed in sequential order. For example, the Pentateuch was the last to appear among extant editions, and it is the only one in the set to have been undertaken without collaboration with William Seres. The thickness of these books varies, of course, but they form a uniform series in terms of length and width. All of them are printed in rather small long primer black-letter type (10-point). Even though the New Testament contains a few lines more than the other books, each part of this set employs essentially the same *mise-en-page*. In printing the Pentateuch under the patronage of the Duchess of Suffolk, a notable sponsor of religious reform, Day included a preface that claims to address "the commodity of these poor" by enabling them to purchase part or all of the Bible and explains that folio Bibles are too costly for poor readers (and hearers) "to whose chief comfort and consolation the Holy Ghost hath caused them to be written." He notes that the high cost of single-volume Bibles, which appear in folio or quarto format, are too expensive for buyers whose funds are limited: "Consideringe also, thayt the bookes contaynynge the same: beynge together in anye one volume ... are of so highe price that the pore ... are not able to bye them." Printing the Old Testament in parts, he notes, means "that they whiche are not able to bie the hole, may bie a part."[57]

Several editions published by John Day departed from the prevailing practice of placing notes in the margins by removing them to the end of each chapter. This is the case, for example, in four volumes of the printer's six-part octavo Bible. The preface to the 1548 octavo Tyndale New Testament co-published with William Seres explains that the appending of notes enabled readers to "better fynde the thynges noted" ($\pi 2^r$). This style of annotation enabled commentators to tailor the length of their remarks to the requirements of particular texts. The Day and Seres folio edition of Becke's revision of the Matthew Bible stands out for the notes that it appended to chapters of the Book of Revelation.[58] Several of these notes identify their source as John Bale's exegetical treatise, *The image of both churches*, an edition of which Day and Seres also published around this time.[59] Appended notes allowed for the inclusion of significant exegetical commentary more easily (without disrupting *mise-en-page*) than did marginal annotation.

By July of 1553 when Edward VI succumbed to illness, twenty-three editions of the Bible and fifty-six New Testaments (excluding the Cologne fragment) had been printed in the English language. Publication during Henry VIII's reign shows a trend in which each of the new translations largely supplanted its predecessor, even though copies of the earlier versions undoubtedly remained available for purchase from booksellers well after they ceased to be published. After the first Coverdale New Testament in 1538,[60] only a single Tyndale edition was printed prior to the accession of King Edward.[61] Within months after publication of the first edition of the Great Bible by Whitchurch and Grafton in 1539, the printing of Coverdale, Matthew, and Taverner versions ceased until 1549. The political

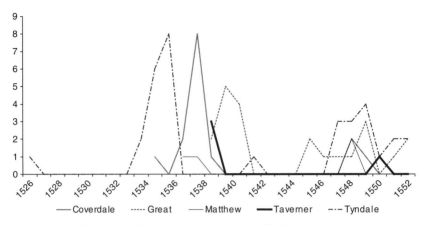

Figure 1 English Bible and New Testament editions published per year from 1526 to 1553, by version. Totals for Tyndale editions include Tyndale, Tyndale–Joye, and Tyndale–Jugge versions; Matthew editions include Matthew and Matthew–Becke versions; and Taverner editions include Taverner and Taverner–Becke versions.

pressures surrounding Bible translation and printing during the rule of Henry VIII make it difficult to attribute this pattern of publication to popular demand.[62] Indeed, the picture of the virtually unregulated (at least for reformist publications) Edwardian marketplace is markedly different (see Figure 1). During Edward VI's reign, translators made only slight changes to the existing Henrician versions: John Day and William Seres published revisions to the Matthew and Taverner versions by Edmund Becke, and Richard Jugge issued editions of the Tyndale New Testament that he revised "using thadvise and helpe of godly learned men."[63] Though the editions published by Jugge, Day, and the Worcester printer John Oswen made Tyndale's New Testament the most reprinted translation under Edward VI (even when counting complete Bibles of the other translations), editions of all of the Henrician versions were being printed throughout the young king's brief reign. The record of extant editions suggests that consumer demand was able to sustain the publication of a diversity of translations in this more open marketplace.

Immediately after the accession of Queen Mary I, the publication of English Bibles came to an abrupt halt. Having been on the throne for just under one month, Mary issued a proclamation on August 18, 1553 forbidding that anyone "prynte any bookes, matter, ballet, ryme, interlude, processe or treatyse nor to playe any interlude, except they have her graces speciall licence in writynge for the same, upon payne to incurre her highnesse indignation and displeasure."[64] Later, on March 4, 1554, she issued her injunctions in which she ordered her bishops to repress "corrupt and naughty" books.[65] Despite these prohibitions, evidence exists that at least one bookseller (and possibly more) continued, in at least 1553–4, to sell English Bibles and other Protestant literature that had been printed during the previous regime. An unknown bookseller's account book records the sale of a sixteenmo edition of a Jugge–Tyndale New Testament with other works for 2s, a copy of one of John Day's Edmund Becke folio editions for 6s, and a copy of the Matthew Bible printed by Nicholas Hill for Robert Toy (this entry may suggest that the record book belonged to Toy) for 11s.[66] The imprisonment of John Day and execution of Bible printers in Antwerp, not to speak of the fate of William Tyndale, attests to the willingness of committed ideologues to court death in order to disseminate banned books.

Not only did Bibles and New Testaments remain on sale despite the Marian prohibition, heterodox individuals who resisted her reestablishment of Roman Catholicism, and conceivably some orthodox individuals as well, retained ownership and continued to read English Bibles and New Testaments. Indeed, at least one of the Protestants who were burnt alive during her reign retained a copy of the New Testament during imprisonment prior to execution. We know this because John Bradford, the notable preacher, entered the following inscription in a sixteenmo edition of the Tyndale New Testament printed in Antwerp for Richard Jugge in 1548.[67] The small size of this book would have facilitated its concealment by a reader who expressly notes that he writes *e carcere* ("from prison") on February 15, 1554, when Bradford was incarcerated in the Tower of London, or soon after his condemnation as a heretic during the following year:

> Mani wolde come to ye oh lorde, but
> few wylle come after the./ many
> wolde have ye rewarde of thy
> sayntes, but very few wyll folowe
> ther wayse. ande yet we know,
> or at ye least we sholde knowe, y^t
> the enterance into thy kyngdome
> & paradyse, is not from a paradise,
> but from a wyldernes, for we

come not from pleasure to pleasure
but from payn to pleasure, or fro*m*
pleasure to payne as thy story
of ye ryche lazarus dothe som thynge set
forthe. e carcere 15 februarii. (5*8ᵛ)

These sentiments concerning salvation are appropriate to one who is preparing for martyrdom. The presence of the initials I.B.I.H. on the gilded
calfskin binding suggests that Joyce Hales, to whom Bradford offered
spiritual counsel, took pains to preserve the book after his death. The
binder's cropping of the leaves in such a way as to excise text from a note
in Bradford's hand (s7ʳ) suggests that this binding postdated his death. If
these presumptions are correct, this book memorializes to the present day
the consolatory function of biblical reading both to a condemned man *in
extremis* and to a woman who had participated in a highly affective spiritual relationship with the martyred reader.

Published in Geneva during the reign of Mary I, the New Testament
printed by Conrad Badius in 1557 was translated for the most part by
the English exile William Whittingham.[68] It is the first major translation
to have been first issued in octavo since the first complete Tyndale New
Testament in 1526. Aside from their shared format, however, these two
editions look quite different. Consuming 58 sheets, Badius's edition of
Whittingham's translation required more paper than any previous octavo
New Testament. And perhaps most notably, it is the first English Bible
to have been printed with only roman and italic type. Although such
fonts had been the norm in Geneva and most of the continent for some
time, the total absence of black letter made Badius's edition a striking
departure from previous English Bibles.[69] This edition is also the first
in English – not the 1560 Geneva Bible as is commonly thought – to
include both chapter and verse divisions. Unlike the latter book, which
begins with a dedication to Elizabeth, the 1557 Whittingham New
Testament immediately reveals its Calvinist leanings with a translation
of John Calvin's epistle "declaring that Christ is the end of the Lawe."[70]
The title page includes a small woodcut of Time leading Truth out of a
cave with the surrounding text, "GOD BY TYME RESTORETH TRVTH
AND MAKETH HER VICTORIOVS," which must have had a particular
resonance for England's exiled Protestants.[71]

By 1560, after Elizabeth's accession, a team of translators in Geneva (including Whittingham) had completed both a new translation of the Old Testament as well as a revision of the 1557 Whittingham New Testament text, which were then issued in a single Bible from Rowland Hall's Genevan press in 1560. Though the 1557 New Testament had included a significant number of discursive marginal notes, there are numerous pages in the 1560 Geneva Bible in which its two columns of scripture are almost entirely surrounded by them, thus creating a *mise-en-page* that is similar to manuscript and early printed commentaries. These notes were vilified and caricatured by critics, and some modern scholars have declared that they betray staunch Calvinist beliefs. Nonetheless, they are less polemical than is commonly assumed.[72] In a departure from the earlier Whittingham New Testament, Hall's Geneva Bible edition contains thirty-three woodcut illustrations including several maps and diagrams.[73] The title page woodcut to the 1560 Geneva Bible, no longer suggesting that Truth need rely on Time for deliverance, shows the Israelites and Egyptians gathering at the parting of the Red Sea as Moses raises his rod, which may function as an emblem for the Exodus of the "Churche of God" out of the Roman Egypt and into Elizabeth's Protestant England.[74]

Shortly after the Geneva Bible's first continental publication, the printing of Bibles and New Testaments resumed in England. In his recently acquired capacity as "Printer to the Quenes Maiestie,"[75] Richard Jugge began to publish octavo editions of the Tyndale New Testament text that he had revised under Edward VI. John Cawood, who had been Mary I's printer and began to share privileges with Jugge under Elizabeth, finished printing the first Elizabethan Bible, a Great Bible quarto, in 1561.[76] In sum, Cawood's Bible output amounted to only five editions of the Great version before his death in 1572. These quarto editions of the Great Bible consisted of one New Testament and four Bibles.[77] Richard Harrison and Richard Carmarden published unauthorized Great Bible folios in 1562 and 1566 respectively.[78] Carmarden commissioned the Rouen printer, Cardin Hamillion, to undertake his edition. Around the same time as this edition, an unknown printer produced the only other Elizabethan Great Bible.[79] It represents the first octavo publication of an English Bible in a single volume. Cawood's quartos were the final editions containing the Great Bible translation.

On October 5, 1568, Matthew Parker, Archbishop of Canterbury, wrote to William Cecil requesting that Richard Jugge be given an exclusive patent to publish a new Bible version, which became known as the Bishops' Bible because of the role played by several prominent Elizabethan bishops in this revision and correction of the Great Bible translation.[80] While its leaves are virtually the same size as those in the largest Great Bibles, the Bishops' first edition, published in 1568, is the largest English Bible of the early modern period in terms of its sheet count; its length demanded that Jugge distribute the labor amongst several printers.[81] Herbert calls this edition "perhaps the most sumptuous in the long series of folio English Bibles" for good reason: in addition to its unprecedented size (one bound copy measures approximately 428 x 295 x 130mm), the first Bishops' Bible was printed in black letter using great primer type (17-point), an opulent size larger than the english type used in the first Coverdale folio, and contains no fewer than 124 woodcut illustrations.[82]

Matthew Parker, who oversaw the production of the Bishops' Bible, made a copy of this book even more ostentatious when he commissioned the binding and decoration of a copy for presentation to Queen Elizabeth. It is bound in the crimson velvet favored by Tudor monarchs with decorative silverwork including clasps, bosses engraved with the Tudor rose, a lozenge bearing the royal arms, and corner plates.[83] In addition to an engraved title-page portrait of the queen,[84] which recalls the depiction of her father on the title pages of the Coverdale and Great Bibles, this Bible contains delicately hand-colored woodcut portraits of two notable patrons who joined Parker in sponsoring publication of this Bible. In the first instance, Robert Dudley, Earl of Leicester, is depicted at the beginning of the Former Prophets (excluding Nehemiah but including Job). This portrayal immediately before Joshua brings to mind contemporary praise of Dudley as a militant Protestant. A hand-colored historiated initial capital at the beginning of Psalm 1 – "Blessed is the man that walketh not in the counsell of the ungodly" – glorifies the religious orthodoxy and learning of the third patron, Sir William Cecil, who was the queen's chief minister. He holds an open book with Hebrew characters lacking Masoretic marks, presumably representative of the Old Testament. The tiny xylographic lettering is in mirror writing, whereby the cutter copied lettering in an artist's drawing as it appeared to the eye, in violation of the necessity of cutting lettering in a wood block in reverse order to render it legible in a printed woodcut.[85]

Parker's role in this project is commemorated by the printing of his heraldic arms at the beginning of the Preface of this Bible. The succeeding Prologue, written by Thomas Cranmer, Parker's predecessor as Archbishop of Canterbury, begins with an elaborate initial capital *C*, whose inclusion of a xylographic *T* commemorates Cranmer's Latin title of *Thomas Cantuariensis*. This initial capital contains Cranmer's coat of arms. Furthermore, the work of different contributors is designated by printed initials. At the end of the Gospel of John, for example, we find the initials *E. P.*, which designate *Episcopus Petriburgensis* (i.e., the Bishop of Peterborough; they are pasted over a misattribution to Parker). It may be that the archbishop's intense interest in printing and his standing as a connoisseur of fine books, for which he commissioned de luxe binding and hand coloration, led to the alteration of two initial capitals for the letter *P* by means of xylographic inclusion of the initials of his Latin title of *Mattheus Cantuariensis*. In their altered state, these initial capitals may suggest that *P* refers to Parker. In line with the Elizabethan regime's distrust of images, some of the continental woodblocks that were used to illustrate the first Bishops' Bible were altered prior to printing to remove anthropomorphic depictions of God the Father. Presumably because Parker had "lost control of the blocks" that had originally come to England from Cologne, the second folio edition of 1572 contains a newly commissioned set of woodcuts that, while fewer in number, are larger in size.[86] Like the 1568 edition's images, these depict a tetragrammaton instead of anthropomorphic images of God. After the second folio edition, Jugge's title page, which prominently features a portrait of Elizabeth, did not reappear.[87]

Because of his inability to meet the demand for Bibles in the wake of Cawood's death, Jugge's patent for publishing Bibles was restricted in 1575 to quarto Bibles and sixteenmo New Testaments. To this date, Jugge had published five editions of the new Bishops' Bible (three in folio, two in quarto) in addition to four octavo New Testaments of the same. Although Jugge could no longer oversee the publication of folios, William Norton commissioned him, along with Henry Bynneman, as his printer for what became the fourth folio of the Bishops' Bible.[88] Under his revised patent, Jugge published two additional quartos and the only sixteenmo Bishops' New Testament before his death in 1577.[89]

The second and third editions of the Geneva Bible were printed on the continent in 1562 (a moderately sized folio) and either 1569 or 1570 (a second quarto); none were printed in England until Christopher Barker secured his patent to print Geneva editions from the Privy Council in 1575, shortly after Matthew Parker's death. Despite the fact that he lacked his own press at this time, Barker was able to publish an octavo Geneva New Testament later in this year after hiring Thomas Vautroullier to print it.[90] Perhaps more importantly for the history of the English Bible, Barker then printed the first edition (also in octavo) of Laurence Tomson's revision of the Geneva New Testament on his recently acquired press the following year.[91] This translation was the most often reprinted in New Testament editions during the decades leading up to the publication of the KJB. For his revision, Thomson followed closely Theodore Beza's Latin translation, also taking over his notes to replace those from the original Geneva version. In addition to these, which Barker printed in the margins in a roman font, Tomson added his own notes, which are differentiated from the others by being set in italic type.[92]

When Jugge died in 1577, Thomas Wilkes became the Queen's Printer. No books were ever issued with his imprint (Bibles or otherwise), however, because Barker purchased the title for what he described as a "great somme" roughly a month later.[93] No longer the patent holder only for Geneva Bibles, Barker from this time monopolized Bible and New Testament publication in London, although printers in Edinburgh, Cambridge, and Dort produced editions derived from the Geneva version.[94] No Bishops' editions were ever printed outside of London, though the King's Printers continued to issue octavo New Testaments of the translation through 1619.[95] When Christopher Barker died in 1599, his son Robert took over his position as Queen's Printer, in which capacity he published the KJB in 1611.

In a decision often ignored by scholars, Christopher Barker introduced a Geneva Bible folio in 1578 that rendered its scriptural passages using black-letter type.[96] In the following year, he then published the first two black-letter Geneva quarto editions.[97] Although these and subsequent black-letter Geneva quartos lacked the illustrations present in counterparts set in roman type, they remained steady sellers well into the second decade of the seventeenth century. In fact, neither of the Barkers ever published an edition of the 1560 Geneva translation in a quarto using roman type for the body text. Instead, they issued roman quartos of the Geneva–Tomson version through 1601 and then the Geneva–Tomson–Junius through at least 1611. Editions employing black-letter fonts dominated the quarto market (thirty-three black-letter editions as opposed to thirteen roman), but with the exception of one edition,[98] all octavo Geneva copies were printed in roman. Among editions of Geneva versions before 1612 in all formats, thirty-nine were in black letter and forty-seven were in roman. Among New Testaments, only three were printed in black letter, as opposed to thirty-eight in roman. Although roman Geneva editions outnumber those in black letter for both Bibles and New Testaments, the additional variability of version and format within this set make the reasons for this difference quite complex. By the late sixteenth century, readers would almost certainly have been adept at reading both black-letter and roman typefaces,[99] but it may be that the Barkers (and/or the printers they deputized) judged that roman text, which was quickly becoming the norm for many types of English publications during the final decades of the sixteenth century, was more legible in comparison to black-letter at the small sizes desired for the very popular smaller format editions. On the other hand, although at least one English printer used nonpareil (6-point) black-letter type in the sixteenth century,[100] it may have been the case that roman nonpareil fonts of the type used in the Barkers' smallest New Testaments were simply easier to obtain by English stationers who purchased their type or type matrices from the continent. Regardless of the causal factors, however, it remains that only one edition of any Geneva version was printed in black letter in a format smaller than quarto,[101] despite the fact that small-format editions constitute just over half of the total number of editions printed: sixty-four in octavo or smaller formats versus sixty-three larger editions. In quarto and folio format, however, forty-one extant black-letter editions outnumber twenty-two extant roman editions by nearly two to one. Once the first edition of a version in a particular format had been printed, it would have been easiest to set the next edition using the original as a model. More than economy, legibility, or even, perhaps, consumer preference, this fact likely explains, for example, why quarto Bibles of the original Geneva translation remained in black letter under the Barkers, and quarto Geneva–Tomson and Geneva–Tomson–Juninus Bibles remained in roman. The changes between subsequent quarto editions of each version tended to be minimal; a few select editions printed by the Barkers seem to have served as the templates for later ones. Ultimately, even though the particular circumstances governing decisions about format and typography remain somewhat unclear, it is certain that the Barkers found it profitable to publish a variety of Geneva versions in diverse formats and – in many cases – fonts in this period.

In 1582, Catholic exiles at the English College in Rheims introduced their own English translation in a quarto edition that resembles the first Geneva editions in its adherence to roman and italic fonts.[102] This version, which proclaims on its title page that it provides a "discoverie of the CORRUPTIONS of divers late translations, and for clearing the CONTROVERSIES in religion," found an unlikely outlet in Protestant England when it was published in folio editions edited by the Puritan polemicist William Fulke beginning in 1589. Bearing the imprints of Royal Printers, Fulke's editions (there were two before 1611) include both the Rheims and Bishops' New Testaments in adjacent columns, supplemented with an elaborate paratextual system dedicated to denouncing the "impietie ... heresie, treason and slander" of the former.[103] Although two continental quarto editions of the Rheims translation were produced prior to 1611, readers in England might consult it more readily through the Fulke editions.[104] These highly polemical books are also the only ones in which the Bishops' version was printed in a non-black-letter font. Printed with roman type, the Rheims version appears in the left column whereas the Bishops' is on the right in italic. Nearly thirty years after John Fogny printed the first Rheims New Testament, members of the English College (now back in Douai) completed this project by producing the Old Testament in two thick quarto volumes.[105]

Robert Barker published the first edition of a modified Tomson New Testament in 1602.[106] This new version retained Tomson's translation with few variations,[107] but replaced its notes on the Book of Revelation with those from French Calvinist Franciscus Junius's commentary, which had been translated into English and printed in a standalone edition in 1596.[108] In the standard Geneva–Tomson version, the annotations in Revelation are sparse and non-polemical in comparison with the original Geneva text; they do not, for example, explicitly identify the Whore of Babylon with either the Antichrist or the Church of Rome.[109] Arguably as antipapal as those from the first Geneva Bible, the notes in the Geneva–Tomson–Junius version more than compensate for the Geneva–Tomson's lack. Indeed, throughout much of Revelation, they consume more of the page than the Scripture upon which they comment. While ultimately not reprinted as frequently as the standard Geneva–Tomson version, editions with the Junius notes account for roughly one-fourth of Bibles and New Testaments based on (and including) the 1560 Geneva translation that were printed from 1602 through 1611. That Robert Barker continued to print the Geneva–Tomson–Junius version in addition to the others (often in complete Bible editions) attests to consumers' particular interest in the Book of Revelation during this period.[110]

Produced in a full range of formats, the largest editions of the Geneva Bible were folios published in 1578 and 1583.[111] Along with other trade guilds, The Merchant Taylor's Company purchased a volume of the 1578 edition for use in its Common Hall, indicating the Geneva Bible's perceived suitability for (semi-)public as well as private use. In the printed circular advertising this first Geneva pulpit-size folio edition, Barker advertises it not so much in terms of its translation as in its extensive paratextual apparatus, which most notably includes "large notes and expositions."[112] Although earlier New Testaments had been published in sixteenmo editions, none were smaller until John Legate, printer to the University of Cambridge, printed a 32mo Geneva–Tomson edition around 1590.[113] It is notable in the case of Geneva Bibles that smaller format editions such as Legate's could not contain the same apparatus of discursive marginal notes that scholars have tended to associate inextricably with the Geneva text. For example, in moving from octavo to a sixteenmo, Geneva–Tomson editions lose virtually all of their commentary: the remaining marginalia are almost entirely scriptural cross-references. In fact, no Geneva–Tomson–Junius editions exist in a format smaller than octavo, possibly because smaller books could not accommodate the heavy annotations in Revelation that the version required. Of the extant Geneva New Testament editions that the Barkers published in London through 1611 (including both the Geneva–Tomson and Geneva–Tomson–Junius editions), just over 60 percent are smaller than octavo.[114] If it is true that these smaller-format editions were cheaper than their larger counterparts by virtue of the fact that they tended to require less paper, then the poorer or more frugal the buyer, the less likely it was that they would have had access to explanatory (and sometimes polemical) marginalia in their own copy. In light of this, the assumption that reading versions of the Geneva translation necessarily involved an encounter with (polemical) exegetical glosses cannot be maintained. For a very significant number of Elizabethan New Testament owners, the small-format books that they purchased would not have contained a pedagogical apparatus. In a very real sense, they were *sola scriptura.*

Unlike large-format books designed for reading from lecterns (e.g., first editions of the Coverdale, Great, and Bishops' Bibles), books in the smallest formats printed with eye-straining type lent themselves to reading in privacy as well as in church.[115] Their low cost, small size, and high use value made them relatively ephemeral, and the preservation of some extant examples may be attributable to the existence of fine bindings or association with notable individuals. Such is the case with a black-letter sixteenmo copy of the Geneva–Tomson New Testament owned by Elizabeth I that is printed with brevier type.[116] The black cloth binding bears pietistic mottos embroidered with silver thread, and the front flyleaf bears a holograph inscription in the queen's fine italic hand:

> August
> I walke many times into
> the pleasant fieldes of the
> holye scriptures. Where
> I plucke vp the goodlie
> greene herbes of sentence
> es by pruning: Eate the*m*
> by reading: Chawe the*m*
> by musing: And laie them
> up at length in the hie
> seate of memorie by gather
> ing them together: that
> so hauing tasted thy sweet
> enes I may the lesse per
> ceaue the bitternes of this
> miserable life

This inscription has the appearance of verse, but it may simply be a private reflection in prose. In accordance with the multiple senses of the word *reflection* as both visual image and inward meditation, these words offer insight into the queen's reading practices. After "plucking" and "pruning" (i.e., selecting) "green herbs" (i.e., scriptural verses), it is her practice to "eat" and "chew" (i.e., read and meditate) upon them prior to memorization with the goal of consoling herself against the travails of worldly existence by "tasting" (i.e., internalizing) their "sweet" lessons. This inscription might constitute a topical reference to a particular month during the life of the queen or perhaps be part of an otherwise unknown or lost calendric cycle. This text is neither cited nor included in bibliographies of Elizabethan verse or collections of the writings of Elizabeth I. It should come as no surprise that she is known to have read and inscribed this modest sixteenmo, whereas she may have never read the deluxe copy of the Bishops' Bible given to her by Archbishop Parker.

In a practice carried over from earlier Geneva Bible quartos, the small-format Geneva–Tomson New Testaments enabled readers to commission the binding together of devotional books in different configurations. Different publishers appear to have encouraged this practice by employing the same *mise-en-page* in different books produced by different printers in different years. In a three-book collection preserved at the Bodleian Library,[117] for example, a 24mo New Testament published by Robert Barker in 1607[118] constitutes one side of a minuscule devotional library that is bound *dos-à-dos* with a 24mo Book of Common Prayer published by Barker in 1606[119] and a 24mo copy of the *Whole Book of Psalms* published by the Company of Stationers during the following year.[120] The absence of marginal notes or cross-references facilitated the miniaturization of these conjoined books, whose pages were uniformly set in forty-six lines of roman type. Bound in gold-tooled red calfskin, with gilt and gauffered edges, this set affords no evidence of rebinding. In a small handful, it contains all of the books that a worshipper would need to attend church services. The manner of their binding would have appealed to a reader who looked upon these books as inseparable from daily existence indoors, out of doors, in church, or in manifold other private or public settings. In another instance, a 24mo Geneva–Tomson New Testament (1609) with gilded and gauffered edges is bound *dos-à-dos* with *The Whole Booke of Psalms* (1610). Decorated with silver spangles, the fine white satin cover is embroidered with delicate multi-colored silk, satin, and gilt silver stitchwork.[121] Making even more strenuous demands on the eyesight of readers is the pairing of the Geneva–Tomson New Testament (1593) and *Whole Booke of Psalmes* (1595) in a volume that measures 78 x 55 x 39mm. Printed with nonpareil (6-point) type (the derivation of its name from the French word for "peerless" reflects the fact that this type size is among the tiniest in common use), these 32mo books are bound in red morocco leather with gilded tooling. The crown and initials "CR" on both covers refer to their binding during the reign of *Carolus Rex* (presumably Charles II).[122]

From the publication of the 1557 Whittingham New Testament through approximately 1570, the marketplace of English Bibles and New Testaments supported a number of versions often simultaneously, much as it did under Edward VI. The Whittingham New Testament, Geneva Bible, and Bishops' Bible editions provided new translations that supplemented the Great and Tyndale versions that stationers began printing once again following the reestablishment of Protestant theology under Elizabeth I. Under Matthew Parker's patronage, however, the Bishops' Bible became the official text of the Church of England, rendering Henry VIII's Great Bible obsolete. Though the record lacks clarity because a series of editions published by Jugge lack dates (not one of his New Testaments is dated), it appears that he ceased publication of his octavo Tyndale New Testaments very shortly after Parker earned for him the exclusive patent for Bishops' editions, which he used to publish not only folios of the new translation but also octavo New Testaments. Counting Bibles and New Testaments, the Bishops' translation went into 39 editions (41 if we include Fulke's Rheims–Bishops editions) through 1611. In comparison, the Geneva version and its variants were issued in 127 editions (128 including the Whittingham New Testament). These became the best selling of English Bibles almost immediately after Christopher Barker began publishing them in 1575. Taken together, the two Barkers published 114 of these and 23 of the Bishops'. During the years following 1578, editions of Geneva versions always outnumbered those of the Bishops' version (see Figure 2). As discussed above, the 3 Geneva versions differ in significant ways that may make grouping them together somewhat disingenuous. Of the 127 Geneva editions published through 1611, the original 1560 version accounts for 71 of them, the Geneva–Tomson 47, and the Geneva–Tomson–Junius 9. The Geneva and Geneva–Tomson versions each individually account for more editions than the Bishops', as does the Geneva–Tomson–Junius in the period beginning with the first 1602 edition. Because of its near ubiquity, the Geneva Bible (and its variants) often provided preachers with the biblical quotations they used in sermons delivered from the pulpit. Despite the Great and Bishops' Bibles' use as the sanctioned translations for church reading, preachers who in all likelihood had a copy of the Geneva Bible in their studies would have consulted it

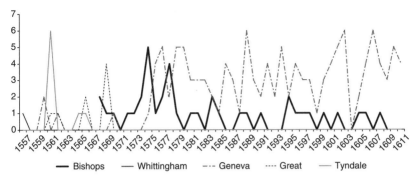

Figure 2 English Bible and New Testament editions published per year from 1557 to 1611, by version. Totals for Geneva editions include Geneva, Geneva–Tomson, and Geneva–Tomson–Junius versions.

while preparing to preach.[123] Even the translators' preface to the reader in the KJB uses some Geneva readings instead of its own.[124]

Like the first Bishops' Bible and the Great Bible before it, the 1611 first edition of the KJB is a monumental pulpit folio printed in a large black-letter font,[125] though it is worth remembering that the Bishops' Bible was ultimately larger. While copies of these two Bibles would have occupied virtually the same area on a pulpit, the first Bishops' folio edition consumes 409 sheets compared to the King James's 366. Aside from its woodcut initials and borders, the King James folio also eschews the "sumptuous" illustrations of the Bishops' Bible for a more austere *mise-en-page*. In a notable departure from the Geneva versions that remained popular for some time after its publication, the pages are not flanked by exegetical marginalia.[126] Like other versions (and smaller Geneva editions), however, it does include annotations in the margins indicating scriptural cross-references as well as some alternative translations of phrases and short passages.

In addition to his two large folios, Robert Barker also published a third edition of the KJB in 1611: a duodecimo New Testament.[127] Although it is not as slight as the smallest Geneva–Tomson editions, this small-format edition used just under 7 percent of the paper required for the first folio. With its nearly simultaneous publication in two formats, the KJB continued the Bible market's longstanding tendency to furnish large pulpit folios for use in churches in addition to affordable small-format New Testaments for private consumption, a trend that began with the editions of the Coverdale version. We should be mindful, at the same time, that small-format books were capable of refined embellishment. This is the case in a copy of the 1611 duodecimo that is bound together with a *Whole Book of Psalms* published by the Company of Stationers during the following year.[128] About the size of a very narrow deck of cards, it is bound with an elegantly floriated embroidered cover and has gilded and gauffered edges.[129] Although the 1611 editions of the King James were printed in black letter, Barker published four New Testament editions of the new version in roman type during the following year. Like the Geneva versions, the King James quickly went into a large variety of formats and editions, although the largest pulpit folios retained black letter at least through the outbreak of the English Civil Wars.[130] In 1649, most likely after Charles I's execution on January 30, the Company of Stationers published a particularly curious edition: a King James quarto with Geneva notes (including Junius's Revelation commentary) printed in the style of earlier roman-type Geneva Bibles.[131] It was only after the KJB became firmly established well into the seventeenth century that the Geneva Bible – remembered, apparently, more for its notes and humble material form than its translation – underwent transition from the most widely read and popular English Bible version to one that symbolized Puritanism and, as it would seem, an anti-Royalist agenda.

Afterword

This study relies very heavily on the *STC* for its information concerning the dating and determination of Bible and New Testament editions. Because we have limited our scope to complete English Bibles and New Testaments from 1525 to 1611 (*STC* numbers 2063–2217 and 2823–2909.5, minus the editions of Erasmus's *Paraphrases* and Fulke's Bishops–Rheims New Testament editions), we have opted to exclude both polyglot New Testaments that include English translations (*STC* 2792.5–2792.7) and Latin–English New Testaments (*STC* 2815–2821). Despite the fact that John Cawood published a Latin–English New Testament in 1550 (*STC* 2821), for example, we have accordingly attributed a total of only five editions to him in our above discussion. We also do not include the Bible in six parts published by John Day and William Seres as a complete Bible edition, though we include *STC* 2087.6 among New Testaments for 1550.[132]

The *STC* attempts to remain agnostic about dating, simply providing the dates from imprints and colophons when available. When an edition prints more than one year as its date of publication, as is often the case in Geneva editions with separate Old and New Testament title pages, we employ the latter in our tabulations and graphs. It is for this reason, for example, that we do not include *STC* 2218 in our study. Although the title page to the New Testament reads 1611, the colophon provides a date of 1612, which more likely represents the year when it became available for purchase. When extant copies provide no date, the *STC* speculates in one of five ways. In the case of editions for which the *STC* simply suggests a date within brackets, those for which a query immediately follows the date (e.g. [1566?]) and those preceded by "*c.*" (e.g. [*c.* 1566?]), we include the edition under the year that the *STC* provides. Among the New Testament editions in our sample, the *STC* assigns two with bounded ranges: *STC* 2873.5 and *STC* 2875. We have included these editions under the median date (1570 for *STC* 2873.5's [1568–72?] and 1574 for *STC* 2875's [1573–5?]). The final type of date is much more difficult to resolve satisfactorily. In some cases, the *STC* can only suggest a *terminus a quo*, leaving the latest possible year of its publication uncertain. This affects seven editions in our survey, most troublingly a set of five Tyndale–Jugge New Testament editions (four octavos, one sixteenmo) that all have 1561 assigned as their earliest possible print year. In the absence of better information, we have included editions with date attributions of this sort under the earliest possible year of their publication. In the graph of Bible and New Testament editions from 1557 to 1611 (Figure 2), the spike of Tyndale editions in 1561 is an unfortunate, though unavoidable, consequence of this practice. It seems unlikely that Jugge continued to publish his Tyndale–Jugge New Testaments after he began issuing Bishops' editions around 1568, which may provide a likely stopping point for these elusive editions. Lastly, for those editions that were reissued in multiple years, we use the date of their earliest issue. The most notable example of this is a Coverdale Bible quarto (*STC* 2079.8), which was printed in Zurich in 1550 but reissued in both 1550 and 1553 with cancel preliminaries; we record it in the year 1550.

DMH provides the text block measurements cited in this study. In the absence of comprehensive data indicating the precise type of paper employed for each Bible and New Testament edition, these provide the most reliable measurement for assessing the leaf size of a book, especially given that the process of trimming leaves (often multiple times through rebindings) has created significant variation among extant bound copies.

Better than paper size, text block measurements represent the smallest leaf size – and, thus, bound size – possible without text loss. Sheet counts have been calculated in one of three ways. In many cases, DMH provides the number of folios (leaves) in an edition; when these are absent, DMH sometimes retains a full collation; for editions not in DMH or in cases where DMH lacks a collation, we have used those provided in the *ESTC* when available.

NOTES

1 E.g. S. L. Greenslade, "English Versions of the Bible, 1525–1611," in *The Cambridge History of the Bible: The West from the Reformation to the Present Day*, ed. S. L. Greenslade (Cambridge: Cambridge University Press, 1963), 141–74; David Norton, *A History of the Bible as Literature*, 2 vols. (Cambridge: Cambridge University Press, 1993); David Daniell, *The Bible in English* (New Haven, CT and London: Yale University Press, 2003). Unless otherwise noted reference is to first editions of pre-1900 books. In the absence of pagination, we provide signature references from which we have omitted the abbreviation sig. Quotations from early printed books observe modern use of i/j, u/v, and w and silently expand tildes in the original to "m" or "n" as appropriate. Contractions are expanded and so noted with italics in transcriptions from manuscripts. Book titles are supplied in abbreviated form with modernized spelling. This essay refers in silence to the following fundamental resources: A. W. Pollard, G. R. Redgrave, W. A. Jackson, F. S. Ferguson, and Katharine F. Pantzer, comps., *A Short-Title Catalogue of Books Printed in England, Scotland, and Ireland, and of English Books Printed Abroad, 1475–1640*, 2nd edn. rev. and enlarged, 3 vols. (London: Bibliographical Society, 1976–91) (*STC*); *English Short Title Catalogue*, http://estc.bl.uk (*ESTC*); Thomas H. Darlow, and Horace F. Moule, eds., S. Herbert rev. and exp., *Historical Catalogue of Printed Editions of The English Bible 1525–1961* (London: The British and Foreign Bible Society, 1903/1968) (DMH, to which *STC* provides cross-references and corrections); Ruth S. Luborsky and Elizabeth M. Ingram, eds., *A Guide to English Illustrated Books*, 2 vols. (Tempe, AZ: Medieval and Renaissance Texts and Studies, 1998) (L&I); and *Oxford Dictionary of National Biography*, www.oxforddnb.com. For cautions concerning our use of *STC*, see the Afterword at the end of this chapter. Details concerning hand-press production methods and technical terms are based on Philip Gaskell, *A New Introduction to Bibliography* (New York and Oxford: Oxford University Press, 1972), 5–185. Because of their frequently indistinguishable titles, quotations from Bible editions are cited only by *STC* and DMH numbers (when available). We are indebted to James Bracken, Alan Coates,

Alan Farmer, Steven Galbraith, David Norton, Nigel Ramsey, and Michael Webb for valuable consultation concerning issues under investigation in this essay.

2 John N. King, *Voices of the English Reformation: A Sourcebook* (Philadelphia: University of Pennsylvania Press), 353. We have no way of knowing whether this text refers to an English translation. Indeed, the book might have been a Greek New Testament of the kind that Lady Jane Grey inscribed prior to her beheading at the Tower of London or a scriptural translation into Latin or a foreign vernacular language.

3 See Beth Quitslund, *The Reformation in Rhyme: Sternhold, Hopkins and the English Metrical Psalter, 1543–1603* (Aldershot: Ashgate, 2008) and Hannibal Hamlin, *Psalm Culture and Early Modern English Literature* (Cambridge: Cambridge University Press, 2004).

4 Colin H. Jory argues, contrary to the traditional publication date of 1525, that the aborted print run began in the early months of 1526. Though Jory's argument remains unpublished at the time of printing, Gergely Juhász discusses a few of its specifics in Chapter 4 of this volume.

5 Daniell, *The Bible in English*, 108–11, et passim.

6 *STC* 2824.

7 *STC* 2823.

8 Early type size names could refer to a small range of sizes, making any attempt to translate them into more precise modern measurements somewhat misleading. With the caveat that point measurements are ultimately anachronistic, approximate translations from period font sizes into point sizes are provided in parentheses to assist modern comparisons.

9 For an argument that challenges the assumption that the use of smaller format (i.e., quarto instead of folio) necessarily resulted in less expensive books, see Joseph A. Dane and Alexandra Gillespie, "The Myth of the Cheap Quarto," in *Tudor Books and Readers: Materiality and the Construction of Meaning*, ed. John N. King (Cambridge: Cambridge University Press, 2010), 25–45.

10 *STC* 2832.

11 *STC* 2825.

12 *STC* 2824, T2^{v}.

13 *STC* 2826.

14 See Gergely Juhász, "Some Neglected Aspects of the Exegetical Debate on Resurrection and the Immortality of the Soul Between William Tyndale and George Joye in Antwerp (1534–1535)," *Reformation* 14 (2010): 1–48. Against the dominant interpretation, Juhász argues that although some of Tyndale's language comes close to charging Joye with denying bodily resurrection at the Second Coming, a closer examination of the evidence reveals that Tyndale was

aware that the position advanced by Joye's translation concerned the immortality of the soul, not resurrection.

15 *STC* 2827.

16 British Library (BL) G 12180.

17 BL C.23.a.8, C.23.a.8* (*STC* 2826).

18 See Gaskell, *A New Introduction*, 136, especially note 43.

19 E.g., BL C.23.a.5 and C.23.a.21.

20 While small-format Bibles and Psalters with luxury bindings were often associated with women, it is only with caution that one can make such a correlation with a Bible from 1534, since no larger format English editions had yet been printed (with the exception of the aborted Cologne quarto).

21 *STC* 2831.

22 Guido Latré, "The 1535 Coverdale Bible and Its Antwerp Origins," in *The Bible as Book: The Reformation*, ed. Orlaith O'Sullivan and Ellen N. Herron (London: The British Library & Oak Knoll Press, 2000), 89–102.

23 See J. B. Trapp and Hubertus S. Herbrüggen, *"The King's Good Servant": Sir Thomas More, 1477/8–1535*, exhibition catalogue (London: National Portrait Gallery, 1977), no. 144.

24 *STC* 2063, +2ᵛ.

25 *STC* 2063.3. At least one extant copy contains Nicolson's prelims, but with its title page dated 1536 (*STC* 2063.5).

26 *STC* 2064. It remains unclear whether the first Bible printed entirely in England was Nicolson's folio or his Coverdale quarto of the same year (*STC* 2065).

27 *STC* 2065.

28 Herbert suggests that Matthew more likely stands for William Tyndale, since it was his name, not Rogers's, that "was then dangerous to employ" (DMH 34).

29 See DMH 34.

30 If the five Taverner-derived editions in Day and Seres's series of partial Bibles (discussed below) are included, the number increases to fourteen. Unlike Becke's revisions to the Matthew text, Taverner's are significantly more thorough, making his text, for Daniell, constitutive of a new version (Daniell, *The Bible in English*, 219). While it remains unclear precisely how much difference is necessary for distinguishing a revision from a substantially new translation, by 1551 Day was selling it (modified by Becke's further revisions) as "set furth according to T. Mathewes translacion" (*STC* 2088, title page). Daniell's language seems to suggest that Taverner's text was intentionally excluded from the list of the versions approved for consultation by the translators of the KJB, though it may be that it was simply not fully recognized – as Tomson's extremely popular revision of the Geneva New Testament was not – as a distinct translation. Erring

on the side of distinction, however, we differentiate the Matthew and Taverner texts throughout the rest of this chapter.

31 See Daniell, *The Bible in English*, 204 and 428.

32 Church of England, *Injunctions for the clerge* (London: Thomas Berthelet, 1538), *STC* 10086, fol. 1 (unnumbered).

33 As cited in A. G. Dickens and Dorothy Carr, eds., *The Reformation in England to the Accession of Elizabeth I* (London: Edward Arnold, 1967), 82.

34 For detailed accounts of the title pages of the Coverdale and Great Bibles, with illustrations, see John N. King, "Henry VIII as David: The King's Image and Reformation Politics" in *Henry VIII and His Afterlives*, ed. Mark Rankin, Christopher Highley, and John N. King (Cambridge: Cambridge University Press, 2009), 34–41.

35 *STC* 2069.

36 Herbert refers to *STC* 2070 as the second edition of the Great Bible, calling *STC* 2069 but a reprint of the first edition, *STC* 2068. As Herbert himself notes, however, *STC* 2069 constitutes a new typesetting with some correction and revision (DMH 52). By these criteria, it constitutes a free-standing edition. Both *STC* 2069 and *STC* 2070, which were printed by different stationers, state that they were finished in April 1540, however, which complicates determination of chronology.

37 *STC* 2070.

38 Church of England, *Iniunccions geuen by the Kynges Maiestie, aswell to the Clergie as to the Laitie of this Realm* (London: Richard Grafton, 1547), *STC* 10087.5, B1^r.

39 King, *Voices of the English Reformation*, 125.

40 With the exception of Tyndale's Pentateuch (*STC* 2350 and *STC* 2351, 2351 a 1534 reissue), printed in 1530 with portions in roman type previous Bible and New Testament editions had reserved roman and italic type for use on title pages and in paratextual material. It was not until Whittingham's New Testament in 1557 that a dedicated edition employed roman type throughout.

41 See Zachary Lesser, "Typographic Nostalgia: Playreading, Popularity and the Meanings of Black Letter," in *The Book of the Play: Playwrights, Stationers, and Readers in Early Modern England*, ed. Marta Straznicky (Amherst: University of Massachusetts Press, 2006), 99–126.

42 *STC* 10087.5, B4^r.

43 STC 2854–2854.6. See E. J. Devereux, "The Publication of the English *Paraphrases* of Erasmus," *Bulletin of the John Rylands Library*, 51 (1969): 348–67; and John N. King, *English Reformation Literature: The Tudor Origins of the Protestant Tradition* (Princeton: Princeton University Press), 94–5, 124, 130–1.

44 Anne Stanhope was the wife of Edward Seymour, Duke of Somerset (also known as Protector Somerset), the elder uncle of Edward VI, who governed England in a monarchal manner until his downfall on October 11, 1549.

45 *STC* 2866. The preceding observations on typography are based on this edition.

46 *STC* 2862 and 2862.5. On the English book trade and dissemination of Protestant books during the reign of Edward VI, see King, *English Reformation Literature*, 76–113, 122–38, et seq.

47 *STC* 2852.

48 Books printed by Crom during 1537–9 included two English New Testaments (*STC* 2836 and 2842) and a Bible published by Grafton and Whitchurch (*STC* 2066). On Bible printing in Antwerp, see *Tyndale's Testament*, ed. Paul Arblaster *et al.* (Turnhout: Brepols, 2002), 3–54, et passim.

49 *STC* 2852, 2867–70.

50 *STC* 2077. The Day–Seres partnership endured at least during 1548–50.

51 See John N. King, "John Day: Master Printer of the English Reformation," in *The Beginnings of English Protestantism*, ed. Peter Marshall and Alec Ryrie (Cambridge: Cambridge University Press, 2002), 190, et passim; and Elizabeth Evenden, *Patents, Pictures and Patronage: John Day and the Tudor Book Trade* (Aldershot: Ashgate, 2008), 15, 20, et passim.

52 *STC* 14018 (1560), A3^v.

53 *STC* 2088.

54 STC 2083–2086.5.

55 *STC* 2088, *3^v.

56 STC 2087–2087.6. Evenden mistakenly identifies them as sixteenmos in *Patents, Pictures and Patronage*, 15 and 21. On a methodological issue posed by this series of editions, see note 132.

57 *STC* 2087, A1^v.

58 *STC* 2077.

59 *STC* 1298. The *STC* suggests *c.* 1550 as the date of the Day and Seres edition of *The image of bothe churches*. It may be that the appeal in their 1549 Matthew–Becke edition to "[l]oke more of thys, in the Image of both the churches, gathered by Iohn Bale" (*STC* 2077, T6^v) is designed as an advertisement for their upcoming edition. Surely both books would have been simultaneously available for purchase in the shops of Day and Seres after they were in print.

60 *STC* 2836.

61 *STC* 2848. The *STC* estimates that the Antwerp printer Matthias Crom printed this edition sometime after 1542. If the attribution to Crom is correct, then the edition has a *terminus ad quem* of approximately 1546, the year during which Crom almost certainly died.

62 This is not to say that subsequent editions of a particular translation were not motivated by customer demand, but that the dramatic shifts from one version to the next that occurred under Henry VIII were motivated primarily by political forces rather than rapid changes in preference among consumers.

63 *STC* 2867, *2ᵛ.

64 Queen Mary I, *By the quene. The quenes highnes* [etc. Against controversy in religion, and preaching and printing without license] (London: J. Cawood, 1553), fol. 2 (unnumbered).

65 Quoted in John N. King, "The Account Book of a Marian Bookseller, 1553–1554," *British Library Journal* 13 (1987): 36.

66 *Ibid.*, 48–55. See entries 18, 42, and 92.

67 Bodleian (Bodl.) MS. Eng. th. g.3 (*STC* 2852; DMH 70).

68 *STC* 2871. See Daniell, *The Bible in English*, 279.

69 Compositors employed roman type for scriptural passages in Erasmus's *Paraphrases*, but they employed black letter as the work's dominant font (see above).

70 *STC* 2871, *2ʳ. See Daniell, *The Bible in English*, 279.

71 On the contemporary Protestant appropriation of Queen Mary's motto of *Veritas filia Temporis* ("Truth, the daughter of Time"), see John King, *Tudor Royal Iconography: Literature and Art in an Age of Religious Crisis* (Princeton: Princeton University Press, 1989), 228–31.

72 Daniell, *The Bible in English*, 304–14.

73 *Ibid.*, 303.

74 This woodcut is reprinted in Exod. 14 with annotations indicating that the figure represents God's "succour" in times of need as well as the necessity of "faith and pacience." See also L&I, 2093/1.

75 *STC* 2872.

76 *STC* 2094.

77 The attribution of the Great New Testament (*STC* 2873.7) to Cawood remains uncertain because the only copy is imperfect.

78 *STC* 2096 and *STC* 2098.

79 *STC* 2098.5.

80 Bruce, J. and T. T. Perowne, eds., *Correspondence of Matthew Parker: Comprising letters written by and to him, from A.D. 1535, to his death, A.D. 1575* (Cambridge: Cambridge University Press, 1853), 337.

81 *STC* 2099. *STC* 2099.2 is the same edition with a reissued title page that reads "The. holie. Bible" instead of the first issue's "The. holie. Bible. conteynynge the olde testament and the newe." Each copy required 409 sheets; the text block alone measures 356 x 238 mm.

82 See I. M. Green, *Print and Protestantism in Early Modern England* (Oxford and New York: Oxford University Press, 2000), 68.

83 Folger Shakespeare Library (FSL) STC 2099 Copy 3 (the copy is actually of STC 2099.2). For an illustration and description of this cover, see Frederick Bearman, Nati Krivatsy, and J. Franklin Mowery, *Fine and Historic Bookbindings From the Folger Shakespeare Library* (Washington, DC: Folger Shakespeare Library and Harry N. Abrams, Inc., 1992), 130–1.

84 For a reproduction and discussion, see King, *Tudor Royal Iconography*, 108.

85 For reproductions of the hand-colored portraits of Dudley and Cecil, see *Elizabeth I: Then and Now*, ed. Georgianna Ziegler (Washington, DC: Folger Shakespeare Library, 2003), 43.

86 Margaret Aston, "The Bishops' Bible Illustrations," in *The Church and the Arts*, Studies in Church History 28 (Oxford: Blackwell, 1992), 276–84.

87 Instead, later editions employed a variety of more traditional ornamental title-page borders. The first and second quarto editions (*STC* 2105 and *STC* 2108) also depict Elizabeth on their title pages, but later editions include no portrait. In fact, the third and fourth quarto editions use the same block as the first and second, but with the portrait of Elizabeth excised. See R. B. McKerrow and F. S. Ferguson, *Title-page Borders Used in England and Scotland 1485–1640* (London: Bibliographical Society, 1932), 112 (entry 127).

88 *STC* 2110.

89 *STC* 2875a5.

90 *STC* 2877.

91 *STC* 2878.

92 On the Geneva–Tomson notes, see also Daniell, *The Bible in English*, 352.

93 Edward Arber, *A Transcript of the Registers of the Stationer's Company of London 1554–1640* (London and Birmingham: privately printed, 1875–94), vol. 1, 115.

94 See *STC* 2125, 2155, 2184.5, 2209 and 2889, 2901, and 2903.

95 In the Rheims–Bishops' folio editions, the Bishops' translation remained in print through 1633. The 1619 octavo, however, was the final free-standing edition.

96 *STC* 2123.

97 *STC* 2126 and *STC* 2127.

98 In or around 1577, an unknown publisher produced the only black-letter octavo New Testament of a Geneva version, an edition of the Geneva–Tomson–Junius translation (*STC* 2879.1). According to the *STC*, it contains neither marginal notes nor commentary.

99 Keith Thomas has declared that "Black-letter literacy … was a more basic skill than roman-type literacy" in "The Meaning of Literacy in Early Modern England," in *The Written Word: Literacy in Transition*, ed. Gerd Baumann (Oxford: Clarendon Press, 1986), 99. For a rebuttal of this claim, see Lesser,

"Typographic Nostalgia," 103. Elizabethan books that use black-letter for the text block also employ roman and italic fonts for paratextual material as well as their title pages. This indicates that proficiency in reading multiple fonts would have been necessary by the time the Barkers were printing their Geneva editions.

100 A nonpareil black-letter font appears in John Day's 1569 metrical psalter in 32mo (*STC* 2440).

101 See note 98.

102 *STC* 2884.

103 This quotation appears on the title page of *STC* 2888.

104 Though it is a relatively small folio (its text block measures 241 x 155 mm), the first Fulke Rheims–Bishops' edition required 262 sheets of paper – more than two and a half times the 100 sheets used in the Rheims quarto – making it a costly publication.

105 *STC* 2207. The two volumes of the Douai Old Testament required 283 sheets of paper.

106 *STC* 2902. According to Daniell, the first Geneva–Tomson–Junius edition was printed in a complete Bible in 1599 (*The Bible in English*, 369). Though there are extant editions of the Geneva–Tomson–Junius that read "1599" on their title pages, these are in fact seventeenth-century editions published in Amsterdam. See the head note to *STC* 2174–80. Before the publication of the revised *STC*, Herbert had recognized that "[t]he nominal date, 1599, is probably untrue in every case," further observing that these editions very closely resemble a known 1633 edition from Amsterdam, *STC* 2309.

107 *STC* 2092.

108 Franciscus Junius, *The Apocalyps, or Revelation of S. John* (London: John Legate, 1596), *STC* 2990.

109 *STC* 2879, 3L5ᵛ. All of the notes in Tomson's Revelation appear in an italic font, indicating that they are his notes, not Beza's.

110 Counting both New Testaments and complete Bibles, there were nine editions from 1602 to 1611 with the Tomson–Junius New Testament, eleven with the Tomson, and nineteen with the original 1560 Geneva version.

111 *STC* 2123 and *STC* 2136. Both are black-letter editions.

112 Arber, *A Transcript*, vol. 2, 749.

113 Extant documents from officials at The University of Cambridge indicate that the Stationers' Company complained, in 1591, against Legate's alleged breach of Barker's patent. A letter to Lord Burghley (Arber, *A Transcript*, vol. 2, 819–20) directly mentions only the Stationers' Company's objection to Legate's 1591 Geneva Bible octavo (*STC* 2155), though a letter sent from the Vice-Chancellor to the Chancellor of Cambridge concerning the charges

includes New Testaments (ostensibly the 32mo Geneva–Tomson) among the books that the Stationers' Company accused Legate of printing "secretly and unlawfully" (W. W. Greg, *A Companion to Arber* [Oxford: Clarendon Press, 1967], Doc. 148–51).

114 Twenty-two of the Barkers' extant editions are in formats smaller than octavo, whereas fourteen are octavo or larger.

115 Although smaller-format Bishops' editions would have allowed churchgoers to follow the same translation being read from the pulpit, it seems likely that some owners of the popular small-format Geneva–Tomson editions also would have carried their copies to church.

116 *STC* 2881.5 (c. 1580). Bodl. Arch. G e.48 (formerly MS e. Mus. 242). This imperfect copy lacks the Gospels.

117 Bodl. C.P. 1606 g.1.

118 *STC* 2905.5.

119 *STC* 16331.

120 *STC* 2524.7.

121 FSL STC 2907. For an illustration, see Bearman *et al.*, *Fine and Historic Bookbindings*, 135.

122 FSL STC 2892.

123 See Norton, *A History* (1993), 224ff.

124 See, for example, the preface's use of "Except I know the power of the voyce" from 1 Cor. 14:11 instead of the KJB's "Therefore if I know not the meaning of the voice."

125 *STC* 2216. In the same year, a second edition – known as the "She" Bible for its correction of the first edition's erroneous use of "he" in Ruth 3:15 (the translators did not know it was an error, as "he" corresponded to the Hebrew they were using) – was also published.

126 Although they are typically bound with copies of this edition, John Speed's *Genealogies* (*STC* 23039) constitute a distinct bibliographic entity. When bound before Genesis after the title page and other preliminaries, as was often the practice, Speed's work prefixes complex woodcut tables as well as a two-leaf map in a manner that makes copies of King James folios appear more elaborate and deluxe.

127 *STC* 2909.

128 STC 2544.2.

129 Bodl. Arch. A.f.122.

130 See, for example, *STC* 2339 (1640).

131 DMH 620. This Bible does include the standard dedication to James, but in this respect it is consistent with many Bible editions published in the years of the Commonwealth and Protectorate, even some by John Field, printer to

Parliament and, subsequently, Cromwell. An edition with the King James text and Geneva notes was first published in Amsterdam in 1642 – after the Civil War had begun – but in folio without the recognizable Geneva Bible *mise-en-page* (Wing B2202).

132 Though Day and Seres certainly seem to have thought of the series as one that could form a complete Bible, they primarily seem to have intended piecemeal sale, encouraging that customers "may bie a part" only (see note 57, above). The appearance of the Pentateuch in 1551 under Day *sans* Seres after the others suggests that an earlier edition may have been lost, but unless more are missing, the fact that the individual volumes were issued across multiple years almost certainly means that the particular editions were made available for sale as they were printed. It would not have been possible to buy a complete set until August of 1550, at the very earliest. More importantly, there is no indication that Day and Seres ever intended for the series to be sold as a single book; in fact, it seems that the entire point is that the individual volumes were to be purchased independently of the others. Based on extant copies, no set was ever issued with a general title page, a feature that we might expect to find if Day and Seres intended to sell the volumes together as a set.

4 | Antwerp Bible translations in the King James Bible

GERGELY JUHÁSZ

The history of the King James Bible (KJB) starts with William Tyndale. Admittedly, Tyndale was not the first person to translate the Bible into English, and he had neither the time nor the opportunity to prepare a translation of the entire Bible.[1] Nonetheless, without William Tyndale the KJB would not be as it is today. His role in the genesis of the Authorized Version and in any subsequent English Bible is impossible to overestimate.[2] And while the opinions of scholars about the exact percentage that is incorporated from Tyndale's wordings into the KJB vary between 76 and 90 percent (though in different biblical books), all of them agree that a substantial portion of the Authorized Version is a verbatim rendering of William Tyndale's translation.[3] To put it somewhat bluntly: by modern standards of authorship, the KJB would be regarded as a form of plagiarism.

William Tyndale was born around 1494 in Gloucestershire, studied and was ordained to the priesthood in Oxford, and worked later as a private tutor in his native county. Around 1523 Tyndale applied for financial support and approval from the renowned humanist scholar Cuthbert Tunstall, bishop of London, for the preparation of a new translation of the New Testament from a Greek source text.[4] Such an approval by the diocesan or local council had been required for all new translations of the Scripture into the vernacular since the Constitutions of Archbishop Thomas Arundel, approved by the Provincial Council of Oxford (1407) and promulgated at the London Council of St Paul's (1409).[5] The Constitutions also prohibited reading and possessing any unlicensed recent translations of the Bible (explicitly mentioning those associated with John Wyclif).[6] The introduction of such a strict control on Bible translation in England was exceptional, as outside the realm, throughout Europe, biblical translations in the vernacular proliferated.[7] With the advance of Luther's teachings, however, and in the wake of Lollardy, a climate in which the Scripture in the vernacular was perceived by the English authorities as a weapon to advance one's own ideas and as a threat not only to the religious but also to the social and political order, Tunstall politely refused to support Tyndale's undertaking. After about a year spent in London, Tyndale moved to the Continent to realize his translation.

First he went to Germany, met Luther in Wittenberg, and started to print his own unlicensed New Testament translation in Cologne in the form of a quarto. The printing took place probably in the premises of Peter Quentell, and (at least part of) the expenses were covered by Frans Birckman, whose brother, Arnold Birckman, was in a printing–publishing partnership with Quentell.[8] The Birckman family was a well-established bookseller family, with shops and business partners in Cologne, Basel, Hagenau, Paris, Antwerp, and, most importantly, in London, "In St Paul's Churchyard at the sign of St Augustine" ("in cimiterio sancti pauli sub intersignio sancti Augustini"). They played an important role both in supplying books for English customers and in publishing the works of English authors (e.g., John Fisher's and Henry VIII's anti-Lutheran Latin treatises) for an international readership. Writing from Cambridge on December 21, 1513, Erasmus claimed that Frans Birckman is the person who imported nearly all books into England.[9] By 1525/26 the German bookseller had been active on the English book market for at least twenty years: Custom Rolls show that Birckman received two consignments of printed books in England in July 1503,[10] and from 1504 onward he supplied the English market with Missals according to the Salisbury use, printed in Paris and in the Low Countries.[11] To seek financial and logistical support from him was thus an obvious choice. But when the printing was advanced almost as far as the end of the Gospel of Mark, the business was discovered, so Tyndale left Cologne, taking the already-printed sheets with him to Worms, where the people, as the contemporary account has it, "Lutherized in full fury" ("ubi plebs pleno furore Lutherizabat").[12] Contrary to the traditional dating of 1525, the study of the Australian scholar Colin Jory suggests that the printing in Cologne cannot have started prior to January 23, 1526 and that Tyndale must have left Cologne by April 8, 1526.[13] In Worms, at the press of Peter Schoeffer, the second son of Gutenberg's successor (also called Peter Schoeffer) and the grandson of Johann Fust (Gutenberg's business associate and Peter Schoeffer the elder's father-in-law), a new, octavo edition was issued, the first printed complete New Testament in English, during the summer of 1526.[14] It is not impossible that Schoeffer also printed the missing quires to complete the quarto volume, but some of the Cologne prints must have also been sold separately.[15]

Birckman, who probably did not want to lose out on the business, commissioned one of his Antwerp business partners, Christopher van Ruremond (sometimes also called Christopher van Endhoven), to issue another edition.[16] Given that copies of the Antwerp edition had reached England before the end of November 1526, the Antwerp publication must have been prepared in collaboration with the printing in Worms. In all likelihood, when Tyndale left Cologne, he agreed with Birckman that a parallel edition was going to be issued in Antwerp (where Frans Birckman resided), and that the German bookseller would cover the cost of printing in both places.[17] This is because it is unlikely that Tyndale could have afforded the expenses, and the fact that no later Worms edition came forth could suggest that Schoeffer had not invested (much) money in the affair. Accordingly, the pages printed in Worms must have been sent immediately to Antwerp and the two editions were published quasi simultaneously. In this way Birckman could ring-fence his financial interests against any substantial loss if anything went wrong in either place, and made it more difficult for the censors to trace the place of publication or stop the printing completely. Apparently Birckman did not entirely live up to his obligation, for after his death (around 1529), his heirs were sued in Antwerp by Jan Silverclinck, the representative of the van Ruremonds, for

25 large Flemish pounds and 10 shillings as the rest of the 28 pounds, 17 shillings and 3 pennies for the business of buying or dispatching of 725 New Testaments printed in the English language, which the same petitioner [Jan Silverclinck], as he asserted, had sold and dispatched to the aforementioned late Frans and for which he subsequently received only 20 Carolus-guilders once from the same Frans.[18]

Antwerp was the ideal place for printing clandestine English books. The very fact that the van Ruremonds could sue the heirs of Birckman for the costs of a banned publication[19] and that they could win the case is telling about the tolerant attitude of the city authorities towards religious dissent.[20] And contrary to David Daniell's opinion,[21] there is no evidence that the Antwerp edition would have been inferior to the one printed in Worms. In fact, the Antwerp printers were renowned for the quality of their work and had more than a considerable share of the English book market.[22] As opposed to the Worms edition, the Antwerp English New Testaments contained a liturgical "kale[n]dare in the beginning / co[n]corda[n]ces in the marge[n]t / & the table in the[n]de."[23] Although George Joye (of whom more will follow later) claimed that no English-speaking corrector was involved in the printing and therefore the printer "so corrupted the boke that the simple reder might ofte tymes be taryed & steek,"[24] his claim is unlikely to be completely true, for the 1532 reprint, which according to Joye was also prepared without an English-speaking corrector, contained a translation of the liturgical readings from the Old Testament, which, of course, would have been impossible to produce without an English-speaking collaborator.[25] It is also noteworthy that the 1532 edition has the New Testament books in the canonical order, as opposed to Tyndale's Worms edition, which followed Luther's New Testament in introducing a canon within the canon and relegating Hebrews, James, Jude, and Revelation as unnumbered items to the end of the New Testament, in the same way that the Apocrypha (Deutero-canonical books) were placed at the end of the Old Testament.[26] The rearrangement of the books according to the canonical order was undoubtedly meant to protect the printer from possible charges of heresy and to appeal to a larger number of potential readers.

In the meantime Tyndale moved to Antwerp, where a thriving community of the English Merchants Adventurer welcomed him.[27] Their English House and the privileges attached to it, the city's excellent geographic position, its renowned book trade, and, not unimportantly, the lenient behavior of the authorities towards religious dissent made Antwerp very attractive to any English Protestant who sought refuge on the Continent. The possibility of smuggling books into England from the city's busy harbor was probably also influential for Tyndale's decision. In Antwerp Tyndale started to work on the translation of the Old Testament. In 1530 he published the translation of the Pentateuch, the following year his translation of Jonah came out, and in 1534 a revised edition of Genesis saw the light of day. It seems that there was some kind of agreement about the division of the work between him and one of his fellow exiles, the Cambridge scholar George Joye, a former fellow of Peterhouse.[28] The latter prepared the translations of Psalms (1530, 1534), Isaiah (1531), Proverbs (1533), Ecclesiastes (1533), Jeremiah (1534), and Lamentations (1534).[29] All these translations were the first printed English versions ever of these biblical books, and Joye was also the author of the first Protestant prayer book in English.[30] In 1534, however, the understanding between Tyndale and Joye came to an abrupt end, when Joye agreed to do the proofs for the forthcoming fourth edition of Tyndale's New Testament from the van Ruremond press, because Joye's corrections turned out to be a revision of some theological importance (August 1534).[31] Joye's changes in Tyndale's New Testament were regarded by Tyndale as meddling with his text, and this moved him to publish his own revision in November 1534. The following year Joye's revision of Tyndale's New Testament was republished by the van Ruremond house, and at the same time Tyndale's final revision appeared in print. But soon afterwards a complot was orchestrated to capture three persons considered to be the most dangerous leaders of the Antwerp Protestant circle: Tyndale, Joye, and Robert Barnes. Barnes was at the time in England; Joye was tipped off, fled to Strasbourg, and eventually returned to England; but Tyndale was arrested and, a year later, probably on September 6, 1536, was executed as a Lutheran heretic.[32] In the only surviving letter from prison, he asked to be allowed to continue to work on his translation of the Old Testament, and tradition has it that he was granted permission. While in prison, his New Testament was reprinted several times in Antwerp.

The year when the debate between Tyndale and Joye became public, Miles Coverdale and John Rogers, two other Cambridge alumni, arrived in Antwerp.[33] While Coverdale came to the Low Countries already with Lutheran convictions, Rogers arrived as the chaplain to the English House; during his stay in Antwerp he became a Protestant under Tyndale's influence. Both of them were to play a prominent role in the history of the English Bible. In 1535, during Tyndale's incarceration, Coverdale published the first complete printed English Bible, probably in Antwerp.[34] Its New Testament, Pentateuch, and the Book of Jonah were revisions of Tyndale's by Coverdale, and for the rest of the Old Testament Coverdale provided a fresh translation "out of fyue sundry interpreters." Besides the Vulgate these are usually understood as being Luther's Bible, the Zürich Bible, and Sante Pagnini's Latin version, to which additionally Erasmus's Latin New Testament, the Zürich Psalter, or the Worms Bible are sometimes named, though no satisfactory identification has been made.[35] Given its Antwerp origin, however, it would make more sense to look among the Dutch Bible translations as possible sources for Coverdale. Coverdale's Psalter was eventually incorporated into the Book of Common Prayer and has thus influenced Anglican Liturgy profoundly. However, since Coverdale did the proofs for Joye's 1534 Psalters he was thoroughly familiar with them, as is apparent from a comparison of his Psalter with Joye's works. Therefore Joye influenced Protestant piety with his Primers and Psalm translations to a much larger degree than is usually acknowledged.

In 1537 John Rogers published another English version in Antwerp. This version, the Matthew Bible, named after Thomas Matthew, the fictitious name of its translator, incorporated Tyndale's hitherto unpublished Old Testament translations (from the Book of Joshua to 2 Chronicles), some of which Tyndale must have produced during his long imprisonment. The rest of the Old Testament followed Coverdale's translation. In the same year the Coverdale Bible was reprinted in England with royal license by James Nicolson of Southwark, being the first Bible ever printed in England. A year later, on September 5, 1538 Cromwell's injunction ordered the clergy to provide and set up in every church a copy of "the bible of the largest volume in English" for people to read.[36] To meet the injunction, the Great Bible (named after its size) was published in 1539, a revision of the Matthew Bible by Coverdale, which accommodated some readings from the Vulgate to make it more acceptable to a conservative readership. Henry VIII's license and Cromwell's injunctions thus released the Antwerp translations of Tyndale and Coverdale into the English churches and into the hands of the English people. And although Henry later backslid and introduced restrictions on the possession and reading of the English Bible, the authority of the Great Bible remained unchallenged for two decades.

In 1560 the appearance of the Geneva Bible, produced by a group of English scholars while in exile in Geneva, marked the beginning of a new era. This Bible became one of the most influential versions in the history of English Bibles.[37] Its Old Testament was meant to bring the Great Bible's text closer to the Hebrew. Its New Testament was also a revision (previously a separate New Testament had been issued), although compared to the Old Testament, less revision was necessary, and Tyndale's phrases were retained to a much higher degree than Coverdale's. Just as the translations of Tyndale, Coverdale, and Joye resembled very much the Latin and vernacular biblical editions in Antwerp, the Geneva Bible copied not only the external features (font, woodcuts, and maps) of the French Geneva Bibles but incorporated many of the historical, philological, and theological notes of the French editions.[38] Some of its language and especially the copious paratextual elements (many of which reflect Puritan and Calvinist theology) were perceived as antimonarchical in England, and as a response the Bishops' Bible was issued in 1568. Initially, the various parts of this Bible, revised by different bishops, reflected much variation in quality and translation strategy, but on the whole it was a less radical revision of the Great Bible than the Geneva Bible.

The Bishops' Bible went through several revisions, and in some parts "it ought to be thought of as a new version."[39] It never gained the same popularity as the rival it was meant to replace. Its true importance lies in the fact that the 1602 edition formed the basis for the KJB, as was stipulated by the rules set up for the translators of the Authorized Version.[40] It was in this way that the clandestine work of the early pioneers of English Bible translation arrived from Antwerp to Robert Barker, the King's Printer in London. To illustrate this journey from Antwerp to London, just two random examples will suffice:

Isaiah 6:1:

Joye (1531): The yeare in the whiche Ozias the kynge dyed: I see the Lorde sittinge in an highe seate all aboue / and the trayne of his robe fylled ye temple.

Coverdale (1535): In the same yeare yt kynge Osias dyed, I sawe the LORDE sittinge vpon an high and glorious seate, and his trayne fylled ye palace.

Geneva (1560): In the yere of the death of King Vzziah, I sawe also the Lord sitting vpo[n] an high throne, and lifted vp, and the lower partes thereof filled the Temple.

Bishops' (1568): In the yere that kyng Oziah dyed, I sawe also the Lorde sitting vpon an high and glorious seate, and his trayne filled the temple.

KJB (1611): In the yeere that King Uzziah died, I saw also the Lord sitting vpon a throne, high and lifted vp, and his traine filled the Temple.

Hebrews 11:35:

Tyndale (1526): The wemen receaved their deed to lyfe agayne. Wother were racked / and wolde nott be delivered / thatt they myght receave a better resurreccion.

Joye (1534): The wemen receaued their deed to lyfe agayne. Some were racked / and wolde not be delyuered / that they myght receaue rather the better lyfe.

Tyndale (1534): And the wemen receaved their deed raysed to lyfe agayne. Other were racked and wolde not be delyvered that they myght receave a better resurreccion.

Joye (1535): The wemen receaued their deed from lyfe agayne. Some were racked / and wolde not be delyuered / that they myght receave rather the better lyfe.

Coverdale (1535): the wemen receaued their deed agayne from resurreccion. But other were racked, and accepted no delyueraunce, that they mighte optayne the resurreccion that better is.

Geneva (1560): The women receiued their dead raised to life: other also were racked, and wolde not be deliuered, that they might receiue a better resurrection.

Bishops' (1568): The women receaued their dead, raysed to lyfe agayne: Other were racked, not lokyng for deliueraunce, that they might receaue a better resurrectio.

KJB (1611): Women receiued their dead raised to life againe: and others were tortured, not accepting deliuerance, that they might obtaine a better resurrection.

Henry's royal license, Cromwell's injunction, the large number of editions, the printers' commercial success, and the incorporation into later editions, ultimately including the KJB (and its derived versions), all testify to the fact that the Antwerp Biblical translations became a huge success. This is mainly due to their intrinsic qualities, and the degree of their eventual absorption into the King James Bible also reflects their literary quality and proximity to the source text. Tyndale's translations, as the ones most prominently present in the KJB, clearly testify to his superb use of spoken English. David Daniell's works frequently draw attention to Tyndale's outstanding linguistic talents.[41] Tyndale's preference for monosyllabic Anglo-Saxon words over polysyllabic and Romance expressions, his feeling for rhythm, his awareness of the diverse genres and registers, and his effort to render the various Greek styles in appropriate corresponding English make Tyndale's translation not only an inspirational read but also a pleasing one, even to present-day readers. Daniell has repeatedly pointed out the many expressions that were coined by Tyndale, and Coverdale's merits are also frequently acknowledged. Less known is the fact that quite a few of Joye's formulations were also kept or reintroduced in later versions (e.g., "backslide" (Jer 3:6), "sauing helthe" (Ps. 67:2), "a mess of pottage" (Prov. 15:17), and the proverb "Pryde goth before a fall/ and a fall foloweth a proude mynde" (Prov. 16:18).[42]

Closely connected to this is one of the characteristics of Tyndale's biblical works, namely Tyndale's "naturalizing" and "modernizing" translation strategy, to use the terms of James S. Holmes's theory of translation.[43] This meant among other things that in the case of some of the *realia* Tyndale "converted" foreign entities (e.g., measurements, money units) into English ones, which resulted in a text much easier to understand for the uneducated.

At the same time both his language and his translation strategy offended the authorities in England. They claimed that Tyndale's "filthy" language was not worthy of the New Testament,[44] and that he wilfully mistranslated theologically loaded words. It is common knowledge, for example, that Tyndale was criticized by Thomas More for translating the Greek word ἐκκλησία as "congregation" instead of the usual term "church." More was convinced that Tyndale, following in the footsteps of Luther, differed from the traditional usage in order to advance his own theology.[45] It is less well known, however, that his fellow Protestant translator, George Joye, must have had the same impression. Apparently Joye, too, thought that Tyndale's emphasis on the etymological correspondence of certain words between the source and the target language ignored the connotations that the word in the source text had acquired by the time of the writing of the New Testament. For example in his revision of Tyndale's New Testament, Joye changed Matthew 16:18, where Tyndale's version read: "And I saye also vnto the / yt thou arte Peter: and apon this rocke I wyll bylde my congregacion," into "And I saye also vnto the / that thou arte Stone. And apon this same stonne / I wyll bylde my chirche." While Joye agreed with Tyndale that the official Roman Catholic Church could not be the Church Christ founded or wanted, he was clearly dissatisfied with Tyndale's "congregation," a term that did not carry the same theological connotations as *ecclesia* did in this passage according to Joye. Therefore he rendered *ecclesia* with "church," but dissociated the true Church from Peter and the Pope, as Peter's successor, by rendering the pun on Πέτρος and πέτρᾳ in the Greek twice with "stone" in English. Later versions were divided in their usage: the translators of the Geneva Bible opted for the traditional "church," while the Bishops' Bible retained Tyndale's "congregation." Remarkably, the rules laid down for the translators of the KJB stipulate that its wording should follow the "old" and most commonly accepted ecclesiastical usage, and that thus the translators should employ for example the word "Church" instead of "congregation" (rules 3–4). Indeed, the general tendency of the translators of the KJB is clearly historicizing and exoticizing, and as such just the opposite to Tyndale's own goals. A similar tendency is detectable in the reintroduction of the word "charity" instead of Tyndale's "love" in 1 Corinthians 13 by the revisers of the Bishops' Bible.

Tyndale's seemingly innocent "naturalizing" and "modernizing" translation strategy could also cause theological problems. For example, in the account about the Temple Tax (Matthew 17:24–7), Tyndale translated the two occurrences of the Greek δίδραχμα (two-drachma) with "poll money" and "tribute" (v. 24), and the Greek στατῆρα (*stater* v. 27) with "a pece of twelve pens" in 1526 and, perhaps due to inflation, with "a pece of twentie pence" in 1534.[46] By doing so, however, the meaning, that would have been obvious to any Greek reader, namely that the silver coin *stater* was four drachmas worth, and thus covered the entire temple tax for both Jesus and Peter, was not evident from Tyndale's version. Later versions realized this and solved it by introducing paratextual elements. While keeping "polle money," "tribute," and "a piece of twentie pence," the Geneva Bible inserted the following notes at vv. 24 and 27 respectively: "The Greke word is (didrachma) w[ich] was of value about 10 pence of olde sterling monie, & Israelites payed it once by the Lawe, Exo.30,13, and at this time they payed it to the Romai[n]s"; and "The worde is (Statera) w[hich] co[n]teineth two didrachmas, & is valued at about 5 grotes of olde sterling."[47] The translators of the KJB, which uses "tribute" twice in v. 24 and "a piece of money" in v. 27, likewise felt it necessary to clarify to the reader in two marginal notes at the appropriate verses: "Called in the originall Didrachma, being in valew fifteene pence"; and "Or, a stater. It is halfe an ounce of silver, in valew two shillings sixe pence, after fiue shillings the ounce."

Joye's translation strategy was similar to Tyndale's, but linguistically he was less talented. He, too, preferred a target-language- and target-culture-oriented translation strategy, and his translations were also characterized by modernizations and naturalizations. On one point, however, they differed radically. In his controversy about Joye's correction of Tyndale's New Testament for the van Ruremond press, Tyndale accused Joye of putting a theological gloss into the text when he translated the forms and cognates of the Greek verbs ἀνίστημι and ἐγείρω with expressions referring to the immortality of the soul instead of the bodily resurrection. In his defense, Joye replied that he preferred to include everything necessary for the understanding of the text in the text itself, and not to put anything in the margins. The glosses, he argued, if they are absolutely necessary, should only give further elucidation to an already understandable text. But according to his Protestant principle the text of the Scripture is self-explanatory, and therefore the translation should be self-evident, too. An ideal translation of the Bible needs no glosses or marginal notes according to Joye: "I wolde the scripture were so puerly & plyanly [sic] tra[n]slated that it neded nether note, glose nor scholia, so that the reder might once swimme without a corke."[48] In that respect the Geneva Bible was clearly in favor of inserting notes, but rule 6 of the instructions for the translators of the KJB prescribes that no marginal notes are allowed, "only for the explanation of the Hebrew or Greek words, which cannot without some circumlocution so briefly and fitly be expressed in the text."[49] This presupposes not only an exoticizing and historicizing translation strategy (e.g., transliteration of Hebrew and Greek *realia*) but also the practice that most (if not all) necessary explanatory notes should be included in the translation itself in order to make it a comprehensible text on its own.

The choice of source texts of the Antwerp reformers also appealed to many of their targeted readers. While Wyclif still maintained that Jerome's translation was authentic, that Jerome's holiness guaranteed that there was no difference between the meaning of the Hebrew and the Latin text,[50] and that the assistance of the Holy Spirit guaranteed its preservation by the Church, Tyndale decided to base his translations on Hebrew and Greek sources because he mistrusted the Vulgate. In his time two printed Greek texts of the New Testament were available: Cardinal Ximénez de Cisneros's Complutensian Polyglot Bible, of which the New Testament was printed in 1514 but was circulated only after 1521; and Erasmus's Greek New Testament (first published in 1516, revised in 1519, 1522, 1527, and 1535). As Erasmus's edition was first on the market, was printed in Basel, and was cheaper and in a handier format than the chunky volumes of the Complutensian, this became the source text for most contemporary Bible translators; it eventually became the standard or received Greek text (*textus receptus*) until the end of the nineteenth century. Tyndale used Erasmus's second and/or third edition.[51] By doing so he was the first person in the history of English Bible translation who based his New Testament on a Greek text. Since humanists and reformers questioned the reliability of the Vulgate, this authenticated his translation in the eyes of many. But to choose Erasmus's text instead of the Complutensian Polyglot was, in light of modern textual criticism, an unfortunate decision since the former's Greek text was much inferior to the Greek of the latter.[52] It is also a well-known fact that Erasmus translated passages back from the Latin into Greek in the case of the last verses of Revelation (which were initially not available to him in Greek) as well as in many other instances whenever he mistrusted his Greek sources.[53] Apparently Tyndale must also have had some reservations vis-à-vis Erasmus's text, because it is obvious from his work that he kept an eye on Luther's German translation as well as on the Vulgate, especially where these diverged from the Greek of Erasmus, and that he chose to accommodate readings that could not be justified by Erasmus's text. For example, Tyndale decided (on the basis of the Vulgate's text) to leave out the doxology at the end of the Lord's Prayer (Matt. 6:13) in his first edition of the New Testament. Although Tyndale supplied the doxology in his 1534 edition (and henceforward it was incorporated in subsequent Protestant English Bible translations and made its way into the Authorized Version), his original assessment was confirmed by modern scholarship which established that the Vulgate's Latin in that case (as in many others) reflects a Greek text that is older and closer to the (presumable) original than the late Byzantine Greek manuscripts Erasmus used. With regard to Tyndale's Hebrew sources, one can only conjecture that he used the second edition of the Flemish Daniel Bomberg's Rabbinic Bible (1524/5).[54]

As opposed to Tyndale, neither Joye nor Coverdale knew Greek or Hebrew. And although they both recognized the importance of the Vulgate,[55] they, too, sought to validate their translations in the eyes of their readers by the *Hebraica veritas*, even if they did not translate directly from the Hebrew. Accordingly, Joye used Martin Bucer's and Huldrych Zwingli's Latin translations as source texts for his Old Testament translations, and he warned in his preface to Isaiah that the reader should not judge it on the basis of the Vulgate text but on the

Hebrew. Similarly, his Psalter was "purely & faithfully translated" after Feline's [i.e., Martin Bucer's] text from the "Ebrue verite / in the which tonge Dauid / with the other syngers of y[e] Psalmes firste sung them."[56] And in his *Apologye*, he usually quotes Erasmus's Latin translation of the New Testament and not the Vulgate. As has been observed, Coverdale also made sure that his readers knew that his Bible was translated "out of fyue sundry interpreters."

The Geneva Bible was the first English Bible that was revised on the basis of Hebrew and Greek texts for both Testaments. With regard to its source language texts, the translators consulted the Complutensian Polyglot, Robert Estienne's 1550 edition of the Greek New Testament (the innovation of which they followed when they also introduced verse numbers), Theodore de Bèze's 1566 Latin translation of the New Testament, Sante Pagnini's 1528 Latin translation of the Old Testament, and Bomberg's Third Rabbinic Bible edited by Sebastian Münster.[57] The 1557 Geneva New Testament printed words and phrases in italics that are not explicitly in the source text but were deemed necessary in English for a correct understanding of the text, and thus distinguished for the first time in the history of the English Bible between the translators' additions and the wordings of the source text. By putting additions in Roman type, as opposed to the surrounding black-letter type, the Authorized Version followed (although inconsistently and incompletely) the practice of distinguishing between the original morphemes contained in the source text and morphemes added by the translators.[58]

Paradoxically, opting for Hebrew and Greek source texts (or derivatives from them) also gave grounds for criticizing the translations. Surely Catholics were aware of the fact that the Vulgate was "but a translation," yet as has been observed in Wyclif's remark, the authenticity and reliability of the Latin Bible was believed to be safeguarded by the holiness of its translator and the guarantee of the Holy Spirit through the Church. Accordingly, rejecting the Vulgate and choosing source texts that were preserved by the "schismatic Eastern Church" and by the "Jews who rejected Jesus" meant schism and the rejection of the Incarnate Word of God.[59] In their eyes, the Greek and Hebrew texts available were corrupted due to the corrupt character of their keepers, and their translation necessarily brought about moral corruption in the reader. On that issue Catholics and Protestants remained in fundamental disagreement, precisely on grounds of their shared commitment to preserve the authentic Word of God. The history of the English Bibles in the course of the sixteenth century shows an ever diminishing dependence on the Vulgate and a turn to Greek and Hebrew source texts. The only exception to that rule is, of course, the Catholic Douai–Rheims Bible.

By way of summary it can be stated that probably no other individual has shaped the KJB as much as William Tyndale did. While on the run and hiding from authorities on the Continent, he created a superb version of the New Testament in English. In Antwerp, Tyndale, Joye, and Coverdale produced the first fruits of early modern English biblical scholarship. Their works went through many revisions, and thus the road from Antwerp to London, passing by Geneva, was one of a long process of careful corrections and emendations which were all carried out in order to bring the Word of God ever closer to the reader. Joye envisioned this clearly when he wrote,

And I doute not but there be, & shal come aftir vs, that canne & shall correcke our workes and translacions in many places & make them miche more perfayt & better for the reader to vnderstande, and shulde we therfore brawll & wryte agenst them ...? god forbyde, but rather thanke them and geue place as Paule teacheth.j.Corinth.xiiij."[60]

Therefore he called upon the English authorities: "Burne nomore goddis worde: but me[n]de it where it is not truly translated."[61]

We have seen that Tyndale's translation, characterized by a certain uncompromising radicalism, was gradually molded and balanced by opposite tendencies. Besides Tyndale's linguistic genius, it is perhaps precisely this tension between Tyndale's radicalism and the Geneva Bible's nonconformist nature, on the one hand, and the mollifying efforts of Coverdale, the translators of the Bishops' Bible, and those of the Authorized Version, on the other – the tension between Tyndale's modernizing and naturalizing, on the one hand, and the historicizing and exoticizing tendencies of the Geneva Bible and the KJB, on the other – that gives the majestic character to the KJB. The KJB is truly "the culmination of a sequence of work begun by William Tyndale and continued by Miles Coverdale, the Great Bible, the Geneva Bible, the Bishops' Bible and the Rheims New Testament."[62] On its way from Antwerp to London through Geneva, the English Bible incorporated the best of all prior scholarship.

NOTES

The author wishes to thank Paul Arblaster, Guido Latré, Anne O'Donnell and Colin Jory for their invaluable help. My sincere thanks go also to Gabrielle Christenhusz for proofreading my chapter on such a short notice. All the remaining mistakes in the article are faults of the author.

1 The first partial written translations of the Bible into Anglo-Saxon (or Old English) were produced in the course of the seventh century AD, by the Venerable Bede and by Saint Aldhelm, Abbot of Malmesbury. In his *Historia ecclesiastica gentis Anglorum* Bede also mentions how the seventh-century monk Cædmon turned biblical passages from both the Old and the New Testaments into verse in his metric-poetic translation. Unfortunately none of these works, executed from the Latin, have survived. One of the first existing biblical texts of some length in Old English is the so-called Vespasian Psalter, an eighth-century, richly illuminated Latin Psalter, with an interlinear Anglo-Saxon word-for-word translation, that dates back to the ninth century AD. During medieval times, many partial translations and glosses were produced in Old and Middle English. Some of these, such as the tenth-century Lindisfarne Gospels with their renowned illustrations, Abbot Ælfric of Eynsham's Heptateuch (an abridged version of the first seven books of the Old Testament dating just after the year 1000), or the Psalter of Richard Rolle (d. 1349), hermit of Hampole, have survived, but many of them are known only indirectly or not at all. Since the general level of literacy was extremely low and the price of books forbiddingly high, these translations were mainly prepared for the clergy and for monasteries, abbeys, and chapterhouses, either to improve the understanding of the Latin text or as preaching and catechetical aids to help the religious in their pastoral tasks. Others were produced for educated, well-to-do lay persons, for the nobility, princes, or monarchs, for use in private devotion. There were also many metrical versions and poetic paraphrases of the most important biblical accounts and teachings. These benefited the common people to a much larger degree, as they were easily remembered by the illiterate. Most important were, however, the oral bible translations (produced extemporaneously during every solemn liturgy or otherwise), the inter-semiotic translations (interpretation of the verbal signs by means of signs of nonverbal systems, such as paintings, glass windows, statues, among which the so-called *biblia paupera*), and the mystery plays, paraliturgical performances, processions, hymns, and religious songs containing the most important elements of salvation history. The first complete translation of the Bible into English was produced in the fourteenth century, and is associated with the name of John Wyclif. The first translation (*c.* 1381) was revised a few years later (1388). The Wycliffite Bibles were also the first biblical translations that gained popularity among the common people.

2 "The significance of Tyndale's translation is that it became the basis of later official [English] versions" (Gareth Lloyd Jones, *The Discovery of Hebrew in Tudor England: A Third Language* [Manchester: Manchester University Press, 1983], 116). "The career of the English Bible from Tyndale *via* the King James and the (British and American) Revised Versions down to the New International Version (1973–78) including especially the Revised Standard Version (1952), has been more than is generally realized: a variation on the theme of Tyndale's composition" (Harry M. Orlinsky and Robert G. Bratcher, *A History of Bible Translation and the North American Contribution*, Centennial Publications [Atlanta, GA: Scholars Press, 1991], 34).

3 Based on a study of eighteen sampled passages from those portions of the Bible which were translated by Tyndale, Nielson and Skousen proposed the overall figure of 83 percent for the entire Bible. Their study suggests the figures of 76 percent for the Old Testament and 84 percent for the New Testament (Jon Nielson and Royal Skousen, "How Much of the King James Bible Is William Tyndale's?," *Reformation* 3 [1998]: 49–74). The study by Nielson and Skousen is uncritically copied by other scholars. It should be noted however that these numbers are only indicative, as this study is based on a very limited sampling of the texts, most of the passages chosen for their familiarity. The methodology used by the authors is defendable, but not necessarily the best. Their study also indicates that the King James Version and the Wyclif Bible, two supposedly independent translations made from different source texts and from different languages, have about 70 percent in common (it is not entirely clear from their study which edition of the Wyclif Bible they used). Westcott suggested the estimates of nine tenths (90 percent) for 1 John and five sixths (83 percent) for Ephesians (Brooke Foss Westcott and William Aldis Wright, *A General View of the History of the English Bible*, 3rd edn. [London and New York: The Macmillan Company, 1905], 158, n. 151). Donald Coggan accepted the figure of 90 percent: Coggan, *The English Bible*, (London: Published for the British Council and the National Book League by Longmans, Green & Co., 1963), 19. Butterworth's calculation of 18 percent is misleading as he based his calculation on matching clauses and phrases only. At the same time, he frequently emphasizes that Tyndale's wording has made it into the KJB essentially without change: Charles C. Butterworth, *The Literary Lineage of the King James Bible, 1340–1611* (Philadelphia: University of Pennsylvania Press, 1941), passim., e.g., 56–64.

4 Sometimes authors speak about "the original Greek text" of the New Testament. The autographs (original manuscripts in Greek) of the New Testament are lost, and the available manuscripts show an enormous number of variant readings. Hence, *the* original Greek text of the New Testament does not exist. Modern biblical scholarship uses an artificially and eclectically reconstructed text, based on

the principles of textual criticism. As will be apparent in this chapter, Tyndale, Coverdale, the Geneva Bible, the Bishops' Bible, and the KJB used a variety of Greek (and Hebrew) texts.

5 The text of the propositions is available on-line in the original Latin: Chancellor Archbishop Arundel, "Constitutions," www.umilta.net/arundel. html (Last consulted November 6, 2009).

6 Thomas More understood the wordings of the Constitutions as implicitly sanctioning earlier bible translations, and claimed to have seen orthodox English Bibles. It is more likely he saw Wycliffite Bibles that were used in an orthodox way (e.g., in private devotion or in the liturgy).

7 A similar local restriction on possessing and reading heretical Bible translation was introduced in Toulouse and Tarragona (1234). These local regulations were, however, the exceptions that proved the rule. For example, the entire Bible had been translated and printed in German even before Luther was born. And by the time he published his first New Testament edition in 1522 there had been at least eighteen editions of the complete German Bible. Additionally, ninety editions of the Gospels and Sunday readings and some fourteen printed German Psalters existed by that time. Throughout Europe there were about 70,000 Bibles, 120,000 Psalters, and 100,000 New Testaments printed in various languages before Luther's stand in 1517. See: Gergely Juhász, "Cat. 57. *Das Newe Testament Deutzsch*, [Translated by Martin Luther] (Wittenberg, Melchior & Michel Lotther, 1524)," in *Tyndale's Testament*, ed. Paul Arblaster, Juhász, and Guido Latré (Turnhout: Brepols, 2002), 116; Gergely Juhász, "The Bible and the Early Reformation Period," in *Tyndale's Testament*, ed. Arblaster *et al.*, 27. Cf. M. H. Black, "The Printed Bible," in *The Cambridge History of the Bible: The West from the Reformation to the Present Day*, ed. S. L. Greenslade (Cambridge: Cambridge University Press, 1963), 423; Orlinsky and Bratcher, *A History of Bible Translation and the North American Contribution*, 31.

8 Richard Rex has called into question Quentell's participation in the business on the basis of Quentell being "the leading Catholic printer and publisher of the decade," but Rex does not suggest any other alternative. Rex, "The English Campaign against Luther in the 1520s: The Alexander Prize Essay," *Transactions of the Royal Historical Society*, 5th ser., 39 (1989): 103. Recent studies by Andrew Hope, John Fudge, and Colin Jory confirmed the likelihood of Quentell's involvement and that Frans Birckman paid (at least partially) the costs of printing and that his presence on the English market was decisive for Tyndale: Andrew Hope, paper presented at the Tyndale Society Conference "Tasting the Word of God," Worcester, March 8–10, 2007; Colin H. Jory, "The Tyndale Cologne Affair Revisited," personal communication by email, April 1, 2009; John D. Fudge, *Commerce and Print in the Early Reformation*, The Northern World 28

(Leiden: Brill, 2007), 143–61. (I am most grateful to Colin Jory for sending me the pre-publication version of his excellent study.) That Birckman could have played some role in the publication was already sensed by Anderson, as Jory has pointed out. Christopher Anderson, *The Annals of the English Bible*, 2 vols. (London: W. Pickering, 1845), vol. 1, 55–6.

9 "Qui libros ferme omnes solitus est huc importare" (Desiderius Erasmus Roterodamus, *Opus Epistolarum Des. Erasmi Roterodami*, ed. Percy Stafford Allen *et al.*, 12 vols. [Oxford: Clarendon Press, 1906] vol. 1, 547, Ep. 283). Erasmus had a low opinion of Frans Birckman and satirized him as a spider weaving webs of intrigue and deception, overcharging his customers, falsifying the bookkeeping, applying all sorts of business tricks as well as intercepting and opening other people's letters, etc. Erasmus, "Philetymus et Pseudocheus in Colloquia," in *Colloquia: Opera Omnia Desiderii Erasmi Roterodami*, ed. Léon-Ernest Halkin (Amsterdam: North-Holland, 1972).

10 Henry Robert Plomer, *Wynkyn De Worde and His Contemporaries from the Death of Caxton to 1535: A Chapter in English Printing* (London: Grafton, 1925), 32.

11 M. E. Kronenberg, "Notes on English Printing in the Low Countries (Early Sixteenth Century)," *The Library* ser. 4, 9.2 (1928): 144.

12 Joannes Cochlaeus, *Commentaria de actis et scriptis Martini Lutheri Saxonis, Chronographice, Ex ordine ab anno domini M.D.XVII. usq[ue] ad Annum M.D.XLVI. Inclusiuè, fideliter conscripta* (Apud S. Victorem prope Moguntiam [Mainz]: Franciscus Behem, September 1549), 134.

13 Jory, "The Tyndale Cologne Affair Revisited." Jory bases his calculations on until-now-neglected information intimated by Cochlaeus (that the whole business coincided with Henry receiving Luther's letter on March 20, 1526), on the speed of printing, and on biographical data on Cochlaeus. Jory also points to the fact that the date of 1525 for the Cologne printing was first suggested in 1845: Anderson, *The Annals of the English Bible*, 52, cf. 48. Jory explains how Anderson and Tyndale's later biographers (Fry, Arber, Demaus, Pollard, Mozley and Daniell) arrived at 1525 as the date for the Cologne incident. His proposition seems not implausible, though difficulties with the dating remain.

14 On Peter Schoeffer, see: Josef Benzing, "Peter Schöffer d. J. zu Worms und Seine Drucke 1518–1529," (*Wormsgau* 5 (1961/2): 108–18); Hellmut Lehmann-Haupt and Monika Estermann, *Peter Schöffer Aus Gernsheim Und Mainz* (Wiesbaden: Reichert, 2002); Holger Nickel, *Literatur, Kunst und Wissenschaft in Den Inkunabeln. Hundert Jahre Gesamtkatalog der Wiegendrucke. Tagungsakten* (Mainz: Gütenberg-Gesellschaft, 2006); Cornelia Schneider, *Peter Schöffer: Bucher für Europa*, Schriftenreihe des Gutenberg-Museum 2

(Mainz: Gutenberg-Museum, 2003); Eric Marshall White and Paul Needham, ed., *Peter Schoeffer, Printer of Mainz: A Quincentenary Exhibition at the Bridwell Library, 8 Sept.–8 Dec. 2003* (Dallas, TX: Bridwell Library, 2003); Lotte Hellinga, "Peter Schoeffer and the Book-Trade in Mainz: Evidence for the Organization," in *Bookbindings and Other Bibliophily: Essays in Honour of Anthony Hobson*, ed. Dennis E. Rhodes (Verona: Edizioni Valdonega, 1994).

15 Cf. Jory, "The Tyndale Cologne Affair Revisited."

16 Cf. George Joye's words: "Tindal aboute.viij. or. ix. yere a goo translated and printed the new testament in a mean great volume ... And a non aftir the dwche men gote a copye & printed it agen in a small volume." Joye, *An Apologye made by George Ioye to satisfye (if it maye be) w. Tindale: to pourge & defende himself ageinst so many sclaunderouse lyes fayned vpon him in Tindals vncheritable a[n]d vnsober Pystle so well worthye to be prefixed for the Reader to induce him into the vnderstaning of hys new Testame[n]t diligently corrected & printed in the yeare of oure lorde .M. CCCCC. and xxxiiij. in Nouember* ([Antwerp]: [Catherine van Ruremond], February 27, 1535), sig. C4r. Joye's words about the original publication seem to refer to a quarto edition, and thus support the suggestion that some of the copies of the Cologne fragmentary publication were expanded to form a complete New Testament.

17 In his unpublished paper, delivered at the 2007 Conference of the Tyndale Society, Andrew Hope was the first to suggest the possibility that the Antwerp publications were not "pirate" editions but commissioned by Birckman.

18 "xxv ponden, x schellingen grooten vlems eens als reste van xxviij ponden, xvij schellingen, iij penningen ter saken van den coope oft overleveringe van vij^c xxv nyeuwe testamenten gedruct in engelsche tale die deselve aenleggere soe hij seyde den voersegde wijlen Franse vercocht ende gelevert hadde ende daerop hij van den selven Franse maer ontfangenen hadde 20 Karolusguldenen eens." "Vonnisboek," (Antwerp: Stadsarchief Antwerpen, 1530), fol. 70v. My translation in the main text. A photographic reproduction is published in Arblaster *et al., Tyndale's Testament*, 153.

19 Andrew Hope, "Ban on Possession of English New Testaments: Antwerp, 1527," in *Tyndale's Testament*, ed. Arblaster *et al.*, 151–2.

20 Cf. Arblaster, "Totius Mundi Emporium: Antwerp as a Centre for Vernacular Bible Translations, 1523–1545," in *The Low Countries as a Crossroads of Religious Beliefs*, ed. Arie-Jan Gelderblom, Jan L. de Jong, and Marc van Vaeck (Leiden: Brill, 2004), 9–31.

21 David Daniell, *The Bible in English: Its History and Influence* (New Haven, CT and London: Yale University Press, 2003), 144.

22 Dirk Imhof *et al., Antwerp, Dissident Typographical Centre: The Role of Antwerp Printers in the Religious Conflicts in England (16th Century)*, Publikaties van het

Museum Plantin-Moretus En het Stedelijk Prentenkabinet 31 (Gent: Snoeck-Ducaju, 1994).

23 Joye, *An Apologye*, sig. C4r.

24 *Ibid.*

25 Demaus's biography contains a facsimile reproduction of the title page of a now lost 1532 Antwerp edition of Tyndale's New Testament, which lists "The Epistles taken out of the Olde Testament." R. Demaus and Richard Lovett, *William Tyndale: A Biography: A Contribution to the Early History of the English Bible*, new, revised edn. (London: The Religious Tract Society, 1886), opposite 352. It would be interesting to know who supplied the Old Testament readings for the printer.

26 See photographic reproduction in Arblaster *et al.*, *Tyndale's Testament*, 148.

27 On the English Merchants Adventurer in Antwerp see Oskar De Smedt, *De Engelse Natie te Antwerpen in de 16e eeuw (1496–1582)*, 2nd edn., 2 vols. (Antwerpen: De Sikkel, 1950).

28 On Joye's life see Butterworth and Allan Griffith Chester, *George Joye, 1495?–1553: A Chapter in the History of the English Bible and the English Reformation* (Philadelphia: University of Pennsylvania Press, 1962).

29 Partridge thought that the fact that Tyndale did not translate Psalms was "because this was a task allotted to Coverdale" (Astley Cooper Partridge, *English Biblical Translation*, The Language Library [London: Deutsch, 1973], 56). Note, however, that Coverdale did not arrive in Antwerp until 1534, and by that time Joye had prepared three different translations of the Psalter, and for some thirty of the Psalms a fourth with possibly a fifth, now lost, translation.

30 No copy of the first edition (1529) has survived. Second edition: Joye, *Ortulus anime. The garden of the soule: or the englisshe primers* (Argentine [*vere* Antwerp]: Francis Foxe [*vere* Merten de Keyser], 1530).

31 A common misconception has to be rectified by emphasizing that Joye's changes were by no means motivated by his purported denial of the bodily resurrection (which he never denied). In fact, he replaced Tyndale's "resurreccion" by some other expressions referring to the immortality of the soul only in twenty-two, carefully chosen, places. The majority of the instances (seventy-three) where Tyndale had "resurreccion" were left unaltered. For Joye's motivations and further details on their debate see Juhász, "Translating Resurrection: The Importance of the Sadducees' Belief in the Tyndale–Joye Controversy," in *Resurrection in the New Testament*, ed. Reimund Bieringer, Veronica Koperski, and Bianca Lataire, Bibliotheca Ephemeridum Theologicarum Lovaniensium 165 (Leuven: Leuven University Press and Peeters, 2002), 107–21; Gergely Juhász, "Some Neglected Aspects of the Debate between William Tyndale and George Joye (1534–1535)," *Reformation* 14 (2009): 1–47.

32 Contrary to common conviction, Tyndale was not executed for translating the Bible (although his translation efforts contributed indirectly), as this was not an offence in the Low Countries. See Juhász and Arblaster, "Can Translating the Bible Be Bad for Your Health? William Tyndale and the Falsification of Memory," in *More Than Memory: The Discourse of Martyrdom and the Construction of Christian Identity in the History of Christianity*, ed. Johan Leemans, Annua Nuntia Lovaniensia 51 (Leuven: Peeters, 2005). Also, the traditional date of October 6 is the result of a misunderstanding. See Arblaster, "An Error of Dates?," *Tyndale Society Journal* 25 (2003): 50–1; Arblaster, "Cat. 119. Comptes Des Confiscations 1533–1538, Fo. 9v–10r. Expenses for Tyndale's Imprisonment and Trial," in *Tyndale's Testament*, ed. Arblaster *et al.*, 176–7.

33 On Miles Coverdale and John Rogers see: Henry Guppy, *Miles Coverdale and the English Bible 1488–1568* (Manchester: Manchester University Press, 1935); James Frederic Mozley, *Coverdale and His Bibles* (London: Lutterworth Press, 1953); *Tindale's Triumph, John Roger's Monument: The Newe Testament of the Matthew's Bible, 1537 A.D.*, The Martyrs Bible Series, 2 (Houston, TX: John Wesley Sawyer, 1989); Joseph Lemuel Chester, *John Rogers, the Compiler of the First Authorised English Bible: The Pioneer of the English Reformation, and Its First Martyr, Embracing a Genealogical Account of His Family, Biographical Sketches of Some of His Principal Descendants, His Own Writings, Etc. Etc.* (London: Longman, Green, Longman and Roberts, 1861).

34 The place of printing has been disputed, but Guido Latré suggested that it was first issued in Antwerp by the same Merten de Keyser who published several of Tyndale's and Joye's translations, the second complete one-volume Dutch Bible (1528), as well as the first complete French Bible (1530): Latré, "The First English Bibles in Print (Antwerp, 1526–38)," *Tyndale Society Journal* 19 (2001): 35–7; Guido Latré, "The 1535 Coverdale Bible and Its Antwerp Origins," in *The Bible as Book: The Reformation*, ed. Orlaith O'Sullivan (London and New Castle, DE: The British Library and Oak Knoll Press in association with The Scriptorium: Center for Christian Antiquities, 2000), 89–102.

35 E.g., Edgar R. Smothers, "The Coverdale Translation of Psalm LXXXIV," *The Harvard Theological Review* 38.4 (1945): 245–69. Heinz Bluhm argued that Coverdale only followed Tyndale and Luther, but his findings are unconvincing, and some of his claims are unsound (e.g., that the Zürich Bible was a mere reprint of Luther's). Bluhm, "'Fyve Sundry Interpreters,' the Sources of the First Printed English Bible," *The Huntington Library Quarterly* 39.2 (1976): 107–16.

36 Juhász, "Cat. 90. The New Testament of Oure Savyour Iesu Christ, Translated by Miles Coverdale, (Antwerp, Matthias Crom, 1538)," in *Tyndale's Testament*, ed. Arblaster *et al.*, 143.

37 Traditionally the name of Coverdale, who was also in Geneva at that time, is connected with it, and also the names of William Whittingham, Christopher Goodman, Anthony Gilby, Thomas Sampson, and William Cole.

38 David Price and Charles Caldwell Ryrie, *Let It Go among Our People: An Illustrated History of the English Bible, from John Wyclif to the King James Version* (London: Lutterworth, 2004), 84.

39 David Norton, *A Textual History of the King James Bible* (Cambridge: Cambridge University Press, 2005), 35. Cf. Edgar J. Goodspeed, *Problems of New Testament Translation* (Chicago: University of Chicago Press, 1945), iii.

40 The document stipulating the rules for the translators of the KJB is preserved in more than one manuscript, with slight variations in phrasing and spelling. The content in modernized spelling is best reproduced in Norton, *A Textual History of the King James Bible*, 7–8.

41 Daniell, *William Tyndale: A Biography* (New Haven, CT: Yale University Press, 1994), passim. e.g., 135–43; Daniell, *The Bible in English*.

42 Joye's translation of Psalm 91:5 ("Thou shalt not nede to be afrayde of nyght bugges") in his *Psalter of Dauid* (1530, reprinted in 1534) was retained in the Coverdale Bible, in the Matthew Bible, and in the Great Bible, and hence these are called the "Bugge Bibles." More on Joye's happy findings see: Butterworth and Chester, *George Joye*, passim.

43 According to Holmes's theory, there is a diachronic axis (the historical distance between the source text and the metatext) and there is a synchronic axis (the cultural differences regardless of their historical settings). Along the diachronic axis, the translator can opt for preserving the historical element (historicizing) or for adapting it to the times of the metatext (modernizing). Along the synchronic axis, the translator can opt for preserving the foreign element (exoticizing) or for adapting to the target culture (naturalizing, familiarization, domestication). These options are made, Holmes emphasizes, on a case by case basis. James S. Holmes and Raymond Van den Broeck, *Translated! Papers on Literary Translation and Translation Studies*, Approaches to Translation Studies 7 (Amsterdam: Rodopi, 1988), 48.

44 It was not the English language that was regarded as "filthy," but Tyndale's homely use of the language was regarded as disgraceful, not unlike many people resenting modern Bible translations today because of their "secular" or "unelevated" language. Of course many present-day translations do lack the linguistic qualities of Tyndale's translation.

45 E.g., in Matt. 16:18 Luther's New Testament read: "vnnd ich sage auch dyr, du bist Petrus, vnnd auff disen felß will ich bawen meyne gemeyne". Tyndale claimed that he merely followed More's friend, Erasmus, who also used *congregatio* in

his Latin translation. This is however not entirely true, for Erasmus's translation of Matthew 16:18 reads: "At ego quoque tibi dico, quod tu es Petrus. &
super hanc petram ædificabo meam ecclesiam" (1522). As Anne O'Donnell has
shown in her forthcoming excellent study, Tyndale is less than honest in claiming to have followed Erasmus in this practice, as only a fraction of the occurrences of ἐκκλησία in the New Testament are translated with *congregatio* by
Erasmus. In fact, the Dutch Humanist retains the Latin term *ecclesia* in most of
the cases: O'Donnell, personal communication by email 2009.

46 For the rendering of verse 27 Tyndale was probably influenced by Luther,
whose 1522 translation read "zins groschen" twice in v. 24 and "eyn halben
gulden" in v. 27.

47 The 1545 edition of the Luther Bible (the last one during Luther's life) still has
"Zinsgrosschen" twice in v. 24, but v. 27 has "Stater" with a similar explanatory
note on the value of the coin.

48 Joye, *An Apologye*, sig. C7r. On Joye's translational strategy see: Juhász, " 'That
the reder might once swimme without a corke': George Joye's Translation
Strategy in His Biblical Translations," in *"Wading Lambs and Swimming
Elephants": The Bible for the Laity and Theologians in the Medieval and Early
Modern Era*, ed. Wim François and August Den Hollander, Bibliotheca
Ephemeridum Theologicarum Lovaniensium (Leuven: Peeters and Leuven
University Press, 2010).

49 Norton, *A Textual History of the King James Bible*, 7–8.

50 "Inter nostros libros latinos et suos hebreos non est in sensu diversitas" (John
Wyclif, *De Veritate Sacrae Scripturae: Now First Edited from the Manuscripts with
Critical and Historical Notes*, ed. Rudolf Buddensieg, 3 vols., [London: Wycliffe
Society, 1905], vol. 1, 233–4).

51 That in his New Testament translation Tyndale included the celebrated passage
about the three heavenly witnesses in 1 John 5:7 (usually taken as a proof of the
teaching on the Holy Trinity) does not necessarily prove that he relied (exclusively) on the third (1522) edition of Erasmus's New Testament, which was the
first among the editions to include this verse. (Cf. Gilbert Tournoi, "Testamentum
Novum [Basel, Johann Froben, July 1522]," in *Tyndale's Testament*, ed. Arblaster
et al., 89.) Some of Tyndale's wordings seem to reflect the Greek of the second
(1519) edition. Whether this is due to Tyndale's dependence on Luther's translation (which was based on the Greek of the 1519 edition) or to Tyndale's own
use of that edition is impossible to discern.

52 Juhász, "The Bible and the Early Reformation Period," 27–8.

53 It is only in Erasmus's fourth (1527) edition that the Dutch scholar supplied the
Greek text for the last verses of Revelation from the Complutensian. *Ibid.*

54 The first parts of the Hebrew Bible were published between 1477 and 1487 in Italy. The first complete Hebrew Bible saw the light of day in 1488 in Soncino, Italy, and was reprinted in 1491–3 in Naples and in 1494 in Brescia. The first Christian edition of the Hebrew text of the Old Testament was again Cardinal Ximénez's Complutensis, followed by the three editions of the Rabbinic Bible by Daniel Bomberg: the first edited by Felix Pratensis (1516–17), the second by Jacob ben Chayyim (1524/5) and the third by Sebastian Münster (Juhász, "Cat. 38. *Biblia Rabbinica*, vol. 3, the Later Prophets [Venice, Daniel Bomberg, (c. 1526)]," in *Tyndale's Testament*, ed. Arblaster *et al.*, 94). See also: David Werner Amram, *The Makers of Hebrew Books in Italy: Being Chapters in the History of the Hebrew Printing Press*, repr. edn. (London: Holland Press, 1963); Price and Ryrie, *Let It Go among Our People*, 35.

55 In 1537 Coverdale published a diglot of the Vulgate New Testament alongside a revised translation of Tyndale's. Joye incorporated some of the Vulgate's readings in his own translations as well as in his revision of Tyndale's New Testament.

56 Joye, *The Psalter of Dauid purely and faithfully translated aftir the texte of feline* (Argentine [*vere* Antwerp]: Francis foxe [*vere* Merten de Keyser], January 16, 1530), A1v.

57 Price and Ryrie, *Let It Go among Our People*, 84.

58 Norton, *A Textual History*, 49.

59 Cf. Ilona N. Rashkow, "Hebrew Bible Translation and the Fear of Judaization," *The Sixteenth Century Journal* 21.2 (1990): 217–33.

60 Joye, *An Apologye*, sig. D5v.

61 Joye, *The Prophete Isaye/ Translated into Englysshe/ by George Joye* (Straszburg [*vere* Antwerp]: Balthassar Beckenth [*vere* Merten de Keyser], May 10, 1531), A7v.

62 Norton, *A Textual History*, 3.

5 | Philip Doddridge's New Testament
The Family Expositor (1739–56)

ISABEL RIVERS

On October 22, 1724, the 22-year-old dissenter Philip Doddridge, who was then ministering to a farming congregation in Leicestershire and devoting much of his time in his rural seclusion to his studies, wrote to his friend and mentor Samuel Clark, minister at St. Albans, about his current reading. After describing the works on divinity he was immersed in, he went on to another related topic that was also giving him "a great deal of pleasure": "I am drawing up, but only for my own use, a sort of analytical scheme of the contents of the epistles of the New Testament." Doddridge's great-grandson and editor of his letters added a note suggesting that this might be considered the origin of *The Family Expositor*.[1] His former student, editor, and biographer Job Orton described this as Doddridge's "Capital-work," noting that "He had been preparing for this Work from his Entrance on the Ministry, and kept it in View in the future Course of his Studies."[2] From these beginnings emerged the six substantial volumes of *The Family Expositor: or, A Paraphrase and Version of the New Testament. With Critical Notes; and a Practical Improvement of each Section*, published over a period of seventeen years, with the last three volumes appearing posthumously.

Doddridge was a highly influential contributor to the principal genres of eighteenth-century religious literature: his many publications in his lifetime and after included polemical essays, sermons, devotional works, biographies, hymns, and academic lectures, several of which went through multiple editions and were extremely successful.[3] In these works, following in the footsteps of his mentor Isaac Watts, he developed a rhetoric of the affections that was designed to arouse the reader to holy action. The *Expositor* in particular, which can be seen to embody the concerns of the evangelical revival of the mid eighteenth century with the religion of the heart and the appeal to a wide range of audiences, was much admired and enormously influential up to the mid nineteenth century, but, like many of Doddridge's other publications, it has largely disappeared from view, and the extent of its influence on popular Bible reading, scholarly interpretation, and translation has gone unrecognized.[4] This chapter tries to open up this ambitious and unusual book to scrutiny. It explores the evolution of the work in the course of Doddridge's various professional activities, its complex structure, and his aims and the audiences he wrote for. It looks in detail at his judgments on and revisions of the King James Bible, assesses the uses he made of paraphrase, and explores some striking examples of his literary analysis of the narrative books of the New Testament.

The origins and publishing of *The Family Expositor*

In order to understand why the *Expositor* took the shape it did it is important to be aware of Doddridge's varied roles and the different audiences he engaged with. As minister of Castle Hill Church in Northampton from late 1729 until his death in 1751, and at the same time tutor at his own academy, providing a higher education for dissenting laymen and training future ministers, Doddridge had a range of responsibilities, pastoral, tutorial, and scholarly. He was concerned with people of all ages and educational and social levels. In addition to his regular services he visited families, catechized children, and preached in outlying villages; in his academy he gave a huge range of lectures on subjects ranging from algebra and Jewish antiquities to divinity and Biblical exposition; he kept up with the interests of the learned world, making careful notes on his reading, and writing scholarly and critical papers for journals; in his regular summer tours he often preached by invitation to prominent London congregations. He wanted to be taken seriously as a scholar, yet he was aware that his ministerial duties led him away from scholarship. At the same time, he saw all these activities as a part of the main effort of his life, which was to encourage practical religion.[5]

This range of approaches informed the ways in which he taught the Bible in his academy. Thus in his three-year course of lectures to his ministerial students, published posthumously in 1763 by his former student and assistant Samuel Clark Jr., the concluding five parts on Divinity cover the credibility of the Old and New Testaments; the Scripture doctrine of the existence and nature of God and the divinity of the Son and Spirit; the fall and redemption; the duties required by the Gospel; and the Scripture doctrines of angels, the future state, and the resurrection.[6] The students were required to read a wide range of extracts from biblical commentators and theologians, and Doddridge also enumerated and appraised the best of them in three of his *Lectures on Preaching*, first published in 1804.[7] He passed on some of these suggestions in a letter to John Wesley of June 18, 1746 which Wesley later published in his *Arminian Magazine*.[8] But this academic and scholarly approach to the Bible took place alongside pastoral and evangelical exposition outside the lecture room. In an important lengthy manuscript account of the teaching methods of his own tutor, John Jennings, Doddridge described how Jennings did this:

In his Family Expositions he not only us'd to give us the Sense of the sacred Authors, which he frequently did with a Surprizing Ease and Dexterity, but he made it his Endeavours to revive and awaken serious Impressions on our Minds by Warm and lively practical Exhortations suited to the Passage of Scripture he spoke from and the Character and Circumstances of those to whom he address'd his Discourses.[9]

We can safely assume that Doddridge imitated Jennings in this as in many other respects.

We know from several sources, including a letter to the Connecticut minister Daniel Wadsworth of March 6, 1741, how much he emphasized the practical as well as academic instruction of his students. He explained to Wadsworth how he combined both in his biblical expositions:

I think it of Vast Importance to instruct them carefully in the Scriptures, & not only endeavour to establish them in the great truths of Christianity, but to labour to promote their practical influence on their hearts; ... [in addition to lectures] I have also every Morning an Exposition of a Chapter of the Old Testament and in the Evening in the New they reading the Chapter from the Original. I also give them once a week critical notes on the N: T which they transcribe as they do my other MSS Lectures ...[10]

In his "Further Advices relating to Exposition," lecture 16 of the *Lectures on Preaching*, he gave a number of suggestions to his students for the most effective ways of teaching the Bible to their congregations. Here the emphasis is primarily practical but with a judicious element of the academic, for example:

§ 2. Let free family exposition be part of your daily work. In this, labour at practical improvement chiefly, not neglecting, however, proper hints of criticism ...

§ 3. Have a private meeting once a week for exposition; – at these meetings, enlarge chiefly on the most devotional parts of scriptures, in an experimental way.[11] Indulge your private meditations on these occasions freely ...

§ 11.5. Aim in all at practical improvement. – Labour to shew the *spirit* of the writer, and for that purpose keep in your own mind and that of the people, the character of the author, and the particular *circumstances* in which he wrote.

§ 12.6. When you correct our version [i.e., the King James Bible], do it modestly ...

§ 13.7. Endeavour to make your exposition pleasant; to do this avoid dry criticism ...[12]

In the surviving records we can see Doddridge preparing the *Expositor* for publication over a number of years, drawing on the multiple methods he used as a tutor and pastor to his students and people. His second biographer, Andrew Kippis, who was a student at the Northampton academy in the early 1740s, made clear that Doddridge's weekly critical lectures on the New Testament formed part of the material of the *Expositor*: "In these were contained his observations on the language, meaning, and design of the Sacred Writings, and the interpretations and criticisms of the most eminent commentators. Many of these observations occur in his Family Expositor."[13] Doddridge first gave his mentor Samuel Clark an account of his plan for the *Expositor* on March 24, 1736: "a fresh translation, with paraphrase interwoven, and references to the most considerable writers, to be published in octavo, the first two volumes containing the Harmony of the Evangelists and perhaps Acts."[14] He tried to fit writing the *Expositor* daily into his very crowded timetable, anxious about completing the task he had set himself: he wrote to Clark on New Year's Day 1737, voicing his fear that he might die soon, "My Family Expositor goes on almost every day; and I press on the faster in it, that I may leave the portion on the Evangelists complete"; on the same day in his private reflections he vowed "To read some portion of Scripture, and if possible to write some of my Family Expositor every morning."[15] His plans for the format altered. He told Clark on April 17, 1737 that he hoped to have two editions, one in quarto with critical notes, and one in duodecimo or small octavo without notes "like the *Spectators* ... for the Service of poorer Families."[16] (In the event this cheap version did not materialize until 1765.) Volumes 1 and 2, containing the harmonized Gospels and the elaborate critical apparatus, appeared in quarto format in 1739 and 1740, with their respective prefaces dated November 27, 1738 and August 9, 1740. Volume 3, containing Acts and a good deal more scholarly material, including a substantial index by Doddridge's ministerial friend Edward Godwin, was not published until 1748, though the preface was dated December 11, 1746. It was the last to appear in Doddridge's lifetime.

In the last two years of his life the sense of both urgency and achievement mounted. In his reflections at the end of 1749 he noted: "I have actually written some of my Family Expositor every day this year, having been urged to it by a solicitation to print much earlier than I intended." He had now completed his notes on the epistles and begun those on Revelation, and transcribed (from shorthand for the press) Romans and the first six chapters of 1 Corinthians. At the end of 1750 he wrote optimistically about his health and surveyed his various activities with pride. "I have now, through the fourth year, been enabled every day to write some of my Family Expositor": he had finished his notes on Revelation and completed much of his transcription to the end of 2 Thessalonians. In his reflections for the beginning of 1751 he promised God "I will still go on with my Family Expositor, the publication of which I shall look upon as the great work of some ensuing years," noting that he hoped to complete the transcriptions up to the end of 2 Peter.[17] But from May onwards he became increasingly unwell, and at his death on October 26, 1751 there was still much left to do. Orton oversaw the publication of volumes 4, Romans to 2 Corinthians (1753), 5, Galatians to Philemon, and 6, Hebrews to Revelation (both 1756). In the "Advertisement to the Reader" prefixed to volume 6 Orton explained that Doddridge had completed the transcription of the material for volumes 4 and 5, and part of the transcription of Hebrews and 1 and 2 John; Orton himself and others (unnamed) had transcribed from Doddridge's shorthand the remainder of the epistles and Revelation. In some places Orton was obliged to interpret Doddridge's marginal "Hints" and add notes. He assured the reader in his anxiety to defend the work's authenticity that though some of Doddridge's phrases had been varied, the sentiments remained unchanged.[18] This lengthy editorial process involved the sometimes difficult collaboration of Orton with Philip Furneaux, Godwin, and Clark Jr., though this was concealed from the contemporary reading public.[19]

Structure, aims, and readers

In the three volumes published in his lifetime, Doddridge covered the narrative books of the New Testament: the four Gospels and the Acts of the Apostles. The title pages drew attention to the extent and boldness of Doddridge's editorial interventions, and he emphasized the term "history" on the title pages of the first two.[20] The following analysis concentrates on these three volumes; it begins by considering how Doddridge arranged his material, the readers he designed it for, and how he thought his book should be used.

The first readers could have been forgiven for being perplexed by the work's structure and *mise-en-page*. The whole New Testament is divided into sections (usually part of a chapter, but in volumes 1 and 2 often containing parts of different chapters from different Gospels). The Gospels altogether consist of 203 sections (with some verses from Acts 1 included in the last section), and Acts of 60 sections. Each section is in four parts: the text of the King James Bible (KJB) (which Doddridge refers to as the received or common translation) in the inner column or margin; his own version, in italics, interwoven with his lengthy paraphrase, as the main text in a larger font; footnotes to the text, in the same font as the KJB text; and the improvement (suggested prayer and meditation) at the end of each section in the larger font of Doddridge's version and paraphrase. In this layout Doddridge's version, paraphrase, and improvement are clearly more prominent than the KJB; at the same time, the text in the margin is easily legible and set off by the spaces between each verse (so it can hardly be said to be downgraded). Each section has a title, which also specifies which verses of which chapters are included; in addition, each page has a heading, a short sentence summarizing in five or six words the contents of that page. (See Illustration 3.)

The volumes also contain a good deal of explanatory material in addition to the notes. In volumes 1 and 2 there are two tables preceding the main text, designed for the reader who wants to work out how Doddridge's harmony relates to the traditional order of the Gospels: "A Table of the Chapters in this Volume, directing to the Sections where they are placed," and "A Table of the Sections in their Order, shewing the Disposition of the Harmony." The first table enables the reader to go straight to a particular chapter of a particular Gospel, which would otherwise be impossible; the second table

die (*f*), *before he had ſeen the* great *Anointed of* S E C T. I I.
the Lord, i. e. the Meſſiah.

Luke II. 27, 28, 29, 30, 31, 32.

27 And he came by the Spirit into the Temple: And when the Parents brought in the Child Jeſus, to do for him after the Cuſtom of the Law,

27 *And he came, under the* ſecret, but powerful, *Impulſe of the Spirit, into the Tem-ple,* juſt at the Juncture of Time, *when his Parents brought in the Child Jeſus* into the Court of Iſrael there, *that they might do for him according to the Cuſtom,* which the Authority *of the* Divine *Law* had required and eſtabliſhed in ſuch Caſes.

28 Then took he him up in his Arms, and bleſſed God, and ſaid,

28 *And* when the pious Simeon had diſcovered him by his Prophetick Gift, and ſaw that well-known Prophecy accompliſhed, (Hag. ii. 7.) that the Deſire of all Nations ſhould come into that ſecond Temple, *he* was tranſported at the Sight of this deſirable Child, and *took him* with a ſacred Rapture *into his Arms, and praiſed God, and ſaid,* with the higheſt Ele-vations of Devotion and Joy, 29 *Now, oh* my Sovereign *Lord* and Maſter, I thank-fully acknowledge, that *thou diſmiſſeſt thy Servant* to the Repoſe of the Grave *in Peace;* and I can die with Pleaſure, ſince thou haſt dealt with me *according to* the gracious En-gagements of *thy Word* to me; 30 *For mine Eyes have* at length *beheld* him, whom thou haſt appointed as the great Inſtrument of *thy* long expected *Salvation:* 31 Even that Salvation, *which thou haſt prepared* to ſet *before the Face of all Nations,* as the glo-rious Object of their Faith and Hope; 32 Ordaining him to be *a Light for the en-lightening of the Gentiles,* and for revealing of the Way of Life to them that fit in Dark-neſs, as well as giving him to be the Conſo-lation *and the Glory of thy People Iſrael,* who have the Honour of being peculiarly related to him.

29 Lord, now letteſt thou thy Servant depart in Peace, according to thy Word:

30 For mine Eyes have ſeen thy Salvation,

31 Which thou haſt pre-pared before the Face of all People;

32 A Light to lighten the Gentiles, and the Glory of thy People Iſrael.

33 *And*

(*f*) *That he ſhould not die.*] Our Tranſlation, *that he ſhould not ſee Death,* is moſt literal; but I did not apprehend the *Antitheſis,* between *ſeeing Death,* and *ſeeing Chriſt,* to be intended as at all material, and therefore did not retain the *Hebraiſm.*

(*g*) A

Illustration 3 Philip Doddridge, *The Family Expositor*, vol. 1 (1739), 63.

enables the reader to see at a glance exactly how Doddridge has rearranged the Gospels. In addition, at the end of volume 3 there are five appendices with new pagination, consisting of (1) "Additional Notes on the Harmony of the Evangelists"; (2) a dissertation on "Sir Isaac Newton's Scheme for reducing the several Histories contained in the Evangelists to their proper

Order"; (3) a dissertation on "The Inspiration of the New Testament"; (4) a "Chronological Table" of events in the Gospels and Acts, with two columns of dates alongside, one the year of the Roman emperors from Augustus to Nero, the other the year AD (for example, Jesus preaches the Sermon on the Mount in AD 30, year 16 of the reign of Tiberius; Paul preaches in Athens in AD 52, year 12 of the reign of Claudius); and (5) a note on the time when the historical books were written. The appendices are followed by two indexes in a small font in double columns: the first an index of the Greek words and phrases in the notes; and the second a "General Index" to the three volumes, 173 pages long, "Referring chiefly to such Articles, as are not pointed out by the running Contents, or Chronological Table."

Doddridge had thought carefully about the function and readership of this very complex book. He set out his aims in the characteristically lengthy preface to volume 1. The title explained his original design, "which was chiefly to promote *Family Religion*, and to render the reading of the *New Testament* more pleasant and improving, to those that wanted the Benefit of a learned Education, and had not Opportunity or Inclination to consult a Variety of *Commentators*." He acknowledged that there had been an alteration in his plan (presumably in part attributable to his experience of biblical exposition to his students), but he insisted "that is still the leading View of the greater Part of the Work." The purpose of the paraphrase was to explain the text to readers "who hardly know how to manage Annotations." By interweaving his own italicized version with the paraphrase, he had made it impossible for the paraphrase to be read without the text, and thus claimed to answer the objection made of previous paraphrases that it was difficult to tell which was which. The aim of the harmony, which had caused him great pains, was to digest the history of the evangelists into one series. He emphasized the originality of his work: he had made his first draft with little help but the Greek Testament, "which I endeavoured to *harmonize*, to *translate*, to *paraphrase*, and to *improve*, just as if none had ever attempted any thing of that Nature before me," and had then compared his work with that of his predecessors (vol. 1, ii–iii; italics in the preface reversed).

The notes, he claimed, were not part of his original scheme: he was persuaded to add them by his friends. He explained the various functions they served: several were inserted out of gratitude to friends who had helped him; some were there to justify his version and paraphrase; some explained his reasons for changing the order; some consisted of

"Observations on the Beauty and Force of various Passages" which had not been noted elsewhere; and some referred to other commentators who confirmed his own interpretations. The notes were generally short (by Doddridge's standards at least), and were not intended to be critical essays. He hoped they would be a guide to young students. He drew attention to a larger work on natural and revealed religion to be published after his death (presumably his *Course of Lectures*). He had tried to make the notes to the *Expositor* "easy and entertaining, even to an *English* reader" (i.e., with no classical training), but in the preface he directed students to philological works to help them (vol. 1, iv–v).

Doddridge thus supposed a general reader for the paraphrase, and a student reader for the notes. In his account of the improvement he was describing a crucial part of the work designed for all readers, and here his evangelical aims came to the fore. The improvement is entirely practical, consisting of exhortations and meditations "all in an *Evangelical Strain*." Doddridge laments that this is not "in the present Taste" (but it could be argued that he went some way toward creating that taste: he was endeavoring to counter the widespread moralist tendency in contemporary religion). The object of the New Testament is to make readers see Christ "not as a generous *Benefactor* only, who having performed some Actions of heroic Virtue and Benevolence, is now retired from all Intercourse with our World," but "as an ever-living and ever-present *Friend*." Seen from such a perspective, the elaborate apparatus of interpretation with which Doddridge presents the reader is strictly speaking unnecessary (though he does not quite say that): "The *New Testament* is a Book written with the most consummate Knowledge of Human Nature; and tho' there are a thousand latent Beauties in it, which it is the Business and Glory of true Criticism to place in a strong Point of Light, the *general Sense* and *Design* of it is plain to every honest Reader, even at the very first Perusal" (vol. 1, v–vi).

In the Advertisement immediately preceding section I, Doddridge gave clear advice on the order in which the book was to be read in families. (It should be borne in mind that this might have several meanings: the head of the household might be reading to his wife, children, and servants, or the minister might be reading to such a group, or the tutor might be reading to his students.)[21] First, the passage of Scripture should be read in the KJB in the margin, unless the family had their own Bible in front of them; then Doddridge's new version in italics should be read by itself (as we shall see, this was not always easy to do); then the paraphrase and the improvement should be read. The person officiating should choose some of the notes of general interest to read after the relevant paragraph; other notes might be made the subject of conversation after the reading, but this would depend on "the State and Character of the Families in Question" (vol. 1, xxviii).[22]

Doddridge envisaged his readers belonging to different kinds of groups of different education and abilities, but at the same time they would gain the impression from the paratextual material that they were members of a broad national community of readers of both sexes embracing different ranks and religious denominations across the country. Doddridge dedicated volume 1 to the Princess of Wales, and his lengthy lists of subscribers (in volumes 1, 2, 4, and 5) included members of the aristocracy, the Archbishop of Canterbury, bishops and clergy, Fellows of Oxford and Cambridge colleges, Scottish professors, and dissenting ministers in addition to the large number of provincial commoners.[23] What brought them together as attentive readers of the New Testament in Doddridge's conception was not only their enhanced understanding but their emotional transformation, as he explained in the preface to volume 3: "For surely the Breast of every well-disposed Reader, under the Influences of that *Blessed Spirit* which guided the *Sacred Penmen* in these lively and well-chosen Narrations, must by every Page of them be inflamed with some devout Passion" (vol. 3, viii).

Doddridge and "our received translation"

Dodddridge had strong views about the strengths and limitations of the KJB and how it could be improved. He defended his new version in the preface to volume 1:

There are so few Places, in which the general Sense will appear different from *our received Translation*, that some will perhaps think this an unnecessary Trouble: But I can by no means repent it, as it has given me an Opportunity, of searching more accurately into several Beauties of Expression, which had before escaped me; and of making some Alterations, which tho' they may not be very material to the Edification of Men's Souls, may yet in some Degree do a farther Honour to *Scripture*; raising some of those Ornaments, which were before depressed; and sufficiently proving, that several Objections urged against it were intirely of an *English* Growth. (vol. 1, ii–iii)

Doddridge implies here that his alterations were largely for literary ends, though this is not entirely the case. A few examples will indicate the reasons he gave for retaining or altering the KJB text on different occasions.

Clearly some of the changes Doddridge made were for reasons of taste, and to draw attention to ways in which the translation might reflect the patterns of modern English prose. Indeed, he implied that he had restrained himself in this respect. In section LXXII, having altered the direct speech of Matthew 9:30 ("and Jesus straitly charged them, saying, See that no man know *it*") to read "*And Jesus gave them a strict Charge, that they should tell no Man*," he added the following note, boldly suggesting a comparison with the most famous writer of his day:

Our *Version* is more *literal*, but the Sense is perfectly the same. I intended the *Variation* only as a *Specimen* of several of the like kind, which I think might be made, in a Manner which would better suit the Genius of *our Language*, tho' (perhaps thro' an Excess of Tenderness,) I have not ventured to take, even such *little Liberties* as these. See *Mr. Pope's Note* on *Homer's Iliad* ... (vol. 1, 448)[24]

Elsewhere Doddridge did not hesitate to point out where he thought the translators were wrong. One of his most important comments on what he saw as a serious mistranslation is in section CLXXII, "CHRIST *at the Conclusion of the Passover institutes the Eucharist.*" Doddridge's version and paraphrase of Matthew 26:28, harmonized with Mark 14:24 and Luke 22:20, reads:

This Cup of Wine *is*, that is, it represents *my Blood*, which is the great Basis *of the New Covenant, [or]* is itself the Seal of *the New Covenant* established *in my Blood (d), which is shed for you, [and] for many* more, as the great Ransom to be paid *for the Forgiveness of Sins*;

Note (d) explains that the word "testament" used in Jesus's speech and in the title of the whole book is misconceived:

I have rendered the Word διαθηκη, *Covenant*, rather than *Testament*, or *Will*, because it is evidently the more usual Signification of the Word; and because *the Old Covenant*, to which *the New* is opposed, cannot with any Propriety be called *a Testament*, with Reference to the *Death of any Testator*, which is the Idea chiefly insisted on by those, who would retain our common *Version* here. And by the Way, it appears on this Principle, that the *Title* of our *Bible* is improperly and obscurely rendered, by a Piece of Complaisance to the *Old Latin Versions*, of which they were by no means worthy. (vol. 2, 445)[25]

Section CLXXXIX, "CHRIST *being delivered up by* Pilate *to the Rage of the People, bears his Cross to* Calvary, *and is there nailed to it*," provides a good example of Doddridge carefully explaining why he has kept to the language of the KJB in one case and altered it in another. In his version of Mark 15:28, which quotes Isaiah 53:12, he retains the term "transgressors" for the reason given in the note:

I chuse in *Quotations* from the *Old Testament*, to keep as close to our *English Version* of the Passage quoted, as the *Greek* will allow me, that the Memory of the Hearer may assist him in distinguishing the *Text*; else I should have rendered ανομων, *Criminals*.

Conversely, Doddridge rewords Luke 23:34 to read "Father, forgive them, for they know not what they are doing," justifying on grammatical grounds his change to one of Jesus's best-known sayings:

This is one of the most striking Passages in the World. While they are actually nailing him to the Cross, he seems to feel the Injury these poor Creatures did to their own Souls, more than the Wounds they gave him and as it were to forget his own Anguish, in a Concern for their Salvation. I render τι ποιουσι, *what they are doing*, as thinking that *Version* most expressive of the present Circumstance; and indeed it is the exact Import of what *Grammarians* call the *Present Tense*. (vol. 2, 560)[26]

In section CXCI, "CHRIST, *having recommended his* Mother *to the care of* John, *and suffered many Agonies and Indignities on the Cross, expires*," Doddridge complains that the translators have obscured the differences in vocabulary in the accounts of the moment of Jesus's death. His version of the end of Luke 23:46, harmonized with Matthew 27:50, Mark 15:37, and John 19:30, reads: "*And when he had said thus, declining his Head, he* voluntarily *dismissed* or delivered up *his Spirit, and expired*." The note comments: "The *Evangelists* use different Words in expressing *our Lord's Death*, which I a little wonder that *our Translators* render in the same Manner, *he yielded*, or *gave up the Ghost*." Doddridge points out that the correct translation of Mark and Luke is "*he expired*," of John "*he yielded up his Spirit*," and of Matthew "*he dismissed his Spirit*." He prefers the last because it shows that this death was unique: Jesus "*died* by the *voluntary Act* of his own Mind, according to the *Power received from the Father*" (vol. 2, 573–4).

The uses of paraphrase

Doddridge suggested in the Advertisement to volume 1 that for family reading his version should be read out before the paraphrase, but in practice for the private reader the two are difficult to separate. The overwhelming impression is of the transformation of the terse prose of the KJB into a much more complex medium in which the new fuller version is embedded, surrounded by material that variously explains the meaning, provides contextual information, modernizes the language, and draws out the beauties of each verse. Doddridge was well aware of the problems. For example, in section XCI, "CHRIST *descending from the Mountain on which he was transfigured, drives out an Evil Spirit...*," Doddridge paraphrases Mark 9:24, "Lord, I believe; help thou mine Unbelief":

Lord, I do from my Heart *believe* that thy Power is unlimited; yet such is my Frailty, that when I look on this Spectacle of Misery, my Faith is ready to fail me again: *Help* me therefore against *my Unbelief*, by mitigating the Circumstances of the Trial, or communicating suitable Strength to my Soul.

In the note Doddridge admits that the force of the translation is diluted, yet insists that the process is necessary:

It seems an Inconvenience inseparable from this Method of *Paraphrasing*, that sometimes (as in the present Instance,) some lively and strongly pointed Sentences should lose something of their Spirit by it; yet keeping the *Original* thus distinct, may in Part remedy it; and on the whole, many of these Expressions are so full of Meaning, that the general Laws of *Interpretation* require, that they should be unfolded. (vol. 2, 11)

In this case, the explanatory paraphrase is relatively straightforward. Many examples could be provided of Doddridge unfolding the translation in far more elaborate and sometimes surprising ways. For example, in section IV, "*The Angel* Gabriel *is sent to the Virgin* Mary, *to inform her of the Conception of* CHRIST *by her, in which she humbly acquiesces*," Doddridge's paraphrase of Luke 1:32–3 helpfully cites several passages of the Old Testament that unveil Gabriel's prophecies of the child's kingdom. In paraphrasing Mary's response in verse 38, Doddridge adds an element of excitement and danger to the narrative that is not present in the original: "I thankfully accept the Honour, of which I confess I am unworthy, and humbly resign my Reputation, and even my Life, to the Divine Care and Providence, while I wait the Accomplishment of thy Prediction." In the note Doddridge draws attention to "the Severity of the *Mosaic* Law against those, who had violated the Faith of their Espousals," citing Deuteronomy 22:23–4; the reader is thus encouraged to imagine that Mary could have been stoned to death (vol. 1, 22–3).[27]

Some of Doddridge's attempts to draw out meaning in his paraphrases seem ill-judged on literary grounds. In section V, "Mary *visits* Elizabeth; *her Faith is confirmed by it, and she breaks out into a Song of Praise*," his paraphrase of the Magnificat (Luke 1:46–55) further illustrates his attempt to develop Mary's character. In Doddridge's hands verse 48 in the KJB, "For he hath regarded the low Estate of his Handmaiden," becomes a story of eighteenth-century social distinctions: "*For*, notwithstanding all the Meanness of my Circumstances, and the obscure Condition that I live in, yet *he hath looked* with a distinguishing Regard, and most surprizing Condescension, *upon the low Estate of his Handmaid*." In the note he usefully points out the echoes of many passages in the Old Testament in Mary's song, but naively assumes that these derive from her own reading, rather than from Luke's deliberate shaping of the narrative: "It is observable, that most of these Phrases are borrowed from the *Old Testament*, with which the pious Virgin seems to have been very conversant; especially from the Song of *Hannah*, in which there were so many Passages remarkably suitable to her own Case" (vol. 1, 27).

Several examples could be adduced of Doddridge attempting unsuccessfully to bring out the beauties of the original by elaborating them: in section X the praises of the heavenly host (Luke 2:14), following the angel's revelation of Jesus's birth to the shepherds, are embarrassingly bombastic, with the paragraph concluding "Eccho it back, oh ye mortal Abodes, to ours! On Earth Peace! Benevolence and Favour unto Men", and in section XL Doddridge seems to lose all sense of proportion in his lengthy treatment of the Lord's Prayer (Matt. 6:9–15), disregarding the injunction in his own version of Matthew 6:7: "*But when you pray, do not use a vain Multiplicity of Words*" (vol. 1, 56–7; 245–8).

Conversely, other paraphrases are genuinely illuminating. For example, in addition to the many passages that illustrate the long-established verbal and narrative links between the Old and New Testaments, there are others that enable Doddridge to clarify his own theological or ecclesiological interpretations as a moderate Calvinist dissenter. In section CXX, on the parable of the Great Supper, he carefully rewords the lord's injunction to the servant, "Go out into the Highways and Hedges, and compel them to come in" (Luke 14:23), which had been used for centuries as a key text in support of religious coercion. Doddridge's paraphrase is designed to undermine this reading: "*Go out* then *into the Roads* without the City, and rather than fail, look for the poorest and most helpless Travellers, who are sheltering themselves under Trees *and Hedges*; *and* if Importunity be necessary to such, *press them* that you find there by the most earnest Invitation *to come in* ..." In the accompanying note he rebukes Augustine, argues for a change in the translation, and shows that one important purpose of paraphrase (paradoxically) is precision of interpretation:

Nothing can be more apparently weak, than to imagine with *St. Augustin*, and many others, that these Words can justify the Use of *Compulsion* and Force *in Religious Matters*... There is an *Ambiguity* in the *English Word* [*press,*] which much more exactly answers to that in the *Original*, than the Word *our Translators* use: And it seems to me the Part of a faithful *Translator*, especially of the *Sacred Writings*, to preserve the *Ambiguities* of the *Original*; tho' a *Paraphrase*, which speaks only a Man's own Sentiments, may sometimes venture to determine them. (vol. 2, 151)

The New Testament narrative

In the preface to volume 2 Doddridge warned his friends against reading the edition as though it were a secular text: "It had been much better, on both Sides, that the Work should never have been undertaken or perused, than that these *Divine Authors* should be treated like a Set of *Profane Classicks*; or that the Sacred and Momentous Transactions they relate, should be handled and read, like an invented Tale, or a common History" (vol. 2, iv). Nevertheless, it is clear that Doddridge was deeply interested in the evangelists' handling of the narrative, what could be deduced about them from their self-presentation, and their portrayal of the principal heroes, Jesus and Paul. In blatant disregard of Doddridge's warning, this section will briefly consider some of his more striking literary interpretations of the Gospels and the Acts of the Apostles.

One of Doddridge's aims in harmonizing the Gospels was to improve the way in which the narrative was ordered. He begins in section I with Luke's address to Theophilus (Luke 1:1–4) as a preface to the whole, followed in section II by John's *"very sublime and emphatical Account, of the Deity, and Incarnation of* CHRIST*"* (John 1:1–14), before embarking on Luke's nativity narrative. It is not possible to analyze here the complex process of interweaving that Doddridge undertook, but two effective examples of reordering can be pointed out. Thus in section CLXXXIX he chose to move the account of Judas's suicide (Matt. 27:3–10) in order not to interrupt the story of Christ's passion (vol. 2, 556). The paraphrase to section CXCIII begins "HAVING thus finished the Account of the Death of Jesus, it may be convenient here to mention the miserable End of that perfidious Disciple, by whom he was betrayed into the Hands of his Enemies" (vol. 2, 586). For a different reason he brought together in section XIX of Acts the two accounts of Paul's conversion, the third-person narration by (supposedly) Luke (Acts 9:1–9), and part of Paul's own first-person retelling of the event to Agrippa (Acts 26:16–18), so that Christ's words could be incorporated in the original story and the drama intensified. Doddridge notes: "I hope, I need make *no Apology* for giving the Reader, in the *first View* of this wonderful and delightful Story, a full Account of it in a Kind of *Compound Text*" (vol. 3, 135). Paul's whole speech to Agrippa (Acts 26 entire) then follows in its proper place in section LVI.

Doddridge includes some fascinating observations about the different characteristics of the evangelists as narrators. In section LXXII he notes, "I endeavour in this Work, to give the Reader as exact a View as possible, of the (very consistent) *Varieties*, with which different *Evangelists* record the *same Facts*" (vol. 1, 444). He observes that Mark's narration of the death of John the Baptist (Mark 6:14–29), "which is by far the most circumstantial, is very much *animated*" (section LXXVII, vol. 1, 492). He emphasizes the evangelists' modesty in depicting themselves as participants in their narratives, focusing particularly on John and Luke. In section CXCIV, on the resurrection and the empty tomb, he comments on John's portrait of himself as the anonymous "other Disciple … who saw, and believed"

(John 20:8), taking for granted the tradition that the evangelist and the beloved disciple were the same person. Doddridge takes this "as a modest Intimation" that John was the first to believe in the resurrection: "Much of the Beauty of *John's* Manner of Writing consists in such Hints as these, which shew the Temper of that excellent Man; and were he to be considered merely as a *Human Historian*, add great Weight to his Testimony" (vol. 2, 598). Doddridge identifies one of his favorite passages in section CCI, "Christ's *Discourse with* Peter *at the Sea of* Tiberias," the conclusion of the last chapter of John, when Peter turns and sees the disciple Jesus loved following (John 21:20):

There is a Spirit and Tenderness in this plain Passage, which I can never read without the most sensible Emotion. *Christ* orders *Peter* to *follow him*, in Token of his *Readiness* to be *crucified* in his Cause. *John* stays not for the *Call*; he rises, and *follows* too; but he says not one Word of his Love, and his Zeal. He chose that the Action only should speak that; and when he records this Circumstance, he tells us not what that Action meant; but with great Simplicity relates the Fact only. (vol. 2, 637)

Similarly Luke as the narrator of Acts is characterized by Doddridge as modest and oblique in his manner of referring to himself. In section XXXVI, in which the apostles respond to Paul's vision of the man of Macedonia, Doddridge points out that this is the first time in which the narrator draws attention to himself (Acts 16:10). In the paraphrase Luke's authority as narrator is emphasized – "this is a Circumstance which the Author of this Book well remembers, for he attended Paul in this Journey, and can relate what follows from his own Knowledge" – but in the note Doddridge makes clear that Luke never states this directly: "Nor does he indeed, throughout *the whole History*, once mention *his own Name*, or relate any one Thing which *he said* or *did* for the Service of Christianity," a characteristic he shares with "the rest of the *Sacred Historians*, who every one of them shew the like amiable Modesty" (vol. 3, 252–3).

In Doddridge's interpretation of the New Testament history, the narrators efface themselves because what matters is the stories they tell of their heroes, Jesus and Paul. Doddridge assumes that some of his own readers respond to the heroic values of Homeric epic and the aesthetic values of eighteenth-century criticism, and he therefore occasionally presents the heroes of the New Testament in these terms, but far surpassing other literary exemplars. Jesus's account of the Last Judgment in section CLXVI (Matt. 25:31–46) evokes the following comment:

I hope every Reader will observe, with what Majesty and Grandeur *our Lord* speaks of himself in this *Section*, which is one of the noblest Instances of the *true Sublime*, that I have anywhere read; and indeed few Passages in the Sacred Writings themselves seem to equal it. (vol. 2, 408)

Jesus's voluntary surrender after his betrayal by Judas in section CLXXXVIII, in full knowledge of what was to come (John 18:4), easily trumps the bravery of Achilles:

The *Criticks* are in Raptures at the Gallantry of *Achilles*, in going to the *Trojan War*, when he knew, (according to *Homer*,) that he should fall there: But he must have a very low Way of thinking, who does not see infinitely more Fortitude in *our Lord*'s Conduct on this great Occasion, when this Circumstance, so judiciously, tho' so modestly suggested by *St. John*, is duly attended to. (vol. 2, 507)

On one crucial occasion Doddridge decides to supplement the modesty of the evangelists: where in section CXCIV the narrative tells only of the angel rolling back the stone (Matt. 28:2–3), Doddridge boldly inserts in his paraphrase the moment of the resurrection as the ultimate heroic act that the Gospels fail to supply: "And, at the very same Time, Jesus, like a sleeping Conqueror, awaking on a sudden, burst asunder the Bands of Death, and sprung up to a new and immortal Life" (vol. 2, 595).

In Doddridge's account Paul is second only to Jesus as hero. In the improvement to section LI of Acts, referring to Paul before the Sanhedrim (Acts 23:1), he asserts: "NEXT to the History of *the great Captain of our Salvation*, as recorded by the Holy Evangelists, none of *the Christian Heroes* of whom we read makes a brighter Figure than *Paul*" (vol. 3, 368). Paul before Agrippa, in Doddridge's improvement to section LVI (Acts 26), combines "the Seriousness and Spirituality of the *Christian*, the Boldness of the *Apostle*, and the Politeness of the *Gentleman* and the *Scholar* (vol. 3, 407). In a telling note to the last verse of Acts in section LX, Doddridge singles out Paul's writings as "his most glorious Monument," and commits himself to his edition of the epistles as "one of the greatest Honours which can be conferred upon me, and the most important Service my Pen can perform for the *Church of Christ*" (vol. 3, 435). This self-dedication reminds the careful reader of the strongly autobiographical element that runs right through Doddridge's exposition.

The later history of the *Family Expositor* cannot be told here, though there are ample materials for it in the responses of readers in Doddridge's lifetime and after, both admiring and critical, in the large number of new editions from the 1760s to the 1830s, and in the range of later biblical commentaries that drew on his work, for example by Thomas Haweis, John Fawcett, Samuel Green, and Adam Clarke. *The Family Expositor* has faded out of sight since the mid nineteenth century, but that is largely because the medium through which it has exercised its greatest and most lasting influence has hitherto remained unrecognized. John Wesley acknowledged in the preface to his *Explanatory Notes upon the New Testament* (1755), a work designed for a more popular readership than *The Family Expositor*, that he had borrowed observations freely from Doddridge among others; he decided against naming his sources in order not to distract the reader, though admitting he "had transcribed some [notes], and abridged many more, almost in the Words of the Author."[28] In fact Wesley did more than this: his edition of the New Testament is to a large extent a revision of the KJB, and much of his version (as well as his notes) comes from Doddridge. Wesley's *Explanatory Notes* in the revised edition of 1760–2 became a standard doctrinal source for Methodism and has therefore remained a living and much reprinted text. *The Family Expositor* has been less fortunate. This chapter has tried to illustrate some aspects of the range and literary ambition of this multi-faceted work, the most original and impressive of the commentaries by eighteenth-century evangelicals.

NOTES

1 *The Correspondence and Diary of Philip Doddridge, D. D.*, ed. J. D. Humphreys, 5 vols. (London: Henry Colburn and Richard Bentley, 1829–31), vol. 1, 429, 427 (hereafter *Correspondence*); G. F. Nuttall, *Calendar of the Correspondence of Philip Doddridge DD (1702–1751)* (London: Her Majesty's Stationery Office, 1979), letter 149 (hereafter *Calendar*).

2 Job Orton, *Memoirs of the Life, Character and Writings of the late Reverend Philip Doddridge, D.D. of Northampton* (Salop: J. Cotton and J. Eddowes, 1766), 143.

3 For an overview of his career see Isabel Rivers, "Doddridge, Philip (1702–1751)," *Oxford Dictionary of National Biography* (Oxford: Oxford University Press, 2004). See also Rivers, "Religion and Literature," in *The Cambridge History of English Literature, 1660–1780*, ed. John Richetti (Cambridge: Cambridge

University Press, 2005), and Rivers, *Vanity Fair and the Celestial City: Dissenting, Methodist and Evangelical Literary Culture in England, 1720–1800* (Oxford: Oxford University Press, forthcoming).

4 Little critical work has hitherto been undertaken on the *Expositor*; exceptions are Geoffrey F. Nuttall, "Philip Doddridge, John Guyse and their *Expositors*," in Cornelis Augustijn *et al.*, *Essays on Church History presented to … J. van den Berg* (Kampen: J. H. Kok, 1987), and John H. Taylor, "Doddridge's 'Most considerable work': *The Family Expositor*," *Journal of the United Reformed Church History Society*, 7.4 (2004): 235–52. See also Ian Green, *Print and Protestantism in Early Modern England* (Oxford: Oxford University Press, 2000), 124.

5 For an exploration of some of these tensions see Isabel Rivers, *Reason, Grace, and Sentiment: A Study of the Language of Religion and Ethics in England, 1660–1780*, 2 vols. (Cambridge: Cambridge University Press, 1991–2000), vol. 1, ch. 4, "Affectionate Religion: Watts, Doddridge, and the Tradition of Old Dissent."

6 Doddridge, *A Course of Lectures on the Principal Subjects in Pneumatology, Ethics, and Divinity*, ed. Samuel Clark (London: J. Buckland, J. Rivington, R. Baldwin, L. Hawes, W. Clarke and R. Collins [and others], 1763), Parts 6–10, lectures 111–230. On Doddridge's teaching methods see Rivers, *The Defence of Truth through the Knowledge of Error: Philip Doddridge's Academy Lectures* (London: Dr. Williams's Trust, 2003).

7 *The Works of the Rev. Doddridge, D.D.*, ed. Edward Williams and Edward Parsons, 10 vols. (Leeds: Edward Baines, 1802–5), vol. 5, lectures 14–16.

8 "A Scheme of Study for a Clergyman," *Arminian Magazine*, 1 (1778): 419–25.

9 University of London Senate House Library MS 609: [P. Doddridge], "An Account of Mr Jennings's Method of Academical Education with some Reflections upon it In a Letter to a Friend who had some Thoughts of Reviving it Written in the Year 1728," ff. 36–7; transcription by Tessa Whitehouse at www.english.qmul.ac.uk/drwilliams/pubs/index.html. See David L. Wykes, "Jennings, John (1687/8–1723)," *Oxford Dictionary of National Biography*.

10 *Calendar*, letter 663, 131–2.

11 "Experimental" (in the sense of "experiential") is a key word in Puritan and evangelical religious terminology: see Rivers, *Reason, Grace, and Sentiment*, vol. 1, 167.

12 Doddridge, *Works*, vol. 5, 477–9.

13 *Biographia Britannica: or, the Lives of the most eminent Persons who have flourished in Great-Britain and Ireland, from the earliest Ages, to the present Times*, 2nd edn., ed. Andrew Kippis, 5 vols. (London, 1778–93), vol. 5 (London: John Nichols, 1793), 280. Kippis's biography first appeared as vol. 1 of the 7th edn. of *The Family Expositor* (London: T. Longman [and others], 1792).

14 *Calendar*, letter 443, correcting from the ms. the version in *Correspondence*, vol. 3, 219.

15 *Correspondence*, vol. 3, 224; vol. 5, 378. Humphreys collected together in volume 5 Doddridge's private writings, transcribed from shorthand by Thomas Stedman.

16 *Calendar*, letter 456; *Correspondence*, vol. 3, 234. Doddridge's relations with his booksellers, Richard Hett and James Waugh, his successful efforts to obtain subscribers, and the sales, distribution, and reception of the *Expositor* can be traced through the *Calendar* (there is unfortunately no index of books).

17 *Correspondence*, vol. 5, 488, 513, 516.

18 Doddridge, *The Family Expositor: or, A Paraphrase and Version of the New Testament: With Critical Notes; and a Practical Improvement of each Section*, vol. 6, ed. Job Orton (London: J. Waugh and W. Fenner, 1756), iv–vi.

19 Their authorship of the introductory sections in volume 6 was identified in the *Monthly Repository*, 13 (1818): 734–5. The posthumous publication history of the *Expositor* as revealed by the manuscript letters of the Doddridge circle is studied in full by Tessa Whitehouse, "The Doddridge Circle and the Booksellers: Publishing Philip Doddridge's *Family Expositor*, 1739–61," *The Library*, 7th series, 11.3 (2010).

20 Doddridge, *The Family Expositor: or, A Paraphrase and Version of the New Testament. With Critical Notes; and a Practical Improvement of each Section. Vol. I. Containing the Former Part of the History of our Lord Jesus Christ, as recorded by the Four Evangelists, Disposed in the Order of an Harmony* (London: printed by John Wilson for Richard Hett, 1739). The title page of volume 2 is virtually identical except that the subtitle specifies *the Latter Part of the History* ... and the publication date is 1740. Volume 3 after the uniform title continues: *Containing the Acts of the Apostles; with additional Notes, on the Harmony of the Evangelists; and Two Dissertations* (London: printed and sold by J. Waugh, 1748). Further citations of these volumes appear in parentheses in the body of the text.

21 See the use of the term "family" on pp. 126–7.

22 Doddridge thanked Godwin here for proofreading and ensuring that the new version was typographically distinct from the paraphrase, as well as for improving his manuscript.

23 Doddridge's subscription lists have been studied by Alan Everitt, "Springs of Sensibility: Philip Doddridge of Northampton and the Evangelical Tradition," *Landscape and Community in England* (London: Hambledon Press, 1985).

24 Pope's note to *The Iliad of Homer*, vol. 2 (London, 1716), Book II, verse 665 (not p. 665 as Doddridge states), explains that he has omitted some short speeches, "expressing only the Sense of them," because they do not appear natural in English.

25 The version (as explained above), is in italic, the paraphrase in roman. In the notes Doddridge uses italic with a different signification, for emphasis.

26 The Greek should read ποιουσιν.

27 Doddridge develops this story further in section V, note (a) (vol. 1, 25).

28 John Wesley, *Explanatory Notes upon the New Testament* (London: William Bowyer, 1755), v. The reception of *The Family Expositor* and Wesley's debt to Doddridge are examined in Rivers, *Vanity Fair and the Celestial City*.

6 | Postcolonial notes on the King James Bible

R. S. SUGIRTHARAJAH

> The English race is emphatically "The people of the Book" – and
> that book an alien one. JAMES BAIKIE[1]

> In truth, I do not know what this book is, but I perceive that
> everything in it is against us. W. J. HEATON[2]

> Where is the white man's Book of Heaven?
> HELEN BARRETT MONTGOMERY[3]

On the Richter scale of English national affection, the King James Bible (KJB) is way at the top like the late Queen Mother. The lovers of the KJB often lapse into quasi-spiritual terminology when extolling its virtues and achievements. Listen to the words of William Canton, the passionate historian of the Bible Society: "The blind had a new world opened to them. Hospitals were supplied with small volumes suitable for the sick-wards, and many a little book was afterwards found under the pillow of the dead. In prisons, penitentiaries, workhouses, the Bible wrought wonders."[4] Those of a generation that knew the Bible would have readily recognized this as a reworking of what is now known as the Nazareth Manifesto recorded in Luke's gospel (Luke 4:16–21). The reported words of Jesus have been re-sacralized in order to applaud the emancipatory potential of the English Bible. A new and intimate contact with the divine has been established through the real presence of the KJB. The Galilean has found his voice again in this English book, and the sterling liberative program of Luke's Jesus is now seen as the work of the Englishman's book.

Textual takeover

The KJB is probably the only Bible in the world which has come to have an ethnic tag attached to it. No version is so closely associated with the people for whom it was translated. The French, the Germans, the Tamils, the Samoans, and countless other ethnic communities have their own versions, but these are not typically perceived as emblems of national identity.[5] The English, on the other hand, who pride themselves on not having a written constitution, embrace, celebrate, and zealously assert the KJB as their own "national book."[6] In the clarification of this identity, the KJB has served as the ideal artifact. It has always been described and referred to as "our English Bible" (W. Macneile Dixon), "the national epic" (Thomas Huxley), "the English national epic" (Peter Levi), "our Eastern Book," "our own Holy Book" (Monier Monier-Williams), "the greatest of English classics," and "the most venerable of the national heirlooms."[7] Dixon claimed that the English Bible "rooted itself in England as a native tree, like one of her own oaks."[8] This rootedness in English culture, in Dixon's view, makes the KJB, "so national, so representative, so English."[9] The fact that it became the religious icon of a wider English-speaking community led Americans to call it "our American Bible" or "the American Book."[10] Such high praise was not confined only to an earlier generation of commentators. Even a contemporary media personality such as Melvyn Bragg, best known for television programs that explore fine arts (especially literature) for a popular audience, has called it "the English Word of God."[11] While all these accolades have been heaped on the English Bible, it is intriguing to think its original was entirely elsewhere among west-Asian and eastern Mediterranean peoples before an English Church and its needs came into existence.

The KJB is a supreme example of how a text that began life elsewhere might find a new incarnation. The historical events, cultural treasures, religious traditions, and moral laws of the Hebrews and Greeks were transmuted into a definitive aspect of English culture. In the history of translation, the KJB is very probably one of the most successful examples of a text finding a new and potent life in a wholly new environment. Sidney Dark audaciously claimed that it was the genius of the English who "moulded the writings in Hebrew, Aramaic and Greek, and made them in English even nobler than they were in their original."[12] Such a nationalistic claim was not an isolated case. A. Clutton-Brock stated that the resultant version had been "naturalized in the west" and "what the Jew long ago begot" was "fathered" by Englishmen.[13] For Dixon, the end-product had "the air of an original" about it, so much so that it should be "read like an English book without a hint of style suggestive of a foreign source."[14] The question remains – how did this text that emerged in hot, dusty West Asia come to be seen as the book of "England's green and pleasant land"?

The clue to this takeover could be traced back to the way the translation activity was organized by the group appointed by King James I. The translators were divided into six sub-groups, and strangely they were not called committees but companies. They were variously known as the Oxford Company, the Cambridge Company, and the Westminster Company. Each company did not have a secretary but a director. The habit of calling the committee of revisers a "company" continued when a new revision was mooted for the KJB. C. J. Cadoux, in his account of the history of the Revised Version, noted that "the members of the committee had already allotted themselves to the Old or the New Testament Company."[15] The word "company" in Elizabethan and Jacobean England was, to quote Adam Nicolson, a "powerful" one.[16] Besides referring to a group of actors, the "company" also meant trading and investment organizations. These companies emerged at a time when Europe was "discovering" a new world – a world which offered potential commercial opportunities.

There were a number of companies at that time trading with different parts of the world. The first company to form was the Muscovy Company in 1555, followed by the Eastland Company for the Baltic in 1579, the Guinea Company for Africa, and finally the East India Company in December 1600. These mercantile companies began as trading ventures, and some of them eventually ended up colonizing and ruling the countries they traded with. Their aim was to bring back goods to England. The employment of the word "company" to describe a group of translators is both intriguing and revealing. For Nicolson, such an application was a "real innovation," and the working practices of the English bible translators had a "hint of efficient, modern commercial organization."[17] Such a picture offers only a partial story of such commerical companies. What Nicolson fails to note is that there is another side to commercial companies, namely, that they are by nature competitive and even predatory. They acquire, enlarge, and take over. Companies not only transact business but are also in the business of acquiring power and effective control of the product. This was exactly what the Bible translators were unwittingly engaged in. Instead of dealing with goods, they were dealing with texts. While the commercial companies of their time were importing cotton, silk, indigo, and spices, these six companies of translators were transferring the textual ideas of the

Jews and ancient Christians and turning them into an English product, "an English book without a hint of style suggestive of a foreign source."[18]

The recent portrayals of the KJB in the nineteenth and twentieth centuries can be seen as very much in keeping with colonial rhetoric, enacting a standard colonial appropriation. In the first place, the rhetoric of appropriation works with the notion that the natural resources of the colonized, such as lands, belong rightfully to "'civilization' and 'mankind' rather than to the indigenous peoples who inhabited those lands."[19] Substitute texts for lands and you will see an exemplary case of appropriation. Translated to theological hermeneutics, the moral and religious values of another people are there for the benefit of humankind. For Matthew Arnold, the nineteenth-century cultural critic who rebranded the KJB as a literary text, "all great spiritual disciplines" exist for "man's perfection or salvation."[20] Phrased more frankly, the British have every right to benefit from the cultural and religious riches of another people. Arnold found a much-needed balance for English life in the contrastive pair of Hebraism and Hellenism. Hebraism was about rules, duty, and obedience, whereas Hellenism was about knowing, morals, virtues, and beauty. Although there were subtle variations between these two trends of thinking, their "final end and aim" was that "we are all 'partakers of the divine nature.' "[21] The rhetoric of appropriation works by claiming that the basic values of the "other" are identifiable with those of western civilization and that their "acquiescence to the colonial system" represents "approval of Western ideals."[22] Arnold incorporates both Hellenistic and Hebraic values as those of the English. He writes: "Hellenism is of Indo-European growth; and Hebraism is of Semitic growth; and we English, a nation of Indo-European stock, seem to belong naturally to the movement of Hellenism."[23] He then goes on to claim that in spite of differences, "the genius and history of us English, and our American descendants across the Atlantic," are knitted in some sort of special way "to the genius and history of the Hebrew people."[24]

A second way in which the rhetoric of appropriation works is by seeking identification with the story of the "other." The story of the Hebrew people was made rhetorically equivalent to the story of the English. The Hebrew Scriptures provided archetypes to work with and language to express the English consciousness of nationality for which no models or language existed before.[25] The Hebrew Scriptures lent themselves to such a nationally inspired interpretation. The Bible was made into the English people's book by seeing the events in the Hebrew Bible as "bound into the national life."[26] Thus Hensley Henson, the Bishop of Durham, provides historical incidents from English political life to demonstrate how these resonate with and parallel events in the story of the biblical Hebrews. He sees the revolt of the English monarch against the Pope as an act of "the Lord's Anointed," and similarly the rebellion of the Puritans against the monarch as having a precedent in the Hebrew prophets who castigated the misrule of their kings. After an interval, "the time-honoured association of the English Bible with English politics" was renewed in the modern era. Plagued by social and economical issues, Christian socialists found an "effective ally" in the Hebrew prophets, not as foretellers of future events but as social reformers. Henson's contention was that this close association was something unique to the English: "On the continent there was no parallel to this intimacy of the connexion between the Bible and the course of political development."[27] Such a contention is debatable, but it is indicative of certain popular views of the English Bible.

Thirdly, the rhetoric of appropriation works on the basis of simultaneously denying and discrediting the agency of the "other" and reifying and exaggerating the role of the master/colonizer. The standard orientalist accusations are reproduced by the admirers of the English Bible. The "other" is not reliable and not capable of producing anything worthwhile. This is a kind of hermeneutical negation that clears space for the colonizers to rescue the story and script it and make it their own. In this way, the appropriated story is fitted into a manageable and meaningful scheme. The "other" is not only made redundant, but the new owners become the new curators of the story. Nicolson follows the customary colonial procedure when he claims that "the standard of scholarship among Christ's disciples was despicable."[28] The Gospel writers were discredited for getting their facts wrong – Mark for muddling Isaiah with Malachi, Matthew for misquoting Hebrew and the Septuagint and for attributing the words of Jeremiah to Zephaniah, and Paul for messing up quotations from Isaiah. Their language, too, was found wanting. The Greek of the New Testament was "coarse and clumsy."[29] Nicolson even brings in later ecclesiastical authorities to reinforce his allegation. He cites Erasmus, who found New Testament Greek "countrified and simple."[30] He disparages not only the message but also the messenger, quoting the militant sceptic Charles Bradlaugh who claimed that the Gospels were "concocted by illiterate, half-starved visionaries in some dark corner of a Graeco-Syrian slum."[31] After diminishing the ancient scribes and their scripts as unworthy and unreliable, Nicolson resorts to the other colonial habit of monumentalizing the role of the master. This is achieved by emphasizing the erudition and excellence of King James's translators. In contrast to the biblical writers, the royal translators are seen as men of eminent scholarship. For instance, John Reynolds, the prime mover behind the translation project, was praised for his memory and reading which were "near to a miracle." Miles Smith had Hebrew at his fingertips and Richard Brett was "skilled and versed to a criticism in the Latin, Greek, Chaldee, Arabic and Ethiopic tongues."[32] Nicolson then assures us of the authenticity of their work. These king's translators were "clever, canny, resourceful and energetic," but most importantly, unlike the original compilers, they did "not distort the source of [their] authority."[33] Finally, their importance is strengthened by according them a quasi-mystical status. The original writers of the Bible were alleged to be known as God's secretaries. Nicolson makes the royal translators their heirs. "Secretaryship," writes Nicolson, is "one of the greatest shaping forces behind the KJB."[34] These royal secretaries are "loyal" and "utterly disposed to the uses of the divine will." They were in fact rendering a service which sought to be utterly submissive to King James and faithful to the text. They thought of themselves as instruments of God. As secretaries, they had no authority of their own, but were entirely dependent on the master. The implicit message was that the Hampton Court translators could not get it wrong because they were not the authors but were simply executing God's will.

Recent books on the Book and their hermeneutical blind spot

The last two decades have seen a spurt of publishing of books on the English Bible.[35] It is no coincidence that there has also been – at a time when the US administration was projecting itself as the new imperium – a crop of books on empire, lending new credence to the old adage that the Bible and empire go hand in hand. The subject matter of these books on the English Bible often overlap. They tell how the translation project was caught up in internecine ecclesiastical battles, and of the power of the monarchy and nobility. However, these erudite volumes are notable in sharing two features. One is their unanimous passionate defense of the translatory brilliance of the KJB and their relentless attack on any new versions. The other is their hermeneutical blind spot regarding the role the KJB has played in modern colonialism.

Almost all of these books on the English Bible devote a great deal of space to evaluating the KJB in relation to versions which appeared before or since the 1611 Bible. The consensus is that by comparison recent translations are acts of willful cultural vandalism. These modern translations are in the "language of the memo,"[36] their style "mundane, tensionless and mystery-free."[37] In contrast, "the seventeenth-century phrases seem richer, deeper, truer, more alive, more capable of carrying complex and multiple meanings than anything the twentieth century could manage."[38] Even David Daniell, who prefers the Geneva Bible to the KJB, concedes that the book by the Hampton Court translators will outlast the new upstarts. In order to discredit the modern versions, these writers call in cultural conservatives like T. S. Eliot and Philip Larkin to lambast them. Their preference for the KJB over the new arrivals is often based on the simple and purely subjective reason that the KJB is venerably archaic and enticingly more familiar. As Nicolson puts it, "the old, for the English, is holy and beautiful."[39] It is part of the English consciousness to "hunger for the archaic" and "search for the ancient and the primitive," a "deeply retrospective habit of mind which searches for meaning in the past."[40] These commentators work on the assumption that only seventeenth-century English is capable of bringing out the complex and multiple meanings of the original Hebrew and Greek texts. It is not clear why the Bible could be transmitted only through the English of the Jacobeans except that it was the "language of patriarchy," "of an instructed order," and "of authority."[41]

The attitude to colonialism in these books on the English Bibles is intriguing. When they mention colonialism, it is mainly the American colony to which they refer. America is given importance because, as Alister McGrath claims, it represented "far the most important English-language community of faith outside the British Isles."[42] When other colonies are referred to, it is always in the context of Bible translation. McGrath makes mention of the fact that "whenever English language versions of Christianity sprang up" they were "nourished" by the "definitive" translation of the KJB.[43] Christopher De Hamel and Daniell draw attention to the translation activities that went on in the colonies. They record only minimal historical details, reinforcing the idea of a missionary as a heroic translator. Like the colonial explorers taming the land, missionary translators are portrayed as single-handedly mastering the obscure and difficult languages of the natives. Daniell refers to the work of John Eliot (North America), Robert Morrison (China), and William Carey (India) without any reference to the local pundits and *munshees* who played an essential and well-recorded role. They furnish astonishing figures to demonstrate how the Word of God was translated into many of the world's vernaculars. They maintain a deadly silence as to how these vernacular versions simultaneously enriched and enfeebled the local languages.

What these books on the English Bible fail to acknowledge and explain is how the empire played a critical role in reviving the fortunes of the KJB. The final triumph of this version over its rivals was not achieved by its own "unassisted" merits as Hensley Henson claimed.[44] It owed this success to the empire. It is now fairly well known that it was the commercial politics of the time rather than the literary merit of the KJB which led to its ultimate ascendancy.[45] Less well known (or at least acknowledged) is that the emergence of Britain as an imperial power facilitated this eventual popularity. The eighteenth- and nineteenth-century British military and economic expansion was "preceded and accompanied by missionary work based on the King James Bible."[46] It was during this time that Britain discovered her role as a nation with a mission. The colonial literature of the time was full of the new destiny of Britain. She was seen as the new Cyrus liberating benighted peoples. Chosen as God's instrument to preach the gospel to the heathen, the British saw themselves as trustees of these colonies. The KJB contributed to this new nationalistic mood. As Liah Greenfield has shown, it carried an unusually high use of the word "nation." It appears 454 times in the KJB in contrast to 100 occurrences of *natio* in the Vulgate. The Hebrew terms *uma*, *goi*, *leom*, and *am*, are all translated as "nation" in the KJB, whereas in the Vulgate they are rendered as *populus*. The Greek terms *ethnos* and *genos* are sometimes translated as *natio* in the Vulgate, but very often other terms such as *populus*, *genus*, and *gens* are employed.[47] The English translation of "nation" had multiple meanings and was especially "used to designate a tribe connected by ties of kinship and language, and race."[48] The Bible was susceptible to a "nationally inspired interpretation" which facilitated the British to perform their new chosen role. By the eighteenth century, in this new political and ecclesiastical context, the popular sixteenth-century Geneva Bible with its basic ingredients of individualism, martyrdom, and future life, was found to be redundant. The Geneva Bible was seen as seditious and as a dissenter's Bible, whereas the "whole purpose" of the KJB "had been nation building."[49] An "embattled religious minority" with its Geneva Bible had now given way to a confident nation on the verge of building the largest empire the world had known. The KJB, with its accent on nation, national election, and establishment values, seemed to be the right text for the imperial occasion. A translation which stemmed from its "loyal belief in that divine-cum-regal authority"[50] now assumed its preordained role as the book of the empire.

These recent books on the English Bible hardly touch on the twentieth century. Of nearly 900 pages of Daniell's erudite book, only 30 are devoted to it. Daniell focuses on providing a scholarly survey of the Bible's impact on Victorian culture. He describes the near universal knowledge of the KJB, its influence on scientists like Charles Darwin, the heroic efforts of Arnold to treat it as literature, and Romantic poets like William Blake who saw in the Bible a "visionary illumination." But what goes unmentioned is how the imperialist enterprise permeated and sustained that culture. Robust textual challenges to the Bible in the Victorian era were posed not only by the Higher Criticism and Darwin's *On the Origin of Species*, as these books claim, but by the "discovery" and publication of the fifty volumes of the Sacred Books of the East. These sacred texts challenged the preeminence of the Christian story. Since then, to use words that Benjamin Jowett employed in a different context, "the book in which we believe all religious truth to be contained" has become "the most uncertain of all books." Such a destabilization occurred not because the Bible was "interpreted by arbitrary and uncertain methods,"[51] as Jowett claimed, but because of the presence of the sacred scriptures from the East which embodied in them moral values which were once thought of as exclusive to the Christian Bible.[52]

Cloning texts, colonializing minds

In the colonies, the KJB acted as a cultural powerhouse which determined the values and accuracy of various vernacular versions. Its hold was such that it led to the production of versions analogous to the English Bible. The vernacular Bibles were made to look like clones of the KJB. The British and Foreign Bible Society, which circulated only the KJB, made it a policy to bring out translations in Indian vernaculars which would do what the "Authorized Version had done in English" so that the translated book would become the "prized heritage of the Indian Church."[53] The Jaffna Auxiliary Bible Society's record shows how the parent society in Madras virtually bullied the translators in Ceylon (now Sri Lanka) to comply with the benchmark represented by the Authorized Version. The resolution of March 5, 1841 of the Madras Auxiliary Bible Society states that there should be a "fixed standard of translation" and "that such a standard is possessed in the authorized English version."[54] The resolution went on to propose that because the translators lacked tools, had no access to books, and had not kept abreast of the latest critical ideas, they should "adhere to the sense adopted in the English version" rather than "justify an appeal to the Textus Receptus, of the Hebrew and Greek originals."[55] Such a restrictive process required that all vernacular versions should adopt the "position of words, arrangements of sentences and punctuation" of the English Authorized Version,[56] and this was applied to the translation projects in the rest of India as well. The result was that each Indian vernacular had its own authorized version known as the Union Version. These Union Versions were ecumenical enterprises, a progressive act at that time. Nevertheless, the production of the Union Versions had two troubling consequences. First, they replaced all existing translatory efforts. For instance, there were already in existence in Tamil a number of Bible translations done by the Danish missionaries Bartholomaeus Ziegenbalg (1683–1719), Johann Fabricius (1711–91), and Charles Rhenius (1790–1838). The Union Version brought out by the Bible Society in 1868 under the chief reviser Henry Bower (1812–85) displaced these earlier efforts. Secondly, these nineteenth-century Union Versions in the course of time attained the status of an original and came to be regarded as the final revealed truth. Almost all the Indian vernaculars had their own Union or Standard Versions. Any deviation from them or any attempt at new translations was seen as desecrating the oracle of God. The KJB became the ideal benchmark. Even the spirituals of slaves in the US contained a preponderance of biblical verses from the KJB.[57] The KJB was responsible for creating and perpetuating a standard of singular, absolutist, and irrecoverably fixed textual authority and reference.

The KJB created a colonial mindset where an extremely literal reading of the written Word of God had replaced the more flexible indigenous ways of articulating sacred stories through songs, chants, rituals, folktales, and visual forms. The British and the Foreign Bible Society's annual reports routinely make clear the importance of the written word: "To the spoken must be added the written word. The missionary who takes the Gospel to Africa, India or China soon discovers that he cannot make progress beyond a certain point without putting that Gospel in a written form into the hands of the people."[58] Instead of cohabiting with nonwritten indigenous forms, the KJB introduced a fixed textual form as the ultimate authority. The textualized written word was now seen as God's word, the word of God. This also paved the way to thinking that no religious truth was valid unless it appeared in a textual and printed form. Religious truths represented in nonverbal and nonwritten formats came to be viewed as inferior.

The continuation of this colonial legacy of privileging literal reading came up recently when the question of homosexuality and same-sex marriage erupted in the Anglican Communion. Ironically, when Archbishop Akinola of Nigeria accused the Western Churches of being colonialist and thrusting their version of Christianity on Africa, he was, in fact, simply parroting the colonial teaching of the literal reading of the written word.

The introduction of Christianity as a book-religion by missionaries in the colonies, especially in India, had its repercussions. Hindus and Buddhists, who were more accustomed to and comfortable with both oral and written forms, were now faced with a situation where their sacred stories were bound in fixed written volumes and classified as their "Bibles." Max Müller called his fifty-volume Sacred Books of the East "forgotten bibles," and his rival and fellow comparativist Monier-Williams termed them the "bibles of non-Christian systems."[59] These "forgotten bibles" gained the authority and status of canonical texts. Indians who were raised on the pluralistic and different variant versions of the Ramayana and the Mahabharata were now presented with "authorized" and expurgated versions of these stories. Other forms of religious expression were subordinated to these written texts. More worryingly, from now on, their interpretation was no more in the hands of a Hindu council or a Buddhist sangha. Once these religions had been made into book religions, they were subjected to a modernistic scrutiny. This meant searching for the original and authentic words and discarding later accretions as not integral to the tradition, and subjecting them to the severest philological and historical investigation. As

Müller could claim, any interpreter "can take any word, a hundred, or a thousand words" of these forgotten bibles and "analyze them, or take them to pieces."[60] Now the temptation was to take these "forgotten bibles" for the religion of Hindus and Buddhists. The total reliance on a text as the supreme authority in the colonies had its roots in presenting the KJB as the book of the Christians.

Colonial reception: materiality and mimicry

The reception history of the KJB in the colonies is a complicated one. To the disappointment of the early missionaries, the "natives" did not always receive the book with the reverence it deserved. Hailed as the "word of God in English" and as a "national shrine built only of words,"[61] it was at times treated with disdain and disrespect. For the "natives," the English Man's Word of God was both a textual and a material object of practical serviceability. They not only found in its pages spiritual sustenance but also used the pages for non-spiritual purposes. The British and Foreign Bible Society's annual reports routinely documented not only how the Bible brought notable transformation in the lives of the colonized but also how the physicality of the book was put to use. This latter included its being used as wrapping paper for cigars, medicine, sweetmeats, and cartridges. William Colenso (1811–99), the brother of the famous John Colenso, who worked as a printer in New Zealand, recalled how he came across a cartridge rolled up in a piece of printed paper. To his astonishment, it was a leaf of an English Bible which had the chilling words of Barzillai the Gileadite, recorded in 2 Samuel 19:34: "How long have I to live?"[62] The medicine that was sent to the English children who were trapped during the Indian Revolt of 1857 was wrapped in a paper which had the words of Isaiah 51:12–14, "I, *even* I, *am* he that comforteth you ... The captive exile hasteneth that he may be loosed, and that he should not die in the pit, nor that his bread should fail."

Another use to which the "natives" often put the English Man's book was as a totem which had the power to protect and ward off danger. The missionary's book was hawked by Maoris as a charm to keep them safe from bullets and as an aid in dispatching enemies.[63] When the canoe of a group of Tahitians overturned, they were not afraid of the sharks because secured to their mast were Bibles carefully wrapped in cloth. A Maori fighting party was reluctant to attack a village because it had a printed Bible. People bought St. John's gospel saying that it was the best prayer to expel mice, rats and moles. As Homi Bhabha has put it, in such usages the "founding object" of the Western world became "eccentric" and lost its "representational authority."[64]

The "noblest monument of English prose" was not always received with awe and wonder. It was mimicked, tampered with, altered, and redrafted. One of those unfazed by the majesty of the text was J. C. Kumarappa, a rare Indian Christian, who openly joined Gandhi's freedom movement and became his economic adviser. During the independence struggle, Kumarappa was imprisoned, and the colonial authorities left him with only the KJB to read. What he did with the English Man's book was to mimic its textuality in order to mock and undermine both the colonial administration and their Christianity. He did this in a number of ways. He filled in the gaps and added a phrase or a word in the original to make the text more relevant to the multi-faith reality of India. For instance, he added "neither Hindu, nor Muslim, neither Zoroastrian, nor Christians" to the famous Pauline passage that there was neither Greek nor Jew[65] – an addition which would have been beyond the imagination of the Hampton Court translators or most missionaries, who were all brought up on different varieties of the single faith – Christianity.

Kumarappa also respectfully mimicked some of the celebrated passages of the KJB in order to reflect what was going on politically at that time in India, and on other occasions, he redrafted biblical verses in order to undermine and expose the brutality of the British. When the Indian freedom fighters were beaten up by the colonial police, Kumarappa rephrased the familiar words of Jesus in Matthew 25 which summed up poignantly what discipleship was about: "I was beaten with lathis and ye came not to dress my wounds, I fell down unconscious and ye gave me no water to refresh me, I was stripped naked and was indecently handled but ye raised not your voice in protest, I was dipped into saline mud and ye came not to lift me out, I was thrown amongst the thorns and you came not to rescue me."[66] The privations listed in the Matthean passage were now replaced by the sufferings of the Indian freedom fighters. The subtext was palpably clear. Kumarappa was reminding the colonial authorities that it was Jesus, in the form of the Satyagrahis, that they were abusing. When imprisoned protesters died from fasting, he reformulated the immortal words of Paul, "Persecution has lost its sting and jail its victory. Suffering is the Satyagrahi's goal." Similarly, he parodied Jesus's lament, substituting Europe for Jerusalem: "O Europe, O Europe, ye that suppress meek and mild nations and live on their life-blood, ye that controvert and distort My teachings and thereby exploit the ignorant, how often would I have gathered thy children together, even as a hen gathered her chickens under her wings, and ye would not! Behold, your countries are left unto you desolate."[67] Nicolson's proud and pompous claim for the English of the KJB that it was not the "language of mothers, or the man at the market stall,"[68] or "the English you would have heard on the street,"[69] was transformed into the speech of the colonial subaltern. Kumarappa brought the anguish and pain of the street into the text.

Kumarappa played with the text not only for political purposes but also to ridicule the type of Jesus imparted by colonial Christianity. Thus the answer Jesus gave to the disciples of John the Baptist when they asked him who he was became transformed: "Look at my Western clothes, look at my cropped head, look at my Western manners; my table is laden with beef and pork, and my house is decorated with things gathered from the four corners of the earth. I go to church on Sundays and have a pew in front; our names are drawn from the saints in the Bible; I wear a cross round my neck or on the watch chain, and read the Bible morning, evening and night, and pray to God that the hungry may be fed." To such a declaration, Jesus's answer is obvious: "I know ye not; not everyone that saith unto me, Lord, Lord shall enter into the Kingdom of Heaven but He that doeth the will of my father which is in heaven."[70] Such ridicule was Kumarappa's way of telling the missionaries of the irrelevance of their version of the faith.

Kumarappa often added inverted commas to these "re-biblicized" verses in order to give the impression that they were part of the KJB, and thus make them appear integral to the hallowed text. Using the style and substance of the text which had become the standard bearer of the empire and Christianity, Kumarappa subverted it. He negotiated "its own authority through a process of interactive 'unpicking' and incommensurable, insurgent relinking."[71] He was engaged in the Bhabhian subaltern mimicry, subversion, and menace. The most revered book – the KJB – now found itself "almost the same, but not quite."[72]

Finally, moving from the master to the masses

What of the future? Will the KJB last the next 400 years? It all depends on what the custodians of the book want it to be. The KJB as a unifying narrative providing a common interpretative reference for English-speaking people is no longer tenable at a time when the believer is replaced by the consumer/customer, and there is a "customer-generated" Bible to suit every interest.

When a religion is in trouble, the reformers generally go to the founding text for clues to its revival, but now the aged book is itself in trouble. The greatness of a text is its ability to reinvent itself. In the nineteenth century, when scientific theories of the time and the newly emerging Higher Criticism undermined the authority of the Bible, the KJB was able to reincarnate itself as a literary text in a single Victorian cultural context. Now, in a changed – multicultural, post-literary, and postcolonial – milieu, the English Man's Bible has to come up with a different story. The KJB has long been associated with the ruling establishment. It was seen as monarchist and episcopal. "One of the consistent driving forces" of the KJB "is the idea of majesty," claimed Nicolson.[73] It used to be marketed in the colonies as "the book your Emperor reads." Now, in the postcolonial context, the book is marketed as the book the celebrities read. Recent marketing of the KJB in single books by the Canongate Press is illustrative of this. The survival of the KJB depends on its giving up its elitist, majestic, ceremonial, stately, celebratory, and establishment image, and recovering the counter-message that is enshrined in the narrative – the message that worried ordinary people care about: justice, compassion, tolerance, rightness, responsibility, goodness. In this way, the KJB can shed its stateliness and majesty and align itself with other sacred texts of the world which also strive for these human and universal qualities. The Bible is permeated by counter-narratives and variants which resonate with the tragedies and triumphs of ordinary people. The KJB should relinquish its association with the master class and move with the masses. To slightly alter the words of Jorge Luis Borges, a book that does not contain its counter-book is not worth preserving.

NOTES

1 James Baikie, *The English Bible and Its Story: Its Growth, Its Translators and Their Adventures* (London: Seeley, Service & Co., 1928), 8.

2 W. J. Heaton, *The Bible of the Reformation* (London: Francis Griffiths, 1913), 4.

3 Helen Barrett Montgomery, *The Bible and Missions* (West Medford: The Central Committee on the United Study of Foreign Missions, 1920), 133.

4 William Canton, *The Bible and the Anglo-Saxon People* (London: J. M. Dent & Sons, 1914), 219.

5 While some might argue that the Luther Bible had a substantial impact on German national identity, the KJB is often seen as having the unique status of having not been translated by a single individual but rather being the product of a slow and careful process of the work of many translators over a period of time, like English laws, and in this respect being distinctively English. See Sugirtharajah, *The Bible and Empire: Postcolonial Explorations* (Cambridge: Cambridge University Press, 2005), 226–7. See also Krishan Kumar, *The Making of English National Identity* (Cambridge: Cambridge University Press, 2003), 103–4.

6 Adam Nicolson, *Power and Glory: Jacobean England and the Making of the King James Bible* (London: HarperCollins, 2003), 236.

7 H. W Hoare, *The Evolution of the English Bible: Historical Sketch of the Successive Versions* (London: John Murray, 1901), 3.

8 W. Macneile Dixon, "The English Bible," in *The English Bible: Essays by Various Authors*, ed. Vernon F. Storr (London: Methuen, 1938), 44.

9 *Ibid.*, 49.

10 David Daniell, *The Bible in English: Its History and Influence* (New Haven: Yale University Press, 2003), 768.

11 Melvyn Bragg, *12 Books That Changed the World* (London: Hodder and Stoughton, 2006), 265.

12 Sidney Dark, "Christianity and Culture," *The New Green Quarterly* 2.2 (1936): 86.

13 A. Clutton-Brock, "The English Bible," in *The English Bible*, ed. Storr, 78.

14 Dixon, "The English Bible," 54. While this claim is contested by scholars who note the ways in which the KJB Hebraized the English language, it nonetheless reflects a widespread popular attitude about the Englishness of the KJB.

15 C. J. Cadoux, "The Revised Version and After," in *The Bible in Its Ancient and English Versions*, ed. H. Wheeler Robinson (Oxford: Clarendon Press, 1940), 242–3.

16 Nicolson, *Power and Glory*, 70.

17 *Ibid.*, 71.

18 Dixon, "The English Bible," 54.

19 David Spurr, *The Rhetoric of Empire* (Durham, NC: Duke University Press, 1993), 28.

20 Matthew Arnold, *Culture and Anarchy: An Essay in Political and Social Criticism* (London: Smith, Elder and Co, 1889), 90.

21 *Ibid.*, 90.

22 Spurr, *The Rhetoric of Empire*, 33.

23 Arnold, *Culture and Anarchy*, 101.

24 *Ibid.*, 101–2.

25 See Kumar, *The Making of English National Identity*.

26 Herbert Hensley Henson, "Introductory Essay," in *The English Bible: Essays by Various Authors*, ed. Vernon F. Storr (London: Methuen, 1938), 9.

27 *Ibid.*, 9.

28 Nicolson, *Power and Glory*, 82.

29 *Ibid.*

30 *Ibid.*

31 *Ibid.*

32 J. Isaacs, "The Authorized Version and After," in *The Bible in its Ancient and English Versions*, ed. Robinson, 196–234; 198.

33 Nicolson, *Power and Glory*, 184.

34 *Ibid.*

35 Benson Bobrick, *The Making of the English Bible* (London: Weidenfeld & Nicolson, 2001), Alister McGrath, *In the Beginning: The Story of the King James Bible and How It Changed a Nation, a Language and a Culture* (London: Hodder and Stoughton, 2001), Christopher De Hamel, *The Book: A History of the Bible* (London: Phaidon Press, 2001), and Nicolson, *Power and Glory*.

36 Nicolson, *Power and Glory*, 234.

37 *Ibid.*, 236.

38 *Ibid.*

39 *Ibid.*, 237.

40 *Ibid.*

41 *Ibid.*, 154.

42 McGrath, *In the Beginning*, 290.

43 *Ibid.*

44 Henson, "Introductory Essay," 5.

45 See Sugirtharajah, *Postcolonial Reconfigurations: An Alternative Way of Reading the Bible and Doing Theology* (St. Louis, MO: Chalice Press, 2003), especially 61–2.

46 McGrath, *In the Beginning*, 290.

47 Liah Greenfeld, *Nationalism: Five Roads to Modernity* (Cambridge, MA: Harvard University Press, 1992), 53.

48 *Ibid.*, 52.

49 Nicolson, *Power and Glory*, 230.

50 *Ibid.*, 189.

51 Benjamin Jowett, "On the Interpretation of the Scripture," in *Essays and Reviews*, 6th edn. (Longman, Green, Longman, and Roberts, 1861), 372.

52 See Sugirtharajah, *Postcolonial Reconfigurations*, 28–31.

53 J. S. M. Hooper, *The Bible in India with a Chapter on Ceylon* (London: Oxford University Press, 1938), 11.

54 *A Brief Narrative of the Operations of the Jaffna Auxiliary Bible Society in the Preparation of a Version of the Tamil Scriptures* (Jaffna: Strong and Asbury Printers, 1868), 16.

55 *Ibid.*, 17.

56 *Ibid.*

57 Daniell, *The Bible in English*, 707.

58 *Tell the World* (London: The British and Foreign Bible Society, 1933), 56–7.

59 Monier Monier-Williams, *The Holy Bible and the Sacred Books of the East* (London: Seeley and Co., 1887), 30.

60 Max F. Müller, "Forgotten Bibles," *Last Essays: Essays on the Science of Religion* (London: Longman, Green and Co., 1901), 6.

61 Nicolson, *Power and Glory*, 70.

62 William Colenso, *Fifty Years Ago in New Zealand* (Napier, 1888), 42.

63 C. J Parr, "A Missionary Library: Printed Attempts to Instruct the Maori 1815–1845," *Journal of Polynesian Society* 70 (1961): 445.

64 Homi K. Bhabha, *The Location of Culture* (London: Routledge, 1994), 92.

65 J. C. Kumarappa, *Christianity, Its Economy and Way of Life* (Ahmedabad: Navjivan, 1945), 52.

66 Kumarappa, "A Day of Prayer," *Young India*, June 19, 1930, 261.

67 Kumarappa, *Practice and Precepts of Jesus* (Ahmedabad: Navjivan, 1945), 37.

68 Nicolson, *Power and Glory*, 195.

69 *Ibid.*, 211.

70 Kumarappa, *Christianity, Its Economy and Way of Life*, 65–6.

71 Bhabha, *The Location of Culture*, 185.

72 *Ibid.*, 86.

73 Nicolson, *Power and Glory*, 189.

7 | From monarchy to democracy

The dethroning of the King James Bible
in the United States

PAUL C. GUTJAHR

In 1986, the New International Version (NIV) accomplished what dozens of other American translations had been unable to do: dethrone the King James Bible (KJB) as the bestselling Bible version among American Protestants, a position it had held for nearly three hundred and fifty years.[1] The impressively long reign of the KJB in the United States is important for many reasons, but its relatively recent migration from the center of American biblical culture is particularly interesting for the way in which it echoes the American political trope of democracy replacing monarchy. When Americans wrote and signed the Declaration of Independence in 1776 and then ratified the Constitution over a decade later, they turned away from Britain's monarchal tradition with its pronounced emphasis on aristocracy in favor of governance which emphasized more common rule. The story of Bible translation and usage in the United States tells an eerily similar tale. At the end of the twentieth century, the remarkable reign of the KJB in America finally gave way to an ever-increasing number of new biblical translations which ultimately offered American Bible readers not a single authoritative voice, but a multitude of voices to guide them. Monarchy had once again been replaced by democracy.

The KJB, however, had not been intended as a regal, elite translation to be read only by a chosen few. Its translators had always wished it to be a translation capable of being "understood even of the very vulgar."[2] This desire for a vernacular Bible still echoes today as the quest for an intellectually accessible translation in a common idiom stands as the single most important driving force in contemporary American Bible translation and publishing.

The reign of the King James Bible

By the 1640s, the KJB had established its reign as American Protestants' favorite version of the Bible. Its prominence, however, did not mean that it went entirely unchallenged by other translation efforts. In the nineteenth century alone, American biblical scholars offered their country some thirty new translations.[3] The most important challenge to the KJB's dominance came in 1881 when a committee composed of both English and American scholars published the Revised Version of the New Testament. Spurred by a feeling that Elizabethan English was becoming archaic to the point of obscurity and a belief that advancements in biblical archaeology and textual scholarship demanded an updated version of the KJB, thirty-two Americans set to work along with a sixty-seven member British committee to create a new translation first of the New Testament and then of the entire Bible.[4] It was a monumental and much-publicized effort. Public interest in the Revised Version (RV) was so intense that the release of its New Testament became the publishing event of the century. Even before its release, one million orders were placed for the new version. Three million copies were issued within the first twelve months of its appearance, and newspapers such as the *Chicago Times* and the *Chicago Tribune* reprinted the entire New Testament in their Sunday sections over a number of weeks.[5]

Four years later, the RV committee released their entire version of the Bible. Even with the initial excitement the revision ignited, Americans found themselves uneasy with the new translation. They did not like its Britishisms, how it changed the wording of many of their most beloved passages, and the lack of the rhythmic majesty so resplendent in the KJB.[6] The RV had taken the KJB as its guide, but it had changed too much to make it quickly embraced by the millions of Bible readers who had been weaned on the KJB. By the turn of the twentieth century, it is estimated that no more than 10 percent of American Protestants had transferred their loyalty from the stalwart and dependable KJB to the new RV.[7]

Not discouraged by the lukewarm response garnered by the RV, new English translations of the Bible occurred with ever greater frequency in the opening decades of the twentieth century. In 1901, an American revision committee published their own variation of the RV, adapting its language to the American context and also paying special attention to the syntax and original languages of the Scriptures. The result was the American Standard Version (ASV), a version which many American Protestants would revere throughout the century as the gold standard of translation accuracy. Sentences may have been awkward in their word order and certain words continued to ring a rather archaic note as the ASV maintained close ties to Elizabethan English, but such choices were made under the guiding principle that this version would offer its readers the most literal, word-for-word translation of the Scriptures available. It was a translation principle that later came to be known as "formal equivalence." The ASV enjoyed more success than the RV, being more widely used in both Britain and the United States after its release.[8]

Between the appearance of the ASV and the end of the Second World War, Americans put forth twenty-one new English translations of the Bible. The 1920s and 1930s each produced seven separate new translations. The next pivotal moment in American Protestant Bible translation did not occur, however, until 1946 when a committee under the leadership of Dr. James Moffat, a professor of Church History at Union Theological Seminary in New York City, published the New Testament of what would become known as the Revised Standard Version (RSV). The RSV was a reworking of the language and syntax of the ASV in light of modern scholarship. The RSV New Testament was well received by both Protestant clergy and lay readers, and initial impressions of its popularity boded well for it being a translation which would finally unseat the long-admired and much-read KJB.

Such hopes ended in 1952 when the RSV committee released its entire translation of the Bible. The RSV's Old Testament quickly came under considerable criticism from conservative Protestants who were appalled by the way in which the translators had consistently made choices to separate the Old Testament from the New. Old Testament passages traditionally used as prophecies to credential Jesus as the Messiah were reworded so as not to overdetermine connections between Jesus and the Old Testament. The most famous passage found objectionable by conservative Protestants was found in Isaiah 7:14, where the RSV translators chose to render the Hebrew word "Almah" as "young woman" rather than "virgin."[9] Conservative Protestants argued that this choice, although within the bounds of linguistic acceptability when it came to the actual languages, highlighted a pattern whereby the RSV translators consistently ignored the prophetic connections between the Old and New Testaments. The RSV slowly gained acceptance in Protestant circles in the coming years, but its base readership lay largely among mainline denominations, not more conservative evangelical groups which still found its general interpretative trajectory troubling.[10]

The controversy surrounding the RSV did bring into vivid relief just how much American Protestants were not a single unified entity as Bible readers. The KJB had united American Protestants throughout almost the entire nineteenth century, but as new translations appeared and gained ever-wider Protestant acceptance, such unity receded in the opening decades of the twentieth century. Slowly, American ties to the KJB began to fray. Although by the mid twentieth century many in the more conservative Protestant camp (largely denominated as "Fundamentalists" and "Evangelicals" with their high view of the Bible and their stress on maintaining a personal relationship with Jesus Christ) still favored the KJB as their Bible of choice, a wide spectrum of Protestants increasingly chose to adopt a variety of the newer Bible translations. By the 1950s, the KJB may have still dominated the American biblical landscape, but it was no longer the absolute sovereign it once had been.

The decline of the king

New translations continued to appear in the wake of the RSV. The 1950s saw no fewer than nine American translations appear, but it was not until the mid 1960s that two new versions of the Bible arrived and challenged the KJB through a new emphasis in biblical translation work. The first of these editions was a translation commissioned by the American Bible Society. Its formal name was Today's English Version (TEV), but to millions who read it in its initial paperback New Testament release, it became known by the title that adorned its cover, *Good News for Modern Man*. The American Bible Society released *Good News for Modern Man* in 1966 and advertised it as a Bible which communicated the sacred words of God in a "language common to both the professor and the janitor, the business executive and the gardener, the socialite and the waiter."[11] The *Good News* enjoyed astounding success. The Society initially printed 150,000 copies of *Good News* which almost immediately sold out. Within one year, 5 million copies had been distributed; in the next twenty years, 75 million copies of the TEV were in circulation.[12]

The *Good News* was the work of Dr. Robert G. Bratcher in consultation with a larger committee appointed by the American Bible Society. Bratcher's goal was to use language common to the educated and the uneducated to communicate the Gospel message. He adopted the translation theory of one of his American Bible Society colleagues, Eugene Nida, who served as executive secretary of the Society's translations department. Nida had posited a method of biblical translation he first called "dynamic equivalence" but would later refine and rename "functional equivalence."[13] Functional equivalence distinguished itself from formal equivalence by its desire to translate the biblical text thought-for-thought, rather than word-for-word. The aim of functional equivalence was to capture the original meaning of the text, not necessarily its exact wording and syntax. Its main goal was to make the biblical message accessible to contemporary readers, not to capture every nuance of the Bible's message.[14]

From its inception, Bratcher targeted those in mainline Protestant churches and Americans who were less biblically literate as his primary audience. Bratcher had not designed the TEV to penetrate deeply into the conservative Protestant Bible market. His concern remained with a less biblically literate reader. With this type of reader in mind, he had decided not to create a translation based on the original languages. He simply modernized the language and thinking already present in other English translations. From the outset, this strategy made the more conservative Protestants suspicious, as they took great pride in arriving at the Bible's text through work in ancient languages such as Latin, Greek, and Hebrew. They did not consider a translation which simply updated the language of another translation to be a serious and accurate work of scholarship. Such English-to-English renderings became known in Protestant circles as "paraphrases" rather than translations.

As the popularity of the *Good News* grew, conservative Protestants took careful aim at Bratcher's translation work, pointing out numerous moments where they believed he had compromised the Gospel message in his attempt to reach a wider, less theologically literate audience. Bratcher's critics never tired of bemoaning his choice to use modern, non-jargon-filled language. For example, Bratcher frequently excised from his translation the phrase "the blood of Christ," leading to the TEV being nicknamed the "bloodless Bible." Ultimately, Bratcher's own views of Scripture proved his undoing among more-conservative American Protestants when, at the 1981 Southern Baptist Convention, he declared that "no one seriously claims that all the words of the Bible are the very words of God."[15] Such an unequivocal statement against the soundness of biblical inspiration infuriated his foes. Conservative Protestants called for a boycott of the American

Bible Society, a call that resulted in Bratcher being forced to resign from his post in the Society.

The year after *Good News* came out, Kenneth Taylor, a Baptist layman who worked for the Christian publishing house Moody Press, released a New Testament paraphrase he called *The Living Bible*. Taylor had wished to create a Bible he could read to his children without the need to offer extensive explanations of difficult theological concepts or obscure wording. In the same spirit of Bratcher's *Good News*, Taylor used simple, common language with a high explanatory emphasis to render the Bible intelligible. Working from the ASV, Taylor released his translation of the epistles of Paul in 1962 and named it *Living Letters*. Billy Graham distributed *Living Letters* through his crusades, setting the groundwork for the popularity of Taylor's New Testament in 1967 and his entire Bible in 1971. Taylor's *The Living Bible* proved immensely popular. For three years, 1972–4, it was the fastest selling book in America. By the late 1990s, more than 40 million copies were in circulation.[16]

With their wholehearted adoption of functional equivalence, the TEV and *The Living Bible* highlighted the reality that all biblical translation work is by necessity interpretative. The question was not whether a translation had its own interpretative bias, but what exactly that bias might be. Functional equivalence tends to allow translators greater interpretative freedom in their work because it is a strategy which stresses the intelligibility of the text over a strict adherence to the wording of the most reliable manuscripts. As a result, functional equivalence permits a greater depth of interpretation to be present in the final product; the theological predilections of those responsible for the translation become more prominent in the text itself. For example, the Arminian Baptist beliefs of Kenneth Taylor show themselves throughout *The Living Bible*, as is evident in his translation of passages such as Acts 13:48 where he renders the (formal equivalent) ASV wording "as many as were ordained to eternal life, believed" into "as many as wanted eternal life, believed." In regard to the issue of predestination, the two passages could not be more different. In the ASV version, the Calvinist notion of God choosing who will be saved and who will be damned is preserved. Taylor switches to an Arminian emphasis by placing the choice for eternal life not with God but with each believer.

The move toward functional equivalence and its greater emphasis on rendering pronounced biblical interpretations through its translation choices set much of the stage for the New International Version (NIV), the translation which would eventually topple the KJB from its sales pinnacle in the mid 1980s. It is important to note that the NIV was not solely responsible for dethroning the KJB as the most popular Bible edition among Americans. The dozens of translations that had been introduced since the RV had all played a part in deposing the monarch as they gathered their own devoted followings and fractured the Bible marketplace. Each new translation chipped away at the foundation that had so long supported the King James as America's Protestant Bible. The NIV simply became the most popular version of the later twentieth century, and as such became the version which proved finally able to remove the King James from its throne.

As attested by their vast similarities, the NIV was actually a stepchild of the RSV.[17] Its translation was inaugurated in 1965 by a group that wished to repristinate the biblical text as the RSV had attempted to do, but this time with a greater emphasis on biblical inerrancy.[18] The NIV translation committee's self-conscious and public professions of faith in the absolute correctness and reliability of the biblical manuscripts upon which they based their work did much to help make the NIV a resounding success among conservative American Protestants.[19] The NIV committee had also made other choices to appease their conservative constituency. They restored the word "virgin" in Isaiah 7:14, and they took every opportunity to highlight connections between Old Testament messianic prophecies and the Christ of the New Testament.[20] Led by the initiative of Burton L. Goddard, the translators also strove to present the Bible in a more contemporary idiom, noting that "unless Christian families and churches use the Scriptures in modern English form, more and more of our young people are going to be strangers to the Gospel."[21] Such decisions paid rich dividends. When the first NIV Bibles appeared in 1978, they were an immediate success. The NIV's initial 1.2 million press run sold out in advance. Within the decade it became the single best-selling English Bible translation in the United States, and by 1996 over one hundred million copies of the NIV were in circulation.[22]

The NIV committee's commitment to a more contemporary idiom helped the NIV become a translation which ultimately tilted toward functional over formal equivalence. Although the translation committee paid close attention to the original languages, it also felt greater freedom to offer its readers explanatory, paraphrastic translations of troublesome, obscure passages in an attempt to give its version greater narrative flow. Such paraphrastic interpretations worked against potential multiple meanings that gave richness and a wider range of interpretative possibilities to the biblical text. The closing down of interpretative options becomes clear in how the NIV translates verses such as Habbakuk 2:2. The RSV translated it thus: "Write the vision; make it plain upon tablets, so he may run who reads it." NIV translators worked hard to make the verse clearer to the contemporary reader by avoiding ambiguity as much as possible: "Write down the revelation and make it plain on tablets so that a herald may run with it." The RSV had retained the double edge of the passage's meaning by translating the Hebrew as "he may run who reads it." In Hebrew there are two possible meanings: a herald might run quickly with the message, or someone might be able to quickly read the writing on the tablets. The NIV translators flattened the interpretative possibilities of the passage by portraying the first interpretation as the passage's only meaning. Such choices enhance the NIV's narrative flow, but the interpretative possibilities of the text have been narrowed. The NIV translators constantly made such explanatory choices, thus producing an English translation which, in the end, leaned far more toward functional equivalency than any of its translators were willing to admit.[23]

While the quest to present Bible readers with a readily understandable vernacular translation reached all the way back to the KJB, the NIV became a shining example of the contemporary cost of such a mission as the NIV offered its readers ever-narrower and more-focused lines of interpretation. As the voice of the KJB receded in American culture, not only did a multiplicity of scriptural voices become more prominent, but also these voices were increasingly inflected with distinct interpretative stances.

Niche Bibles: the rising democratic voice

Nowhere was the rise of common idiom Bible translations more evident than in the growing number of niche – or speciality – Bible editions which followed in the wake of the NIV. Bible publishers adopted new publishing technologies which revolutionized their industry in the 1980s, and thus the very decade when the NIV overtook the KJB in terms of overall sales proved to be a watershed moment in Bible publishing. Using the new publishing technologies, American publishers produced an ever-wider array of Bible formats to accompany the proliferation of new English translations of the sacred text. To an unprecedented degree, publishing innovations helped make the 1980s the moment when the sovereign voice of the KJB found itself drowned out by the polyvocality produced by the appearance of dozens of niche Bibles in the American marketplace.

At the heart of the new publishing technologies lay computerization. Publishers switched from traditional methods of offset printing to computers and their digital printing processes.[24] Computers vastly increased the speed and ease with which a translation could be completed. By the mid 1980s English Bible translations were appearing at the unheard-of rate of one or two every year. New technologies also created a greater range of possibility in Bible formatting. Computers facilitated a new era of ease when it came to laying out and typesetting various Bible editions. Time-intensive and cumbersome tools such as light tables, large sheets of graph paper, tape, glue, rulers, and scissors became obsolete. Editors found it easy to manipulate features such as sidebars, illustrations, color-coded fonts, and marginal commentary using new computer software. By the early 1980s, new Bible translations could be transformed into niche Bibles in a fraction of the time that it would have taken just a decade before as editors manipulated the creation and placement of specialized study aids, highlighting, illustrations, and concordances to make unique Bible editions for specific readerships.

In considering the wide adoption of computer technology in American Bible production, it becomes essential to note that of the forty-eight English translations that followed in the wake of the appearance of *Good News for Modern Man* in 1966, the most popular new translations have been products of the functional equivalency approach.[25] Five versions are particularly noteworthy: The New Century Version (1987), Contemporary English Version (1995), New Living Bible (1996), Holman Christian Standard Bible (2004), and the New English Translation or NET Bible (2005). The New Century Version has been the translation of choice for Thomas Nelson's immensely popular New Testament magazines *Revolve* and *Refuel*; the American Bible Society produced and then used its worldwide distribution network to popularize the Contemporary English Version; the Southern Baptists have sponsored through their Sunday School Board The Holman Christian Standard Bible; Tyndale publishers heavily marketed their New

Living Bible to America's non-denominational mega-church and emerging church movements; and Dallas Theological Seminary undertook the NET Bible project with the specific hope of providing a globally accessible internet Bible translation.

The intersection of functional equivalence with the revolutionary changes in publishing has made the last forty years an era dominated by highly interpretative, niche Bibles. The practice of adding marginal notes and commentary to Bibles dates back centuries, but never before have Bibles reached their readers in so many different editions as they have in the wake of the publishing revolution of the late twentieth century.[26] As American Bibles have rolled off the presses in the last few decades, they have not only contained translations bent toward greater intelligibility but also have increasingly been accompanied by ever-more sophisticated, interpretation-laden layouts. Editorial teams carefully craft different editions to appeal to specific audiences to a degree never before seen. Niche Bibles are ever-more common and sport names that reveal their specific target audiences: *The Couples Bible, One Year New Testament for Busy Moms, Extreme Teen Study Bible, Policeman's Bible,* and the *Celebrate Recovery Bible.* The heavy apparatus, mixed with translations that increasingly favor a highly interpretative functional equivalency, have helped set the stage for Bible editions which are more interpretatively direct than ever. At the same time, these Bible editions and their interpretative stances are by no means coherent; they are as diverse as the audiences they are attempting to reach.

In this new, incredibly diverse Bible marketplace, the singularity of the King James Bible's voice has become a thing of the past. Monarchy has given way to democracy, and the American Bible marketplace has become democratic in a dual sense. First, the Bible itself speaks with a democratic multivocality as a plethora of different Bible editions offer Americans new translations further enhanced by a wide range of specialty apparatus. Second, Americans have found themselves able to exercise their own voice within the Bible marketplace. Publishers respond as Americans "vote" with their wallets for distinct Bibles that meet specific life situations, whether those situations be divorce recovery, adolescence, drug addiction, or the love of a particular sport. As the twentieth century gave way to the twenty-first, Bible publishers found that publishing technologies and distribution networks had evolved to such an extent that they could produce smaller press runs of particular Bible editions and still turn a profit. Smaller Bible press runs became economically viable as publishers grew able to identify specific audiences and then target them with sophisticated marketing and distribution strategies.[27] In this way, the American Bible has become ever-more democratic in its ability to be of the people, by the people, and for the people.

Conclusion: the *Light Speed* or the Bible lite?

The Bible presents a great paradox for publishers. Although it is a terribly difficult book to understand, there remain millions of people who wish to read it.[28] Over the past half century, American Bible producers have chosen to address this voracious appetite in two distinct ways. First, they have produced English Bible translations which have leaned toward the heavily interpretative functional equivalency approach. Second, they have created increasingly specialized Bible editions to appeal to an increasingly fragmented American Bible audience. While these two approaches have served to democratize the production and reception of the biblical text, they have not been without consequences. Americans may still wish to read the Bible, but as for the amount and quality of reading they are actually doing, this has become an ever more vexing question to try to answer.

Perhaps no biblical edition better captures the current spirit of the age when it comes to American Bible reading than *The HCSB Light Speed Bible*. *The Light Speed Bible* was a finely tuned response to a biblical culture characterized by the fact that 91 percent of American adults own at least one Bible, but half of those Bible owners rarely or never read the sacred volume. When queried, 40 percent of American Bible owners declared that the book was too hard to understand, and 59 percent felt they simply didn't have enough time to read their Bible.[29] Holman Publishers of Nashville, Tennessee created *The HCSB Light Speed Bible* as the perfect edition to help busy people read this complex and challenging book.

The HCSB Light Speed Bible used as its core translation The Holman Christian Standard Bible, a slightly more literal translation than the NIV but still firmly in the functional equivalency camp. William Proctor, the editor of *The HCSB Light Speed Bible* fused this common idiom translation with an aggressive Bible reading plan. For decades various Bible editions had offered systematic reading plans that allowed a person to finish the Bible in a set amount of time, most commonly a year, but Proctor had no patience with such a slowly attained goal. Through his Bible edition's special format and reading instructions, Proctor promised his readers that they might "expect to take about 12–24 hours or a little longer to read every word of the Old and New Testaments" and enjoy a comprehension rate of "70 percent on basic, factual multiple-choice evaluations."[30]

With such promises of high speed and comprehension, *The HCSB Light Speed Bible* positioned itself as the ultimate user-friendly Bible version for busy, Bible-phobic Americans. Here was a Bible edition which one could completely read and understand in less than a day. *The HCSB Light Speed Bible* exemplifies the impetus behind common idiom translations and the proliferation of niche Bibles: quick, intelligible access to one of the most challenging books ever written. Accessibility, efficiency, and ease of use have clearly become key values in the production and consumption of American Bibles.

In generations past, one of the earmarks of religious reading was its intensive, repetitive nature. Readers read the same biblical book or the same passage again and again over a period of days, weeks, and even years in an attempt to wrestle the meaning from a text for themselves. While not every reader might have so intensively engaged with the Bible, today's American Bible publishers facilitate a far less self-reflective approach to the book as they stretch to make the biblical text accessible through the use of translation strategies which foreground heavily interpretative translation and formatting strategies.[31]

By any measure, the Bible is a demanding book which requires readers to struggle to acquire its meaning. Attempts to make it easily digestible are laudable in one respect, but such attempts need to be considered in light of the fact that the move to provide interpretative clarity always compromises the complex message found in a book that thrives on complexity and ambiguity. Centuries of debate about the Bible's meaning have given birth to hundreds of religious traditions, and such debate testifies to the complexity of the biblical text. Reading and interpreting the Bible has never been easy, and in the end, maybe it should not be. Flattening out the interpretative possibilities of any given verse and then adding additional commentary to clarify that verse robs the Bible of important layers of meaning. The growing trend toward functional equivalent translations and specialized apparatus decreases the opportunity for a reader to appreciate the true richness of the biblical text.

The consequences of the receding presence of the KJB in American culture are both profound and difficult to measure. What is clear is that the multivalent, layered meanings which characterize the KJB differ significantly from what is found in today's biblical marketplace. Not only is the popularity of the KJB dying in America, but with it is American biblical culture's ability to benefit from the many-layered riches found in the Bible.

NOTES

1 Daniel Radosh, "The Good Book Business," *The New Yorker* (December 18, 2006), 56.

2 King James Bible (London: Robert Barker, 1611) "The Translators to the Readers" 11.

3 Paul C. Gutjahr, *An American Bible: A History of the Good Book in the United States, 1777–1880* (Stanford, CA: Stanford University Press, 1999), 193–4.

4 A good overview of the Revised Version translation project can be found in Peter J. Thuesen, *In Discordance with the Scriptures* (New York: Oxford University Press, 1999), 43–55.

5 Margaret Hills, *The English Bible in America* (New York: American Bible Society, 1962) 295; Ken Cmiel, *Democratic Eloquence: The Fight over Popular Speech in Nineteenth-Century America* (New York: William Morrow and Company, Inc., 1990), 216–17.

6 Hills, *The English Bible in America*, 295–296; 309–10; Cmiel, *Democratic Eloquence*, 220; Lori Anne Ferrell, *The Bible and the People* (New Haven, CT: Yale University Press, 2008), 226.

7 Cmiel, *Democratic Eloquence*, 219.

8 Hills, *The English Bible in America*, 332.

9 Thuesen, *In Discordance with the Scriptures*, 95–6.

10 Hills, *The English Bible in America*, 401.

11 Folder "Historical Essays TEV – Secondary Material," RG 53, Box 2, Historical Essays, Studies Nos. 10–15, American Bible Society Archives, New York, NY, 2.

12 *Ibid.*, 2; 12.

13 Nida set forth his method of "dynamic equivalence" translation in such important books as *Message and Mission: The Communication of the Christian Faith* (NY: Harper and Brothers, 1960) and *Toward a Science of Translating, with Special Reference to Principles and Procedures Involved in Bible Translating*

(Leiden, Netherlands: Brill, 1964). Nida later saw his "dynamic equivalence" theories and methods much abused and wished to distance himself from that particular school of translation. He then began to associate himself with the term "functional equivalence."

14 Radosh, "The Good Book Business," 55–6.

15 Robert Martin, *Accuracy of Translation* (Carlisle, PA: Banner of Truth, 1989), 15.

16 Kenneth N. Taylor, *My Life: A Guided Tour* (Wheaton, IL: Tyndale House Publishers, 1991), 381.

17 Robert G. Bratcher, "The New International Version: A Review Article," *Duke Divinity School Review* 44 (1979): 177, 164.

18 Thuesen, *In Discordance with the Scriptures*, 134–5.

19 *Ibid.*, 136.

20 *Ibid.*, 149–50.

21 Burton L. Goddard, "The Crucial Issue in Bible Translation," *Christianity Today* 14 (July 3, 1970): 13.

22 Richard Kevin Barnard, *God's Word in Our Language: The Story of the New International Version* (Colorado Springs, CO: International Bible Society, 1989), 180. Thuesen, *In Discordance with the Scriptures*, 151.

23 Martin, *Accuracy of Translation*, 12.

24 For an overview of the technological changes in printing during this period, see Edward Webster, *Print Unchained: Fifty Years of Digital Printing, 1950–2000 and Beyond – A Saga of Invention and Enterprise* (New Castle, DE: Oak Knoll Press, 2000), 129–81.

25 See the Chronology of English Bible Translations since 1957 at the end of this volume for a bibliography of more recent American Bible editions.

26 Ferrell, *The Bible and the People*, 83, 241.

27 One can find a helpful discussion of the phenomenon of selling smaller lots of a particular good to more targeted audiences in an age of computerization in Chris Anderson's *The Long Tail: Why the Future of Business is Selling Less of More* (New York: Hyperion, 2006). Anderson argues that the widespread use of computer technology has moved marketing from an emphasis on the blockbuster to an emphasis on niche products. In his words, "the mass market is turning into a mass of niches" (5). While Anderson is mainly interested in music, book, and movie sales in his analysis, his argument has clear implications for Bible sales as well.

28 Ferrell, *The Bible and the People*, 4.

29 John Wilson, "The Living Bible Reborn," *Christianity Today* 40 (October 28, 1996): 35.

30 William Proctor, ed. *The HCSB Light Speed Bible* (Nashville, TN: Holman Bible Publishers, 2005), 16, 18.

31 Certain strains of this reasoning can be found in Paul J. Griffiths, *Religious Reading: The Place of Reading in the Practice of Religion* (New York: Oxford University Press, 1999), 182–8. Here, Griffith blames global capitalism in part for the wide-scale extinction of thoughtful religious reading practices.

PART III

Literature and the King James Bible

8 | Milton, anxiety, and the King James Bible

JASON P. ROSENBLATT

If God is Milton's father, and his scriptural word is the strongest of all precursor texts, then the King James Bible (KJB) is the most intimidating version of that text. In Milton's *Doctrine and Discipline of Divorce*, the Mosaic law enshrined in the Bible occupies the place usually reserved for Christ as the incarnation of deity: "the law is [God's] reveled will, ... herein he appears to us as it were in human shape, enters into cov'nant with us."[1] Milton is both the most learned and most biblico-centric of the great British poets. He read the Old Testament in Hebrew (and the relevant parts of Ezra and Daniel in Aramaic, which he called Chaldee),[2] the New Testament in Greek, as well as the Latin translations of both the Vulgate and the Protestant Junius–Tremellius Bible, the latter used with some frequency in his prose. Although Milton's third wife, Elizabeth Minshull, owned a Geneva Bible of 1588, there is no evidence that her husband used it. The only edition of the Bible that bears incontrovertible signs of Miltonic ownership is a 1612 printing by Robert Barker of the King James Bible, with seven entries and various marginal notations in Milton's own hand.[3]

James H. Sims has painstakingly counted 1,364 individual biblical citations in *Paradise Lost* and *Paradise Regained* alone, recorded by Milton's editors from Patrick Hume in 1695 to Merritt Hughes in 1957, and he has added 816 citations of his own.[4] And Michael Bauman has provided an index to more than 9,000 biblical quotations, citations, and allusions (to the last of which he has taken a conservative approach) in Milton's highly original work of systematic theology, *De doctrina Christiana*.[5] What follows in this essay are three mere snapshots of Milton and the Bible, taken in youth, middle age, and (if, with Shakespeare as the standard, early modern poets over fifty can still be called old) old age. The focus is on the poet's anxiety or conspicuous lack of it in relation to the KJB.

In his earliest surviving letter, Milton thanks his tutor, Thomas Young: "The Hebrew Bible, your very welcome gift, I have long since received."[6] Whether or not he had it in his possession when he wrote his earliest surviving poems, paraphrases of Psalms 114 and 136, composed at age fifteen, he certainly didn't bother to consult it, nor was he obsessed with the translations in any other Bible in his possession. Psalm 114, on the wonders of the Exodus, is fraught with meaning. Dante used it, in his letter to the Can Grande della Scalla, to illustrate the fourfold method of biblical interpretation: the literal (the exodus of the Children of Israel from Egypt); the allegorical (redemption accomplished by Christ); the moral or tropological (the soul's conversion from sin to grace); and the mystical or anagogical (the leave-taking of the soul from the corruption of this world to the freedom of eternal glory). It begins its celebration of liberation by alluding to Exodus 1:5, the seventy souls of the house of Jacob/Israel that had originally gone down to Egypt: "When Israel went out of Egypt, the house of Jacob from a people of strange language."

In the freedom of his paraphrase, even of this first verse, Milton blithely substitutes Abraham for Jacob and the small island of Pharos, just off the coast of Alexandria, for Egypt; and he omits any reference to "a people of strange language":

> When the blest seed of *Terah's* faithful Son,
> After long toil their liberty had won,
> And past from *Pharian* fields to *Canaan* Land,
> Led by the strength of the Almighty's hand …[7]

These are Milton's songs of innocence. Their very shortcomings as translation are signs of his youthful exuberance. Some of his verbal flourishes, including his compound epithets, are less evocative of Homer than of the bombastic texture of Joshua Sylvester's enormously popular translation of *Du Bartas: His Devine Weekes and Workes*: "froth-becurled head," "Golden-tressed Sun," "thunder-clasping hand." Also inspired by Sylvester's *Du Bartas* are such embellishments as "*Erythrian* main" for the Red Sea and "Walls of Glass" for the divided sea at the climax of the Exodus. Milton would use the image of the "Crystal wall of Heav'n … op'ning wide" in *Paradise Lost* (6.860) to connect the drowning of Pharaoh and his legions with the sinking down to hell of Satan and his legions to conclude the war in heaven. Milton can imitate Sylvester's *Du Bartas*, but he can casually outdo him as well: "The floods stood still like Walls of Glass, / While the Hebrew Bands did pass" (Ps. 136:49–50).

Polyglot Milton can choose among Bibles, but by 1648 he finds the authority of the KJB irresistible. Scholars have illuminated the politico-religious context of the 1648 metrical translations of Psalms 80–8, in particular the competition among translations to be adopted as the national psalter. Milton's use of the common meter, alternating lines of eight and six syllables, might have been prompted by the desire to offer his translations to the commission charged with revising the psalter.[8] What remains perplexing and unexamined is the purpose behind Milton's marginal transliterations of the Hebrew and his abrupt abandonment of them. Anxiety over the KJB may have something to do with it. In the 1645 edition of his poems, Milton placed the two early Psalm paraphrases just after the Nativity Ode and with justifiable pride added a head-note to Psalm 114: "This and the following *Psalm* were done by the Author at fifteen years old." Once we examine the uses of the marginal Hebrew translations, the defensiveness of the head-note to the 1648 translations might become clearer: "April, 1648, J. M. *Nine of the Psalms done into Meter, wherein all but what is in a different Character* [italics], *are the very words of the Text, translated from the Original.*"[9]

Walter Savage Landor's judgment of these psalm translations overstates, as such quips always do: "Milton was never half so wicked a regicide as when he lifted up his hand and smote King David."[10] But the sentence immediately following contains some truth about the poet who preferred above all set forms of prayer the "prompt eloquence" (*Paradise Lost* [*PL*], 5.149) of original expression: "He has atoned for it, however, by composing a magnificent psalm of his own in the form of a sonnet ["On the Late Massacre at Piedmont]." In the translations of 1648, Milton writes in fetters *and* chains, the form determined by the psalter's conventional meter and the content shaped by a religiously motivated desire for accuracy as well as by the authoritative power of the KJB. Milton's head-note plainly indicates that when the reader removes the italicized portions of the 1648 Psalms, what remains is a literal translation. And when the reader compares Milton's un-italicized text with the KJB, the influence of the latter will be evident.

The various marginal notations – eighteen separate transliterations of Hebrew words and phrases,[11] eight literal English translations that Milton explicitly states come directly from the Hebrew, and one Latin translation – all are signs of the anxiety of that influence. Almost all are a direct response to the KJB. The limits within which Milton must work resemble those imposed on the forty-six scholars whose job it was to amend the KJB translation in process by one of their colleagues, as they are described in John Selden's teasingly brief account, almost certainly based on eyewitness information supplied by his friend, Lancelot Andrews:

> The English translation of the Bible, is the best translation in the world, and renders the sense of the original best … The translators in king James's time took an excellent way. That part of the Bible was given to him who was most excellent in such a tongue (as the Apocrypha to Andrew Downs) and then they met together, and one read the translation, the rest holding in their hands some Bible, either of the learned tongues, or French, Spanish, Italian, etc. If they found any fault they spoke; if not, he read on.[12]

Like the learned translators, Milton is holding in his hand a Hebrew Bible and listening to the words of the KJB, waiting for the word or phrase that will give him a (limited) opportunity to express himself by improving or correcting that "best translation in the world" – and, absent that opportunity, at least to prove that he can follow along. The aesthetic results of such anxiety have already been sufficiently commented on by others.

There will never be a definitive explanation of Milton's shifts in the margins of the 1648 from Hebrew to English to Latin or for the total absence of marginal notations in the 1653 translations of Psalms 1–8. (By then Milton may simply have given up trying to compete.) And any explanation, even of a single notation, is bound to be speculative. But it may be helpful to attempt to categorize those notations. A very few of them, the most ambitious, seem to offer very slight improvement on the KJB text. This might explain the first marginal notation, on Psalm 80:2b, which the KJB translates as "Before Ephraim and Benjamin and Manasseh stir up thy strength, and come *and* save us." Milton's version differs slightly:

> In Ephraim's view and Benjamin's,
> > And in Manasse's sight,
> > Awake* thy strength, come and *be seen*   *Gnorera
> > *To* save us *by thy might.*

Milton substitutes "Awake" for "stir up," and calls attention to it with the transliteration "*Gnorera.*"[13] He might legitimately consider his substitution to be slightly closer to the biblical Hebrew root עור ('wr), "rouse oneself, awake."[14]

The same can be said of the second transliteration. The KJB renders 80:4 as: "O Lord God of hosts, how long wilt thou be angry against the prayer of thy people?" Milton has his eye on that rendition:

Lord God of Hosts how long wilt thou,
   How long wilt thou declare
Thy *smoking wrath, *and angry brow*   *Gnashanta.
   Against thy peoples praire.

Milton's substitution might be closer to the root of the biblical original עשׁן ('shan), "vb. denom. smoke, be wroth." And where the KJB in 85:6 translates the two words תשׁוב תחיינו (*tashuv t'chayenu*) as "revive," Milton's poetic rendition, "turn ... and revive," and his marginal note, "**Heb. Turn to quicken us*," more literally convey the meaning of the two separate imperatives. A Miltonic translation in 85:3b might be slightly more literally accurate than that of the KJB's "thou hast turned *thyself* from the fierceness of thine anger." Milton is less abstract:

Thine anger all thou hadst remov'd,
   And *calmly* didst return
From thy †*fierce wrath* which we had prov'd   †*Heb. The burning heat*
   Far worse than fire to bear.   *of thy wrath*

Brown translates the missing Hebrew phrase חרון אף (*charon aph*) as "burning anger"; the root חרה (*charah*) means "burn, be kindled, of anger."

The last example is from 86:2 (KJB: "Preserve my soul; for I *am* holy"). Milton's notation may actually be superior:

Preserve my soul, for †I have trod   †*Heb. I am good, loving,*
   Thy waies, and love the just. ...   *a doer of good and holy things,*

Brown translates the missing Hebrew word חסיד (*chasid*) as "kind, pious, godly," and Milton's notation comes closer than the KJB to capturing the various meanings of that word. This example provides a transition to the second category of notations: those that point to multiple meanings of a single word. Biblical poetry is, after all, considerably more difficult to translate than biblical narrative, enriched by the ambiguity of polysemy.

The KJB translates 83:2a as "For, lo, thine enemies make a tumult." For "tumult," Milton substitutes two related words:

For lo thy *furious* foes *now* *swell
And *storm outrageously,   *Jehemajun

The root word, הָמָה (*hamah*) is defined as "murmur, growl, roar, be boisterous … turbulent," and Brown cites Jeremiah 5:22, המון גליו (*hamon galav*), the roar of waves. Milton's "swell" and "storm" also evokes Jeremiah 51:22, where a great throng is represented under the figure of an overwhelming mass of waves.

In the next verse, 83:3, the single sense of the KJB seems perfect: "They have taken crafty counsel against thy people, and consulted against thy hidden ones." Milton achieves mixed success with his translation:

Against thy people they †contrive   †*Jagnarimu*
    †Their Plots and Counsels deep,   †*Sod*
*Them to ensnare they chiefly strive   **Jithjagnatsu gnal*
    *Whom thou dost hide and keep.   **Tsephuneca.*

KJB's "crafty counsel" is more accurate than Milton's "contrive their plots," and the root of *Jagnarimu*, ערום (*'rum*), is the same word used to describe the "subtile" serpent of Genesis 3:1. But Milton's *Tsephuneca*, which he translates as both "hide" and "keep," is more or less supported by Brown's צפן (*tzafan*), "hide, treasure up." Robert Alter's translation "protected ones" clarifies the relation between hiding and keeping.[15]

The conspicuous multiple definitions of a word allow Milton very infrequent opportunities to part from and to assert himself against the KJB, as in 80:6 (KJB: "Thou makest us a strife unto our neighbors: And our enemies laugh among themselves"). Remove the italics, and the debt is obvious, but Milton obscures the debt with three separate definitions of a word, none of them the one chosen by the KJB:

A strife thou mak'st us *and a prey*
    To every neighbour foe,
Among themselves they *laugh; they *play,   **Jilgnagu.*
    And *flouts at us they throw.

Milton's "flouts" ("flout: A mocking speech or action; a piece of mockery, jeer, scoff" [*OED*]) is closer to the Hebrew root לעג (*l'g*), "mock, deride, have in derision." Milton can have it both ways, with his own translation as well as that of the KJB ("laugh"). And while the KJB translates ילעגו למו (yil'gu lamo) as "laugh among themselves," because למו (lamo) is a poetic form of "them, to them," Milton can have the enemies both "laugh among themselves" and "mock us," the latter a variant reading in two manuscripts and three ancient translations.

In Milton's translation of 82:6, the corruption of justice by human beings entrusted with executing it undermines the very foundation of the world:

They know not nor will understand,
 In darkness they walk on,
The Earths foundations all are *mov'd
 And *out of order gon.   *Jimmotu

Milton's double translation is close to the KJB's ("all the foundations of the earth are out of course)," but it also provides the literally correct meaning of ימוטו (yimotu), "be shaken, moved, overthrown." And where the KJB reads 88:4b as "I am as a man *that hath* no strength," Milton seems to be relying on a lexicon that translates איל (eyal) as potency as well as strength:[16]

I am a *man, but weak alas,   *Heb. A man without manly strength
 And for that name unfit.

Some of Milton's attempts at plural signification are unpersuasive. There seems to be no basis for Milton's augmentation of the KJB's correct translation of נאות אלהים (neot Elohim) in 83:12 ("the houses of God") as both "Gods houses" and "palaces," despite his marginal insistence that "*Neoth Elohim bears both*."[17] And where the KJB provides a correct translation of 88:7b ("thou hast afflicted *me* with all thy waves"), Milton's poetic version reads:

*Thou break'st upon me all thy waves,   *The Heb. bears both
 *and all thy waves break me.

The first is correct, and the second isn't so much wrong as it is an unnecessary and not at all literal near-recapitulation of the first. It signifies most of all an attempt at expression through difference. More is also less when Milton translates "*Lev jachdau*" (his own marginal note on 83:5, literally "[with] one heart") as "with all their might, / And all as one in mind," which is no improvement on the KJB's "with one consent." The most radical example of difference in the entire translation appears in the last marginal notation. KJB translates 88:15 as:

> I *am* afflicted and ready to die from
>   *my* youth up;
> *while* I suffer thy terrors I am distracted.

In Milton's distribution of the verse over six lines, he translates מנער (*mi'noar*) not as "from my youth," as in the Hebrew or Septuagint or Vulgate but rather as "on account of shaking":[18]

> That am already bruis'd, and †shake   †*Heb. prae Concussione*
>   With terror sent from thee.
> Bruz'd, and afflicted and *so low*
>   As ready to expire,
> While I thy terrors undergo
>   Astonish'd with thine ire.

The last category, whose examples include but are by no means limited to most of Milton's extensive marginal annotations for Psalm 82, consists of transliterated Hebrew words whose sole purpose seems to be to call attention to the fact that the translator is working with the original language of these psalms. The emphasis in these pages on Milton's annotations should not obscure the fact that most of the words in his translation come from the KJB. The poet may advertise his individuality by translating *mi'noar* in 85:3 in a radically different way, but he never engages with truly difficult words, such as the verb *'afunah* in the very same verse, which is anomalous, its meaning uncertain. Milton translates it as "Astonish'd," which is not exactly distant from the KJB's "distracted."

Although they are intrinsically interesting, the 1653 poetic renditions of Psalms 1–8 lack marginal notations, which are a barometer of anxiety in the earlier translations. Their head-notes, unlike those of 1648, highlight not accuracy of translation but rather dating and prosody. Although Milton dated only Psalm 1 1653, the head-notes to Psalms 2–8 indicate that they were composed on successive days between August 8 and 14, shortly after Cromwell had dissolved the Rump and a month after the first meeting of the new Nominated Parliament, which Milton would at the time have regarded as "th' assembly of just men" (Ps. 1:5). These psalms anticipate themes – including the promotion of the Son and Satan's rebellion – that Milton would develop in his great epic. Composed only a year and a half after he lost his sight, Psalm 6:7 alludes to blindness ("mine Eie / Through grief consumes, is waxen old and dark"), adding "dark," which is missing from the KJB translation ("Mine eye is consumed because of grief; it waxeth old"). But even when Milton departs, as here, from the KJB, it remains the touchstone by which to measure the accuracy of his own translation.

These meditative psalms express, sometimes with raw emotion, the anxieties and hopes that Milton must have felt deeply: faith in the perfection of God's system of rewards and punishments; the desire for protection from slandering enemies, such as those who attacked his treatises advocating divorce and defending the regicide.[19] And what words more powerfully reproduce the affliction of clinical depression than Psalm 6:

> I am weary with my groaning;
> all the night make I my bed to swim;
> I water my couch with my tears.
> Mine eye is consumed because of grief;
> it waxeth old because of all mine enemies.   (KJB 6:6–7)

> Wearied I am with sighing out my dayes,
>   Nightly my couch I make a kind of Sea;
> My bed I water with my tears; mine Eie
>   Through grief consumes, is waxen old and dark
> Ith' mid'st of all mine enemies that mark.   (Milton's version)

The head-note of Psalm 2 includes "*Terzetti*," pointing to the *terza rima* of Milton's rendition and, less directly, to the achievements in versification of Psalms 1–8. Each psalm is an experiment in a special meter. But despite the originality and variety of meter, the reversed feet in iambic lines, the enjambment, and the run-on stanzas, the voice remains that of the psalmist. We need only turn to the magnificent poetry of book 7 of *Paradise Lost* to note the difference. In this book the scriptural weave is thicker than anywhere in the first half of the epic, and quotations from the King James Bible are everywhere. But the voice is that of the Miltonic bard:

> Heav'n op'n'd wide
> Her ever-during Gates, Harmonious sound

On golden Hinges moving, to let forth
The King of Glory in his powerful Word
And Spirit coming to create new Worlds.   (7.205–09)

Open, ye everlasting Gates, they sung,
Open, ye Heav'ns, your living doors; let in
The great Creator from his work return'd
Magnificent, his Six days' work, a World.   (7.565–8)

Passages such as these, which echo Psalm 24 (KJB: "Lift up your heads, O ye gates; and be ye lifted up, ye everlasting doors; and the King of glory shall come in"), remind us more effectively than the dedicated psalm translations of the words of Milton's early anonymous biographer: "And Davids Psalms were in esteem with him above all poetry."[20]

The epic voice alludes to Psalm 19:5, in which the sun "is as a bridegroom coming out of his chamber, and rejoiceth as a strong man to run a race" (KJB):

First in his East the glorious Lamp was seen,
Regent of Day, and all th' Horizon round
Invested with bright Rays, jocund to run
His Longitude through Heav'ns high road: the gray
Dawn, and the *Pleiades* before him danced
Shedding sweet influence.   (7.370–5)

There are other allusions and references in this book to Psalms, ranging from the brief but important "tabernacle" (7.243–9; Ps. 19:4) that contains the *Ur-Licht* from the first day until the sun is created on the fourth, to the lengthy elaboration of the "glad precipitance," the rush of waters to separate themselves from the land (7.290–306; Ps. 104:8–10). But of course the text of the KJB that shapes all that is most memorable in book 7 is Genesis 1–2. Where Milton, in the 1648 psalm translations, distributes the biblical verses, the angel Raphael, "Divine Interpreter," compresses them, reducing them to their constituent elements and then outdoing them with the energy and magnificence of his interlinear poetic commentary.

The rest of this essay examines the various strategies by which Milton in book 7 overcomes his Great Original, not his "better teacher" Spenser, *pace* Harold Bloom,[21] but the rival transcriber of the words of God the Father, the King James Bible. Milton, then, does not compete, as the strongest contemporary secular poets do, for a qualitatively identical sort of originality. Even so, *mutatis mutandis*, one of Bloom's revisionary ratios illuminates Milton's method:

The later poet, in his own final phase, already burdened by an imaginative solitude that is almost a solipsism, holds his own poem so open to the precursor's work that at first we might believe the wheel has come full circle, and that we are back in the later poet's flooded apprenticeship, before his strength began to assert itself ... But the poem is now *held* open to the precursor, where once it *was* open, and the uncanny effect is that the new poem's achievement makes it seem to us, not as though the precursor were writing it, but as though the later poet himself had written the precursor's characteristic work.[22]

The KJB floods the psalm translations of 1648; but in book 7 of *Paradise Lost*, Milton holds his poem open so that the King of Glory may come in.

And when the KJB enters as an invited guest, it reciprocates with its own invitations for substitution and elaboration, most simply through direct repetition (e.g., "Let there be light: and there was light") or, following a divine creative command, "and it was so" (Gen. 1:7, 9, 11, 15, 24, 30), along with its variant, "it was good" (Gen. 1:4, 10, 12, 18, 21, 31 ["very good"]). And in each instance Milton follows the divine imperative by eschewing mere repetition, describing instead with a burst of energy and movement just *how* it was:

> Let there be Light, said God, and forthwith Light
> Ethereal, first of things, quintessence pure
> Sprung from the Deep ....   (243–5)

Although lines 387–98, on the creation of water-creatures and birds, repeat the key words of Genesis 1:20–3, the tone is exuberant rather than anxious, and again the interlinear commentary jumps in with "forthwith," easily outdoing the direct scriptural verses, faithfully reproduced, that by all the laws of hierarchy should have outranked them:

> Forthwith the Sounds and Seas, each Creek and Bay
> With fry innumerable swarm, and Shoals
> Of Fish that with thir Fins and shining Scales
> Glide under the green Wave, in Sculls that oft

> Bank the mid Sea: part single or with mate
> Graze the Seaweed thir pasture, and through Groves
> Of Coral stray, or sporting with quick glance
> Show to the Sun thir wav'd coats dropt with Gold,
> Or in thir Pearly shells at ease, attend
> Moist nutriment, or under Rocks thir food
> In jointed Armor watch.   (399–409)

Milton's delight in fecundity manifests itself in the beauty of this poetry: the comic elegance of "in thir Pearly shells at ease, attend / Moist nutriment"; the mimetic alliteration of "Glide under the Green Wave"; soon after, "on smooth the Seal, / And bended Dolphins play" (409–10) on the smooth sea, their grace highlighted by contrast with the galumphing sea monsters, "Wallowing unwieldy" (411). Leviathan, "Hugest of living Creatures" (413), symbolized Satan in a notable homily in book 1 (200–8), capsizing a boat and drowning its sailors with one flick of its tail, thus demonstrating the catastrophic effects of placing one's faith in evil. But in book 7 Leviathan is a huge bathtub toy, who stretches out innocuously "and at his Gills / Draws in, and at his Trunk spouts out a Sea" (415–16).

Milton makes the KJB translation of Genesis 1 even more concise, enfolding it within his capacious rhetorical and poetic blanket. The poet asserts his autonomy and liberty by making it a central theme of the book. When, on the sixth day, the animals spring from their earthly matrix, creation and freedom occur simultaneously:

> now half appear'd
> The Tawny Lion, pawing to get free
> His hinder parts, then springs as broke from Bonds,
> And Rampant shakes his Brinded mane; the Ounce,
> The Libbard, and the Tiger, as the Mole
> Rising, the crumbl'd Earth above them threw
> In Hillocks; the swift Stag from under ground
> Bore up his branching head: scarce from his mould
> *Behemoth* biggest born of Earth upheav'd
> His vastness.   (463–72)

Beholden to no one – certainly not to the earth that held them prisoner – these animals birth themselves through their own strenuous efforts. But even more striking than this passage regarding the self-begetting animals is the description of what John Rogers calls the "parturient earth":

> The Earth was form'd, but in the Womb as yet
> Of Waters, Embryon immature involv'd,
> Appear'd not: over all the face of Earth
> Main Ocean flow'd, not idle, but with warm
> Prolific humor soft'ning all her Globe,
> Fermented the great Mother to conceive,
> Satiate with genial moisture, when God said,
> Be gather'd now ye Waters under Heav'n
> Into one place, and let dry Land appear.　　　　　(276–84)

The last lines of the excerpt reproduce the KJB translation of Genesis 1:9: "And God said, Let the waters under the heaven be gathered together unto one place, and let the dry *land* appear." But that verse is almost an afterthought, hardly equal to the autogenetic process described in the lines that precede it, which Rogers brilliantly explicates, helpfully separating active verbs ("Appear'd," "flow'd") from verbal adjectives ("involv'd," "Satiate"):

An "Embryon immature" at first, "involv'd," or surrounded, by "Main Ocean," the earth is warmed by the generative humor of this "Womb … of Waters." Softened and made porous, the earthly globe soaks up the saturating powers of the amniotic abyss, maturing, through something like endosmosis, into a womb herself. Over the course of five lines, this globe has metamorphosed from "Embryon" to "Great Mother" and through a process of fermentation is made to conceive. … What is it that this Great Mother conceives? The answer to this question is at once simple and absurd: the earth conceives and generates the very embryo that was her former self.[23]

The lines that follow "Immediately" (285) from 1:9, a lengthy elaboration of the verse's last words, "and it was so," join those that precede it in transforming biblical prose into Miltonic poetry. As if the self-generating earth weren't enough to absorb our attention, the lines that enact the gathering of waters induce a *hysteron proteron* effect that can be as dizzying as watching a movie on rewind. In this lengthy passage, embryonic maturation (277) precedes conception (281), which in turn precedes the image of sexual intercourse between the tumescent mountains and hills and the murmuring maternal waters: "the Mountains huge appear / Emergent, and the broad bare backs upheave / Into the Clouds" (285–7); "So high as heav'd the tumid Hills, so low / Down sunk a hollow bottom broad and deep, / Capacious bed of waters" (288–90).

"Forthwith," "Immediately," and "At once" are key words in book 7, an attempt to replicate the kinetic energy of creation. They initiate the interlinear poetic commentary that follows almost every verse in Genesis 1 – "almost," because the Bible's first verse, "In the beginning God created the heaven and earth" (KJB), which appears in the epic's opening lines, "In the beginning how the Heav'ns and Earth / Rose out of *Chaos*" (1.9–10), is conspicuously absent from the creation account of book 7. The propulsive force of that account imitates a dynamic, evolving nature that never achieves stasis, while the opening lines of both the Bible and the epic describe a completed act.

Anyone familiar with the KJB text of Genesis 1 and 2 can see that it organizes Raphael's story of creation in book 7. But the most memorable passages of that story appear in the commentary, which celebrates the beauty of the book of nature while, more subtly, presenting doctrinal statements that occasionally betray their generic origins in commentaries on Genesis by Milton himself in his *De doctrina Christiana* and in other sources. It is noteworthy that Matthew Poole, the author of *Synopsis Criticorum*, whose eclecticism generally extends to those authorized patristic, scholastic, and Reformation sources one expects to find in the most exhaustive seventeenth-century scriptural commentaries, characterizes Milton as an "ingenious and learned" expositor rather than as a poet. In his *Annotations upon the Holy Bible* (1683), Poole reads books 9 and 10 of *Paradise Lost* as biblical exegesis rather than as epic, and he closely paraphrases the long dialogue between Satan and Eve as a sort of *midrash*, "in which there is nothing absurd or incredible," on Genesis 3:1.[24]

In these doctrinal statements, which have been discussed elsewhere,[25] Milton weighs in on such questions as whether the angels existed before the hexaëmeron (253–60) and whether or not it is permissible to play music on the Sabbath (592–99). More important, unlike traditional commentators on creation, Raphael, the angelic narrator, forbears emphasizing Christ's recreation. He resists strategies that would diminish the physical, present creation by signaling the ultimate inconsequentiality of its loss. Although faith in Christ's redemption of humankind compensates for the

Fall, it also weakens the attraction of an earthly paradise. The result, in book 7, of the poet's forbearance is the celebration of a visible, palpable universe – a celebration that is, in comparison with Christian commentaries on Genesis, purer in its sense of longing.

In book 7, Adam knows the Son only as his creator and as the hero of the war in heaven. Behind the wall of paradise, in the epic's middle books, the Miltonic bard tries to keep inoperative postlapsarian experience, particularly the Christian experience of salvation in a crucified messiah. The attempt to block off even the fallen reader's experience bears directly on the question of free will in paradise. To know Christ as redeemer is to cast the shadow of determinism over paradise by making the sin that requires redemption a foregone conclusion. It is significant that the only truly overt reference in book 7 to the New Testament has nothing to do with Christian redemption. Milton manages at once to paraphrase closely the KJB on Mark 4:39 ("And he arose, and rebuked the wind, and said to the sea, Peace, be still") and to demonstrate technical mastery with a pause after "Deep" that makes these the most metrically interesting lines in the book:

> Silence, ye troubl'd waves, and thou Deep, peace,
> Said then th' Omnific Word, your discord end. (216–17)

Christian expositors of Genesis 1:26 ("Let us make man in our image"; *PL* 7.519) take the plural *Elohim* and "Let us" as evidence of the mystery of the Trinity. Although, in his speech at the beginning of book 7, God "to his Son thus spake" (138), here he "to his Son thus audibly spake" (518). The audibility of God's speech to the Son registers Milton's disagreement with the overwhelming majority of exegetes, who declare that the Trinity deliberated with itself. The adverb suffices to bring the account into accord with Milton's position in *De doctrina*: "The word Elohim, although it is plural in number, is applied even to a single angel, (in case we should think that the use of the plural means that there are, in God, more persons than one)" (*YP*, vol. 6, 234).

Milton's insistence on the primacy of the Father as the principal cause in the act of creation, the Son acting as instrumental or less principal cause, bears on his radical sense of autonomy and freedom. According to Milton's subordinationist beliefs, developed in *De doctrina* 1.5, the Son, neither co-eternal nor co-essential with the Father, is "By Merit more than Birthright Son of God" (*PL* 3.309). The Miltonic correlatives of merit and birthright are limitless, and they include good works (merit) and grace (birthright), free will and determinism, Cromwellian republicanism and divine right monarchy.

The thematic importance of human freedom in book 7 goes far toward explaining why Denis Saurat, in his pioneering study of Milton's thought, would read as he does God's parting words to the Son, who is about to ride out on his creative mission into Chaos:

> Boundless the Deep, because I am who fill
> Infinitude, nor vacuous the space.
> Though I uncircumscrib'd myself retire,
> And put not forth my goodness, which is free
> To act or not, Necessity and Chance
> Approach not mee, and what I will is Fate.   (168–73)

Saurat asserts that these lines reveal Milton's belief in the kabbalistic theory of creation by retraction (Heb. *tzimtzum*). He sees Milton attributing immensity and infinity to God, who is "no creator external to his creation, but Total and Perfect Being, which includes in himself the whole of space and the whole of time."[26] But if God is absolute, perfect, and infinitely large, with neither power nor reason to change into a less perfect state, how can he have created the imperfect human being? Saurat claims that Milton finds his answer in the *Zohar*: "According to his eternal plans, God withdraws his will from certain parts of Himself, and delivers them up, so to speak, to obscure latent impulsions that remain in them. Through this 'retraction' matter is created; through this retraction, individual beings are created. The parts of God thus freed from his will become persons."[27]

God might be represented as an infinite circle who retracts, as it were, to the circumference, withdrawing "from Himself into Himself," abandoning a region within Himself to emptiness, thus allowing a space in the middle for the creation of human beings. Saurat sees this theory as beautiful, for the separation of God's will from humankind implies a gift of freedom to every individual. There are many problems with this theory, including its absence from the *Zohar*. It is rather a post-Zoharic kabbalistic myth developed in the sixteenth century by Isaac Luria. Where would Milton have encountered this theory? And the lines in question might simply be God's answer, mediated belatedly by the angel Raphael, to Adam's earlier question:

> what cause
> Mov'd the Creator in his holy Rest
> Through all Eternity so late to build
> In *Chaos* [?]   (7.90–3)

Luckily for Adam, Raphael does not resort to Calvin's response to those who ask what God was doing before creation: creating hell for the inquisitive. Rather, God is explaining that his inactivity is the result entirely of his own will, and that this divine passivity owes nothing to necessity and chance.

Even if Saurat is completely mistaken about the meaning of these lines, his assumption of an affinity between Milton's thought and creation by retraction might well have been encouraged by the emphasis throughout book 7 on human autonomy and liberty. (And at the very least, Saurat's theory reminds us that God the Father chooses to retire for most of the six days of creation.) For other readers, the idea of a transcendent God who withdraws the divine presence from human beings might not seem beautiful at all, and it would be inimical to Milton's explicit theological views, in particular to his belief in creation *ex Deo*. Although, as Gershom Scholem points out, the kabbalists did not explicitly say that the act of retraction (*tzimtzum*) was a divine type and prefiguration of exile, "the analogy seems obvious": "It is surely no accident that the doctrine of *tzimtzum*, the first inklings of which appeared among the kabbalists of Gerona in the thirteenth century, struck root and blossomed only at a later period, when the problem of exile had become central to religious consciousness."[28]

There are far more incontrovertible signs in book 7 of Milton's exultant poetic freedom, including the various metaphors of creation, whether magical (the divine word calling creation into being instantaneously [176–9]), sexual (276–89), geometrical (the Son's golden compasses [224–31]), or musical, like Amphion raising the walls of Thebes by the music of his lyre (182–91, 602–32). Indeed, Milton frames the creation with angelic song, creating, as he does elsewhere in *Paradise Lost*, an original psalm complete with that book's characteristic synonymous parallelism:

> Great are thy works, *Jehovah*, infinite
> Thy power: what thought can measure thee or tongue
> Relate thee.   (602–4)

Milton's anxiety-free use of the KJB in book 7 can be seen as part of a general sense of joyous creativity. The discussion of his poetic commentary has taken us away from the biblical text, to which we return by means of a word that reminds us of the neglected poignancy of his description of "this World / Of Heav'n and Earth conspicuous" (62–3) – conspicuous ("clearly visible, easy to be seen, obvious or striking to the eye" [*OED*]) to us, but not to the narrator, whose celebration of external vision has kept his blindness from us for the duration of the creation account. The word takes us back finally to the invocation of book 3 by a narrator whose blindness is his subject. Book 7 described an earthly paradise:

> Earth now
> Seem'd like to Heav'n, a seat where Gods might dwell,
> Or *wander* with delight, and love to *haunt*
> Her sacred shades.   (7.328–31; emphasis added)

The haunts of the blind narrator of book 3 are immaterial, a world of words:

> Yet not the more
> Cease I to *wander* where the Muses *haunt*
> Clear Spring, or shady Grove, or Sunny Hill,
> Smit with the love of sacred Song; but chief
> Thee *Sion* and the flow'ry Brooks beneath
> That wash thy hallow'd feet, and warbling flow,
> Nightly I visit.   (3.26–32; emphasis added)

And of course these sacred places visited by the blind bard are the books of the Bible, almost certainly in the KJB, a source not of anxiety but of comfort. Enacting his own version of creation by retraction, the narrator compresses the six-days' creation, the wonder of the six evenings and mornings of Genesis 1 that took up an entire book, into three short lines, reminding us that it is lost to him:

> the sweet approach of Ev'n or Morn,
> Or sight of vernal bloom, or Summer's Rose,
> Or flocks, or herds, or human face divine.   (3.42–4)

NOTES

1 *The Complete Prose Works of John Milton*, gen. ed. Don M. Wolfe, 8 vols. (New Haven, CT: Yale University Press, 1953–82), 292. Future references to this Yale prose edition will be abbreviated as *YP*.

2 See *Early Lives of Milton*, ed. Helen Darbishire (London: Constable, 1932), 31, where Milton's nephew Edward Phillips testifies not only to Milton's mastery of Greek and Latin but also to his "attaining to the chief Oriental Languages, *viz.* the *Hebrew*, *Caldee* and *Syriac*, so far as to go through the *Pentateuch*, or Five Books of *Moses* in *Hebrew*, to make a good entrance into the *Targum*, or *Chaldee* Paraphrase, and to understand several Chapters of St. *Matthew* in the *Syriac* Testament."

3 "Notes on Milton's Bibles," in *The Works of John Milton*, gen. ed. Frank Allen Patterson, 18 vols. in 21 (New York: Columbia University Press, 1931–8), vol. 18, 559–65.

4 James H. Sims, *The Bible in Milton's Epics* (Gainesville: University of Florida Press, 1962), 259–78.

5 Michael Bauman, *A Scripture Index to John Milton's* De doctrina Christiana (Binghamton, NY: Medieval & Renaissance Texts & Studies, 1989).

6 *YP*, 1:312. First among the selected letters that Milton permitted to be published in his lifetime, *Joannis Miltonii Angli, Epistolarum Familiarium Liber Unus*, it is dated "*London*, March 26.1625." But the actual date may be closer to 1627.

7 *John Milton: Complete Poems and Major Prose*, ed. Merritt Y. Hughes (New York: Odyssey, 1957), 3. Unless otherwise noted, parenthetic book and line references to Milton's poetry are to this edition.

8 See *Milton: Poetical Works*, ed. David Masson, 3 vols. (London and New York: Macmillan, 1890), vol. 1, 241–5; W. B. Hunter, "Milton Translates the Psalms," *Philological Quarterly* 40 (1961): 485–96; Barbara K. Lewalski, *The Life of John Milton: A Critical Biography* (Oxford: Blackwell, 2000), 213–14.

9 All quotations from the 1648 and 1653 psalm translations are from their first appearance in print, *Poems, & c. upon several occasions both English and Latin, &c. Compos'd at several times. With a small tractate of Education to Mr. Hartlib* (1673).

10 Walter Savage Landor, *Imaginary Conversations*, 6 vols. (London: J. M. Dent, 1891), vol. 3, 230.

11 There seem to be nineteen, because Milton in 83:3 puts the two-word phrase "*Jagnarimu sod*" (lit., "they make crafty [their] counsel") on two separate lines.

12 *The Table Talk of John Selden*, ed. Samuel Harvey Reynolds (Oxford: Clarendon Press, 1892), 9.

13 Contemporary readers of biblical Hebrew might understandably wonder about the ugliness of transliterations such as this one, which change for the worse the word *orrerah* by reading the letter *ayin* (usually pronounced like an *aleph*) as *gn*. (There are a lot of these *gn*'s embedded in words in the margin.) It turns out that Milton's reading may be closer than that of most current readers of Hebrew to the ancient biblical pronunciation of the *ayin*, which probably had a sound resembling a hard *g* – hence, *Gaza* for the contemporary bible reader's *aza*, *Gomorrah* (twin city of Sodom) for *omorah*, and Arabic *Maghreb* ("place of sunset, western") for *Maarav*. In J. Weingreen's *A Practical Grammar for Classical Hebrew*, 2nd edn. (Oxford: Clarendon Press, 1959), the letter *ayin*, represented by the Greek sign for rough breathing ʽ, "is very difficult to pronounce, being produced at the back of the throat, almost like a gulping sound" (3). This may be what Milton is trying to reproduce phonetically.

14 Unless otherwise noted, Hebrew entries are from *A Hebrew and English Lexicon of the Old Testament, Based on the Lexicon of William Gesenius as Translated by Edward Robinson*, ed. Francis Brown, with the co-operation of S. R. Driver, and Charles A. Briggs (Oxford: Clarendon Press, 1907; rpt. with corrections, 1968); cited hereafter in the text as Brown.

15 Robert Alter, *The Book of Psalms: A Translation with Commentary* (New York and London: W. W. Norton, 2007), 294.

16 In *The Complete Hebrew–English Dictionary*, ed. Reuben Alcalay (Ramat-Gan and Jerusalem: Masada, 1981), this phrase from 88:4, כגבר אין־איל, is translated as "powerless, impotent, ineffectual, feeble, weak person." Brown translates *eyal* in this verse as "help," noting that it is a loan word from Aramaic.

17 Brown defines the root נוה (*n'w-h*) as "abode of shepherd, or flocks, poet. habitation ... meadow." This word is translated as "pastures" in the KJB 23rd Psalm: "He maketh me to lie down in green pastures."

18 The justification for this translation is the meaning of *n'r* as both "boy, lad, youth" and as "shake." Luther and the Junius–Tremellius Bible read the verse as Milton does.

19 For insight into the public and personal contexts of these psalms, see Lewalski, *The Life of John Milton*, 297–9.

20 Darbishire, *Early Lives*, 33.

21 Harold Bloom, *The Anxiety of Influence: A Theory of Poetry* (New York: Oxford University Press, 1973), 34.

22 *Ibid.*, 16.

23 John Rogers, *The Matter of Revolution: Science, Poetry, and Politics in the Age of Milton* (Ithaca, NY and London: Cornell University Press, 1996), 116.

24 Poole, *Annotations upon the Holy Bible* (1683; rpt. 1696), Sig. B3r.

25 Jason P. Rosenblatt, *Torah and Law in* Paradise Lost (Princeton: Princeton University Press, 1994), 156–63. Much of the following paragraph is taken from 156.

26 Denis Saurat, *Milton, Man and Thinker* (New York: The Dial Press, 1925), 113.

27 *Ibid.*, 124.

28 Gershom Scholem, *Sabbatai Sevi: The Mystical Messiah*, trans. R. J. Zwi Werblowsky, Bollingen Series XCIII (Princeton: Princeton University Press, 1973), 31.

9 | Bunyan's biblical progresses

HANNIBAL HAMLIN

In Woody Allen's story "The Kugelmas Episode," a bald, hairy, soulless New York Jew, "professor of humanities at City College," solves his mid-life crisis with the help of a magician named The Great Persky.[1] By entering Persky's magic cabinet with a copy of *Madame Bovary*, Sidney Kugelmas is transported into the world of Flaubert's novel and has a torrid affair with its protagonist, who is desperate for love and hasn't yet met the dashing Rodolphe. Later, Kugelmas brings Emma Bovary to New York, but finds her exhausting and expensive. Persky returns her to her novel, and tries to send Kugelmas into *Portnoy's Complaint* but has a heart-attack and dies in the process, having accidentally sent Kugelmas into *Remedial Spanish* instead. The story ends with Kugelmas on the run, pursued by a "large and hairy irregular verb."

John Bunyan, though not without his own sense of humor, was an altogether more serious writer than Woody Allen. Like Sidney Kugelmas, however, Bunyan had the remarkable ability to transport himself into and live inside his favorite book, in his case, the Bible. Bunyan is hardly the first writer to be profoundly influenced by the Bible, nor is he the first to allude to it frequently and intensively in his writing. In English literature alone, writers had been alluding to, paraphrasing, and adapting the Bible from the Anglo-Saxons on. Some of these writers, like Edmund Spenser, may have influenced Bunyan's own practice. The first book of Spenser's *The Faerie Queene* is a complex allegory of St. George (stepping in for the biblical Michael) aiding Una (the Church?) in rescuing her parents, King Adam and Queen Eve, from a dragon. We know Bunyan enjoyed Romances, like the popular *Bevis of Southampton*, so it seems hard to believe he wouldn't have relished a Romance that was also inherently biblical, and Protestant.[2] Indeed, comparisons of *Pilgrim's Progress* to Book 1 of *The Faerie Queene* date back at least to Samuel Johnson.[3] Yet Bunyan's manner of biblical allusion goes beyond Spenser's. Christian's pilgrimage to the Heavenly City, followed later by that of his wife and children, not only alludes to the Bible at certain points, it seems like a journey through Scripture itself. Moreover, Bunyan's spiritual autobiography, *Grace Abounding to the Chief of Sinners*, indicates that this is essentially how he saw his own life, as a continual encounter with Scripture in something like a literal sense.[4] Certainly Bunyan knew the Bible as thoroughly as probably anyone ever has, and he spent much of his time thinking about biblical texts and what they might mean. But, more than this, he seems to have seen everything in the world around him in biblical terms, and he didn't simply apply Scripture to his experience, Scripture thrust itself upon him, sometimes troublingly, and with a peculiar, at times almost physical, force.

Weirdly, in *Grace Abounding*, Bunyan describes even his early, irreligious life in biblical terms, recounting how he said to God, "Depart from me, for I desire not the knowledge of thy ways, Job 21" (8).[5] Would someone not interested in a religious life really address to God his lack of desire? Perhaps only in retrospect, post-conversion. In any case, when Bunyan does begin to take religion seriously, the Bible is constantly present to him. When Bunyan desires God, for instance, Romans 9:16 seems "to trample upon all my desires" (the text cited is "*It is neither in him that willeth, nor in him that runneth, but in God that sheweth mercy*") (20). Another biblical sentence "fell with weight upon my spirit: *Look at the generations of old, and see, did ever any trust in God and were confounded?*" (20). That it is the sentence itself rather than Bunyan that is the agent in this "fall" is indicated by Bunyan's inability to locate it in the Bible: "Well, I looked, but I found it not." The sentence drops upon him, from where he doesn't know. Over a year later, still searching, Bunyan finally finds that the sentence had fallen from Ecclesiasticus 2:10 (21). Furthermore, Luke 14:22–3 "breaks in upon my mind," presenting "sweet words" when Bunyan is in great distress (22). But the Scriptures affect him in diverse ways, positive and negative. Mark 3:13 "made me sick," he writes, and feel "faint and fear," but he is then encouraged when Joel 3:21 "came in upon me" (23–4). In moments of crisis, Bunyan recounts, he cried out bitterly in the words of Psalm 107:16, but then "the Word" of Isaiah 45:5 created "in my heart a peaceable pause" (25). He hears a sermon on the Song of Solomon 4:1, "Behold, thou art fair, my Love, behold thou art fair," in which the preacher urges thinking on the words, "My love."[6] The words "Thou art my Love, thou art my Love" run together twenty times in Bunyan's mind, and when he asks, "Is it true too?" Acts 12:9 "fell in upon me" ("He wist not that it was true which was done unto him of the Angel"). At this point, he writes, "I began to give place to the Word." Romans 8:39 comes into his mind, and he is "much followed by" Luke 22:31, as if the Scripture were dogging his heels (28).[7] In a period of doubt, "that Scripture [Isa. 57:20–1] did tear and rend my Soul in the midst of these distractions" (31).

Sometimes the arrival of a Bible text is attributed to God:

the Lord made that also a precious word unto me, *For as much then as the children are partakers of flesh and blood, he also himself likewise took part of the same, that through death he might destroy him that had the power of death, that is the Devil: and deliver those who through the fear of death were all their life time subject to bondage,* Heb. 2. 14, 15. (34)

But then other passages continue to arrive seemingly under their own steam, as 1 Peter 1:19–20, which "dropt on my Spirit" (35). On the other hand, Bunyan does praise God generally for "leading him into the Scriptures" (36) and writes that God did "lead me into his words" (37), so perhaps he felt it was always God behind the texts that confronted him. As divine messengers, though, the Bible passages sometimes have great force of their own, as when the "Scripture did seize upon my Soul" (Heb. 12:16–17), or when, in torments, "that Scripture in these flying fits would call, as running after me, *I have blotted out as a thick cloud thy transgressions, and as a cloud thy sins. Return unto me, for I have redeemed thee*" (40, 48). Bunyan continues, "I could not return, but fled, though at some times it cried, *Return,* as if it did hollow after me:[8] for I feared to close in therewith, lest it should not come from God, for that other was still sounding in my conscience, *For you know how that after-wards, when he would have inherited the Blessing, he was rejected, &c*" (Heb. 12:16–17 again, about Esau, tricked out of his father's blessing by his brother Jacob).

These lines from Hebrews 12 continue to engage Bunyan, as "that say-ing about *Esau* would be set at my heart, even like a flaming sword, to keep the way of the tree of Life, lest I should eat thereof, and live" (50). Bunyan's allusion to Genesis 3:22–4 here serves as a metaphor to describe yet another biblical text; the first passage seems under the control of the author, but the second is clearly an autonomous agent. Bible verses con-tinue to rend Bunyan's soul asunder (Acts 4:12, p. 51), and others actually strike him down (Rom. 6:9, p. 53). When he exclaims, "*How can God comfort such a wretch as I?*" a text replies to him:

this returned upon me, as an echo doth answer a voice, *This sin is not unto the death*. At which I was as if I had been raised out of a grave, and cryed out again, *Lord, how couldst thou find out such a word as this?* For I was filled with admiration at the fitness, and also at the unexpectedness of the sentence. (54)

The passage that answers him is from 1 John 5:16–17, but it is not identified in *Grace Abounding*, so that, like the earlier sentence from Ecclesiasticus, it seems to arrive on its own, entirely independently of Bunyan's conscious knowledge. Other passages "came rowling into my mind" (Ps. 77:7–9, p. 58) or "darted in upon me" (2 Cor. 12:9, p. 59) or did "with great power suddenly break in upon me" (2 Cor. again, p. 59). Sometimes "the Scripture did now most sweetly visit my soul" (John 6:37, p. 61), but other verses, at other times, are still "fearful and terrible" (63).

At one point, seemingly contradictory passages struggle within Bunyan, those "of Grace" and "that of Esau" (Heb. 12:16–17).[9] These scriptures "boulted both upon me at a time, and did work and struggle strangely in me for a while; at last, that about *Esaus* birthright began to wax weak, and withdraw, and vanish; and this about the sufficiency of Grace prevailed, with peace and joy" (61). The passages fight like the twins Jacob and Esau themselves, who struggle against each other in Rebecca's womb (Gen. 25:24–6). In that story, Esau is born first, but with the feisty Jacob holding on to his heel. In another famous biblical fight, Jacob meets a "man," who seems actually to be God or an angel, and wrestles with him until break of day (Gen. 32:24–32). When "he [the man] saw that he prevailed not against him [Jacob]," he puts Jacob's thigh out of joint, but is forced to bless Jacob and rename him Israel, "for as a prince hast thou power with God and with men, and hast prevailed." So two biblical texts are at war within Bunyan's soul, but he conceives of that struggle in terms of another set of texts concerning Esau, the subject of the Hebrews passage that "kill'd me, and stood like a Spear against me" (64), and his brother Jacob. Like Jacob, the passage of grace "prevails," and the implication seems to be that, like Jacob, Bunyan receives the blessing against all odds.

Ultimately, Bunyan's textual encounters become less terrifying, more comforting. One day, as he is walking through a field, "suddenly this sentence fell upon my Soul, *Thy righteousness is in Heaven*" (65). Texts have fallen on Bunyan many times before, but this seems to have been a different experience, as indicated by his description a few sentences earlier about the passing of the storm within his soul: "And now remained only the hinder part of the Tempest, for the thunder was gone beyond me, onely some drops did still remain, that now and then would fall upon me." The biblical locus for these drops from heaven is the prayer in Isaiah 45:8, "Drop down, ye heavens, from above, and let the skies pour down righteousness." Known as the *Rorate coeli* (from the Vulgate translation) in Catholic and Anglican tradition, this verse is familiar as an antiphon in Advent, the season leading up to the birth of Christ. The text that drops upon Bunyan ("Thy righteousness is in heaven"), while not precisely biblical, invokes the righteousness that comes from heaven in Isaiah's prayer, and drops down from heaven itself in the way expressed by the prophet. In similar fashion, Bunyan thinks later that "the Word should now fall as rain on stony places" (79). For a brief happy time, Bunyan writes, Scriptures are "made to spangle in mine eyes" (67), but it seems likely that depressing doubts, and the texts upon which they are based, continued to plague Bunyan throughout his life. By Psalm 19:13, for instance, Bunyan "was … gauled and condemned" (68). As he himself summarizes,

I have sometimes seen more in a line of the Bible then I could well tell how to stand under, & yet at another time the whole Bible hath been to me as drie as a stick, or rather my heart hath been so dead and drie unto it, that I could not conceive the least dram of refreshment, though I have lookt it over. (93)

The Scriptures continued to wrestle within him, and he wrestled with them.

Bunyan's own elaborate textual adventures (i.e., *with* the text, as well as *in* it) often resemble the fictional biblical allegory Bunyan developed later in *The Pilgrim's Progress*. In *Pilgrim's Progress*, Christian, like Bunyan, lives in the midst of the Bible, and his pilgrimage is a progress through it, in ways even more vivid than those represented in *Grace Abounding*. When we first meet Christian, he is reading a book, and we have no doubt what book this is. He is "*cloathed with Raggs*" that derive from Isaiah 64:6, the margin tells us (the Israelites' "righteousnesses," like Christian's, "are as filthy rags"), he has "*his face from his own House*," showing that he "forsaketh all he hath," as Jesus requires of his disciples in John 14:33 (also in Bunyan's margin), and he bears "*a great burden upon his back*," as does the Psalmist in Psalm 38:4 (again in the margin) (11).[10] Even what seems a spontaneous emotional outcry, *"what shall I do?"* is really a biblical citation: Acts 16:31, as the margin indicates (the keeper of the prison cries to Paul and Silas, "What must I do to be saved?" which is the slightly expanded cry Christian bursts out with on his exit from the City of Destruction, p. 12). *Pilgrim's Progress* is all Bible, all the time.

Not surprisingly, one of the first people Christian meets, when he is walking in the fields (just as Bunyan was when a text fell on him), is Evangelist. Evangelist hands Christian a Parchment-Roll on which is written the counsel from Matthew the Evangelist, "Fly from the wrath to come" (Matt. 3:7). Evangelist then directs Christian to the "Wicket-gate" that derives from Matthew 7's "strait gate" (7:13) and tells him to knock there, literalizing Jesus's instruction in Matthew 7:7, "knock and it shall be opened to you."[11] Evangelist reappears several times in both parts of *Pilgrim's Progress*, but, in a sense, he is always present. Christian may have the Bible in his hand, but it is allegorically all around him too. At the end of the second part of *Pilgrim's Progress*, Mr. Great-heart is able to guide Christiana, her children, and their companions through the "inchanted Ground" even in the dark, because he "had in his Pocket a Map of all ways leading to, or from the Celestial City." It is, we are told, rather "a Book or Map," and in a rare narrative intrusion, the author reflects that "who, that goeth on Pilgrimage, but would have one of these maps about him, that he may look when he is at a *stand*, which is the way he must take" (233). In case we have missed the point, the margin at these lines states clearly "God's Book." The Bible is the essential map, because it is through the Bible that they are walking. A little earlier, when their vision is obscured by "a great Mist and a Darkness," we are told that the pilgrims were "forced for some time, to feel for one another, by Words; for they walked not by Sight" (232). The capitol "W" is essential (confusingly omitted in the Penguin edition), since the pilgrims are not just calling out to each other through the fog. They are guided, here as always, by the Word, by the Map, the Book, the Bible.

Bunyan, who had a healthy sense of humor, sometimes has fun with his own Biblicism, especially in part two. Great-heart tells his company about the encounter between Christian and Faithful with Evangelist, "who prophecyed to them of what Troubles they should meet with at Vanity Fair" (213). Old Honest responds, *"Say you so! I dare say it was a hard Chapter that then he did read unto them?"* Bunyan is having a chuckle here. The

OED includes under the idiom "hard chapter" (s.v. "chapter" 10) a 1696 citation that explains the usage: "We say 'tis a hard Chapter when a man suffers undeservedly," and a later passage from Strype confirms this: "Lady Jane … had a very hard chapter to be set up to be queen, even against her will." Since Bunyan's is the first citation given by the *OED*, it is possible that *Pilgrim's Progress* shaped later usage, but I suspect Bunyan was playing with a popular idiom already current. In effect, he reliteralizes the idiom, playing the figuratively developed "hard chapter" against its concrete origins as a tough biblical text. The joke lies in the fact that Evangelist, who is giving Christian and Faithful a "hard chapter," can hardly do otherwise than give them a chapter, since he is himself a book.

Some places in Bunyan's topography are more thoroughly biblical than others. For instance, though "Vanity Fair" derives its name from the preaching against worldliness of Ecclesiastes ("All that cometh is vanity," the narrator quotes, the margin pointing us to Eccl. 1 and 2:11, 17), many of the details of the fair come from seventeenth-century Bedford and London rather than the Old Testament. On the other hand, the Valley of the Shadow of Death through which both Christian and Christiana must pass is a geographical realization of Psalm 23:4, "Yea, though I walk through the valley of the shadow of death, I will fear no evil: for thou art with me," though some of the valley's features are imported from Jeremiah 2:6, a passage which also refers to a place "of the shadow of death," as the narrator informs us (50). Just in case we might miss the primary relevance of the Psalm text, Bunyan has Faithful recite this verse as he is walking through the valley the verse describes. Christian hears Faithful (though he doesn't yet know it is him), and he receives just the consolation in "the valley" that the verse promises, and which believers have derived from the verse over the centuries (52).

Much of the rest of the beloved Psalm 23 crops up in *Pilgrim's Progress* as well.[12] After passing through Vanity Fair, where Faithful is martyred and Christian gains a new companion in Hopeful, the pilgrims arrive, after some other adventures (including seeing the pillar of salt Lot's wife was turned into, Gen. 19:26), at verse 2 of Psalm 23. They come to a "pleasant River, which *David the King* [or the Psalmist] called the *River of God*" (86). Again, different biblical texts are conflated; the Psalm in question is 65:9, referring to the "river of God," but John, we are also told, called this "The River of the water of life," which he does in Revelation 22:1. (John is shown a "pure river of the water of life, clear as crystal, proceeding out of the throne of God and of the lamb.") These citations are provided in the margin, as is the reference to Psalm 23 in the "Meadow" in which the pilgrims "might *lie down safely*" ("he makes me to lie down in green pastures"). Unmarked is the allusion to the Song of Solomon when "Christian and his Companion walked with great delight." Features from this biblical book, so full of natural delights, and symbolizing (in the traditional allegory) the love of God for the Church, appear regularly throughout *Pilgrim's Progress*. Here the attentive reader recognizes 2:3, "I sat down under his shadow with great delight, and his fruit was sweet to my taste." No surprise, then, that Christian and Hopeful find trees bearing "all manner of fruit." The Meadow is also "curiously beautified with Lilies," one of the most familiar flowers from the Song of Solomon, in which the lover (allegorically Christ) is "the lily of the valley" (2:1) and "feedeth among the lilies" (2:16).

When Christian arrives at the Delectable Mountains, the shepherds are "feeding their flocks," which alludes to a different biblical source: the Nativity story of Luke 2:8, "And there were in the same country, shepherds abiding in the field, keeping watch over their flocks by night" (93).[13] When Christiana arrives at the Mountains in part two, however, the biblical context shifts back again to Psalm 23. This is the place where "the Medows are green all the year long, and where they might lie down safely" (Ps. 23:2 again). Christiana leaves her grandchildren here, "that none of them might be lacking in time to come," echoing Psalm 23:1 (in Miles Coverdale's translation, printed and bound with the Book of Common Prayer [BCP]), "therefore can I lack nothing."[14] They will also "never want Meat and Drink and Cloathing," echoing the King James Bible (KJB) translation of Psalm 23:1, "I shall not want." At the end of part two, when the various pilgrims are called over the River to the Celestial City, Mr. *Ready-to-halt* gets the message that God has sent for him, and "expects thee at his Table to Sup with him in his Kingdom" (240). This is what we expect from Psalm 23, since the Psalmist states that God "preparest a table before me" and that he "will dwell in the house of the Lord for ever" (Ps. 23:5–6).

Like Psalm 23, the Song of Solomon provides further details of the landscape through which Christian and other pilgrims journey.[15] After traversing the "Inchanted Ground," Christian arrives at the "Countrey of Beulah," where he hears "continually the singing of Birds, and saw every day the flowers appear in the earth: and heard the voice of the Turtle in the Land"

(Song of Sol. 2:12, "The flowers appear on the earth, the time of the singing of birds is come, and the voice of the turtle is heard in our land"). This is the land where "the contract between the Bride and the Bridegroom was renewed," referring not just to Isaiah 62, as Bunyan's margin notes, but to the allegorical interpretation of the Bride and Bridegroom in the Song of Solomon. Christian and Hopeful fall sick with desire, crying "*If you see my Beloved, tell him that I am sick of love*" (Song of Sol. 5:8, not cited in Bunyan's margin). In part two, Christiana and her troop reach the same part of the country, where grow "*Camphire* with *Spicknard*, and *Saffron*, *Calamus*, and *Cinamon*, with all its Trees of *Frankincense*, *Myrrhe*, and *Aloes*, with all the chief Spices" (238). Again the margin is blank, but this is an almost exact quotation of Song of Solomon 4:14. All that is missing are the biblical pomegranates, but, conveniently, Christiana already has these with her, part of the provisions packed for their journey by Gaius, who earlier sings a version of Song of Solomon 2:5: "*Drink of his Flagons then, thou, Church, his Dove, / And eat* his *Apples, who art sick of Love*" (206).[16]

A list of biblical allusions in *Pilgrim's Progress* would in fact include most of its text, and refer to most books of the Bible. Appropriately, Revelation provides many details of the Celestial City. The Heavenly Host shouts out Revelation 19:9 as Christian and Hopeful approach the gates: "Blessed are they that are called to the Marriage supper of the Lamb" (123). But, while the source of this passage is noted by Bunyan, subsequent allusions are left to the reader to recognize: the King's Trumpeters "cloathed in white" (Rev. 7:9, "After this I beheld, and lo, a great multitude … clothed with white robes") who shout ("the same multitude cried with a loud voice") and make the "sound of Trumpet" (as do the seven angels with seven trumpets of Rev. 8:2, but Ps. 150:3 also enjoins, "Praise him with the sound of the trumpet").[17] Revelation 22:14 is inscribed in gold letters above the gate, the King commands the gate to be opened, "*That the righteous Nation … that keepeth Truth may enter in*" (Isa. 26:2), and Christian and Hopeful enter to the singing of the great lines, "Blessing, Honour, Glory, and Power be unto him that sitteth upon the Throne, and to the Lamb for ever and ever" (Rev. 5:13–14).[18] Before Christian arrives at the Celestial City, he must cross the River:

They then addressed themselves to the Water; and entering, *Christian* began to sink, and crying out to his good Friend *Hopeful*; he said, I sink in deep Waters, the Billows go over my head, all his Waves go over me, *Selah*. (120)

Even for Bunyan, this is a strikingly textual, and intertextual, moment. Psalm 69 is the source of the waters – "I am come into deep waters, so that the floods run over me" (Ps. 69:2, BCP version) – though Psalm 38 may be the source of the specific phrase "over my head" (Ps. 38:4, "For my wickednesses are gone over my head," BCP version). On the other hand, the billows and waves come from Psalm 42:9, "all thy waves and thy billows are gone over me" (BCP version), though it's possible Bunyan also remembered the similar lament from Jonah 2:3 ("all thy billows and thy waves passed over me"). Christian's sinking and call for help is an allusion to Matthew 14:30, when Peter tries walking on water but "was afraid: and beginning to sink, he cried, saying, 'Lord, save me.'" (For a moment, Christian seems in danger of turning into Little-Faith, since Jesus's response to Peter is, "O thou of little faith, wherefore didst thou doubt?") Most strange is Christian's final word, "Selah." This may point to yet another watery Psalm (88:7): "thou hast afflicted me with all thy waves. Selah" (KJB). "Selah" is a word that appears mainly in the Psalms (a few times in Habbakuk), and its meaning is a mystery even today. The marginal gloss in the Geneva Bible to its first appearance (in Ps. 3:4) is "Selah here signifieth a lifting up of the voice, to cause us to consider the sentence, as a thing of great importance."[19] Thus, as a kind of diacritical marker, like "italics," it is not a word one expects anyone to say aloud. That Christian says it is a sign of just how rooted in the *text* of the Bible Bunyan's writing tends to be.

Which Bible was it, though, that Bunyan lived in? Like most sixteenth- and seventeenth-century Englishmen, Bunyan knew more than one Bible translation. Moreover, tracing which English Bible Bunyan had in mind is not always possible, since Bible translation was a notoriously incestuous business, as the translators' preface to the KJB explained:

wee never thought from the beginning, that we should neede to make a new Translation, nor yet to make of a bad one a good one, (for then the imputation of Sixtus had bene true in some sort, that our people had bene fed with gall of Dragons in stead of wine, with whey in stead of milke:) but to make a good one better, or out of many good ones, one principall good one, not justly to be excepted against.[20]

As a result, a good deal of the KJB is identical to the Geneva, or the Bishops', or even Tyndale. Thus, the allusions to the Song of Solomon (2:10–12) in the land of Beulah could be to either Geneva or KJB, since those texts are identical. Similarly, 1 Corinthians 15:55 ("O Death, where is thy sting? O Grave, where is thy victory?"), which Bunyan quotes in both *Grace Abounding* (74) and the second part of *Pilgrim's Progress* (242) is the same in both Bibles. There are a few instances, though, where KJB and Geneva diverge, and where Bunyan does seem to have the Geneva in mind. In *Grace Abounding*, Bunyan's quotation of Romans 9:16 – "It is neither in him that willeth, nor in him that runneth, but in God that sheweth mercy" (20) – is not exactly like either Geneva or KJB, but it is much closer to the former. KJB has "of him" and "of God," though both KJB and Geneva have "not" instead of "neither." Bunyan's quotation of Mark 3:13 is similarly closer to Geneva: "He went up into a Mountain, and called to him whom he would, and they came unto him" (*Grace Abounding*, 23). KJB has "goeth" and "calleth" instead of "went up" and "called." Bunyan's occasional lack of precision suggests that he was often quoting or alluding from memory, and the few variations in translations indicate that he remembered or conflated different versions.[21] The Psalms were especially likely to come from various versions, since there were so many different translations available, and since the ones most familiar from church worship, unlike the rest of the Bible, were not from either KJB or Geneva but from Coverdale (in the BCP) and the Sternhold–Hopkins Psalter (sung congregationally). Several quotations from or allusions to BCP Psalms have already been cited. In *Grace Abounding*, though, Bunyan quotes the first verse of Psalm 51 in the metrical version of Sternhold–Hopkins (19).[22] In *Pilgrim's Progress*, the verse of Psalm 23 recited by Faithful is from another metrical psalter, perhaps the Scottish Psalter of 1650 (by Francis Rous and William Barton) or the earlier version by Henry Ainsworth (52). Both of these have the Psalmist fearing "none ill," rather than "no evil," which is in all the English Bibles since Coverdale (though Douai has "no evils").

Despite the occasional word, phrase, or verse that Bunyan recalls from other English versions, however, the Bible he clearly knew best was the KJB. The vast majority of identifiable biblical quotations and allusions in *Grace Abounding* and *Pilgrim's Progress* are either decisively KJB or in language shared by KJB and Geneva. The passages from Hebrews (2:14–15, 6:4, 10:26, and 12:16 in *Grace Abounding*, 34, 56; 12:16 in *Pilgrim's Progress*, 99), for instance, that so haunted Bunyan are from the KJB; the Geneva in each verse is markedly different. The many allusions to the Song of Solomon and Revelation in both parts of *Pilgrim's Progress* are also from the KJB. For instance, Song of Solomon 5:8 in both Bunyan (*Pilgrim's Progress*, 119) and KJB is "If you see my Beloved," but in Geneva is "wellbeloved." Both Revelation 22:14 and 5:13–14, quoted at the end of part one, are also distinctly KJB, the Geneva translators having chosen different words and syntax. Some particularly memorable biblical verses are also in Bunyan's ear from KJB. 1 Corinthians 13:1–2, "Though I speak with the tongues of men and angels, and have not charity [etc.]," is cited in *Grace Abounding* in the KJB (83), since Geneva renders the key term as "love." Proverbs 6:6 in *Pilgrim's Progress* (36), "Go to the Ant thou sluggard, consider her ways and be wise," is also from KJB, since Geneva advises going to the "pismire." The visceral, colloquial language of 2 Peter 2:22 obviously appealed to Bunyan, since it is quoted verbatim twice in the first part of *Pilgrim's Progress* (103, 117): "*The Dog is turned to his own vomit again.*" This is the KJB phrasing; Geneva states it as, "The dogge is returned to his owne vomit." Even the critical words inscribed over the Wicket-gate (23), "Knock and it shall be opened unto you" (Matt. 7:8), are in the KJB's exact language, Geneva having "to him that knocketh, it shall be opened."

One of the peculiarities of the history of the KJB is that the English Bible associated most strongly with a monarch and with the established church became the favored Bible of radicals and dissenters such as Bunyan.[23] As David Norton has shown, the KJB was not immediately embraced by English Christians of all sorts, whether churchmen, ordinary worshippers, or writers.[24] Yet the first major English writers who seem predominantly influenced by the language of the KJB are Milton and Bunyan.[25] Milton defended the execution of James I's son, Charles I, and vehemently opposed the established church; Bunyan spent a good portion of his life in prison for his dissenting preaching. How then did the Bible translated "by his Majesty's special commandment" under the general supervision of Lancelot Andrewes and "appointed to be read in Churches" become the Bible of choice of some of the established Church's staunchest opponents?

The answer to this question lies perhaps not so much in matters of theology or church politics as in the vicissitudes of the printing business. Simply put, by the late seventeenth century, the KJB had become *the* English Bible.[26] The last printing of a Geneva Bible in England was in 1616, though editions continued to be printed in and imported from Amsterdam until 1644.[27] Archbishop Laud seems to have been the man most responsible for suppressing the Geneva Bible, though, as Norton points out, Laud tended to use this version himself until at least the late 1620s.[28] Laud's efforts were of course aligned with the interests of the King's Printers, who held the monopoly on printing the KJB. Nevertheless, with the fall of Laud and Charles I and the establishment of the Commonwealth, the Geneva Bible failed to be reinstated to its former position of prominence. Parliament seems to have been no more interested in printing Geneva Bibles than Charles I had been. KJBs were printed throughout the 1640s and 1650s by the Company of Stationers, by John Field, "printer to the Parliament" (five editions in 1653 alone, as well as a KJB New Testament), and by independent printers like James Fletcher, Roger Daniel, Evan Tyler, and Giles Calvert. Doctrinal positions apparently had little to do with these printings. Daniel had been one of the printers to the University of Cambridge, and Tyler was for a time the King's Printer in Scotland, while Calvert, though a member of the Stationers' Company, became the major Quaker bookseller.[29] Calvert's 1653 duodecimo KJB seems to have become known as the "Quaker Bible." Not surprisingly, Calvert's edition eliminates the dedication to King James, while Daniel's 1654 edition includes it, as does Tyler's in 1653, and Field's in 1656, though by this time Field is styled "one of His Hignes printers" rather than "printer to the Parliament," the "Highnes" here being not the King but the Lord Protector, Oliver Cromwell. Further evidence of the security of the KJB's primacy in this period is the printing of several editions containing the Geneva notes. These notes had been one of the bugbears of King James, who famously decreed that no such marginalia should be included in the KJB. They were clearly popular with readers, however, surely because the majority were not particularly polemical but expository. The Geneva Bible was the first "Study Bible" geared to the average, inexpert reader. Although the popularity of the Geneva notes led to their reprinting at least eight times with the KJB text between 1642 and 1715, the fact that the Geneva text was not reprinted with them suggests that there was less attachment to its translation than to its apparatus.[30] The copious marginal references in *Pilgrim's Progress* might suggest to some readers the famous Geneva notes, and they do further add to the book's biblical resemblance. In fact, though, Bunyan's marginalia more closely resemble those in the KJB rather than Geneva.[31] In both *Pilgrim's Progress* and KJB, the majority of the marginalia are biblical cross-references rather than (as in Geneva) interpretative glosses.

In the mid seventeenth century, Bunyan was certainly not singular in living a profoundly Bible-oriented life or in writing biblically saturated literature. In this period, as Christopher Hill has pointed out, the Bible was "the foundation of all aspects of English culture."[32] Milton's *Paradise Lost*, *Paradise Regained*, and *Samson Agonistes*, not to mention his Psalm translations, are fundamentally adaptations of and engagements with the original biblical texts, as are Abraham Cowley's verse retelling of the David story, *Davideis*, the emblems of Francis Quarles, and the poems of George Herbert, Richard Crashaw, Henry Vaughan, and many others. However, none of these writers seems quite to have found Kugelmas's magic cabinet.[33] The scriptural intensity of *Pilgrim's Progress* is due to Bunyan's progress through the Bible in his daily life. In part, this mode of biblical living seems derived from the peculiar Puritan, or more generally Protestant, thinking about the inherently allegorical nature of this world. As Thomas Luxon has described it, Protestants drove Catholic allegorical scriptural exegesis out the door, while letting a different conception of allegory, under other names, in through the window.[34] Luther and others famously rejected the medieval tradition of the fourfold meaning of Scripture, favoring instead the Bible's "literal" sense. Yet, since the real, literal meaning of the Bible is that which points not to the kingdoms of this world but to the Kingdom of Heaven in the next one, both the Bible and the world are conceived essentially, if not explicitly, as allegories of the life to come. No wonder, then, that Bunyan is continually confronted by Scripture in Bedford every day. If one reads both the Word and the World (the Book of Scripture and the Book of Creation) in the same allegorical fashion, as ephemeral signs of eternal verities, it is easy to muddle the two texts together; both require interpretation in terms of the eternal reality to which they point. *Pilgrim's Progress* is one more fiction pointing in the same direction, a guide for those who find the hard chapters of the Bible and the World a little too tough.

NOTES

1 Woody Allen, "The Kugelmas Episode," *Side Effects* (New York: Ballantine, 1975), 61–78.

2 Michael Davies, *Graceful Reading: Theology and Narrative in the Works of John Bunyan* (Oxford: Oxford University Press, 2002), 279–91. The monster Apollyon seems to derive from *Bevis*.

3 "There is reason to think he had read Spenser," remarks Johnson. James Boswell, *Life of Johnson*, World's Classics (Oxford: Oxford University Press, 1980), 529. See also Harold Golder, "Bunyan and Spenser," *PMLA* 45.1 (1930): 216–37.

4 As John Knott puts it, "Bunyan appears more completely at the mercy of texts that act upon him in unpredictable ways." " 'Thou must live upon my Word': Bunyan and the Bible," in *John Bunyan: Conventicle and Parnassus: Tercentenary Essays*, ed. N. H. Keeble (Oxford: Clarendon Press, 1988), 158.

5 *Grace Abounding to the Chief of Sinners*, in *Grace Abounding with Other Spiritual Autobiographies*, ed. John Stachniewski, with Anne Pacheco (Oxford and New York: Oxford University Press, 1998). All further citations are from this edition.

6 Citations from the King James Version are taken from *The Bible: King James Version with Apocrypha*, ed. David Norton (Harmondsworth: Penguin, 2006). The Penguin text is taken from Norton's 2005 edition, *The New Cambridge Paragraph Bible* (Cambridge: Cambridge University Press).

7 Even this notion may be biblical, since in Ps. 23, goodness and mercy are said to "follow" the Psalmist all the days of his life. Perhaps biblical verses can do the same.

8 Stachniewski and Pacheco gloss "hollow" as "call, often in hunting" (242).

9 This passage from Hebrews was clearly critical for Bunyan. It comes up in *Pilgrim's Progress* too, when Hopeful cites it to Christian in a foolish defense of Little-Faith selling his "Jewels" (99).

10 John Bunyan, *The Pilgrim's Progress*, ed. Cynthia Wall (New York and London: W. W. Norton & Company, 2009). All further citations are from this edition.

11 Various straight and narrow ways recur throughout the book, as in the plain called Ease that "was but narrow" (83).

12 For an extended discussion of Bunyan's use of Ps. 23 in the context of other, related early modern literary uses and Renaissance pastoral, see Hannibal Hamlin, *Psalm Culture and Early Modern English Literature* (Cambridge: Cambridge University Press, 2004), 166–68.

13 Bunyan's syntax at the beginning of this sentence – "Now there was on the" – also clearly echoes Luke's "And there were in the ..."

14 References to Psalm translations other than the KJB are taken from *Psalm 23: An Anthology*, ed. K. H. Strange and R. G. E. Sandbach (Edinburgh: Saint Andrew Press, 1978).

15 See also Brainerd P. Stranahan, " 'With Great Delight': The Song of Solomon in *The Pilgrim's Progress*," *English Studies* 3 (1987): 220–7.

16 Pomegranates are also provided for the pilgrims by Mr. Interpreter earlier in the journey (170).

17 Ps. 150 is alluded to again at the end of part two, when Mr. Great-heart and Mr. Valiant "played upon the well tuned Cymbal and Harp for Joy" (240); Ps. 150:3, 5 (in the BCP version), "praise him upon the lute and harp," "Praise him upon the well-tuned cymbals."

18 This text also provides the climactic ending of Handel's *Messiah*.

19 All citations from the Geneva Bible are from *The Geneva Bible: A Facsimile of the 1560 Edition*, ed. Lloyd Berry (Peabody, MA: Hendrickson Bibles, 2007; repr. from University of Wisconsin Press facs. edn., 1969).

20 "Preface to the Version of 1611," *Records of the English Bible*, ed. Alfred W. Pollard (London, New York, Toronto, and Melbourne: Oxford University Press, 1911), 369.

21 Stranahan argues that "Bunyan never sets himself to recall the precise wording of a given passage, as might be required of a Sunday-school class." This is an overstatement, however, since many of Bunyan's citations are perfectly accurate. "Bunyan's Special Talent: Biblical Texts as 'Events' in *Grace Abounding* and *The Pilgrim's Progress*," *ELR* 11.3 (1981): 329–43; 331.

22 On Sternhold–Hopkins, see Hamlin, *Psalm Culture*, 19–50, and Beth Quitslund, *The Reformation in Rhyme: Sternhold, Hopkins and the English Metrical Psalter, 1547–1603* (Aldershot and Burlington, VT: Ashgate, 2008).

23 Though it never was actually "authorized" by King or Parliament, it is famously known as such.

24 David Norton, *A History of the English Bible as Literature* (Cambridge: Cambridge University Press, 2000), 89–114.

25 On Milton, see Jason Rosenblatt's essay in this volume. Norton points out (*A History* [2000], 176) that Milton owned a 1612 quarto KJB from his early childhood, which shows signs of having been well used.

26 Despite its popular American nickname, the "KJB" was not known in England as the "King James" but as the "Authorized Version" or simply "the English translation of the Bible" (the latter description is John Selden's, cited in Norton, *A History* [2000], 107).

27 David Daniell is incorrect on this, confusing the final continental printing with the final English one. See *The Bible in English: Its History and Influence* (New Haven, CT and London: Yale University Press, 2003), 457–8.

28 Norton, *A History* (2000), 104.

29 See Henry R. Plomer, *A Dictionary of the Booksellers and Printers Who Were at Work in England, Scotland and Ireland from 1641 to 1667* (London: Printed for the Bibliographical Society by Blades, East & Blades, 1907), and Ariel Hessayon, "Giles Calvert," *Oxford Dictionary of National Biography*.

30 Norton, *A History* (2000), 40; Daniell, *The Bible in English*, 489.

31 Despite King James's well-known objection to the Geneva's "bitter notes," and William Barlow's report that at Hampton Court James insisted that "no marginal note should be added" to the KJB (cited in Daniell, *The Bible in English*, 434), the KJB margins are in fact full of notes, just of a different kind than in the Geneva.

32 Christopher Hill, *The English Bible and the Seventeenth-Century Revolution* (Harmondsworth: Penguin, 1993), 7.

33 One exception is an anonymous seventeenth-century Ranter who wrote a scandalous biblical poem discovered in manuscript only in the late twentieth century (Anne Laurence, "Two Ranters Poems," *Review of English Studies*, New Series, 31.121 [1980]: 56–9). The poet writes of "walking on a day" and spying a "gallant City ... Jerusalem new it was," in which there are pastures greene" and a "waterie fountaine." The new Jerusalem is from Rev. 21:2, and the pastures and waters are from Ps. 23, probably in the BCP ("green pastures") or the Scottish Psalter ("pastures green"). The poet wants to get inside the city gates, "to refresh myself or sleepe those Hills between," but he finds them closed. As Noam Flinker points out, the geography in which the poet would fain sleep is a topographical allegory of Song of Sol. 1:13, in which the beloved longs for the lover to "lie all night betwixt my breasts" (*The Song of Songs in English Renaissance Literature: Kisses of their Mouths* [Cambridge: D. S. Brewer, 2000], 136). The locked gate, the specific language of which derives from Isaiah and Revelation, should also be read in terms of the Song of Solomon, in which the beloved is described as a "garden enclosed" (4:12), and she describes how her lover "put in his hand by the hole of the door" (5:4). In typically blasphemous Ranter fashion, the poet wants sex with Jerusalem. Flinker describes the tendency of Ranters and other seventeenth-century radicals to interpret the Song of Solomon literally, as a celebration and endorsement of sexual license. But though Bunyan would have been appalled at the substance of this poem, he would have recognized its biblical mode. It is notable too that even this Ranter turns primarily to the KJB rather than Geneva. Of course, few if any probably read the Ranter poem in the seventeenth century, and no one read it for several hundred years thereafter.

34 Thomas H. Luxon, *Literal Figures: Puritan Allegory and the Reformation Crisis in Representation* (Chicago and London: University of Chicago Press, 1995), ch. 2.

10 | Romantic transformations of the King James Bible

Wordsworth, Shelley, Blake

ADAM POTKAY

When you hear the Bible echoed in a Romantic poet, expect to find it transformed. I start with a biblical echo in William Wordsworth's early poem, *Descriptive Sketches* (1793). In the following passage the speaker rejoices in the "Soft music from th'aëreal summit" (421), and in the absence of man:

> – And sure there is a secret Power that reigns
> Here, where no trace of man the spot profanes …
> An idle voice the sabbath region fills
> Of *Deep that calls to Deep* across the hills,
> Broke only by the melancholy sound
> Of drowsy bells for ever tinkling round;
> Faint wail of eagle melting into blue
> Beneath the cliffs, and pine-woods steady sugh;
> The solitary heifer's deepn'd low;
> Or rumbling heard remote of falling snow.
>
> (424–39, emphasis mine)[1]

In the "Deep that calls to Deep across the hills," a *basso continuo* over which plays an array of "melancholy" (but not saddening) sounds, Wordsworth recalls the first line of Psalm 42:7 – "Deep calleth unto deep at the noise of thy waterspouts" – while signally omitting its parallel line, in which the sound of waters becomes a vehicle for the speaker's despondency: "All thy waves and thy billows are gone over me." Wordsworth's lines reverse the Biblical dynamic; here inner landscape seems to give way to outer. The deeps that concern him are those of nature, not of human spirit, and they call, but not primarily to us, the speaker's witness notwithstanding. Whereas Psalm 42 as a whole uses natural imagery to describe, analogically, the individual's inner striving towards God – "As the hart panteth after the water brooks, so panteth my soul after thee, O God" (v. 1) – Wordsworth, antithetically, describes the elements of nature in relation to one another, "where no trace of man the spot profanes." In short, Wordsworth turns the Bible on its head.

Why, then, quote it at all? First of all, Wordsworth alludes to the King James Bible (KJB) to set his own project in relation to its tenets (here, anthropocentrism), and at least partially against it (for Wordsworth, nature is set over man, or man subsumed into nature). By incorporating well-known lines of the KJB he gives a scriptural sonority to his own poetry; by transforming the meaning of the lines he quotes, he lays claim to a metaphysical heft of his own. Wordsworth reads the Bible *antithetically*, or in a manner that reveals its own tensions or fissures: and in this creative dialogue with the KJB, we shall see, he is at one with most of the other major Romantic poets.

A second attraction of the line from Psalms that Wordsworth employs is its *ambiguity*, a semantic vagueness that contributes to its richness. In Hebrew as in the KJB's corresponding English, it's hard to say precisely what "deep calleth unto deep" means, and so commentaries vary. Most offer a naturalistic interpretation: in Wordsworth's day, a popular gloss of the verse suggested that "when, at the 'sound' of descending 'water spouts,' or torrents of rain, the depths are stirred up, and put into horrible commotion," it is as though "the clouds above [were] calling … to the waters below, and one wave encouraging and exciting another, to join their forces, and overwhelm the despairing sufferer."[2] Nearer our own day, Abraham Cohen offers another naturalistic interpretation of what it means for a deep to call to a deep: "The melting snows from the peaks of Hermon form thunderous waterfalls; and to these are added the rapids of the Jordan."[3] But Robert Alter gets closer to what attracted Wordsworth to the KJB style when he concedes the ambiguity of the forty-second psalm's "deeps": "this could be an associative leap from the heights [of v. 7] to the antithetical depths, from the mountains to the seas"; these "deeps" or "abysses" are "geological or cosmic."[4] Indefiniteness shades into an intimation of infiniteness. Alter's gloss is attuned to the indeterminacy, the sublime affront to clear representation, which attracted Wordsworth to the Hebrew Bible and its King James translation. Wordsworth spells out his anti-iconic aesthetic in his 1815 *Preface* to his *Poetical Works*:

The grand storehouses of the enthusiastic and meditative Imagination, of poetical … Imagination, are the prophetic and lyrical parts of the Holy

Scriptures, and the works of Milton … I select these writers in preference to those of ancient Greece and Rome, because the anthropomorphitism [sic] of the Pagan religion subjected the minds of the greatest poets in those countries too much to the bondage of definite form; from which the Hebrews were preserved by their abhorrence of idolatry. This abhorrence was almost as strong in our great epic Poet … However imbued the surface might be with classical literature, he was a Hebrew in soul; and all things tended in him towards the sublime.[5]

Wordsworth's lines on the anti-iconic sublimity of Milton and "the prophetic and lyrical parts of the Holy Scriptures" are in keeping with Edmund Burke's influential assessment that both these sources evince the sublime of the indefinite or obscure.[6]

They may also be read as a manifesto for the Biblical aesthetic shared by all the major Romantics, with the partial exception of the artist-poet Blake – though it is perhaps significant that Blake scarcely illustrates "Proverbs of Hell," his first major engagement with the Bible. As David Norton notes, the central figures of English Romantic poetry "share a biblical upbringing in a time when a favorable literary opinion of the KJB had become established," being "the first major literary group to have this in common"; I would add that for the most part the literary quality they valued in the KJB was the rhetorical sublimity praised by Longinus and admiring eighteenth-century critics from John Dennis through Robert Lowth and Burke.[7] In this essay, I continue with my examination of Wordsworth's sublime and antithetical use of the KJB, focusing on his poem "Tintern Abbey," and then suggest ways in which his method of allusive sublimity and semantic inversion influences the work of Shelley, and runs parallel to Blake's antithetical or dialectic engagement with the Bible in his "Proverbs of Hell." This antithetical relation to the Bible does not, I should note, necessarily make the Romantics involved in a process of secularization; they can also be viewed, and in the early nineteenth century often were viewed, within the framework of Protestant Dissent to a Church–State establishment that was ratcheting up its authority during the Napoleonic wars.[8]

Yet of the three antithetical biblical echoes I find in Wordsworth's "Tintern Abbey," the poem to which I now turn, the echo that seems most radical in its implications concerns *conscience*, a faculty still dearer to Dissent than to the religious establishment. It is conscience, I would argue, that Wordsworth means to conjure in his richly mysterious phrase "the still, sad music of humanity," for behind it lies the "still small voice" of 1 Kings 19:11–12. This voice that subdues the fire-eating prophet Elijah, rendering him serviceable to God's designs, afterwards became identified as conscience, the voice of God within. Particularly among early evangelicals, the "still small voice" served as a source of enlightenment to which the Christian should listen in composure and silence, outside the din of the public world. Thus William Cowper satirizes the ethics of the third earl of Shaftesbury, which equate the moral sense and the sense of beauty, as (alluding to 1 Cor. 13:1) "tinkling cymbal and high sounding brass / Smitten in vain!"; for "such music cannot charm" the soul where "The STILL, SMALL VOICE is wanted."[9]

Wordsworth asserts such music precisely in lieu of the "still small voice." His music is sometimes the blended sounds of outer nature: e.g., "Soft music from th'aëreal summit" in *Descriptive Sketches*, or the "soothing melody" that begins and ends *The Ruined Cottage*, Ms. D. (15, 531–3).[10] In the 1798 *Lyrical Ballads*, directly after "The Convict" – a poem that laments the "torture" of conscience (130) – we find "Tintern Abbey," in which the still small voice is transformed into

> The still, sad music of humanity,
> Not harsh nor grating, though of ample power
> To chasten and subdue. (92–4)

To read this music as a purely formal version of conscience is to understand why it is not harsh nor punitive (as conscience was popularly held to be[11]), but nonetheless chastens by putting one into an ethically receptive mood, an orientation of responsiveness towards the Other, outside of a Christian (or monarchist) ethics of obedience or, as Wordsworth called it in an Alfoxden fragment, "negative morality."[12] The "still small voice" to which Wordsworth alludes can say "thou shalt not," but music never forbids, though it may prompt to tenderness and fellow feeling. Wordsworth thus uses a KJB echo to suggest, in an indefinite manner, opposition to "harsh and grating" commandments, injunctions, and laws, or the civic arm of religion itself.

A second KJB allusion in "Tintern Abbey" is to a pastoral psalm, the well-known Psalm 23, "The Lord is my shepherd," specifically to verse 4: "Yea, though I walk through the valley of the shadow of death, I will fear no evil: for thou art with me; thy rod and thy staff they comfort me." After the speaker of "Tintern Abbey" has heard "the still, sad music of humanity," and been moved by "a sense sublime / Of something far more deeply interfused" in all things, he turns to a presence that walks beside him, one that would seem at first to be God (or some person of the triune God):

> Nor, perchance,
> If I were not thus taught, should I the more
> Suffer my genial spirits to decay:
> *For thou art with me*, here, upon the banks
> Of this fair river; thou, my dearest Friend,
> My dear, dear Friend, and in thy voice I catch
> The language of my former heart, and read
> My former pleasures in the shooting lights
> Of thy wild eyes. Oh! Yet a little while
> May I behold in thee what I was once,
> My dear, dear Sister! (112–22, emphasis mine)

Why does Wordsworth wait seven lines between the KJB phrase "thou art with me" – referring here to an unidentified "thou" whose presence has not been anticipated in the first 115 lines of the poem – and the identification of that "thou" as his sister? Clearly, I think, he intends by the force of his allusion to make his readers infer that this "thou" is the Lord, and then Jesus-as-Friend, and only gradually disabuse us of this inference: "thy wild eyes" is the first sign that this reading is probably awry. By the time we discover that those eyes belong to his sister (Dorothy, if we read the poem biographically), his sister has been invested with the office and splendor of the Lord of Psalms – and of Paul's Epistle to the Hebrews as well ("For *yet a little while*, and he that shall come will come, and will not tarry," 10:37, emphasis added). She emerges as a new shepherd or comforter, at once naturalized and rendered numinous. That the poem's speaker turns in the following lines to comfort his comforter, indemnifying her against the prospect of future ills, registers a final irony with respect to the Psalm we've had in mind, a final deconstruction of the hierarchical relation between shepherd and sheep, lord and servant.

The poem's third and final KJB allusion comes in the speaker's prayer to Nature on his and his sister's behalf. Nature can (in this valley of the shadow of death) quell the fear of evil, or – as he puts it –

> so impress
> With quietness and beauty, and so feed
> With lofty thoughts, that neither evil tongues,
> Rash judgments, nor the sneers of selfish men,
> Nor greetings where no kindness is, nor all
> The dreary intercourse of daily life,
> Shall e'er prevail against us, or disturb
> Our cheerful faith that all which we behold
> Is full of blessings.   (127–35)

Here Wordsworth conjures both Milton and St. Paul. His "evil tongues" that shall not prevail come, textually, from Milton's proem to book 7 of *Paradise Lost*: "More safe I sing with mortal voice, unchang'd / To hoarse or mute, though fall'n on evil days, / On evil days though fall'n, *and evil tongues*; / … yet not alone, while thou / Visit'st my slumbers Nightly" (24–9) – this "thou" referring to Urania as muse of epic poetry.[13] Wordsworth imagines into being similarly evil tongues and times, as proof of what he and Dorothy can withstand as long as they stand firm in their religion of nature. And to underscore that theirs is truly a religion and a calling, Wordsworth's catalog of negations ("neither … nor … nor … nor") – of all that will not render them apostate – is modeled, as Michael Vander Weele has argued, on a Pauline passage concerning the perseverance of the saints: "Who shall separate us from the love of Christ?… For I am persuaded, that neither death, nor life, nor angels, nor principalities, nor powers, nor things present, nor things to come, nor height, nor depth, nor any other creature, shall be able to separate us from the love of God, which is in Christ Jesus our Lord" (Rom. 8:35, 38–9).[14]

Far more remains to be said of the imprint of the KJB on Wordsworth's poetry, but suffice it to say here that he persistently deploys scriptural allusion in crafting his oppositional (or complementary) religion of nature. We may say of Wordsworth what Wordsworth, in book 1 of *The Excursion*, says of his character, "the Wanderer": "He had early learned / To reverence the Volume which displays / The mystery, the life which cannot die: / But in the mountains did he feel his faith" (244–7).[15]

That Percy Shelley reverenced the major works of Wordsworth is well known, but his own ongoing dialogue with the KJB has drawn less attention.[16] His debt to both sources is readily apparent in "The Retrospect"

(1812), a poem about revisiting a spot in Wales that is modeled on "Tintern Abbey" and that draws on Psalm 139. This Psalm concerns God's protection of the elect wherever they may be: "If I take the wings of the morning, and dwell in the uttermost parts of the sea; Even there shall thy hand lead me, and thy right hand shall hold me. If I say, Surely the darkness shall cover me; even the night shall be light about me" (vv. 9–11). "The wings of the morning" appear to be a piece of pagan imagery, a synecdoche for the goddess of dawn as she rises from the eastern ocean. With these wings in mind, Shelley recalls his visionary flights in the solitude of the night, in flight from false friends who would yoke him to earthly things:

> And early I had learned to scorn
> The chains of clay that bound a soul
> Panting to seize the wings of morn,
> And where its vital fires were born
> To soar, and spurn the cold control
> Which the vile slaves of earthly night
> Would twine around its struggling flight.   (71–7)[17]

Shelley's lines here could be paraphrased: even if darkness covers me, night shall be light about me; the aerial spirit can take flight. Yet Shelley recasts Psalm 139 in terms of individual transcendence, without the evident embrace of divine protection – his allusion to the KJB is thus, as Wordsworth's allusions were, oppositional. Similarly, Shelley alludes as well to Psalm 42, verse 1 – "so panteth my soul after thee, O God" – but here the "panting" (destined to become a favorite Shelley word) is to rise above, to the spirit's primordial fire, but to do so without an external master of that spirit.

Shelley lights in "The Retrospect" on another biblicism that will become a standard part of his poetic repertoire: Christ's "crown of thorns" (Matt. 27:29). In the present of "The Retrospect," the speaker's days are as happy as his visionary nights, because of the love of a new companion (biographically, Shelley's first wife, Harriet Westbrook). She has effected "so bright a change" (143) that

> The gloomiest retrospects that bind
> With crowns of thorn the bleeding mind,
> The prospects of most doubtful hue

> That rise on Fancy's shuddering view,
> Are gilt by the reviving ray
> Which thou hast flung upon my day.   (163–8)

The speaker has in this poem been addressing his own past, but the chiasmic transformation of Christ's singular "crown of thorns" into the plural "crowns of thorn" suggests, as does "the" rather than "a" "bleeding mind," a reference to a retrospect by or of mankind as a whole. This suggestion flowers in the first Act of Shelley's masterpiece *Prometheus Unbound* (1818–20), in which the Chorus of Furies torments Prometheus with a painful vision of human history, torn by fire and dread religious war:

> Joy, Joy, Joy!
> Past ages crowd on thee, but each one remembers,
> And the future is dark, and the present is spread
> Like a pillow of thorns for thy slumberless head.   (560–3)

The "thee" of the Furies' last three lines refers equally well to Prometheus, to personified Joy, or to the Christ addressed earlier as "One … of gentle worth" (546), and the equation of the three seems intentional – any of these figures would be tortured by the vision of history the Furies unfold.

The redemption of history comes through Prometheus's Christ-like endurance and forgiveness.[18] Cosmic rejuvenation stems from Prometheus's act of forgiveness, one that recalls Christ's words upon the cross: "Father, forgive them; for they know not what they do" (Luke 23:34). This verse is evoked by the Furies who tempt Prometheus to despair. According to the last Fury, "Many are strong and rich, – and would be just, – / But live among their suffering fellow men / As if none felt – they know not what they do" (629–31). Christ's act of forgiveness, evoked here under erasure – the line "Father, forgive them" is precisely what the Fury omits – is for Shelley the essence of his teaching and the key to the possible perfection of man and his environment. Only pity for those who act unreflectively within the chain of causal necessity ("they know not what they do") can inaugurate change within that chain; only forgiveness can open up a horizon of possible virtue beyond the calculation of probable evil. Prometheus responds to the final Fury: "Thy words are like a cloud of winged snakes / And yet, I pity those they torture not." These are the words that make the Fury vanish: "Thou pitiest them? I speak no more!" (634).

For Shelley (as earlier for Blake), everything beyond the example of forgiveness advanced under the name of Christianity is a lie and force of destruction. Although an atheist, Shelley adhered to theological ethics, for forgiveness is not an unqualified good in any secular ethics (in which it might be censured for condoning evil-doing or for flouting the moral law). And he remained steeped in the KJB, which, along with his friend Byron (in his closet drama, *Cain: A Mystery*, and elsewhere), Shelley read against the grain. Spirits may take wing with or without God; humans may usefully forgive with or without a God to forgive them.

Another masterpiece of antithetical Bible reading is one that none of the other major Romantics knew: William Blake's *The Marriage of Heaven and Hell* (1790–3), a strange and complex work that is part prose and part poetry, part satire and part prophecy. While called a "marriage," and while its title page depicts a couple in embrace, in this work the devil's party wins all the debates – presumably to offset the one-sidedness of the Bible and Judeo-Christian literature more generally. Here the voice of the devil proclaims:

1 Man has no Body distinct from his Soul, for that calld Body is a portion of Soul discerned by the five Senses, the chief inlets of Soul in this age.
2 Energy is the only life and is from the Body, and Reason is the bound or outward circumference of Energy.
3 Energy is Eternal Delight.[19]

Shortly after this creed of bodily energy we find a section called "Proverbs of Hell." To some degree, these are the contraries of the biblical book of Proverbs: whereas the biblical Proverbs teach prudential wisdom, Blake's Proverbs of Hell celebrate energy, action, and exuberance. The biblical Proverbs claim to show the way to success through conduct that is upright, just, industrious, prudent, and god-fearing. One must avoid excess, overindulgence, and especially (as the book is addressed foremost to men) "strange women," a phrase that would seem to refer to all women who aren't wives or family members. Blake's "Proverbs of Hell," by contrast, commend excess in a variety of forms because – as Blake earlier states the case, *in propria persona* – "without Contraries is no Progression. Attraction and Repulsion, Reason and Energy, are necessary to Human existence" (plate 3). Yet Blake's diabolic proverbs do not simply oppose or invert biblical proverbs: the devil doesn't advise, "be lazy, be unjust, and be drunk." Indeed, the devil doesn't in any clear way advise anything, and in this opposes less the ethics than the didacticism of the biblical Proverbs. Blake's proverbs invite the reader to struggle with their semantic excess, and to glean from that struggle an ethic that is internal rather than imposed.

The "Proverbs of Hell" (plates 7–10) are set out in a list, one that begins benignly: "In seed time learn, in harvest teach, in winter enjoy." But the second proverb, on first sight, may startle: "Drive your cart and your plow over the bones of the dead." Upon reflection, however, the injunction is softened by its very ambiguity: does it mean "desecrate your predecessors," or simply "cultivate the earth and all that your ancestors have brought to it"? Does it urge us to reject the past utterly, or rather to cultivate a present moment that incorporates within it accretions of the past? A similar question can be asked of the gospel injunction that Blake echoes here, one that on first glance seems no less shocking than Blake's: "Follow me," Christ says to a disciple who asks if he can wait till he buries his father, "and let the dead bury the dead" (Matt. 8:22). Thus Blake's proverb prompts us to think not only about it, but also about the Gospel line it obliquely invokes.

And when we think about either injunction, we can't help but notice its quality of excess, of being in excess of a literal command (i.e., it involves hyperbole and/or symbolism) and also in excess of any one reading (ambiguity). But excess, hermeneutic or otherwise, is critical, as we are told in Blake's next proverb: "The road of excess leads to the palace of wisdom." And the prudence that would reign in excess, the prudence that the biblical Proverbs presents as a divine quality – "I wisdom dwell with prudence," speaks Wisdom personified as a woman (8:12) – is thus countered by the following Proverb of Hell: "Prudence is a rich ugly old maid courted by Incapacity."

A subsequent set of diabolic proverbs sound as though they accord well enough with the biblical Proverbs' emphasis on work and industry: "Eternity is in love with the productions of time"; "The busy bee has no time for sorrow"; "The hours of folly are measur'd by the clock, but of wisdom: no clock can measure." (There follows a vegetarian proverb: "All wholsom [sic] food is caught without a net or a trap.") But next comes a proverb that runs athwart the numerous biblical Proverbs on what we would now call "business ethics," in a day before standard coinage, when gold and silver often had to be weighed out during commercial transactions. Proverbs urge time and again to measure justly, using a good scale or "balance" and proper weights: for example, in the antithetical parallelism of Proverbs 11:1, "A false balance is abomination to the Lord; but a just weight is his delight." Blake counters: "Bring out number, weight, & measure in a year of dearth."[20] This compacted expression could be paraphrased: "bring out weights and scales when there's scarcity, presumably of wheat, of grain, of goods." But should care in business dealing be taken only when there's scarcity? What about in years of plenty? Blake's implication here may be that if there's enough to go around, let it go around freely – perhaps according to the ancient Christian principle of "to each according to his need" (Acts 2:45, 4:35). Unless there's real scarcity, don't worry about the minutiae of apportionment. Less Christian-communistic, however, is an alternative interpretation: in years of plenty, it's fine to take advantage of one's customers (they've got the dough). Again, Blake's proverb is in excess of any single or simple meaning – and what matters, finally, is how it "reads its reader," revealing and perhaps transforming her unexamined assumptions, and prompting her to the fruit of suitable action.

Blake's next three proverbs emphasize the reader's self-reliance in both interpretation and action. "No bird soars too high if he soars with his own wings": like Shelley on the "wings of morning" he would seize without a divine protector, Blake endorses soaring in one's own way, subtly echoing and inverting Isaiah 40:31: "they that wait upon the Lord shall renew their strength; they shall mount up with wings as eagles." Blake's bird needs no succor, though the next proverb suggests that he needs to think well on his relation to others: "A dead body revenges not injuries." Conversely, if you're alive you will avenge yourself? Or is it fine to injure someone as long as you don't give that person an opportunity to strike back – that is, by making sure he's dead? Finally, however, an ethical rule seems to inhabit Blake's provocative saying: don't injure anyone *unless* you're ready to kill him – which, upon inspection, you may well find yourself not ready to do. Only in this last interpretation does Blake's "dead body" proverb accord with the altruistic proverb that follows: "The most sublime act is to set another before you." But the ethical turn is one that Blake invites rather than dictates, requiring his reader, on her own wings, to meet him at least halfway. The less careful or differently inclined reader could become a murderer, a Raskolnikov. Yet it would not be the devil's fault.

"He who desires but acts not, breeds pestilence" is Blake's fifth proverb, but he arrives at a more shocking variation in his fourth-to-last: "Sooner murder an infant in its cradle than nurse unacted desires." Read by someone urgently desiring to murder an infant, this proverb could prove a goad to infanticide. But Blake did presumably not imagine a readership of repressed murderers. For the ideal reader, the key word here may be "nurse": if you have a desire you shouldn't or wouldn't act on, then don't nurse it. Cultivate only desires you would see flourish: in this light, Blake's diabolic proverb is not so far from Proverbs 13:12, "Hope deferred maketh the heart sick: but when the desire cometh [when the thing desired comes], it is a tree of life." Still, this ethical reading of "sooner murder an infant" is dependent on a hermeneutic decision to focus on "[don't] nurse unacted desires"; the proverb as a whole, as Blake frames it, is in excess of a simple meaning or moral injunction. But it is only in ambiguity, in opposition, that the ethical choice arises.

True limits arise only from excess: this lesson in reading finds a final summation in Blake's final two proverbs. The first looks self-reflexively at Blake's fostering of self-understanding: "Truth can never be told so as to be understood, and not be believ'd." And the truth, at last, lies in Blake's final proverb: "Enough! Or Too much." "Enough" is the first choice we're offered, and its emphatic punctuation makes it appear the preferable one. "Too much," the road of excess, is a second choice that seems finally to be instrumental to the first, as indeed it is in the earlier proverb, "The road of excess *leads* to the palace of wisdom." Excess isn't urged for its own sake. Blake's motto is not that of the Lone Star Saloon in the Manhattan of my youth: "Too much ain't enough." The wise man knows when enough is enough, or the ethical and/or natural limits of desire. What Blake warns against, in the Proverbs of Hell and throughout his work, is "nursing unacted desires," that is, poisoning oneself with repressed rage and frustration, pining away with frustration; in this sense, *not* acting. But Blake knew that not all desires should be acted upon.

Of Blake's final proverbs I have saved for last his antepenultimate: "Where man is not nature is barren." Does this too have a relation to the KJB? It may seem to extend the anthropocentrism we find in Psalm 8 ("thou hast made … [man] a little lower than the angels") and in the Bible more generally, and in doing so to run counter to Wordsworth's anti-anthropocentric echo of Psalm 42 in his description of a scene "where no trace of man the spot profanes." But Blake's proverb may also be read as splitting the difference between these two extremes, and indeed as revealing the paradox inherent in Wordsworth's passage: the poem's speaker, imaginatively describing the rural scene, is the trace of man. The critic David B. Morris writes of this proverb: "What turns nature barren is not an absence of people, but, specifically, the absence of imaginative vision. Humans who view nature solely through the chinks of the un-liberated five senses will see only a reflection of their own imprisonment .... Where vision is absent, then, man and nature are equally barren; where vision is present, nature and man both reveal their kinship in the infinite, the eternal, and the divine."[21] Supporting this reading is Blake's proverb "A fool sees not the same tree that a wise man sees," as well as his comment elsewhere: "the tree which moves some to tears of joy is in the Eyes of others only a Green thing that stands in the way."[22]

As Mike Goode has recently argued in a provocative article on Blake, proverbs in general tend towards diffusion, subject to excerption and recollection as well as different interpretations among different readers; although directed to shaping lives, they are offered in an ad hoc, accretive, unsystematic, and otherwise shapeless way, and are thus structurally opposite to the systematic regulation of theological orthodoxy.[23] Yet Blake's diabolic proverbs more than other proverbs critically depend on the power of ambiguity or semantic excess to craft a fit reader. Thus what Goode writes of proverbs as a genre is especially true of Blake's Proverbs of Hell: "through their circulation, they carry the potential not just to undermine their own already unsystematic regulatory authority but also, as they do so, to produce cultural hegemonies that compete with and perhaps begin to erode a culture's systematic regulatory authorities."[24]

One such authority in the Romantic era, as I remarked at the outset of this essay, was the Church of England, still closely tied to the state, its doctrine enforced by the increasingly long arm of the law. And it was against the authoritative use of Scripture, rather than Scripture itself, that Wordsworth, Shelley, and Blake, each in his own way, aimed their antithetical engagements. These poets displayed their gratitude for the Bible's rich ambiguities by crafting richly ambiguous lines of their own, lines that never enshrine the "authorized" version but that often echo its sublimities. We may thank them for helping to keep the Bible alive.

NOTES

1 *Descriptive Sketches*, ed. Eric Birdsall with Paul M. Zall (Ithaca, NY: Cornell University Press, 1984); I quote from the 1793 version of the poem. Wordsworth defines "sugh" (437) in a footnote: "a Scotch word expressive of the sound of the wind through the trees."

2 George Horne, *A Commentary on the Book of Psalms*, 3rd edn., 2 vols. (Oxford: Clarendon Press, 1784), vol. 1, 254.

3 *The Psalms: Hebrew Text & English Translation with an Introduction and Commentary* (London: The Socino Press, 1945), 132.

4 Robert Alter, *The Book of Psalms: A Translation with Commentary* (New York: Norton, 2007), 150.

5 Wordsworth, *Prose Works*, vol. 3, ed. W. J. B. Owen and J. W. Smyser (Oxford: Clarendon Press, 1973), 34–5.

6 Part II of Burke's *A Philosophical Enquiry into the Origin of our Ideas of the Sublime and Beautiful* (1757) enumerates the various attributes of the sublime, starting with terror, obscurity, and power, and illustrating these with quotations from sources including Milton, Job, and Psalms.

7 David Norton traces the rise of the Bible's, and particularly the KJB's, literary reputation from 1700 to the Romantic poets and Charlotte Brontë in *A History of the Bible as Literature*, 2 vols. (Cambridge: Cambridge University Press, 1993), vol. 2, 1–175, although he only touches upon Burke's *Philosophical Enquiry*. My quotation from Norton comes from vol. 2, 136.

8 For challenges to seeing Romantic poetics as a process of secularization, see Robert Ryan, *The Romantic Reformation: Religious Politics in English Literature, 1789–1824* (Cambridge: Cambridge University Press, 1997), and Colin Jager, *The Book of God: Secularization and Design in the Romantic Era* (Philadelphia: University of Pennsylvania Press, 2007).

9 William Cowper, *The Task*, book 5, "The Winter Morning Walk," 681–5 (emphasis original), quoted from *The Task and Selected Other Poems*, ed. James Sambrook (London: Longman, 1994), 188. Similarly, William Wilberforce urges: "Rise on the wings of contemplation, until the praises and the censures of men die away upon the ear, and the still small voice of conscience is no longer drowned by the din of this nether world" (*A Practical View of the Prevailing Religious System of Professed Christians in the Higher and Middle Classes of this Country, contrasted with Real Christianity*, 2nd edn. [London, 1797], 235).

10 *The Ruined Cottage and The Pedlar*, ed. James Butler (Ithaca, NY: Cornell University Press, 1979).

11 On the hell of conscience, see for example Fanny Holcroft's ballad "Conscience the Worst of Tortures" (*Monthly Magazine*, April 1798), reprinted in

Wordsworth and Coleridge, *Lyrical Ballads and Related Writings*, ed. William Richey and Daniel Robinson (Boston, MA: Houghton Mifflin/Riverside, 2002), 270–1.

12 Fragment, "There is an active principle alive in all things," l. 73, in *Lyrical Ballads, and Other Poems, 1797–1800*, ed. James Butler and Karen Green (Ithaca, NY: Cornell University Press, 1992), 310. I elaborate on Wordsworth's substitution of music for conscience in "Music vs. Conscience in Wordsworth's Poetry," in *Theory and Practice in the Eighteenth Century: Writing between Philosophy and Literature*, ed. Alexander Dick and Christina Lupton (London: Pickering & Chatto, 2008), 225–38, 279–83.

13 Quoted from Milton, *Complete Poems and Major Prose*, ed. Merritt Y. Hughes, rev. David Kastan (Indianapolis: Hackett, 2005). Wordsworth – and Milton – may have also had in mind Psalm 34:13: "Keep thy tongue from evil, and thy lips from speaking guile."

14 Michael Vander Weele, "The Contest of Memory in 'Tintern Abbey,'" *Nineteenth-Century Literature* 50.1 (1995): 6–26; Vander Weele's Pauline citation appears on 24.

15 Quoted from the 1814 edition in *The Excursion*, ed. Sally Bushell, James A. Butler, and Michael C. Jaye (Ithaca, NY: Cornell University Press, 2007).

16 See, however, Bryan Shelley's useful *Shelley and Scripture: The Interpreting Angel* (Oxford: Clarendon Press, 1994).

17 Quotations of Shelley are from *Shelley's Poetry and Prose*, ed. Donald H. Reiman and Neil Fraistat (New York: Norton, 2002).

18 For a fuller reading of *Prometheus Unbound* in relation to forgiveness and joy, see Adam Potkay, *The Story of Joy from the Bible to Late Romanticism* (Cambridge: Cambridge University Press, 2007), 180–6.

19 *Marriage of Heaven and Hell*, plate 4, quoted from *Blake's Poetry and Designs*, ed. Mary Lynn Johnson and John E. Grant (New York: Norton, 1979).

20 Cf. Wisdom of Solomon 11:20–2, where "measure and number and weight" are attributed to God, as one who both manages natural order, and is as superior to his created world as to "a little grain of the balance."

21 David B. Morris, "Dark Matter(s): Sacramental Humanscape in *The Marriage of Heaven and Hell*," a paper delivered at the American Society for Eighteenth-Century Studies, Richmond, Virginia, March 2009.

22 Blake's letter to John Trusler, August 23, 1799; quoted from *Blake's Poetry and Designs*, 448.

23 Mike Goode, "Blakespotting," *PMLA* 121.3 (2006): 769–86.

24 *Ibid.*, 780.

11 | Ruskin and his contemporaries reading the King James Bible

MICHAEL WHEELER

This chapter focuses upon John Ruskin (1819–1900) as perhaps the most biblically literate of all nineteenth-century writers, who owed much to the KJB in his prose style, which was admired worldwide, and yet who came to understand its limitations as a translation from the Hebrew and Greek. Unique in the range of his interests, which are reflected in his massive *œuvre*, Ruskin is also representative of his age. (His dates coincide almost exactly with those of his monarch, who outlived him by a year.) First, then, let us consider the Victorian age.

Nineteenth-century Britain was broadly Christian, largely Protestant, and, judging by the newspapers, passionately interested in religious news. Individual believers were ready to defend their own doctrinal and sect-arian positions against those who held different views, often with gusto. Before the 1860s, most people believed in the literal truth of the Bible and regarded the Four Last Things – death, judgment, heaven, and hell – as being central to their faith. With the possibility of everlasting punishment in hell fire hanging over you, it was important to be sure that you had access to the means of grace. Religious battles of words raged between different groups, sects, and parties, each of which believed that it had access to a saving truth. Apart from the Roman Catholics (about 5 percent of the population by 1860), all turned to the KJB as *the* authoritative source; and many Catholics had some acquaintance with the KJB.

The impact of biblical criticism and science upon religious belief was everywhere felt and discussed. Religious matters frequently made the headlines, and some religious controversies which ran on for many months, even years, were eagerly followed by readers. Something of the energy expended upon religion in the nineteenth century is reflected in the huge number of religious publications that poured from the new steam presses.[1] Charles Knight worked out that of the 45,260 titles published in Britain between 1816 and 1851 (fewer than in one year today), more than a fifth were on "divinity." As late as the 1880s, religious books still outnumbered any other class. Cheap paper, new printing techniques, and an expanding reader-ship increased the demand for books – once for the minority, now for the million. In an age of strict moral standards, presided over by Victoria and Albert, and of considerable social control by the churches, Sabbatarianism and the Sunday school movement led to a huge demand for religious read-ing matter. The Religious Tract Society's periodical, *Sunday at Home*, for example, founded in 1854, claimed a circulation of 130,000 by 1865. The impact of Evangelicalism on Victorian culture was profound, and much of the popular religious literature of the age reflects a strong urge to proselyt-ize. The opponents of the Evangelicals had no choice but to follow suit.

In 1897, the Religious Tract Society, founded in 1799, sent out from its home depot alone over 38,720,000 items of literature, of which 18,320,000 were tracts. Not all of these were read, as many copies were either thrown away or used as spills for lighting the fire or the tobacco pipe. The British and Foreign Bible Society was founded in 1804. The Society for Promoting Christian Knowledge was older and somewhat moribund, until it woke up to the challenge of the Religious Tract Society and became an organ for the High Church party. By 1867 it was publishing over eight million items per annum. Religious literature was circulated through bookshops, circulating libraries, local churches, chapels and societies, and through hawkers. One young man claimed to have made over eighteen thousand calls in one year and sold almost four thousand books. Religion sold.

The biggest seller, then as now, was the KJB, regarded by many as the true "Word of God," for all its textual errors. The British and Foreign Bible Society distributed about sixteen million English Bibles and Testaments between 1804 and 1854. By 1884 they could offer a New Testament for the price of one penny. Among the more expensive productions were illus-trated Bibles, such as Charles Knight's *Pictorial Bible*, with notes by John Kitto (1836–8, 2nd edn. 1847–9), and Gustave Doré's Bible, published by Cassell (1866–70). Births, marriages, and deaths were entered in specially designed pages in the larger family Bibles, sometimes together with pho-tographs, making the KJB the most personalized printed text in Victorian culture. Family Bibles were clasped in brass and prominently displayed in the home. Ponderous large-print Bibles rested upon the Johannine eagle lecterns in parish churches across the land, where the faithful heard read-ings from the KJB at Morning and Evening Prayer, and, on special feast days, at Holy Communion. Personal Bibles, in black bindings, rested on Anglican and Nonconformist bedside cabinets. Smaller Bibles, tastefully bound in morocco, nestled in ladies' handbags. Copies of the KJB and of Bunyan's *Pilgrim's Progress* were often to be found in the homes of the "deserving poor." The KJB was everywhere.

Ruskin spoke for his generation when describing the language of the KJB as "habitual music."[2] The rhythms and cadences of a Jacobean text which had been antiquated even on publication day could still be heard in the poetry and fiction of writers who witnessed a technological revolution, but who also knew their Bibles well, through regular church attendance and private reading. Those familiar rhythms and cadences conveyed a seriousness and a high moral purpose which Victorian culture embraced and made its own.

Published at the end of the nineteenth century, Frederic William Farrar's study on *The Bible: Its Meaning and Supremacy* (1897) provides a useful source for this discussion, as the Dean looks back at some of the most famous Victorian responses to the KJB. Thomas Babington Macaulay is there, for example, with his rather startling description of the "English Bible" as "a book which, if everything else in our language should perish, would alone suffice to show the whole extent of its beauty and power."[3] So too is William Ewart Gladstone, who believed that, "amid the crowds of the court, or the forum, or the street, or the market-place," the "still small voice of the Holy Bible will be heard, and the soul, aided by some blessed word, may find wings like a dove, may flee away and be at rest."[4]

The aural metaphor is significant, as Victorian writers and Bible commentators often described the KJB in terms of familiar and much loved "music." Equally significant is the tendency towards rhapsodic idealization of the KJB in these two passages. As David Norton has suggested, "'AVolatry' (in preference to 'KJBolatry') has been rife since the 1760s."[5] Norton's own selection of Victorian celebrations of the KJB includes Richard Chenevix Trench's reflections on the "golden mean" of its language and the *via media* of Anglicanism,[6] and Thomas Huxley's famous statement, in his study on the school boards, about the KJB's historical and thus educational significance:

consider the great historical fact that, for three centuries, this book has been woven into the life of all that is best and noblest in English history;

that it has become the national epic of Britain, and is as familiar to noble and simple, from John-o'Groat's House to Land's End, as Dante and Tasso once were to the Italians; that it is written in the noblest and purest English, and abounds in exquisite beauties of mere literary form; and, finally, that it forbids the veriest hind who never left his village to be ignorant of the existence of other countries and other civilisations, and of a great past, stretching back to the furthest limits of the oldest nations in the world. By the study of what other book could children be so much humanised ... ?[7]

Huxley the agnostic does not touch upon what contemporaries such as Dickens, Tennyson, Browning, Christina Rossetti, and Ruskin regarded as the transcendent qualities of the KJB. At the same time, these literary figures were also acutely aware of the impact upon Bible study of the Higher Criticism, and of problems of translation. Similarly, the artists whose work adorned Victorian family Bibles and public galleries held in tension a sense of the mystical which characterizes "sacred art" with the demands of historical and "scientific" authenticity, as the archaeologists and the early photographers revealed how things really looked in the Holy Land. Take, for example, the Aberdonian painter, William Dyce, who went to great lengths to get the local detail right in *St. John Leading the Blessed Virgin Mary from the Tomb* (Illustration 4), exhibited at the Royal Academy in 1860. The dark cactus on the left (*agave americana*) points towards the site of the crucifixion and reinforces the message of the crown of thorns carried by Mary. The same plant is represented in Dyce's *Christ and the Woman of Samaria* (Illustration 5), painted at about the same time, but here both it and the period clothing of the two figures are held in tension with the British landscape in which the encounter is set. Thus Dyce tries to convey in one painting a sense of both the historical Jesus and the immanent Christ – "Christ with us."

AVolatry was far from universal. The historian Henry Hallam, for example, pointed out that the language of the KJB is "not the language of the reign of James I": "It abounds, in fact, especially in the Old Testament, with obsolete phraseology, and with single words long since abandoned, or retained only in provincial use."[8] Biblical scholars frequently referred to shortcomings in the translation from Hebrew or Greek. The great Joseph Barber Lightfoot, for example, wrote on John 4.27 ("And

Illustration 4 William Dyce, *St. John Leading the Blessed Virgin Mary from the Tomb.*

Illustration 5 William Dyce, *Christ and the Woman of Samaria.*

upon this came his disciples, and marvelled that he talked with the woman"):

Here again an error in the English version obscures the sense. Their marvel was, not that He talked with *the* woman, but that He talked with *a* woman. It was a rabbinical maxim, "Let no man talk with a woman in the street (in public), no, not with his own wife."[9]

Farrar argued in *Eternal Hope* (1878) that three words in the KJB which were frequently cited by those who preached the "popular teachings about hell" – "damnation," "hell," and "everlasting" – were "inadequate or erroneous or disputed renderings," and should be changed.[10] Tennyson agreed, and was disappointed late in life when the Revised Version failed to substitute a word like "aeonian" for "everlasting" in Matthew 25.41, as he "never would believe that Christ could preach 'everlasting punishment.' "[11]

Meanwhile new biblical scholarship, following exciting archaeological discoveries in the Holy Land, produced new editions – such as Henry Alford's Greek New Testament (1849–61), a photographic facsimile of the Codex Alexandrinus (1879–83) and Westcott and Hort's New Testament (1881) – and new translations, including the Revised Version (New Testament, 1881; Old Testament, 1885; Apocrypha, 1895). Yet those who produced the Revised Version, which proved to be something of a flop, were instructed to stick as closely as possible to the KJB.[12] Earlier, in 1857, five clergymen of the Church of England published their own translation of the fourth gospel, "after the Authorized Version." The preface, to which all five contributors subscribed, summarized the dilemma in which those who loved the KJB, but who were aware of its limitations and looked for a new translation, found themselves. Some, they wrote, had "experienced much anxiety lest the well known diction, the grave authority, and the general acceptance of the existing Version of the Holy Scriptures were about to receive a shock which would seriously endanger the cause of sound religion in our Church and Nation."[13] The aim of these translators was to exhibit "the actual meaning of the Inspired Word of God" *and* to show that the Authorized Version "is indeed a precious and holy possession, and that the errors of it are very slight and few in comparison of its many and great excellences."[14] It would be "serious and fatal," they thought, to lose "the deep-rooted affection, and earnest confidence of the people in that

'English Bible' which has been the guide and comfort of their Christian life from their childhood upwards."[15]

It was this comfortable familiarity with the KJB that made it possible for Victorian writers to develop a complex art of allusion. As readers of fiction and poetry, rich and poor, but mainly middle-class, knew their KJB, writers could make creative use of biblical allusions, not merely as decoration or to add a touch of pietism, but as important thematic and structural references to the richest intertext of them all. The Victorian novel, for example, uses narrative techniques which owe something to scriptural and confessional forms of narrative, whether spiritual autobiographies or testimonies, tracts or sermons, histories or letters.[16]

One of the most enthusiastic endorsements of the KJB as the corner-stone of the shared culture of Victorian England came from an unlikely witness. In a passage from his life of St. Francis, Frederick Faber, convert Catholic and head of the London Oratory, waxed lyrical on what he called the "uncommon beauty and marvellous English of the Protestant Bible":

It lives on in the ear like a music that never can be forgotten, like the sound of church bells which the convert hardly knows how he can forego. Its felicities seem often to be things rather than mere words. It is part of the national mind and the anchor of the national seriousness. Nay, it is worshipped with a positive idolatry ... The memory of the dead passes into it. The potent traditions of childhood are stereotyped in its verses. The power of all the griefs and trials of a man is hidden beneath its words. It is the representative of his best moments ... It is his sacred thing which doubt never dimmed and controversy never soiled.[17]

Faber's enthusiasm was matched by a writer who began his adult life as an Evangelical who was hostile towards Roman Catholicism and ended it having achieved some kind of rapprochement with the old religion: John Ruskin.

In *The Bible of Amiens* (1880–5), Ruskin, then in his early sixties, reflected upon the importance of St. Jerome's fourth-century translation of most of the Bible into Latin from the original tongues – work which formed the bulk of the Vulgate from the sixth century ownwards. Ruskin writes, "the severity of the Latin language was softened, like Venetian crystal, by the variable fire of Hebrew thought; and the 'Book of Books' took the abiding form of which all the future art of the Western nations was to be an hourly enlarging interpretation" (*Works*, vol. 33, 109–10);

all the future *art* – painting (Giotto, Tintoretto, Holman Hunt) and architecture (St. Mark's, Amiens Cathedral) – as interpretation. *Hourly* interpretation has an autobiographical ring to it, suggestive of those extraordinary notebooks of Ruskin's, most of which are now housed in the Ruskin Library at Lancaster University, containing diary entries, outlines of essays, sermons and books, memoranda, measurements of buildings (especially Venetian), and biblical commentaries – this last, still an area ripe for research.

Ruskin himself was an "hourly interpreter" of the Bible, who echoed in his own work the chiming resonances of his earliest and most influential intertext, the KJB. Famous as an art critic who taught his readers how to see, Ruskin seized and held their attention through the sound of his rolling periods; and those periods were underpinned by the rhythms and cadences of the KJB, as we will see later.

In *Præterita* (1885–9), the fragmentary autobiography written at the end of his writing career, he recorded his gratitude to his mother for the lessons, continued until he was fourteen, which had made every word of the "Scriptures" familiar to his ear "in habitual music, – yet in that familiarity reverenced, as transcending all thought, and ordaining all conduct" (*Works*, vol. 35, 40, 189). He learned the whole of 1 Kings 8 and Deuteronomy 32 by heart, for example, and, as he noted in *Præterita*, "the lower corners of the pages" of his oldest Bible in use were "worn somewhat thin and dark" at these chapters as a result, the learning of Solomon's prayer at the dedication of the temple – a passage also loved by other Evangelicals – and the last song of Moses having cost him "much pains" (*Works*, vol. 35, 42). (Significantly, he also learned four chapters from Proverbs and Psalm 32 – part of the wisdom tradition of the Old Testament.[18]) It would also have been at his mother's instigation that Ruskin, in his own words in *Præterita* (*Works*, vol. 35, 490), "received" his religion from Bunyan and from Isaac Ambrose, the Puritan divine whose most popular work was entitled *Looking unto Jesus* (1658).[19]

At his Evangelical mother's knee, Ruskin naturally became a "Bible Christian," in the sense that he turned to "Scripture" (capital S) as his prime authority. He wrote to Thomas Dale in 1841: "Scripture of course must be the ultimate appeal … our fellows are departing every instant into eternal pain" (*Works*, vol. 1, 395–7). Ruskin's hourly interpretation of the KJB was a matter of (eternal) life and death.[20]

Ruskin went on to say that, while the music of the Bible was habitual, it was also "reverenced" as "ordaining all conduct." As I have suggested, the KJB conveyed a seriousness and a high moral purpose which Victorian culture embraced and made its own. But Ruskin also stated that the English Bible was reverenced as "transcending all thought," implying that the language of the KJB points beyond this earthly life to the sublime mysteries of the heavenly and divine life. It was for this ability to convey both the natural and the supernatural that the KJB was venerated by Ruskin and his contemporaries.

Evidence from the unpublished material in his diary notebooks indicates that in the late 1840s he was turning to Thomas Scott's famous Bible commentary (1788–92) for explanatory notes on texts that he was studying, as other leading Victorians as varied as Cardinal Newman and Bishop Colenso did in their younger days.[21] Scott, a Calvinist, argues in his preface that the "Bible alone, and such books as make it their basis, introduce the infinite God speaking in a manner worthy of himself, with simplicity, majesty, and authority."[22]

Ruskin's approach to his habitual and formative Sunday reading and study, often written up in the diaries, was not dissimilar to Scott's, again described in the preface to his commentary:

The Author having, for many years, made the Bible his daily and principal study; and having bestowed great pains to *satisfy his own mind*, as to the meaning of most parts of Scripture, and the *practical use which should be made of them*; and supposing also that his talent chiefly lies, in speaking plainly and intelligibly to persons of ordinary capacity and information; he adopts this method of communicating his views of divine truth, in connexion with the Scriptures themselves, from which he has *deduced them*. (My emphases)

Working in a similar way, Ruskin's habit was to read the Bible largely unaided by earlier commentaries and to arrive at conclusions only after careful analysis, in the same way that his youthful studies in geology, architecture, and painting were based upon patient and careful observation. His instinct was to investigate primary source material in all these domains. Towards the end of his career Ruskin was "entirely disposed to concur" with Mazzini's comment that he had "the most analytic mind in Europe" (*Works*, vol. 35, 44).

Much as these intellectual qualities were appreciated by his huge reading public, both in Britain and in America, it was his facility as a writer of vibrant descriptive prose that captivated them in the first place, rather as it was the sound of the KJB that worked its special magic upon those who heard it read aloud in church and chapel, and at family prayers in the home. In one of the great set pieces in the first volume of *Modern Painters* (1843), the controversial work with which Ruskin burst onto the literary scene at the age of 24, he presents Turner as a messenger of God (a position from which he later had to retreat). His description of the light that follows the dawn on an isolated mountain draws upon "literary" hymns of the Romantic period which would have been familiar to his first readers, and which were themselves underpinned by the language of the KJB:

Wait yet for one hour, until the east again becomes purple, and the heaving mountains, rolling against it in darkness, like waves of a wild sea, are drowned one by one in the glory of its burning: watch the white glaciers blaze in their winding paths about the mountains, like mighty serpents with scales of fire: watch the columnar peaks of solitary snow, kindling downwards, chasm by chasm, each in itself a new morning; their long avalanches cast down in keen streams brighter than the lightning, sending each his tribute of driven snow, like altar-smoke, up to the heaven; the rose-light of the silent domes flushing that heaven about them and above them, piercing with purer light through its purple lines of lifted cloud, casting a new glory on every wreath as it passes by, until the whole heaven, one scarlet canopy, is interwoven with a roof of waving flame, and tossing, vault beyond vault, as with the drifted wings of many companies of angels: and then, when you can look no more for gladness, and when you are bowed down with fear and love of the Maker and Doer of this, tell me who has best delivered this His message unto men! (*Works*, vol. 3, 418–19)

Four famous hymns written between 1826 and 1834 are present in Ruskin's own hymn of praise. "*New* every *morning* is the love," by John Keble; "Praise, my soul, the King of Heaven, / To His feet thy *tribute* bring," by Henry Francis Lyte; "O worship the King All-glorious above … Whose robe is the light, Whose *canopy* space," by Sir Robert Grant; and "Holy, Holy, Holy! Lord God Almighty!" by Bishop Heber:

> Holy, Holy, Holy! all the Saints adore Thee,
> *Casting down* their golden crowns around the glassy sea;
> Cherubim and Seraphim *falling down* before Thee,
> Which wert, and art, and evermore shalt be.[23]

Heber's morning hymn, for example, is based on Revelation 4 in the KJB, in which the throne of God is described and which ends, "Thou art worthy, O Lord, to receive glory and honour and power: for thou hast created all things, and for thy pleasure they are and were created." Some of Grant's key words – "power," "splendour," "girded," "robe," as well as "canopy" – are also Ruskin's (*Works*, vol. 3, 93, 287, 469, 416), and Grant's last verse, ending, "And sweetly distils in the dew and the rain," would have made a fitting epigraph for Ruskin's chapter on the rain-cloud.

In this Alpine Benedicite, Ruskin describes the mountains in terms of the tabernacle and the temple. Thirteen years later, in the fourth volume of *Modern Painters*, sub-titled "Of mountain beauty," he treats the workings of the God of wisdom, truth, and love more directly and prophetically. The KJB is cited more directly, too, as he explores the idea of God's beneficence in protecting the world that he has created through the heat shield of the encircling firmament:

This, I believe, is the ordinance of the firmament; and it seems to me that in the midst of the material nearness of these heavens God means us to acknowledge His own immediate presence as visiting, judging, and blessing us. "The earth shook, the heavens also dropped, at the presence of God." [Ps. 68:8] "He doth set His bow in the cloud," [Gen. 9:13] and thus renews, in the sound of every drooping swathe of rain, His promises of everlasting love. "In them hath He set a *tabernacle* for the sun;" [Ps. 19:4] whose burning ball, which without the firmament would be seen but as an intolerable and scorching circle in the blackness of vacuity, is by that firmament surrounded with gorgeous service, and tempered by mediatorial ministries; by the firmament of clouds the golden pavement is spread for his chariot wheels at morning; by the firmament of clouds the temple is built for his presence to fill with light at noon; by the firmament of clouds the purple veil is closed at evening round the sanctuary of his rest; by the mists of the firmament his implacable light is divided, and its separated fierceness appeased into the soft blue that fills the depth of distance with its bloom, and the flush with which the mountains burn as they drink the overflowing of the dayspring. And in this tabernacling of the unendurable sun with men, through the shadows of the firmament, God would seem to set forth the stooping of His own majesty to men, upon the *throne* of the firmament. As the Creator of all the worlds, and the Inhabiter of eternity, we cannot behold Him; but, as the Judge of the earth and the Preserver of men, those heavens are indeed His dwelling-place. "Swear not, neither by heaven, for it is God's throne; nor by the earth, for it is His footstool." [Matt. 5:34–5] And all those passings to and fro of fruitful shower and grateful shade, and all those visions of silver palaces built about the horizon, and voices of moaning winds and threatening thunders, and glories of coloured robe and cloven ray, are but to deepen in our hearts the acceptance, and distinctness, and dearness of the simple words, "Our Father, which art in heaven." [Matt. 6:9] (*Works*, vol. 6, 113–14)

Like the preachers at whose feet he sat in the churches of south London for the first forty years of his life, Ruskin exploits the rhetorical power of repetition ("by the …," "by the …"; "as the …," "as the …"; "and all …," "and all …"; "and … and … and") which they all learned from the KJB's translations from the Hebrew in the Old Testament, ranging from the description of the crossing of the Red Sea in Exodus 14, with its repeated "chariots and horsemen," to the seventh chapter of the Song of Solomon, in praise of "thy feet," "thy thighs," "thy navel," "thy belly," "thy two breasts," "thy neck," "thine eyes," "thy nose," and so on.

If *Modern Painters* provides examples of Ruskin's oxygenated descriptive prose at its grandest and most expansive, the opening of the first volume of *The Stones of Venice* (1851), written between the two passages just quoted, is remarkable for its allusive compression, conveying a sense of prophetic urgency:

Since first the dominion of men was asserted over the ocean, three thrones, of mark beyond all others, have been set upon its sands: the thrones of Tyre, Venice, and England. Of the First of these great powers only the memory remains; of the Second, the ruin; the Third, which inherits their greatness, if it forget their example, may be led through prouder eminence to less pitied destruction. (*Works*, vol. 9, 17)

What distinguishes this passage from eighteenth-century "ruin sentiment" is the rhetorical power, prepared for in the pseudo-biblical grandeur of the opening clause, which is derived from Ruskin's use of familiar words and phrases from the KJB: "three thrones" ("and behold, a throne was set in heaven" [Rev. 4:2]); "set upon its sands" ("a foolish man, which built his house upon the sand" [Matt. 7:26]); "Tyre … ruin … destruction" ("Thy riches … shall fall into the midst of the seas in the day of thy ruin," "What city is like Tyrus, like the destroyed in the midst of the sea?" [Ezek. 27:27, 32]). The passage sits at the entrance to a work that is to Protestantize Venice and is to describe St. Mark's – to English eyes an alien structure, Byzantine in style and Catholic in religion – as a "Book-Temple" and a "glorious Bible," dominated by the Cross (*Works*, vol. 10, 141, 82–3, 88).

By 1860 Ruskin had cut his ties with formal Evangelicalism, completed the five volumes of *Modern Painters* and decided upon a new direction for his writing. He no longer wanted to enchant his readers with his heavenly sentence structure, but to teach them how to live and work and have their being. If anything, his grip now tightened upon what we might call the "social gospel," which was prefigured in the wisdom books of the Old Testament. In his controversial economic essays entitled *Unto This Last* (1860), for example, he cast himself in the characteristic prophetic role of a man out of tune with his times, as he took on the role I described in *Ruskin's God* as that of a "Victorian Solomon." Here he is on King Solomon's teaching, or the "Jew merchant's maxims," as he writes, tongue-in-cheek, with that ironic edge that was to characterize his public lectures and, later, *Fors Clavigera*:

Some centuries before the Christian era, a Jew merchant, largely engaged in business on the Gold Coast, and reported to have made one of the largest fortunes of his time (held also in repute for much practical sagacity), left among his ledgers some general maxims concerning wealth, which have been preserved, strangely enough, even to our own days. (*Works*, vol. 17, 57)

From the political economist's perpective, Solomon's Proverbs are secondary to his reputation as a wealth creator: his wisdom is mentioned parenthetically, and his teaching is said to be "left among his ledgers." The reference has the effect of "making strange" Solomon's prophetic teaching in the modern world, in which that teaching had "fallen into disrepute."

Nevertheless, Ruskin intended to "reproduce a passage or two from them," which he promptly did:

He says, for instance, in one place: "The getting of treasures by a lying tongue is a vanity tossed to and fro of them that seek death" [Prov. 21:6]; adding in another, with the same meaning (he has a curious way of doubling his sayings): "Treasures of wickedness profit nothing: but justice delivers from death" [Prov. 10:2] …

Again: the merchant says, "He that oppresseth the poor to increase his riches, shall surely come to want" [Prov. 22:16]. And again, more strongly: "Rob not the poor because he is poor; neither oppress the afflicted in the place of business. For God shall spoil the soul of those that spoiled them" [Prov. 22:22]. (*Works*, vol. 17, 57–8)

At a time of religious turmoil for Ruskin and his contemporaries, in the year of *Essays and Reviews* and only a year after Darwin's *Origin of Species*, these biblical quotations carry all the more weight for being from the KJB, the familiar words of which resonated for writer and readers alike from the days of their spiritual formation.

The title of *Unto This Last* is, of course, taken from the parable of the vineyard, in which the laborers who have been working all day in the hot sun complain when a recent arrival is paid the same as themselves, and the owner responds by saying: "I will give unto this last, even as unto thee" (Matt. 20:14). As in his earlier published works, Ruskin drew out the eschatological meaning of what he had been saying in the closing paragraph of the final essay, imitating the way in which Victorian preachers often ended their sermons:

Raise the veil boldly; face the light; and if, as yet, the light of the eye can only be through tears, and the light of the body [Matt. 6:22] through sackcloth, go thou forth weeping, bearing precious seed [Ps. 126:6], until the time come, and the kingdom, when Christ's gift of bread [John 6:35], and bequest of peace [John 14:27], shall be "Unto this last as unto thee" [Matt. 20:14]; and when, for earth's severed multitudes of the wicked and the weary, there shall be holier reconciliation than that of the narrow home, and calm economy, where the Wicked cease – not from trouble, but from troubling – and the Weary are at rest [Job 3:17]. (*Works*, vol. 17, 114)

To say that Ruskin's prose is steeped in the KJB is no exaggeration, when we have passages like this before us; and this remained true throughout his life. Two other developments in his work after 1860 should be mentioned, however. First, there is a movement from text to artifact, from the black-backed Bible of the early nineteenth-century Evangelicals – heirs to the Reformers – to the illuminated "Bible" that was the medieval cathedral, a movement which, as it were, reverses that of ecclesiastical history and helps to explain Ruskin's self-description in later years as a "Catholic of the

Creeds" (*Works*, vol. 29, 92). Second, the biblical resonances of the earlier work often gave way later to the chopped phrases of Ruskin's own translations from the Greek New Testament, through which he confronted the English Protestant reader with the radical message of the gospel, which for him says more about money and our use of it than either Victorian Churchman or capitalist found comfortable.

From the 1850s onwards, Ruskin's private notes on his Bible reading reflect his close study of the Greek New Testament.[24] They also record his objections to the methods of the KJB translators, and especially their failure to render the same word by the same equivalent (*Works*, vol. 27, xxxxvi). Such reservations emerged in the published writings, particularly after the death of his father, John James Ruskin, in 1864, with whom he had discussed sensitive religious "difficulties" for many years. In the first "Christmas letter" of *Fors Clavigera*, for example, published on December 23, 1871, Ruskin challenged his readers to review their easy assumptions about the truth embodied in the nativity narrative in Luke's gospel. His manner is that of a challenging preacher: "What, then, let me ask you, is its truth to *you*?" (*Works*, vol. 27, 201). He then takes his readers slowly through some of the key verses, using his own translations. These verses include Luke 2:9 (καὶ ἄγγελος κυρίου ἐπέστη αὐτοῖς καὶ δόξα κυρίου περιέλαμψεν αὐτούς, καὶ ἐφοβήθησαν φόβον μέγαν;[25] "And, lo, the angel of the Lord came upon them, and the glory of the Lord shone round about them: and they were sore afraid"):

> "And behold, the Messenger of the Lord stood above them, and the glory of the Lord lightened round them, and they feared a great fear."
>
> "Messenger." You must remember that, when this was written, the word "angel" had only the effect of our word – "messenger" – on men's minds. Our translators say "angel" when they like, and "messenger" when they like; but the Bible, messenger only, or angel only, as you please. (*Works*, vol. 27, 202)

Fors, Ruskin's most humorous work, includes passages in which the joke works better because it touches upon what his more pious Victorian readers would have called "sacred" subjects. Take, for example, the second section of Letter 27, "Christ's lodgings" (March 1873), in which the informality of the epistolary form allows him to have some fun at the expense of the clergy, and thereby startle his readers into new lines of thought. His text is from that part of the farewell discourses in which Jesus reassures his disciples about the place that he is going to prepare for them (ἐν τῇ οἰκίᾳ τοῦ πατρός μου μοναὶ πολλαί εἰσιν [John 14:2]; "In my Father's house are many mansions"):

> If ever your clergy mean really to help you to read your Bible, – the whole of it, and not merely the bits which tell you that you are miserable sinners, and that you needn't mind, – they must make a translation retaining as many as possible of the words in their Greek form, which you may easily learn, and yet which will be quit of the danger of becoming debased by any vulgar English use. So also, the same word must always be given when it *is* the same; and not in one place translated "mansion," and in another "abode." (Compare verse 23 of this same chapter.*) Not but that "mansion" is a very fine Latin word, and perfectly correct, (if only one knows Latin), but I doubt not that most parish children understand by it, if anything, a splendid house with two wings, and an acre or two of offices, in the middle of a celestial park; and suppose that some day or other they are all of them to live in such, as well as the Squire's children; whereas, if either "mona" or "remaining" were put in both verses, it is just possible that sometimes both the Squire and the children, instead of vaguely hoping to be lodged some day in heaven by Christ and His Father, might take notice of their offer in the last verse I have quoted, and get ready a spare room both in the mansion and cottage, and offer Christ and His Father immediately, if they liked to come into lodgings on earth.
>
> * "If a man love me, he will keep my words: and my Father will love him, and we will come unto him, and make our abode with him." [KJB] Our mona, – as in the 2nd verse (John xiv.).
>
> (*Works*, vol. 27, 490)

The fault is not the Jacobean translators', for whom "mansions" meant "abodes" (or "dwelling-places," as modern translations have it), but the Victorian clergy's, who were not teaching the true meaning of the Greek, both literally and analogically.

The transition in Ruskin's own theology, from an early Evangelical emphasis upon the atonement and salvation by faith alone to a "Catholic" emphasis upon the incarnation and salvation by works, was effected partly through his close reading of the Greek New Testament. This in turn drew his attention to the limitations of the "English Bible" as a translation for his generation. The sense of limitation, however, was combined in Ruskin with a deep love for the "habitual music" of the KJB which he shared with his contemporaries. There was a tension between aesthetic considerations associated with the spiritual nourishment provided by traditional language and the need for accuracy in the light of new historical research. This tension in the responses of Ruskin and the Victorians to the glories and challenges of the KJB anticipated the heated debates of the twentieth century and the resultant modern translations that have now displaced the KJB in both church and study. Whereas in 1811 the KJB was considered to be "the (authorized) word of God," in 2011 it is regarded as "the literary Bible."

NOTES

1 On Victorian reading habits, see Richard Daniel Altick, *The English Common Reader: A Social History of the Mass Reading Public, 1800–1900* (1957; rpt. Chicago and London: Phoenix/University of Chicago Press, 1963).

2 *Præterita*, ch. 2: *The Works of John Ruskin*, ed. Edward Tyas Cook and Alexander Wedderburn, Library edn., 39 vols. (London and New York: Allen/Longmans, Green, 1903–12), vol. 35, 40. See also my further discussion of this phrase, below. Further references to the Library edition are given in the text.

3 Frederic William Farrar, *The Bible: Its Meaning and Supremacy*, 2nd edn. (London: Longmans, Green, 1901), 259. The passage is taken from Macaulay's essay on Dryden (1828).

4 *Ibid.*, 266.

5 David Norton, *A History of the Bible as Literature*, 2 vols. (Cambridge: Cambridge University Press, 1993), vol. 2, 176.

6 *Ibid.*, vol. 2, 184.

7 *Ibid.*, vol. 2, 188.

8 *Introduction to the Literature of Europe in the Fifteenth, Sixteenth, and Seventeenth Centuries* (1837–9), cited in Norton, *A History* (1993), vol. 2, 177.

9 *Biblical Essays* (London and New York, 1893), 35.

10 See Frederic William Farrar, *Eternal Hope* (London and New York: Macmillan, 1904), 77 (1st edn. 1878). Trench and F. D. Maurice had presented similar arguments in the 1850s.

11 Hallam Tennyson, *Alfred Lord Tennyson: A Memoir* (Macmillan, 1899), 270 (1st edn. 1897). The RV gives "eternal."

12 See Samuel Hemphill, *A History of the Revised Version of the New Testament* (London: Stock, 1906).

13 John Barrow, *et al.*, *The Gospel According to St. John, after the Authorized Version, newly compared with the original Greek and revised by five clergymen* [John Barrow, George Moberly, Henry Alford, William Gilson Humphry, Charles John Ellicott, ed. Ernest Hawkins] (London: Parker, 1857), i.

14 *Ibid.*, ii.

15 *Ibid.*, iii.

16 See Michael Wheeler, *The Art of Allusion in Victorian Fiction* (London and Basingstoke: Macmillan, 1979).

17 *The Life of St. Francis of Assisi* (1853), 116–17; cited in Norton, *A History* (1993), vol. 2, 183.

18 The subjects of the chapters which Ruskin claims in *Præterita* to have learnt by heart and to have "established [his] soul in life" are as follows: Exod. 15 and 20 (Moses' song after crossing the Red Sea; the Ten Commandments); 2 Sam. 1:17 – end (David's lament over Saul and Jonathan); 1 Kings 8 (Solomon's prayer at the dedication of the temple); Pss. 23 ("The Lord is my shepherd"), 32 ("Blessed is he whose trangression is forgiven"), 90 ("Lord, thou hast been our dwelling place"), 91 ("He that dwelleth in the secret place"), 103 ("Bless the Lord, O my soul"), 112 ("Praise ye the Lord"), 119 ("Blessed are the undefiled"), 139 ("O Lord, thou hast searched me"); Prov. 2, 3, 8, 12 (the benefits of obedience and wisdom); Isaiah 58 (the benefaction of true godliness); Matt. 5, 6, 7 (the Sermon on the Mount); Acts 26 (Paul tells the story of his conversion to Agrippa); 1 Cor. 13, 15 (on "charity" and on the resurrection of the dead); James 4 (on sanctification and judgment); Rev. 5, 6 (the book sealed with seven seals, the four horses, the opening of the sixth seal). Ruskin also had the versified Scottish paraphrases of the Bible to learn (35.41). He continued to learn Bible passages until middle age.

19 For a discussion of Ruskin's religion, and of the particular significance of the wisdom tradition in his life and work, see Wheeler, *Ruskin's God* (Cambridge: Cambridge University Press, 1999).

20 Later in life he wrote disparagingly in *Fors Clavigera* (May 1874) of "evangelical self-worship and hell-worship" (*Works*, vol. 28, 82).

21 See Lancaster MS 5c, Diaries, fol. 94, where Ruskin casually quotes Scott on Matthew 5.3 in his notes; cf. Wheeler, *Ruskin's God*, 18.

22 *The Holy Bible*, with explanatory notes, practical observations, and copious marginal references by Thomas Scott, 9th edn., 6 vols. (London: Seeley, 1825), vol. 1, Preface (n.p.).

23 See *Hymns Ancient and Modern, for Use in the Services of the Church*, standard edn. (London: Clowes, 1916), nos. 4, 298, 167, 160.

24 See, e.g., Lancaster MS 9, Diaries, fol. 38. Ruskin also cites the Vulgate in the 1850s: see, e.g., Lancaster MS 11, Diaries, fols. 30, 32. See also his marginalia in his medieval gospel lectionary in Greek (British Library), which Zoe Bennett discusses in her forthcoming article on Ruskin in *The Oxford Handbook of the Reception History of the Bible*, ed. Michael Lieb, Emma Mason, Jonathan Roberts, and Christopher Rowland (Oxford: Oxford University Press). Ruskin

had studied Greek since boyhood, but did not build upon the little Hebrew that he once learned.

25 Quotations from the Greek are taken from *The New International Version Interlinear Greek–English New Testament: The Nestle Greek Text with the Literal English Translation*, ed. Alfred Marshall (Grand Rapids, MI: Zondervan, 1976).

12 | *To the Lighthouse* and biblical language

JAMES WOOD

The Rainbow (1915) and *To the Lighthouse* (1927) are the most religious of modern secular English novels. But whereas D. H. Lawrence expressly mobilizes a host of biblical motifs (Creation, Eden, the Flood, Resurrection, the Trinity), Virginia Woolf's novel is stealthily biblical, and its visionary power all the stronger for the submersion and ghostliness of its biblical allusions.

Perhaps the central question of *To the Lighthouse* is "what will endure"? In different ways, the Ramsay family, along with various guests, ponder again and again the hopes and anxieties of one of the greatest of the Psalms, 90, the text that most canonically measures man's limited lease on life ("threescore years and ten") against God's cosmic tenure ("For a thousand years in thy sight are but as yesterday when it is past, and as a watch in the night"):

So teach us to number our days …

Make us glad according to the days wherein thou hast afflicted us, and the years wherein we have seen evil.

Let thy work appear unto thy servants, and thy glory unto their children.

And let the beauty of the Lord our God be upon us: and establish thou the work of our hands upon us; yea, the work of our hands establish thou it.
(Ps. 90:12, 15–17)

For the Psalmist, there is God's massive work, and there is our smaller work ("the work of our hands"), and an abiding hope that though our lives are as transient as the grass that grows up only to be cut down in the evening, our children might extend, through succession, our limited lease on the world; perhaps – this is very much Woolf's question, but only more mildly implicit in Psalm 90 – our children *are* our best work?

The Ramsays and their friends have decamped for the summer to a house on the Isle of Skye. Mr. Ramsay, a fierce and melodramatic patriarch, is a thinker much concerned, in his most self-pitying moments, with whether his intellectual work will "last." He is a brilliant philosopher, but not, perhaps, a genius. At times, he fears that he would have done greater work if he had not married; but elsewhere in the book he thinks that his eight children represent "a good bit of work," and perhaps his real achievement.[1] For his wife, Mrs. Ramsay, what will endure is not scholarly or creative work, but the instinctively biological work of her gender: children, the adroit arrangement of remembered moments (a dinner party, a beautiful day at the beach), a house that one might pass on to future generations: the work of our hands.

The novel is arranged in three sections: the first, "The Window," takes place in an unnamed summer, which can be assumed to be shortly before the outbreak of the First World War. The second, "Time Passes," narrates what happens to the summer house during and just after the war, when it is abandoned, neglected, and then restored. In the course of this section, we learn that houses and humans may not endure: Mrs. Ramsay dies, as do her children Andrew (killed on the battlefield in France) and Prue (who dies in childbirth). The third section, "The Lighthouse," describes the return to Skye, ten years after the first section, of some of the original characters: Mr. Ramsay, older and even more self-pitying in his grief than he had been in marriage; two of Mr. Ramsay's surviving children, James and Cam, now teenagers; Augustus Carmichael, a *fin-de-siècle* poet whose fame was briefly revived during the War; and Lily Briscoe, a painter.

It is the novel's third major character, Lily Briscoe, who is Woolf's deliberately complicated bridge between the two extremities of gender embodied by Mr. and Mrs. Ramsay. Childless, unmarried, she cannot compete, and perhaps has no real wish to, with Mrs. Ramsay's superb fertility; but she also confesses to Mr. Ramsay's son, Andrew, that she has no idea what Mr. Ramsay works on. Yet Lily Briscoe is a painter, a creator, and is thus not immune to the kinds of "male" anxieties that persecute Mr. Ramsay – will her paintings turn out to be unimportant, trivial, will they be rolled up and stored, unseen, in an attic? Or will she, as an artist, "make of the moment something permanent," as Mrs. Ramsay, in her different way, made something permanent (161)? The question of endurance has a particular urgency for Lily, because she spends the third part of the novel painting a tribute to the late Mrs. Ramsay, in what turns out to be a long, intense elegy. She thus necessarily reflects, as does the novel, on what

Mrs. Ramsay (and, by implication, all women who produce children, but not books or paintings or scientific discoveries) leaves behind her: "What was the spirit in her, the essential thing, by which, had you found a crumpled glove in the corner of a sofa, you would have known it, from its twisted finger, hers indisputably?" (49).

The novel, then, circles around what could be called a hard war and a soft war – the First World War, which shadows the second and third parts of the book, and the softer war of the struggle between men and women, between rival ways of seeing the world, and ultimately between philosophy and art. Mr. Ramsay is a rather glamorous epistemologist; he works on "subject and object and the nature of reality," as his son, Andrew tells Lily. In this intensely autobiographical book, we might rightly think of Mr. Ramsay as a novelized version of Woolf's demanding father, Sir Leslie Stephen, a distinguished Victorian man of letters; but we might also think of Bertrand Russell, and the philosophical atmosphere of Cambridge just before and after the war, familiar to Woolf through friends and family connections, when Russell could report of Wittgenstein, with amused exasperation, "he thinks nothing empirical is knowable – I asked him to admit there was not a rhinoceros in the room, but he wouldn't."

On the Isle of Skye, the men deal in knowability; they are scientists of reality. In addition to Mr. Ramsay, the house party includes one of Ramsay's students, Charles Tansley, an atheist, and Mr. Bankes, a zoologist. When Lily says that she has no idea what it is that Mr. Ramsay works on, Andrew Ramsay, handed a familiar ticket of female helplessness, obliges with familiar male superiority: "Think of a kitchen table … when you're not there" (23). The women, it is assumed, will confine themselves to matters of family, domesticity, or less precise modes of knowledge than philosophy or politics or science, such as painting and reading.

Against this world of hard male rigor and confident renown, Mrs. Ramsay retaliates with a deliberate feminine airiness – a kind of verbal softening, in which the referent is deliberately removed: she mockingly thinks of Mr. Tansley's thesis as "the influence of something upon somebody"; she characterizes Mr. Ramsay's academic world as "who had won this, who had won that." This conversion of formal names and titles into vague "somethings" and "somebodys" is not a minor verbal parry; the word that probably appears more regularly than any other in the text is the word, or suffix, "thing." We have already encountered Mrs. Ramsay making "of the moment something permanent" and the "essential thing" that one might remember her by. There is also what Mrs. Ramsay thinks of as "the thing she had with her husband" (60). Elsewhere, looking at her parents, Prue Ramsay thinks, "That's my mother ... That is the thing itself, she felt ..." (116). At dinner, in the first section, Lily feels inclined to "pick out one particular thing; the thing that mattered; to detach it; separate it off" (112). In her painting, she longs to grasp "the thing itself before it has been made anything" (193). She characterizes her painting as her "attempt at something" (208).

This kind of female "vagueness" infuriates Mr. Ramsay: "He thought, women are always like that; the vagueness of their minds is hopeless ... They could not keep anything straight in their minds" (167). Lily Briscoe indeed concedes that Andrew supplied her with the image of a kitchen table because she had only a "vagueness as to what Mr. Ramsay did think about" (155). But the novel subversively reclaims the apparent failure of this female vagueness, and converts it into the very measure of artistic success. Perhaps to make a very serious – the most serious – "attempt at something" is to succeed by failing. (Woolf was herself very unsure of her novel's aesthetic success.) When Lily is finally able to complete her painting of Mrs. Ramsay, in section three, it is because she has a kind of vision of the ghost of Mrs. Ramsay: "Suddenly the window at which she was looking was whitened by some light stuff behind it" (201). "Some light stuff" is vague, in a way, as vague as "something"; and yet it is, for a painter, also absolutely palpable and exact: it is what a painter works with; it is paint itself.

You could say, indeed, that one difference between Woolf's artistic generation and the one that preceded it was the difference between the certainty of *things* and the uncertainty of *something*. Edwardian novelists like Wells and Bennett and Galsworthy seemed to have such easy relations with the known; reality, in the late-nineteenth-century naturalistic or realist tradition was full of inventoried things. Ford Madox Ford, Lawrence, Joyce, Katherine Mansfield, and Woolf felt that they had broken with such confidence. Woolf and Lawrence wanted to sharpen reality into the invisible, while the Edwardians blunted it by stubbing it into things – houses, income, furniture, clothes. Woolf was willing to risk what might look like failure: "Tolerate the spasmodic, the obscure, the fragmentary, the failure," she implored her readers, in her manifesto, "Character in Fiction."

Just as aesthetic vision will be willing to dare vagueness, so, in *To the Lighthouse*, religious vision is, here, a daringly vague "attempt at something." In the book's first section, Mrs. Ramsay returns often to an almost mystical desire to grasp the thing itself:

And pausing there she looked out to meet that stroke of the Lighthouse, the long steady stroke, the last of the three, which was her stroke, for watching them in this mood always at this hour one could not help attaching oneself to one thing especially of the things one saw; and this thing, the long, steady stroke, was her stroke. Often she found herself sitting and looking, sitting and looking, with her work in her hands until she became the thing she looked at – that light, for example. And it would lift up on it some little phrase or other which had been lying in her mind like that – "Children don't forget, children don't forget" – which she would repeat and begin adding to it, It will end, it will end, she said. It will come, it will come, when suddenly she added, We are in the hands of the Lord.

But instantly she was annoyed with herself for saying that. Who had said it? Not she; she had been trapped into saying something she did not mean. (63)

Forty pages later, in the great dinner party scene, Mrs. Ramsay again drifts into a visionary experience: she feels that there is something beyond language, something that "partook ... of eternity":

there is a coherence in things; a stability; something, she meant, is immune from change, and shines out (she glanced at the window with its ripple of reflected lights) in the face of the flowing, the fleeting, the spectral, like a ruby; so that again tonight she had the feeling she had had once today, already, of peace, of rest. Of such moments, she thought, the thing is made that endures. (105)

Notice that in both passages, "things" are explicitly not palpable – they are light, they are moments, they are words; but they are not what most of us think of as things. And in both passages, "thing" slips into the vaguer "something," and then back again to a now-renovated "thing" ("the thing is made that endures"). *Thing* has to take on the mystery, the vagueness, of *something* before it can become the thing that endures; thing has to be *made* into something.

What if Mrs. Ramsay's visionary optimism is religious? What if the "something that is immune from change" is God? As she flickers out of her mysticism (almost Buddhist in its selfless identification with the rhythms of the spiritual world), Mrs. Ramsay lands, for a second, in what sounds like traditional Christianity – "We are in the hands of the Lord." Just as quickly, she repudiates the thought; it was not she that said it. On the one hand, "We are in the hands of the Lord" thus takes its place in the novel with all the other flotsam of words, the bits of verse and prose, the mental and spoken thoughts, that float through the novel and jostle each other. As a phrase, as a piece of language, as a formal plea, "We are in the hands of the Lord" belongs aside Mr. Tansley's mean-spirited "Women can't paint, can't write," or Tennyson's "Someone had blundered," or the last line of the Grimm fairy tale that Mrs. Ramsay narrates to her son ("And they are living still at this very time"), or the lines spoken at dinner from "Luriana Lurilee":

> And all the lives we ever lived
> And all the lives to be
> Are full of trees and changing leaves   (119)

These phrases are all, in their different ways, relics; it is not clear that they will endure any longer than the summer house, or Mr. Ramsay's work, or Mr. and Mrs. Ramsay's children. The very island of Skye is, thinks Mr. Ramsay, "a spit of land which the sea is slowly eating away ... the sea eats away the ground we stand on" (44). Lily feels sad looking at the sea, because "distant views seemed to outlast by a million years ... the gazer and to be communing already with a sky which beholds an earth entirely at rest." This is the millennial temporality of God, alongside which empires and flags and wars and Victorian verse and obscure books of philosophy and unseen paintings, and even lives themselves ("all the lives we ever lived ... / Are full of trees and changing leaves") are but as yesterday that is past.[2]

Yet words persist, even if they do not endure forever, and many of the words that persist in *To the Lighthouse* are biblical words, some from the King James Bible (KJB), and others that are still identifiable as "biblical" or "religious," but which are of less precise provenance. One of the novel's central questions turns on what it means to continue to need or make use of a religious language whose content is no longer believed in. Words fail, thinks Lily in section three, as she sits and paints; they "flutter sideways" and miss the object, a familiar enough Romantic and Modernist confession (178). And of course, the failure of language is one of the premises of

Woolf's Modernist plea that we tolerate the spasmodic, the fragmentary, the failure. Nevertheless, insofar as the novel reclaims that failure as a kind of success – the risky glory of an "attempt at something" – it does not really believe that words fail; it believes that the confession that words fail signifies a kind of achievement. Indeed, it takes a certain confidence in words to press down as hard as Woolf does in this book on "thing" and "something." There is something undeniably successful about the vagueness of Mrs. Ramsay's mysticism, just as Lily can say, with some proper sense of triumph at the close of the novel, "I have had my vision."

However, the failure of the identifiably religious or biblical words that occur in the book seems to be of a different order. It is hard to make the case that the inability of "We are in the hands of the Lord" to mean anything to Mrs. Ramsay is some sign of perverse success, some kind of achieved negative theology. Mrs. Ramsay thinks the words, and then immediately disavows them; they represent, she thinks, "a lie":

What brought her to say that: We are in the hands of the Lord? She wondered. The insincerity slipping in among the truths roused her, annoyed her. She returned to her knitting again. How could any Lord have made this world, she asked. With her mind she had always seized the fact that there is no reason, order, justice, but suffering, death, the poor. (64)

Mrs. Ramsay here considers a familiar argument, from the annals of theodicy, for the likely non-existence of God: His existence is incompatible with the suffering world. It is a theme taken up in the novel's second section, "Time Passes." The cadences of this argument ("no reason, order, justice") are shadowed by Matthew Arnold's "Dover Beach," with its cry that the world "Hath really neither joy, nor love, nor light, / Nor certitude, nor peace, nor help for pain," itself perhaps a negative version of the great verse from Revelation 21:4, in which John foresees a new heaven and new earth in which "there shall be no more death, neither sorrow, nor crying, neither shall there be any more pain: for the former things are passed away."

But Mrs. Ramsay's question remains: "Who had said it?" When Mr. Ramsay declaims Tennyson, or Mr. Tansley complains that "women can't write, can't paint," we know who has spoken the words, or spoken and written them. But in the case of "We are in the hands of the Lord," the words *speak Mrs. Ramsay*, and if an unidentifiable voice says, "We are in the hands of the Lord," perhaps that voice is the Lord's? Why would one have need of the words, if the belief is a lie? Just as consoling poetry? But the phrase is not really poetry. There is a telling anxiety, here. The failure of secular words can be seen as a kind of aesthetic success, but the failure of religious words cannot be seen as a kind of religious success, since someone has "trapped" Mrs. Ramsay into invoking a lot of nonsense she doesn't believe in. Yet, the failure of these religious words *is* allowed to constitute some kind of *extra-religious visionary* success. And this extra-religious visionary success is necessarily shadowed by the formal religious belief and language that shaped it. For after all, wouldn't one definition of Mrs. Ramsay's certainty that there is a "coherence" that is somewhere immune from change be … God? Isn't this immunity from change just what the Psalmist is invoking – "a thousand years in thy sight are but as yesterday when it is past"? Mrs. Ramsay dislikes, in the passage I have quoted, "the insincerity slipping in among the truths," but which, precisely, are the truths in that passage, and which are the insincerities? The distinction is not at all clear, and when I read this novel I find myself unable to determine to what extent Virginia Woolf is lucidly presenting Mrs. Ramsay's necessary confusion, or to what extent this necessary confusion of truth and insincerity, of visionary truth and religious "lie," is Woolf's own.

The image of an insincerity slipping in among the truths might put us in mind of the extended description, in "Time Passes," of the "stray airs," "advance guards of great armies," that detach themselves from the body of the wind, and creep into the summer house while it is abandoned for years, during the Great War: "Almost one might imagine them," writes Woolf of those airs, "as they entered the drawing-room questioning and wondering, toying with the flap of hanging wall-paper, asking would it hang much longer, when would it fall?" (126). Sure enough, it is the "Time Passes" section in which we see the novel's language most violently haunted by distant airs, distant melodies or tunes, distant atmospheres; it is in this section that words and cadences from the Bible, and particularly the KJB, slip in among the truths – and slip in so comprehensively that one cannot easily say what is untrue and what is not.

"Time Passes" is a difficult, obscure, and somewhat overwrought piece of writing. It often sounds very different from the novel's two other sections. This distinctiveness has to do not only with the language's biblical saturation, but its heightened, archaic, almost epic intensity, in which can be heard Virgil and Arnold, Tennyson, Masefield, and Shakespeare.

There is a curious instability about the prose, as if it were uncertain what to do with the words at hand; given the archaism of a good deal of the language, it is hard not to feel that the very words being used to describe the passing of time are also being summoned as examples of time's passing, verbal surfaces which themselves have been marked by decay and loss. This is especially true of those words that gesture towards theology and biblical meaning, where the precise sense of the language is often elusive.

This short, twenty-page section, as we have seen, describes the slow decay of the Ramsay's summer house, during the years of the First World War. In abrupt, off-stage announcements, Mrs. Ramsay, Prue, and Andrew die. The house, invaded by wind and weather, falls into disrepair, and very nearly disintegrates, but is rescued and restored by local cleaners, just in time for the arrival, in section three, of a now-depleted Ramsay house party, not long after the war. There are extraordinary descriptions of what can be taken to be the turmoil and catastrophe of war – thuds like artillery shells, the sea boiling with a bloody red color, storms and dark chaos, "as the winds and waves disported themselves like the amorphous bulks of leviathans whose brows are pierced by no light of reason … " (134). Again, the reader hears, as throughout the novel, Arnold's plangent elegy for the withdrawal of religious faith, "Dover Beach," and its images of "confused alarms of struggle and flight, / Where ignorant armies clash by night." Psalm 19 is also audible in this section, with its vision of the Lord thundering, and churning the waters. The book of Job is a steady presence here, too – not just because of the reference to "leviathans," but because Woolf expands on the argument about the failure of theodicy that Mrs. Ramsay had begun in the first part of the novel:

It seemed now as if, touched by human penitence and all its toil, divine goodness had parted the curtain, and displayed behind it, single, distinct, the hare erect; the wave falling; the boat rocking, which, did we deserve them, should be ours always. But alas, divine goodness, twitching the cord, draws the curtain; it does not please him; he covers his treasures in a drench of hail, and so breaks them, so confuses them that it seems impossible that their calm should ever return or that we should ever compose from their fragments a perfect whole or read in the littered pieces the clear words of truth. For our penitence deserves a glimpse only; our toil respite only. (128)

There is a suggestion here of the end of the book of Job, in this idea of God – or "divine goodness" – briefly glimpsed, and then quickly obscured. The parallelism of "For our penitence deserves a glimpse only; our toil respite only," is reminiscent of the Hebraic rhythms of the KJB, especially of the Psalms. The passage continues:

The nights now are full of wind and destruction … Also the sea tosses itself and breaks itself, and should any sleeper fancying he might find on the beach an answer to his doubts, a sharer of his solitude, throw off his bedclothes and go down by himself to walk on the sand, no image with semblance of serving and divine promptitude comes readily to hand bringing the night to order and making the world reflect the compass of the soul. The hand dwindles in his hand; the sea bellows in his ear. Almost it would appear that it is useless in such confusion to ask the night those questions as to what, and why, and wherefore, which tempt the sleeper from his bed to seek and answer.

Again, there is the parallelism of "The hand dwindles in his hand; the sea bellows in his ear," with that Psalmic semi-colon separating the phrases. This is not Mrs. Ramsay's vaguely successful vision of the coherence of things, or moments that endure. On the contrary, this is a vision of the absence of endurance, of "no image," of the incoherence of things. The words plume themselves up, and have a distinctly biblical ring – *bellows, toil, respite, penitence* – but find purchase on nothing, and it is the words themselves that seem like the fragments and "littered pieces," in which it is so hard to find "the clear words of truth."

Repeatedly in this section, Woolf imagines that most Romantic or Victorian of seekers, the person who goes down to the sea to ask for guidance (one thinks of John Masefield's "I must down to the seas again, to the lonely sea and the sky," or Wallace Stevens's later poem, "The Idea of Order at Key West"). This seeker may find an answer, a revelation of sorts, but we shall not know what that answer is:

The mystic, the visionary, walking the beach on a fine night, stirring a puddle; looking at a stone, asking themselves, "What am I?" "What is this?" had suddenly an answer vouchsafed them: (they could not say what it was) so that they were warm in the frost and had comfort in the desert. (131)

Isaiah's cry from the beginning of chapter 40 is perhaps behind this passage, with its language of comfort in the desert:

Comfort ye, comfort ye my people, saith your God.

Speak ye comfortably to Jerusalem and cry unto her, that her warfare is accomplished, that her iniquity is pardoned: for she hath received of the Lord's hand double for all her sins.

The voice of him that crieth in the wilderness, Prepare ye the way of the Lord, make straight ye the way of the Lord, make straight in the desert a highway for our God ...

And the glory of the Lord shall be revealed, and all flesh shall see it together: for the mouth of the Lord hath spoken it.

The voice said, Cry. And he said, What shall I cry? All flesh is grass, and all the goodliness thereof is as the flower of the field;

The grass withereth, the flower fadeth: because the spirit of the Lord bloweth upon it: surely the people is grass. The grass withereth, the flower fadeth: but the word of our God shall stand for ever. (Isa. 40:1–3, 5–8)

As in Psalm 90, God's governance is timeless, while humans wither like grass or flowers (verses repeated almost exactly in the New Testament, in 1 Peter 1:24–5). "Time Passes," and the novel's third section, "The Lighthouse," elaborate on this familiar motif. Mrs. McNab, the cleaner who restores the house to its former health, is almost seventy years old, and weary. "How long, she asked, creaking and groaning on her knees under the bed, dusting the boards, how long shall it endure?" "It" may be the house, her life, or the world itself, after the great fall of the First World War. Woolf nicely blends the banality of domestic housework with the Psalmist's imploring, canonical cry – "Lord, how long wilt thou look on?" (Ps. 35:17); "My soul is also sore vexed: but thou, O Lord, how long?" (Ps. 6:3); "O Lord God of Hosts, how long wilt thou be angry against the prayer of thy people?" (Ps. 80:4).

In these last two sections, Woolf takes the image of flesh as grass and passes it through Whitman, as it were, so that our transient flesh becomes the leaves of grass, further echoing the imagery of Isaiah: "we all do fade as a leaf" (64:6). Indeed, apart from "thing" and "something," no word is as common in the final sections of *To the Lighthouse* as "leaf." The minor Victorian verse that is remembered at dinner in section one likens our brief lives to "trees and changing leaves." Lily, returning to her painting in section three, remembers that at the dinner party in section one, there had been "a little sprig or leaf pattern on the table-cloth, which she had looked at in a moment of revelation" (147). Leaves are here the leaves of our lives, the leaves of books, the leaves of memory, one laid upon the other (rather like Freud's memory-book). James Ramsay, in section three, is described as "Turning back among the many leaves which the past had folded in him" (185). From their boat, on the way to the Lighthouse, the Isle of Skye looks "something like a leaf stood on end" (188). Words themselves are like leaves – "words fluttered sideways and struck the object inches too low."

So much for the obviously biblical language. But what does its presence mean, in a book in which no one professes formal Christianity? An answer, writes Woolf, is vouchsafed those who seek on the shore, but "they could not say what it was." ("Vouchsafe" is a familiar verb from the Book of Common Prayer.) Likewise, Lily Briscoe thinks to herself, in section three, "The great revelation had never come. The great revelation perhaps never did come" (161).[3] What "Time Passes" certainly seems to suggest is that though an antique biblical language is needed to evoke the almost cosmic confusion of the First World War, that same biblical language will not suffice to disclose revelation, because the formal belief that sustained and enriched that language has disappeared; in this sense, when God died, the language of revelation died with Him. It is this post-Christian dimension that makes *To the Lighthouse* both the great elegy for the innocence destroyed by the First World War, and the great farewell, comparable to "Dover Beach," to the last, frail sureties of Victorian Christianity: Mr. Ramsay, after all, is a kind of Moses without God; when, in section three, he gets to his promised land – when he finally sets foot on the rock that bears the lighthouse – he seems to stand there "as if he were saying, 'There is no God.'"

Is this absence of revelation because revelation still exists but is beyond language, is unspeakable; or is it because there can be no revelation without language, and the language for this kind of revelation has disappeared? It is hard to be sure, but I am inclined to think that the novel moves towards the former proposition, not the latter, more structuralist, proposition. The persistence of religious and biblical language in this book may be suggestive not just of human need, and human nostalgia; perhaps it is also suggestive of religious presence – at least of a kind. Just as "someone had blundered," so *someone* said, and not Mrs. Ramsay it seems, "We are in the hands of the Lord." The question remains: "who had said it?"

Woolf, of course, was the daughter of a famous agnostic, who had published the even more famous atheist, Thomas Hardy, as editor of *The Cornhill* magazine. Agnosticism is often hard to distinguish from a certain kind of atheism, which surely leaves its imprint on this book – I mean the structural contradiction of needing to invoke a God who, by rights, one is supposed to have got beyond. God may be dead, but he can't be easily murdered. His ghost, slipping in and out of truths, still whispers to us. And the book is alive, if not quite to this God, then, in an almost Platonic sense, to the idea that there may be a revelation prior to language – "the thing itself before it has been made anything." Woolf disliked the "mysticism" in *A Passage to India*, because, she said, Forster was an artist who did not trust enough in art alone, who "despises his art and thinks he must be something more." But Woolf often gives evidence in her fiction and diaries and essays of looking for "something more," a something lying outside art, and even outside language. At times she seems to have been looking not so much for the aesthetic pattern behind reality, as for a further metaphysical pattern behind the aesthetic pattern. What this further pattern looked like, she couldn't say. It is not necessarily moral; it is certainly not the familiar God of the Old and New Testaments. But she suspected that this reality, this voice, was revealed to her.

She tells us, in her diaries, that she sensed this deeper reality in her moments of insanity. Woolf broke down, mentally, in 1897, in 1904, and most severely in 1913, when she nearly killed herself. In 1926, while finishing *To the Lighthouse*, she was again ill. She had periods of feverish intensity and insight, followed by weeks of depression. But she said that she saw through to some kind of "truth" while ill. "I believe these illnesses are in my case – how shall I express it? – partly mystical." Significantly, she told Forster that her illness had "done instead of religion," and wrote that in periods of intensity, she heard a third voice – not hers, not her husband's, but another's. In September 1926, she wrote in her diary, sounding very like Mrs. Ramsay, of "the mystical side of this solitude; how it is not oneself but something in the universe that one's left with." She continues: "One sees a fin passing out." Five years later, in February 1931, amidst the pleasure of having finished *The Waves*, she writes: "I have netted that fin in the waste of waters which appeared to me over the marshes out of my window at Rodmell when I was coming to an end of *To the Lighthouse*."

Did she *see* a fin in 1926, a mystical bulk; or was the idea of a fin merely her image of precisely what she could not see but only imagine? We cannot know. She herself complains of the difficulty of describing this reality. But it was a reality: "If I could catch the feeling, I would: the feeling of the singing of the real world, as one is driven by loneliness and silence from the habitable world."

This idea, of a real world behind the habitable world, recalls the Victorian Platonism in which Woolf was raised. (Her youthful studies in Greek involved reading Plato with Pater's sister.) But Woolf's version is both a fruit of, and a pit shied at, this Platonism. Victorian Platonism put the good in place of God. This good was an invisible order behind the world of appearances. It could be reached, says Plato in The *Republic*, but only by philosophical thought. Inheriting this tradition, Woolf changes the terms: like her father, she did not believe in God. Rather like the Platonist, she intuited a real world behind the apparent world. But it is not the form of the Good. It is intrinsic, indescribable. And most importantly, it seems that it cannot be reached through philosophical reasoning, but only groped toward, every so often, by that faculty that Plato demoted: the imagination.

At the end of *The Waves*, Bernard casts off "this veil of being" and asks: "What does this central shadow hold? Something? Nothing? I do not know." Importantly, he feels that he has pierced a silent world without need of language or art, "a new world ... without shelter of phrases." This is similar to Lily Briscoe's apprehension, towards the end of *To the Lighthouse*, that beauty is a veil that has to be got beyond: "beauty was not everything. Beauty has this penalty – it came too readily, came too completely. It stilled life – froze it" (178). Lily is here referring to Mrs. Ramsay's beauty, but over the course of the next two or three pages, the definition of beauty begins to expand, and begins to bleed into the larger question of art and art-making. Lily looks over at Augustus Carmichael, the poet, and longs to shake him and ask, "What does it mean? How do you explain it all?" She feels that words fail (it is at this moment that she thinks of words as fluttering sideways and missing their mark). She thinks that nothing lasts, not "you," not "I," not "she." Yet, she reassures herself, words and paint last. But in the very next breath, she concedes that her painting will be rolled up and flung under a sofa. So perhaps it is not this picture that will last, she tells herself, but "what it attempted":

One might say, even of this scrawl, not of that actual picture, perhaps, but of what it attempted, that it "remained for ever," she was going to say, or, for the words spoken sounded even to herself, too boastful, to hint, wordlessly … (179)

As ever, the thought is so diaphanous in this book, that one does it a violence – one literalizes mysticism – by attempting to pin it down. But it does seem that Lily is suggesting that there is a truth outside beauty, a truth that is both beyond and before beauty – where beauty means words, paint, phrases, the very poetics of art-making. The truth that is outside beauty is the "attempt at something" – this will last, this has truth and meaning. Notice that Lily's own phrase, "remained for ever," is not actually spoken by her. She is about to speak it; it is ready to be spoken. But then it sounds too vainglorious, and instead she speaks the words silently, to "hint, wordlessly." Words can be used wordlessly, because there are truths without language.

It might be objected that Lily can use words wordlessly at this moment only because the words have already framed the thought. We can think that something will "remain for ever" precisely because language speaks us, even though we don't ever enunciate the words; just as, when Mrs. Ramsay thinks "We are in the hands of the Lord" and immediately disowns the thought, those words have already spoken Mrs. Ramsay. But I have argued that Woolf's suggestion, in this novel and elsewhere, is that it is not just language that speaks us (biblical and religious language being our special interest, here), but some other extra-linguistic reality – God, goodness, another voice, "the singing of the real world," a fin, even: but certainly *something*. Perhaps we can find our way out of this paradox. This mystical reality, this "something," is, as I say, both *before* and *beyond* art: it precedes art, but it is also made by art. It comes before art because the artwork longs to get hold of "the thing itself before it has been made anything." It comes after art – it is made by art – because the act of art-making is itself visionary, or quasi-religious; art-making is the portal of revelation: there is a truth that exists before the attempt at something; but the "attempt at something" also constitutes that truth, brings it into being. Indeed, the attempt at something is that truth, is that being.

And just as there is a truth both before and beyond language, so there is "an essential thing" which both defines us before we are anyone, and which outlives us: "What was the spirit in her, the essential thing, by which, had you found a crumpled glove in the corner of a sofa, you would have known it, from its twisted finger, hers indisputably?" That spirit, that essential thing, precedes us, and outlasts us, even once the material evidence – the glove, the house, the children, the work – has died. That spirit, that essential thing, belongs to God's temporality; it is measured in millennia. Whether this "essential thing" can be contained within a formally religious tradition is very doubtful. It deserves not the word "God," but only the vaguer, much humbler, "thing." Truth can be looked for but cannot be looked at; and that art is the greatest way of giving form to this contradiction, is what moves us so intensely in this novel. Vagueness is all.

NOTES

1 Virginia Woolf, *To the Lighthouse* (New York: Harcourt, Brace, Jovanovich, 1981), 69. All further citations to the novel refer to page numbers in this edition.

2 In Muriel Spark's novel, *The Prime of Miss Jean Brodie* (1961), a book influenced by *To the Lighthouse*, and similarly preoccupied with questions of endurance and memory, biblical language is also used to play one temporality off against the other. Just after the end of the Second World War, Miss Brodie and Sandy Stranger sit in a hotel: "They looked out of the wide windows at the little Braid Burn trickling through the fields and at the hills beyond, so austere from everlasting that they had never been capable of losing anything by the war" (New York: Harper Perennial, 2009), 57. Psalm 72:3 refers to the mountains that shall bring peace to the people, "and the little hills, by righteousness"; and Psalm 90:2: "Before the mountains were brought forth, or ever thou hadst formed the earth and the world, even from everlasting to everlasting, thou art God."

3 Compare Beckett's play, *Krapp's Last Tape*, whose single protagonist remembers a moment, at the end of a jetty (and in the sight of a lighthouse), "in the howling wind, never to be forgotten, when suddenly I saw the whole thing. The vision, at last." We never know what that "vision" of "the whole thing" really is, because whenever Krapp comes upon this memory in his taped diary, he stops the tape recorder and winds the tape forwards.

13 | The King James Bible as ghost in *Absalom, Absalom!* and *Beloved*

NORMAN W. JONES

In typical ghost stories, the first convincing sign that an actual ghost might be present creates a transformation: it takes an otherwise familiar world and makes it unnervingly and catalytically strange. Sigmund Freud described this sense of familiarity-turned-strange as the uncanny – the *unheimlich* that confronts us with something disturbingly unfamiliar hidden in what seems familiar, the *heimlich*.[1] Thus the ghost of Jacob Marley appears and unsettles Ebenezer Scrooge, thereby preparing him to revise what he thinks he knows about his world and what he values most: before he takes a fantastical journey through Christmases past, present, and future, Ebenezer must first come to terms with the very existence of the ghost, which does not accord with his beliefs about the world.[2] Likewise, the ghost of Hamlet's father sets the play in motion not by revealing a "murther most foul" but, as the opening scene emphasizes, by first challenging Horatio's general system of beliefs with his mere presence: in Hamlet's words, the existence of a ghost suggests "there are more things in heaven and earth, Horatio, / Than are dreamt of in your philosophy."[3] Arguably, the most successful ghost stories don't merely depict a character's experience of the uncanny; they actually create such an experience for many of their readers or audience members.

Two of the most widely acclaimed novels of the twentieth century tell this kind of profoundly uncanny ghost story. Often considered their Nobel-prize-winning authors' respective masterpieces, William Faulkner's *Absalom, Absalom!* and Toni Morrison's *Beloved* are ghost stories of a hauntingly unconventional kind. At the center of each novel's strange-making representational strategies is the King James Bible (KJB) – so much so that, as I elaborate below, the KJB itself haunts these novels as much as any other ghost. Yet the KJB does not merely haunt them. More than that, it defines what it means to be haunted in these novels. Specifically, the KJB helps define the implicit sense conveyed by these novels that the present is inescapably haunted by the past, which is to say that the word *history* names a ghost, as it were, a ghost that constantly threatens to render the present unsettlingly and perhaps catalytically strange to itself.[4]

Both *Absalom* and *Beloved* announce the KJB as a key intertext from their titles onward, as I elaborate shortly; additionally, both cast slavery and racism as America's original sin. As Jim Wallis puts it, the US "was established as a white society, founded upon the genocide of another race and then the enslavement of yet another," and this "original sin has affected most everything about our nation's life ever since."[5] To suggest that US history is haunted by the sins of its founders – using *haunt* as a metaphor – accords with biblical depictions of the relationship between history and ethics. The Decalogue, after all, begins by insisting on the importance of remembering the past. God is defined, in part, as a God of history: "I am the Lord thy God, which have brought thee out of the land of Egypt" (Exod. 20:2). The Israelites are to rest on the sabbath to commemorate God's historical act of creating the world (Exod. 20:8–11). Moreover, the Decalogue insists that past ethical failings – even from the distant past – have an impact on the present: God is described as "visiting the iniquity of the fathers upon the children unto the third and fourth generation" (Exod. 20:5).

Even so, those familiar with the Bible might find it odd that Faulkner and Morrison would choose the KJB as a primary intertext for their respective ghost stories: unless the definition of a ghost story gets stretched far beyond its customary bounds, the Bible is anything but. The KJB uses the word *ghost* in two senses: in the Old Testament, it refers to a person's life-breath or spirit and is used only in the expression "to give up the ghost," meaning to die (e.g., Gen. 25:8); in the New Testament, it is used either in this sense or to refer to the Holy Ghost (e.g., John 14:26). Neither sense of the word denotes the spirit of a dead person returned to haunt the living. Similarly, the word *haunt* appears three times in the KJB and is used only to denote a place frequented by living people (as in 1 Sam. 23:22). The one tale recounted in the KJB that might arguably resemble a modern ghost story is that of Saul and the witch of Endor (the 1960s television series, *Bewitched*, alludes to this story in the name of Samantha's mother, Endora), who has "a familiar spirit" and raises the spirit of Samuel from the dead (1 Samuel 28:7–25). This story has inspired artwork by William Blake and others, but it is not characteristic of the Bible. Witches, wizards, and familiar spirits appear elsewhere in the KJB,[6] as do stories of demonic possession (by "devils" or "unclean spirits," as in Mark 5:2–20). Yet these are not stories about ghosts in the sense of spirits of the dead who haunt the living. Even the story of Saul and the witch of Endor describes less a haunting than a kind of séance.

Absalom and *Beloved* implicitly suggest that the KJB is a fitting intertext for their ghost stories not because of Saul and the witch of Endor, and not simply because the Bible can be said to depict the past as ethically haunting the present (in a metaphorical sense), but also because the Bible – specifically the KJB translation – has itself, as a text, become for some modern readers a kind of ghost. While ancient Christian traditions generally understood the Bible to be a vehicle through which the Holy Ghost inspired the communities who read it together (typically aloud), by the twentieth century, an increasing number of people understood the Bible to be less a text of the living than of the dead – of lower-case ghosts (rather than the Holy Ghost) who haunt the present only metaphorically as denizens of an archaic world almost unrecognizable to the technologically unprecedented modern era. The voices of such ghosts could therefore seem particularly well suited to the archaic language of the KJB.

This is not to say that *Absalom* and *Beloved* exemplify the only or even the dominant modern understanding of the Bible. On the one hand, many Christians still experience the Bible as a living text that speaks directly to the present. On the other hand, many non-Christians don't view the Bible as a kind of ghost: for many, it is merely a corpse. Thus, for example, the KJB does not so much haunt T. S. Eliot's *The Waste Land* but rather functions as one of many zombie-like reanimated corpses wandering aimlessly in a desolate landscape (in which no truly living people remain to be haunted). As David Fuller argues, the KJB in *The Waste Land* "is just one element in the 'heap of broken images'"; if the poem offers any sense of religious consolation, it comes not from the Bible but from the Upanishads.[7] For other modern readers, however, the Bible is not simply a living text and not simply a dead one, either. For many such readers, the sense of distance between biblical past and modern present was exacerbated by the Higher Criticism[8] and its descendants in modern biblical scholarship: the Bible can be seen as a mosaic of ancient texts that have been edited in complex and highly subjective ways, such that the sense of "the immediate presence of 'history'" offered by biblical narratives has become "deferred and mediated."[9] *Absalom* and *Beloved* reflect those modern understandings of the Bible that view it as a collection of voices that speak to the present in important ways but are sufficiently fragmented, mediated, and obscured by historical distance as to seem ghostly. Two of the most influential and critically acclaimed ghost stories of the twentieth century, these novels attest that for many modern readers, the KJB has become quite a fitting intertext for the genre despite the Bible's lack of conventionally recognizable ghost stories.

Originally published in 1936, *Absalom* uses several characteristically modernist representational strategies: it disorients the reader, fragmenting its story by narrating it out of chronological order and by telling and retelling parts of the story retrospectively in the voices of different characters whose versions sometimes conflict with each other. The reader thus learns obliquely and recursively about the story of Thomas Sutpen, a legendary plantation owner in antebellum Mississippi who amasses a fortune from nothing – creating his hundred-square-mile plantation as if by divine fiat, "the *Be Sutpen's Hundred* like the oldentime *Be Light*."[10] Sutpen is motivated primarily by his racist horror at having realized when still young and extremely poor that he and his family, though white, were even lower in the social hierarchy than house slaves. Despite his rags-to-riches success, his fortune and his plantation eventually fall into ruin in the aftermath of the Civil War. The war comes to symbolize Sutpen's own house divided against itself as his son, Henry, rejects his father and repudiates his inheritance – echoing not only the New Testament saying about the "house divided," famously used by Abraham Lincoln to describe the Civil War, but also the Old Testament conflict between David and Absalom alluded to in the novel's title.[11] Henry, the only male heir to his father's estate, goes on to cement his apostasy by murdering the man he loves, Charles Bon – Henry's half brother as well as his sister Judith's fiancé – which echoes the Absalom–Amnon–Tamar story told in 2 Samuel 13.[12] Judith's engagement to Bon threatens not only the incest taboo but also that against miscegenation because Bon's mother, Sutpen's first wife, is partly of African descent (which is why Sutpen, upon discovering it, repudiated that first marriage). Henry afterward flees in shame, never to be seen again by his father.

The novel opens in 1909, with the inheritors of this history telling and re-telling it to each other. The narrative foregrounds the subjective nature of each one's perspective by using a style influenced by stream-of-consciousness writing, which emphasizes the shadowy, self-occluding, and sometimes self-contradictory complexity of each character's psyche. The novel's closing lines, for example, thus convey a breathless sense of self-conflicted desperation in part by eschewing conventional punctuation: Quentin Compson, a young Southerner in his first year at Harvard, protests too much in response to his Canadian roommate Shreve McCannon's accusation that he hates the South: "*I dont hate it* he thought, panting in the cold air, the iron New England dark: *I dont. I dont! I dont hate it! I dont hate it!*" (303). The novel's opening similarly abuses the conventions of grammar to help depict the dark recesses of the elderly Miss Rosa's psyche while doing so in such a way as to leave the obscurity of those recesses still intact. Faulkner suggests but does not fully expose some of the reasons why Rosa, who is soon to take Quentin on a midnight adventure to the haunted Sutpen mansion, is figuratively haunted by Sutpen's story (she played a minor role in it when she was young) – so much so that in telling the story to Quentin, her voice itself seems literally haunted by Sutpen:

> Her voice would not cease, it would just vanish. There would be the dim coffin-smelling gloom sweet and oversweet with the twice-bloomed wistaria against the outer wall by the savage quiet September sun impacted and distilled and hyperdistilled, into which came now and then the loud cloudy flutter of the sparrows like a flat limber stick whipped by an idle boy, and the rank smell of female old flesh long embattled in virginity while the wan haggard face watched him above the faint triangle of lace at wrists and throat from the too tall chair in which she resembled a crucified child; and the voice not ceasing but vanishing into and then out of the long intervals like a stream, a trickle running from patch to patch of dried sand, and the ghost mused with shadowy docility as if it were the voice which he haunted where a more fortunate one would have had a house. (4)

While evoking images associated with a hot Mississippi afternoon, the lines also hint at the uncompromising idealism of a martyrdom at once horrific (resembling a crucified child) and somewhat childish: Rosa casts Sutpen as a "demon" not least for the sin of proposing marriage to her in a way that deeply affronted her honor (4, 223–4).

Absalom is not alone among modernist texts in its propensity for gothic figures that transgress the boundaries between the living and the dead.[13]

Vampires as well as reanimated corpses inhabit *The Waste Land*; similarly, Eliot's "The Love Song of J. Alfred Prufrock" opens with the image of an unconscious "patient etherized upon a table," ready to be cut open.[14] Yet there is a crucial difference between Faulkner's and Eliot's uses of such symbols. In *The Waste Land* and "Prufrock," the horror of the living dead represents a sense of disconnection from history. In *The Waste Land*, only broken "fragments" of history remain; Prufrock finds himself hopelessly unable to identify with heroic characters of Western cultural history such as John the Baptist and Hamlet – he is no Lazarus returned to life "from the dead."[15] In *Absalom*, by contrast, the horror symbolized by ghosts represents an uncanny sense of connection with history in "the deep South dead since 1865 and peopled with garrulous outraged baffled ghosts": not only is Rosa haunted by a ghost, but she herself is figured as a kind of ghost, as is Quentin, "who was still too young to deserve yet to be a ghost but nevertheless [had] to be one for all that, since he was born and bred in the deep South the same as [Rosa] was" (4). If anything, these characters feel too much of a connection with history and their forebears.

The Waste Land's gothic symbolism has prompted some critics to describe its dense collage of fragmentary allusions as creating a sense of being textually haunted: "the speaker is possessed by the writings of the dead," Maud Ellmann avers; the speaker "rehearses his own death as he conjures up the writings of the dead, sacrificing voice and personality to their ventriloquy" such that the poem ultimately "stages the ritual of its own destruction."[16] Yet *The Waste Land* represents an evacuation of the self far beyond the poetics of impersonality Eliot valorized: as Robert Langbaum argues, not only the speaker but also "the characters … are nameless, faceless, isolated … all they have is a sense of loss."[17] *The Waste Land* focuses on the disjunction between past and present, on modernity's loss of any sense of continuity with tradition. The figures of the undead symbolize this loss as being so devastating as to create a sense of death-in-life, a loss beyond that symbolized by ghostly haunting. Put simply, Eliot's poem is no ghost story; as noted above, his fragmentary allusions to the KJB function less as ghosts than zombies. While critics debate the extent to which Faulkner's work thematizes a similar sense of disjunction between past and present (for example, in *The Sound and the Fury*[18]), *Absalom* emphasizes from its title onward a sense of continuity between past and present – indeed a sense of historical repetition that connects past and present.

The undead in *The Waste Land* and "Prufrock" symbolize an inability to act,[19] whereas in *Absalom* and *Beloved*, ghosts symbolize a call to action, even if that action might ultimately be tragic. Like the ghost of Hamlet's father and the ghost of Jacob Marley, Faulkner's and Morrison's ghosts reveal previously occluded histories, thereby bringing past and present closer together, as it were. Quentin sees himself as a ghost not because he feels cut off from the present but because he identifies with figures from the past. Indeed, he identifies strongly with the entire Sutpen history, especially with Henry but also with the legendary Thomas Sutpen himself. Quentin imagines that Sutpen, too, felt the same powerful sense of being haunted by history. In retelling the story of Sutpen's boyhood realization of his low social status, he describes Sutpen as having

discovered, not what he wanted to do but what he just had to do, had to do it whether he wanted to or not, because if he did not do it he knew that he could never live with himself for the rest of his life, never live with what all the men and women that had died to make him had left inside of him for him to pass on, with all the dead ones waiting and watching to see if he was going to do it right, fix things right so that he would be able to look in the face not only the old dead ones but all the living ones that would come after him when he would be one of the dead. (178)

Absalom as a whole tells the story of Quentin's own realization of how he feels similarly haunted by history, called to account by the Sutpen story and especially by the ghost (who turns out to be a living person) he and Rosa discover in Sutpen's "haunted house" late one night in 1909: the aged Henry, Sutpen's son, returned from his self-imposed exile of more than forty years (174).[20]

The novel centers on this discovery of Henry, teasing the reader toward it as a climactic revelation. The first five chapters describe how Rosa summons Quentin to accompany her on a nighttime adventure to the haunted mansion, ominously insisting, "There's something in that house … Something living in it. Hidden in it" (140). Yet before this "something" is revealed, the narrative jumps four months ahead to a late-night conversation between Quentin and Shreve in their Harvard dorm room. The second half of the novel describes how they take turns telling each other the Sutpen family history; only in the closing pages does the reader finally learn that Rosa and Quentin discovered Henry in the haunted house – and that when Rosa returned three months later with an ambulance "to save him," Henry and his half-sister, Clytie (Sutpen's daughter by an enslaved woman), set fire to the decrepit mansion and burned themselves to death (298–301).

Absalom begins by raising vague questions about ghosts and demons whose answers seem connected to whatever is haunting the old Sutpen mansion. The narrative suggests various possibilities as to who (living or dead) might be the source of the haunting – Sutpen, Clytie, or Jim Bond, who is Sutpen's illegitimate great-grandson and (like Clytie) is partly of African descent. Yet the ghost turns out to be Henry, the figure in the Sutpen history with whom Quentin most closely identifies (236, 280). It is as though Quentin meets himself in history by meeting this figure from the past still alive in the present. The encounter is all the more uncanny because Henry is not a literal ghost but an actual person: the past lives on in the present despite what the novel also insists is the otherness of history. In the words of Quentin's father, "We have a few old mouth-to-mouth tales; we exhume from old trunks and boxes and drawers letters without salutation or signature, in which men and women who once lived and breathed are now merely initials or nicknames out of some now incomprehensible affection which sound to us like Sanskrit or Chocktaw" (80). Yet Quentin's encounter with Henry teaches him that the past can be intimately familiar as well as incomprehensibly strange – indeed, can be both at once. Thus Quentin feels permanently haunted by the encounter despite the fact that Henry is not literally a ghost: "Nevermore of peace. Nevermore of peace. Nevermore. Nevermore. Nevermore" (298–9). M. Night Shyamalan's 1999 film, *The Sixth Sense*, chronicles psychologist Malcom Crowe's discovery that he, himself, is no longer alive but is one of the ghosts haunting nine-year-old Cole Sear, whom Dr. Crowe initially takes to be a young patient suffering from hallucinations of being haunted. In *Absalom*, Quentin makes a similar discovery about himself, though on a symbolic rather than literal level. The shocking, otherworldly history of how Henry came to murder the man he loved in the name of misguided racial and sexual taboos – in effect destroying himself for the sake of these taboos, just as his father did before him[21] – is what haunts Quentin, what he "could not pass," because in that story he increasingly recognizes himself (139). Henry's story serves as a call to action and an omen of his own fate.[22]

Published half a century after *Absalom*, Morrison's *Beloved* insists that the ghost story it tells "is not a story to pass on,"[23] much as *Absalom* describes the story of Henry as something Quentin "could not pass": these are stories one cannot get over, cannot "take a pass" and ignore, because they insistently haunt the present even against its will, demanding a response. At the same time, these are also stories that cannot be passed on in the sense that they cannot be told fully or adequately. The stories and the larger history of slavery and racism they represent are like the ghost, called Beloved, whom people try to forget "like a bad dream" though she still haunts them day and night – haunts their sleep, hovers obscurely in their photographs, or leaves uncanny footprints "so familiar" that they fit one's own feet but then "disappear again as though nobody ever walked there" (323, 324). "Although she has claim" on those living in the present because she is part of their history, "she is not claimed" and indeed cannot be claimed: "no one is looking for her, and even if they were, how can they call her if they don't know her name?" (323). The project of Morrison's novel is to invoke the stories of slavery and racism that are hidden and lost within US history and imaginatively claim those lost stories in the spirit of Romans 9:25 (which serves as her epigraph): "I will call them my people, which were not my people; and her beloved, which was not beloved" – to lay claim to and tell these lost stories even while showing why those stories can never be fully claimed or told. In short, the novel aims to leave the reader with a sense of the US as a country whose very weather is haunted by "the breath of the disremembered and unaccounted for" (324).

Beloved was inspired by a historically documented event: in 1856, Margaret Garner escaped with seven other slaves from a Kentucky plantation; they successfully crossed the Ohio River trying to gain their freedom, but the 1850 Fugitive Slave Act allowed the slave owners to capture them even there and return them to their enslavement in Kentucky. When they captured Garner, she chose to kill her four children rather than allow them to be enslaved. She succeeded in killing just one of them, her three-year-old daughter, by slitting the girl's throat. Morrison's complex reimagining of the Garner story takes place years after these tragic events: the Civil War has ended, and Sethe (the Garner figure), now a free woman living in Ohio, is haunted by the ghost of her dead baby girl. The novel explores various characters' struggles to come to terms with the "rough choice" Sethe made to protect her children from slavery (212), especially when the past comes calling, as it were, in the form of Paul D – a man formerly enslaved with Sethe on a Kentucky plantation ironically called Sweet Home – at whose arrival Beloved, the ghost of Sethe's dead child, ceases to be a disembodied poltergeist and instead materializes as a very strange flesh-and-blood young woman.

The novel suggests that one of the reasons why a ghost is such a fitting symbol for the haunting legacy of slavery is that the history of African Americans in the US is ghostly in the sense that it is at once there and not there. African American stories are integral to US history yet have often been underplayed, overlooked, and avoided in white accounts of that history. In addition, as a result of the many ways in which literacy was made unavailable to slaves, there exist only a small number of first-hand accounts of eighteenth- and nineteenth-century African American experiences. Most such experiences remain as a ghostly absence from historical records, testified to only indirectly and uncertainly; even the first-hand accounts that do exist are obscured by the profound racism of the discursive contexts that shaped those accounts.[24]

In a 1993 interview, Morrison praises *Absalom* for how it depicts this ghostly sense of race: "Faulkner ... spends the entire book tracing race, and you can't find it. No one can see it, even the character who *is* black [Charles Bon] can't see it ... It is technically just astonishing ... No one has done anything quite like that ever."[25] Literary influences, like literary echoes, are often conceived of as operating in only one direction, but *Absalom* and *Beloved* suggest that it can be more complicated than that. *Beloved* echoes and is to some extent haunted by *Absalom*; yet *Beloved* can teach us how to speak productively with ghosts. Morrison has acknowledged various ways in which Faulkner has inspired her – especially his representations of history.[26] *Beloved* has also influenced *Absalom* in that it has changed how at least some readers interpret Faulkner. Whereas Faulkner was once often read primarily as an exemplar of modernist formal techniques, Catherine Gunther Kodat argues that, partly as a result of novels such as *Beloved* that teach readers to expand our sense of the possible uses of modernist strategies, Faulkner's novels are increasingly "read for his history – particularly for the ways in which his texts reveal how the southern modernist desire to 'forget' history arises as much from the white ruling class's effort to remain in power during a period of social upheaval as from any individualistic psychosexual trauma."[27] Some readers continue to see *Absalom* as articulating a characteristically modernist pessimism and disillusionment, specifically in contrast to *Beloved*.[28] Yet in one of the most recent critical comparisons of the two novels, Peter Ramos insists that *Absalom* does not ultimately embrace pessimism but, like *Beloved*, "attempt[s] to speak not silence, but that which might otherwise be unspeakable."[29] It is no coincidence that Ramos grounds this assertion in his recognition that *Absalom* is also like *Beloved* in that both are structured as ghost stories. Morrison's more pronounced ghost story arguably teaches us to read *Absalom* as one.

To the extent that *Beloved* directs our attention to *Absalom*'s thematic meditations on history, so, too, does *Absalom* direct our attention to *Beloved*'s form: as Kodat contends,

> In *Beloved*, Morrison realizes that the real target for revision and reclamation is not the author's use of individual black characters, but the very literary language itself. *Beloved* remembers [*Absalom*'s] most striking formal properties – its recursive use of multiple voices, its fragmentation, even its acknowledgment that some stories never can be properly told or forgotten – in order to respectfully, but nonetheless thoroughly and without regret, bury the notion of a "pure" white American modernism.[30]

The KJB constitutes a crucial element of these formal qualities shared by both *Absalom* and *Beloved*. To illustrate, consider another landmark of modernist literature: Ernest Hemingway's *The Sun Also Rises*. An epigraph reveals that its title alludes to Ecclesiastes 1:5, but the KJB's archaic language, quoted in the epigraph – "The sun also ariseth, and the sun goeth down, and hasteth to the place where he arose" – stands in stark contrast to the modern simplicity of Hemingway's title. In effect, the titular allusion suggests the disjunction between the modern world and that depicted in the Bible as much as any continuities between the two. One could argue that *The Sun Also Rises* thematically emphasizes such continuities inasmuch as Jake's world-weary cynicism resonates with Ecclesiastes (and more broadly with the *vanitas* tradition). Yet the novel seems rather to allude to the sentiments expressed in the opening of Ecclesiastes in order to suggest a negation of the vast majority of biblical themes.[31] While *The Sun Also Rises*, like *The Waste Land*, may be said to represent those who find the Bible to be, for the most part, a dead text in the modern world, *Absalom* and *Beloved*, by contrast, represent those for whom "the very 'non-modern' strangeness of the Bible" serves as "an indication of its inexhaustible resources and even a model of art's own creative capacities," as

Ward Blanton argues.[32] Moreover, they represent specifically those who find the strangeness of the Bible commingled with its familiarity in such a way as to produce a haunting sense of the uncanny. Freud associated a sense of the uncanny especially with non-normative sexual desires and expressions, and a comparison of these four texts invites the use of sexuality as a thematic lens. Where *The Sun Also Rises* and *The Waste Land* represent sexuality as far more destructive than productive, *Absalom* and *Beloved* represent sexuality as potentially transformative in dangerous yet nonetheless productive ways.[33] For the purposes of this essay, however, more telling is their respective echoes of the KJB, whereby the text of the KJB itself comes to haunt these novels as an uncanny other.

Some might argue that Hemingway's writing style in *The Sun Also Rises* (and elsewhere) – favoring the concrete over the abstract, and favoring simple, direct, and paratactic grammatical constructions – more closely echoes the KJB's style than Faulkner's style in *Absalom*, which favors abstraction, circumlocution, and hyper-complex grammatical structures built especially on hypotactic layers of subordination and qualification.[34] What such an argument neglects is both novels' characteristically modernist preoccupations with the relationship between past and present – with history – and how this thematic concern informs each one's stylistic choices. While the KJB certainly favors the concrete and the grammatically simple and direct, even in 1611 its language was not that of ordinary speech (as is, for example, the dialogue in *The Sun Also Rises*) but already had a slightly strange, archaic feel: its language was not precisely that of an older form of English but rather its own unique amalgam of the familiar and the unfamiliar, which included genuine archaisms alongside strange new Hebraized English.[35] By the twentieth century its language had come to sound far more archaic, as even those idiomatic and stylistic elements familiar to English speakers in 1611 were now often unfamiliar (though ironically some of the once-unfamiliar Hebraicisms had become familiar[36]). *Absalom* echoes this strangely archaic "feel" of the KJB's language – along with the stately liturgical rhythms that help confer the Authorized Version's sense of authority – not in what Gregory Machacek describes as a slavish and unoriginal "exact duplication" of an earlier text by a later one but as a "more general resemblance," a ghostly echo.[37] This is in part to claim, as Machacek insists, that "allusion is culturally mediated": this particular ghostly echo might not have been recognizable as such in earlier historical moments when the KJB's archaisms might have seemed less pronounced, less strange.[38]

For many twentieth- and twenty-first-century readers, this ghostly echo is clear enough to hear: many critics have identified stylistic echoes of the KJB in *Absalom*. Yet they often disagree about the ways in which the novel achieves these echoes, which disagreement itself speaks to the indirect, suggestive, and even elusive – ghostly – textual presence of the KJB in *Absalom*. Glenn Meeter, for example, argues that this ghostly echo is created by Faulkner's use of concepts that allusively resonate with the kind of mythical, primeval conflicts thematized in the Bible.[39] Robert Alter finds more and more specific intertextual resonances, agreeing with Meeter that Faulkner's style does not directly resemble the KJB's but arguing that the general sense of an echo derives from the novel's mythical representation of history as well as its incorporations of thematic keywords from the Bible, such as "birthright, curse, land or earth, name and lineage, get (as a noun, an archaic term for 'offspring' …), sons or seed, birthplace, inheritance, house, flesh and blood …, bones …, dust and clay."[40]

Maxine Rose insists that *Absalom*'s writing style structurally echoes the Bible's: "Faulkner's grammatical and rhetorical structure is cumulative; each phrase or clause explains or increases or enlarges upon the meaning of the previous one(s). The total effect is that of accumulation and coordination, rather than subordination. Such a structure reflects the basic structure of Hebrew literature."[41] Thus the KJB's frequent use of *and* as a translation of the Hebrew connective transliterated *waw*, forming the following type of paratactic structure: "In the beginning God created the heaven and the earth. *And* the earth was without form, and void; *and* darkness was upon the face of the deep. *And* the Spirit of God moved upon the face of the waters" (Gen. 1:1–2, emphasis added). Rose finds this grammatical structure frequently echoed in *Absalom*, as in the description of how Sutpen "came out of nowhere *and* without warning upon the land with a band of strange niggers *and* built a plantation – (Tore violently a plantation, Miss Rosa Coldfield says) – tore violently. *And* married her sister Ellen *and* begot a son and a daughter" (5, emphasis added). Rose argues that such series of clauses or phrases in *Absalom* also often evince the same kind of parallelism fundamental to biblical poetry, in which each verse consists of two or more statements that work together synonymously (the second restates the first), antithetically (the second contrasts with the first), or synthetically (the second builds on the first).[42] She qualifies this comparison of *Absalom* and the KJB by noting that, while Faulkner himself spoke of his high estimation of the Old Testament, she does not mean to suggest that he "was a deliberate student of Hebrew verse forms (though he may have been)"; she means to identify not an exact likeness but a similarity between the two texts.[43]

Even so, *Absalom*'s stylistic echo of the KJB may be slightly more ghostly than Rose allows. Series of cumulative statements in *Absalom* only sometimes fall into identifiably parallel structures, and when they do, they lack the sustained regularity sufficient to create the sense of a larger pattern one finds in most biblical poetry. Mr. Compson's description of the past as an unsolvable mystery in the present (quoted above), for example, includes what might be considered parallelism: "they don't explain and we are not supposed to know," which is followed by, "We have a few old mouth-to-mouth tales; we exhume from old trunks and boxes and drawers letters without salutation or signature" (80). These lines arguably involve repetitions whereby the second part repeats and slightly expands on the first, but such repetitions do not continue long enough to constitute a pattern. In this case, they are soon followed by a characteristically Faulknerian sentence that does not echo itself only in units of two but builds several layers of successive qualifications: "they are like chemical formula exhumed along with the letters from that forgotten chest, carefully, the paper old and faded and falling to pieces, the writing faded, almost indecipherable, yet meaningful, familiar in shape and sense" (80). In Faulkner's prose, near-restatements and qualifications come in twos, threes, even fours, seemingly at random.

Rose notes that Old Testament grammatical and rhetorical structures "accommodate themselves well to stream-of-consciousness techniques,"[44] which raises the question: do stream-of-consciousness techniques always potentially echo the Bible? More plausibly, such modernist literary strategies – which are well suited to conveying a sense of intertextual haunting in that they readily accommodate fragmented, shadowy allusions – can, especially in narratives such as *Absalom* and *Beloved* that thematically foreground the KJB as a key intertext, be made formally to invoke biblical tones and shadings.

In *Absalom*, this formal invocation of the Bible specifically entails the sense of ancient history speaking to the present with a mythical moral authority that Faulkner frequently contrasts or ironically compares with civic law, which is itself a textual record speaking authoritatively from the past to the present about codes of conduct – as in the phrase, "because of love or honor or anything else under heaven or jurisprudence" (248). Indeed, the novel's hyper-complex grammatical structures and highly abstract, Latinate diction echo not only the Bible but also the exaggerated legalese of Bon's lawyer:

So take this, Sir, neither as the unwarranted insolence which an unsolicited communication from myself to you would be, not as a plea for sufferance on behalf of an unknown, but as an introduction (clumsy though it be) to one young gentleman whose position needs neither detailing nor recapitulation in the place where this letter is read, of another young gentleman whose position requires neither detailing nor recapitulation in the place where it was written. (252)

In the world *Absalom* depicts, it's easy to mistake the legal for the biblical. Thus when Sutpen tries to rectify the "mistake" in his "design" (his plan to become a wealthy plantation patriarch), he makes the additional mistake of consulting a "legally trained" mind rather than considering that his woes might be the result of a more profound "retribution": the "sins of the father come home to roost" (particularly the sin of repudiating his first marriage on racist grounds) (215, 219–220).[45] Sutpen faces the kind of dilemma depicted repeatedly in the New Testament as a conflict between the law and love (the former associated especially with the "scribes and Pharisees" of Matt. 23:1–36): the question of healing or working on the Sabbath (Mark 3:1–6, Mark 2:23–8), of having dirty hands at dinner (Mark 7:1–9), of associating with Samaritans (Luke 10:29–37), and of befriending prostitutes and tax collectors (Mark 2:13–17). *Absalom*'s title likewise represents this conflict: the law condemns David's rebellious son as a traitor to his king, but David rejects this legal view of the situation. Absalom dies because he tries to overthrow the king, but David's lament ignores this culpability and instead casts himself as a loving father instead of a wronged king: "O my son Absalom, my son, my son Absalom! would God I had died for thee" (2 Sam. 18:33). Unlike David, Sutpen never questions the law or sees beyond it.

In contrast to *Absalom*'s emphasis on the law and its relationship especially to patriarchal succession, *Beloved* thematizes maternal lineage: the novel suggests that the repeated physical and psychological dismantling of enslaved African American families also contributed to the silencing and erasure of African American histories, thwarting not only their written but also their oral transmission and preservation. In Paul D's reckoning, Sethe may have chosen Halle to be her husband because of his devotion to family: he purchased freedom for his mother, Baby Suggs, earning the money by working for five years on the one day of the week he was not forced to work at Sweet Home (13). Sethe's mother tried to safeguard their kinship by showing Sethe the unique brand burnt into her skin (72–3). Sethe focuses on a different emblem of connection with her children, one largely unavailable to her own mother: breastfeeding, a union of mother and child perversely violated in what critics describe as the mammary rape of Sethe at Sweet Home (240, 236). Ultimately, kinship serves in part as a metaphor for African American history in the novel.

Many of the characters bear names that constitute attempts to claim and memorialize a family history – names which, at the same time, ironically thus testify to the difficulties faced in trying to make such kinship claims. Baby Suggs named herself after her husband (though they were never allowed to be married): he called her baby, and he was called Suggs (167). Of the characters who were at one time enslaved, Sethe is one of the few who was named by her mother, and her name memorializes the fierce, rough kind of love necessary to create a lasting mother–daughter connection in the world Morrison depicts (retrospectively echoing the kind of love Sethe has for her own children): Sethe's mother was "taken up many times" by white men during and after her forced crossing of the Atlantic (the slave trade's infamous Middle Passage), but she "threw away" all the white babies without giving them names; she gave Sethe the name of the one black man who impregnated her, the only man "she put her arms around" (74). Stamp Paid, a conductor on the Underground Railroad, renamed himself to attest to his forcibly broken family: "Born Joshua, he renamed himself when he handed over his wife to his master's son. Handed her over in the sense that he did not kill anybody, thereby himself, because his wife demanded he stay alive … With that gift, he decided that he didn't owe anybody anything" (218). Sethe is inspired to call her dead baby "Beloved" by a phrase used in the baby's funeral liturgy, "Dearly Beloved" (5). Yet as Sethe's older daughter, Denver, later reveals, Beloved is not the baby's "given name" but rather serves, like so many names in the novel, to memorialize the violence done to her family – a renaming born of violence – as well as Sethe's resistance to that violence (246).

Like *Absalom*, *Beloved* unfolds most of these kinship histories retrospectively and in fragments through the thoughts and retellings of various different characters. The narrative foregrounds their subjective differences especially in each one's attempt to come to terms with Sethe's rough choice as to how to protect her children from slavery. Ella, a neighbor, "understood Sethe's rage in the shed … but not her reaction to it, which Ella thought was prideful" (301–2). Sethe's surviving children, by contrast, seem not to understand their mother's rage in the shed but fear that at any moment she might try to kill them as she killed their youngest sister (242). Paul D insists Sethe "was wrong" (194). Stamp Paid tries to justify Sethe's actions to Paul D: "She ain't crazy. She love those children. She was trying to out-hurt the hurter" (276). Baby Suggs "could not approve or condemn Sethe's rough choice. One or the other might have saved her, but beaten up by the claims of both, she went to bed" (212). At different times, Sethe herself voices aspects of all these reactions: she justifies herself to Paul D by pointing out that her choice did save her children and herself from being re-enslaved (194), but her desperation to explain herself to Beloved (236) leads Denver to conclude, "It was as though Sethe didn't really want forgiveness given; she wanted it refused. And Beloved helped her out" (297). Indeed, when Sethe imagines a slave catcher has come again to take Beloved (it's actually just Mr. Bodwin, a white man who was formerly a conductor on the Underground Railroad), this time she chooses to try to kill the slave catcher instead of her children (308–9, 311–12). The narrative seems bent on keeping the reader from comfortably identifying with any settled perspective on the murder. The murder itself is narrated in a flashback that is pointedly unsettling because it situates the reader in the repugnant position of viewing the event through a slave catcher's eyes (174–8). The casual, familiar tone he takes in describing his work potentially allies the reader with the slave catcher through its colloquial use of "you": "sometimes, you could never tell, you'd find them folded up tight somewhere: beneath floorboards, in a pantry – once in a chimney"; "you" had to be careful to keep them under control or "you ended up killing what you were paid to bring back alive" (174).

Beloved works repeatedly to disorient the reader in such ways, turning what seems at first to be something familiar into something disturbingly unfamiliar. The novel's opening, for example, strangely names Sethe's house merely after its street number and insists the house is possessed by an angry spirit, an actual ghost: "124 was spiteful. Full of a baby's venom" (3). In the introduction to the 2004 reprinting, Morrison attests that, beginning with these opening lines, she "wanted the reader to [feel] kidnapped, thrown ruthlessly into an alien environment as the first step into a shared experience with the book's population – just as the characters were snatched from one place to another, from any place to any other, without preparation or defense" (xviii). The formal disorientation effects help convey the novel's themes, especially that of forcibly denied and dismantled kinship. Thus the novel implicitly asks to be interpreted in much the same way Ella, when she was a conductor on the Underground Railroad, interpreted the stories told by those attempting to escape from slavery: "she listened for the holes – the things the fugitives did not say; the questions they did not ask. Listened too for the unnamed, unmentioned people left behind" (108).

Morrison's use of modernist strategies to create a sense of fragmentation, repetition, and the highly subjective nature of human experience – including a section influenced by stream-of-consciousness writing (248–56) – serves to elaborate the novel's central mystery, the identity of Beloved. While the reader learns the identity of the ghost right away in the opening pages, Morrison is nonetheless able to create a sense of complex mystery about the ghost, ultimately inviting a variety of possible ways of identifying Beloved: the dead baby girl, a demonic "devil-child" who eventually gets exorcised (308), or an African enslaved and brought by ship to the US in the Middle Passage (like Sethe's mother, which suggests a kind of mother–daughter circularity) (88, 248–251). Critics have also identified the ghost in more abstract terms as an embodiment of the crushing psychological and physical oppression of slavery that Sethe has internalized as shame and guilt, for example, or as a Christ-like figure. In these various and variable possible identifications, the ghost-made-flesh symbolizes the novel as a whole in its attempt to represent African American history and the enslavement of so many as a story that is to some extent untellable yet demands to be told.[46]

Beloved frames this history in terms of what Emily Griesinger contends is a realistic depiction of the syncretistic combination of Christian and African spiritual beliefs that shaped nineteenth-century black folk religion.[47] This may help explain why the ghost is genuinely supernatural, which would be consistent with such beliefs. In this syncretistic context, communion with ancestral spirits of the dead becomes what Nancy Berkowitz Bate argues is a specifically Eucharistic sense of communion with the past: the novel "unites two of the ideas inherent in the first Eucharist, remembrance of the beloved and freedom from slavery. A third element of the Eucharist, remission from sin/freedom from the past, is dependent, paradoxically, upon *remembering* that past."[48] The Bible – the language of the KJB – is intimately interwoven with this sense of the past depicted in the novel. As with *Absalom*, the novel is littered with allusions to the KJB: its title, the epigraph from Romans, "go and sin no more" (103, quoting John 8:11), "Spirit willing; flesh weak" (203, from Matt. 26:41), "Sufficient unto the day is the evil thereof" (302, quoting Matt. 6:34). Also like *Absalom*, *Beloved* evinces some ambivalence about the Bible as a text that has been used to uphold a host of oppressions including slavery and racism (which is arguably another reason why it takes on a ghostly, ambiguous presence in both novels). Faulkner reminds his readers that many believe "the Bible said" people of African descent were "cursed by God to be brute and vassal to all men of white skin" (226). Morrison has Baby Suggs critique the Bible as much as preach it: "She did not tell them they were the blessed of the earth, its inheriting meek or its glorybound pure"; rejecting the beatitudes' promise of heavenly reward for earthly suffering (Matt. 5:2–12), she insists "that the only grace they could have was the grace they could imagine … if they could not see it, they would not have it" (103).

One of the most important biblical intertexts in *Beloved* comes from the Song of Solomon: "I am my beloved's, and my beloved is mine" (6:3; see also 2:16).[49] This verse is echoed several times in the opening lines of four successive chapters, two of which are written in a stream-of-consciousness style: "Beloved, she my daughter. She mine"; "Beloved is my sister"; "I am Beloved and she is mine"; and "I am Beloved and she is mine" (236, 242, 248, 253). The last lines of three of these chapters echo their first: "she is mine"; "She's mine"; "You are mine" (241, 247, 256). These chapters articulate the thoughts of Sethe, Denver, and Beloved about their relationships with one another as mother, daughter, and sister. In contrast to the Song of Solomon source of these allusions, the lack of reciprocity in the claim to a loving possession suggests a childish, even destructively obsessive possessiveness in this love, as the fourth chapter ends with a chorus of the three women: "You are mine / You are mine / You are mine" (256). Paul D will later voice an alternative to such possessiveness in response to Sethe's lament that her baby was her "best thing," countering, "You your best thing, Sethe" (321, 322). That the biblical intertext should figure so prominently here, defining the mother–daughter–sister relationships, suggests that the KJB is associated in *Beloved* with the almost pre-linguistic consciousness and subconsciousness generally represented by stream-of-consciousness writing techniques.

The novel's climax reinforces this association, suggesting that the archaic language of the KJB symbolizes an ancient and elemental spiritual power that exists prior to merely human language and that haunts the words of the novel like an ancestral spirit. Thirty women come to 124 to exorcise the ghost and save Sethe, and they do it by singing: "the voices of women searched for the right combination, the key, the code, the sound that broke the back of words" (308). The power of this pre-linguistic sound – the code beneath the words – is characterized in specifically biblical terms as saving Sethe through a kind of baptism: the women's voices become "a wave of sound wide enough to sound deep water and knock the pods off chestnut trees. It broke over Sethe and she trembled like the baptized in its wash" (308). The word "sound" is repeated here deliberately, transformed from a noun into a verb, an action, a power; in a similar repetition, the sound is not only powerful enough to sound (take the measure of) deep water but also becomes (metaphorically) water, washing over Sethe like a wave. Thus the very words of the novel itself are transformed as the line describes how the women "broke the back" of words, transforming their words to tap into some powerful substratum of sound. Through the biblical imagery of baptism used here, and the repeated biblical intertext in the stream-of-consciousness chapters – chapters that similarly "break" and transform ordinary language – the novel represents this sense of a powerful sound hidden or locked beneath ordinary words through both the themes and language of the KJB.

Beloved and *Absalom* situate their narratives in a retrospective relationship to a past horror – Henry's murder of Bon and Sethe's murder of Beloved – that haunts the present not just for its own sake but also as a kind of ghostly representative of a much larger history of oppression and struggle. While the iconic modernist poem, *The Waste Land*, uses the symbolism of the living dead primarily to reinforce the profound sense of fragmentation conveyed by the poem's formal strategies of disorientation, *Beloved* and *Absalom* rather use such modernist disorientation strategies to help create their respective ghost stories. The KJB plays a central role both formally and thematically in creating these ghost stories – plays the role, in a sense, of an intertextual ghost. For writers such as Faulkner and Morrison, the KJB lends itself to being used to help represent a sense of the present as haunted by history – by an uncanny sense of the past as being at once faraway and so close, strange and familiar, in unnerving and ethically challenging ways.

NOTES

The author wishes to thank Debra Moddelmog for her exceptionally helpful comments on this chapter.

1 See Sigmund Freud, *The Uncanny*, trans. David McLintock (New York: Penguin, 2003). Julia Briggs offers a useful overview of ghost stories as a genre in "The Ghost Story," in *A Companion to the Gothic*, ed. David Punter (Oxford: Blackwell, 2000), 122–31.

2 Charles Dickens, *A Christmas Carol* (New York: Simon & Schuster, 2007). The story was originally titled, *A Christmas Carol in Prose, Being A Ghost Story of Christmas*.

3 William Shakespeare, *Hamlet*, 1.5.27, 1.1.23–33; 1.5.166–7 (*The Riverside Shakespeare*, 2nd edn. [New York: Houghton Mifflin, 1997]).

4 Jacques Derrida describes history as a kind of ghost exemplified by the ghost of Hamlet's father (*Specters of Marx*, trans. Peggy Kamuf [New York: Routledge, 1994], 127).

5 Jim Wallis, *God's Politics: Why the Right Gets It Wrong and the Left Doesn't Get It* (New York: HarperSanFrancisco, 2005), 308.

6 See, for example, Exod. 22:18, Deut. 18:10–11, 2 Chron. 33:6, Lev. 20:6, and Isa. 19:3.

7 David Fuller, "T. S. Eliot," in *The Blackwell Companion to the Bible in English Literature*, ed. Rebecca Lemon, Emma Mason, Jonathan Roberts, and Christopher Rowland (Malden, MA: Blackwell, 2009), 667–80; 669–70.

8 See the Introduction for a discussion of the Higher Criticism and its influence.

9 Ward Blanton, "Introduction to Part VI" in *The Blackwell Companion to the Bible in English Literature*, 603–16; 607–8.

10 William Faulkner, *Absalom, Absalom!* (New York: Vintage, 1990), 4. All further references to this novel are cited parenthetically in the body of the text.

11 Mark 3:25 (see also Matt. 12:25 and Luke 11:17), and 2 Sam. 13–18.

12 Absalom killed his half-brother, Amnon, because Amnon raped their sister, Tamar.

13 For an overview of modernist uses of the gothic, see John Paul Riquelme, "Toward A History of Gothic and Modernism: Dark Modernity from Bram Stoker to Samuel Beckett," *Modern Fiction Studies* 46.3 (2000): 585–605. See also Helen Sword, *Ghostwriting Modernism* (Ithaca, NY: Cornell University Press, 2002).

14 See *The Waste Land*, I "Burial of the Dead" (1–76), and V "What the Thunder Said" (378–95; regarding the vampire allusion, see also Riquelme 589 and 604, n. 4); "The Love Song of J. Alfred Prufrock," 2–3 (*The Norton Anthology of English Literature*, ed. M. H. Abrams, 6th edn. [New York: W. W. Norton, 1993]). Faulkner at one point describes Miss Rosa as a vampire (68).

15 *The Waste Land*, 431; "Prufrock," 79–86, 111–19, 94–5. The use of "fragments" in the closing lines of *The Waste Land* resonates suggestively with the instructions Jesus gives to his disciples after the miracle of the loaves and fishes: "Gather up the fragments that remain, that nothing be lost" (John 6:12); in *The Waste Land*, an attempt has been made to gather together and "shore" the fragments of cultural history (especially of texts) "against my ruin," but the attempt seems futile. Similarly, Prufrock imagines himself beheaded like John but ultimately concedes, "I am no prophet" (83).

16 Maud Ellmann, "A Sphinx without a Secret" in *The Waste Land: Authoritative Text, Contexts, Criticism*, ed. Michael North (New York: W. W. Norton, 2001), 258–75; 267, 275. Eliot invites this gothic symbolism for literary citation, allusion, and general influence in "Tradition and the Individual Talent": "we shall often find that not only the best, but the most individual parts of [a poet's] work may be those in which the dead poets, his ancestors, assert their immortality most vigorously" (*The Waste Land: Authoritative Text, Contexts, Criticism*, 114). As Ellmann argues, while Eliot "celebrates the voices of the dead" in "Tradition and the Individual Talent," "he comes to dread their verbal ambush in *The Waste Land*" (267).

17 Robert Langbaum, "The Walking Dead" in *The Waste Land: Authoritative Text, Contexts, Criticism*, 230–5; 231.

18 Warwick Wadlington argues that Faulkner presents a sense of continuity between historical traditions and modernity in "*The Sound and the Fury*: A Logic of Tragedy" in *The Sound and the Fury: An Authoritative Text, Backgrounds, and Context Criticism*, ed. David Minter, 2nd edn. (New York: W. W. Norton, 1994), 358–70. For a contrasting view, see Donald M. Kartiganer, "[The Meaning of Form in] *The Sound and the Fury*," in *The Sound and the Fury: An Authoritative Text, Backgrounds, and Context Criticism*, 324–43.

19 On this point, F. R. Leavis's interpretation remains compelling: the poem "exhibits no progression" – it ends with a figure simply sitting, apparently unable to act; "the thunder brings no rain to revive the Waste Land, and the poem ends where it began" ("The Significance of the Modern Waste Land," in *The Waste Land: Authoritative Text, Contexts, Criticism*, 173–85; 179–80). By contrast, Cleanth Brooks argued against such readings offered by Leavis and F. O. Matthiessen, claiming that *The Waste Land* subtly thematizes redemption and specifically "resurrection" in response to its "basic theme" of modern life as a kind of "death-in-life"; yet Brooks supports his reading by reference to Eliot's later conversion to Christianity, a questionable lens through which to view the poem composed years earlier ("*The Waste Land*: An Analysis," in *The Waste Land: Authoritative Text, Contexts, Criticism*, 185–210; 209, 185, 204–5). Yet the poem offers some grounds for interpreting its biblical allusions and imagery – especially that of the desert – as perhaps suggesting an experience of desolation that leads to a turn or return to faith.

20 For an extended argument that the novel constitutes this kind of self-realization on Quentin's part, see Norman W. Jones, *Gay and Lesbian Historical Fiction: Sexual Mystery and Post-Secular Narrative* (New York: Palgrave Macmillan, 2007), 41–71.

21 Quentin, telling about Rosa's father's view of the Civil War, casts the South as morally misguided like the man described in Matt. 7:24–7 who built his house on sand instead of rock: "the South … erected its economic edifice not on the rock of stern morality but on the shifting sands of opportunism and moral brigandage" (209). In *Absalom*, Sutpen's "house" symbolizes that edifice: both fell as a result of iniquities.

22 Faulkner's earlier novel, *The Sound and the Fury*, offers an account of Quentin's self-destruction that suggests this omen will prove true. Warwick Wadlington contends that Quentin thus plays the role of the traditional tragic hero ("*The Sound and the Fury*: A Logic of Tragedy").

23 Toni Morrison, *Beloved* (New York: Vintage, 2004), 324. All further references to this novel are cited parenthetically in the body of the text.

24 See Dwight A. McBride, *Impossible Witness: Truth, Abolitionism, and Slave Testimony* (New York: New York University Press, 2001).

25 Quoted in John N. Duvall, "Toni Morrison and the Anxiety of Faulknerian Influence," in *Unflinching Gaze: Morrison and Faulkner Re-Envisioned*, ed. Carol A. Kolmerten, Stephen M. Ross, and Judith Bryant (Jackson, MS: University Press of Mississippi, 1997), 3–16; 8. Morrison explores the visible invisibility of blackness in US literature in *Playing in the Dark* (Cambridge, MA: Harvard University Press, 1992).

26 Morrison's 1955 master's thesis explores Faulkner's work, and in an address at the 1985 Faulkner and Yoknapatawpha Conference, she describes how his work inspired her; nevertheless in a 1983 interview with Nellie McKay, she explains that she does not view her work as being "like" Faulkner's. See Duvall's discussion of these statements and of the relationship between Faulkner and Morrison in "Toni Morrison and the Anxiety of Faulknerian Influence."

27 Catherine Gunther Kodat, "A Postmodern *Absalom, Absalom!*, a Modern *Beloved*: The Dialectic of Form," in *Unflinching Gaze*, 181–98; 196.

28 See Philip Goldstein, "Black Feminism and the Canon: Faulkner's *Absalom, Absalom!* and Morrison's *Beloved* as Gothic Romances," *The Faulkner Journal* 20.1/2 (2004/2005): 133–48; and Phillip Novak, "Signifying Silences: Morrison's Soundings in the Faulknerian Void," in *Unflinching Gaze*, 199–216.

29 Peter Ramos, "Beyond Silence and Realism: Trauma and the Function of Ghosts in *Absalom, Absalom!* and *Beloved*," *The Faulkner Journal* 23.2 (2008): 47–66; 48.

30 Kodat, "A Postmodern *Absalom, Absalom!*," 189.

31 While acknowledging the ambiguities that keep readers debating precisely where the moral center lies in *The Sun Also Rises*, S. A. Cowan argues that "Hemingway's use of Ecclesiastes is true ... to the idea that 'all is vanity'": ultimately, the novel endorses Jake's "disillusioned worldly wisdom" ("Robert Cohn, the Fool of Ecclesiastes in *The Sun Also Rises*," *Dalhousie Review* 63.1 [1983]: 98–106; 105).

32 Ward Blanton, "Introduction," 610.

33 Regarding *Absalom*, see Jones, *Gay and Lesbian Historical Fiction*, 41–71. The case is more readily apparent in *Beloved*, primarily in the romance between Paul D and Sethe.

34 Robert Alter argues that Hemingway's style does indeed echo the KJB, though he argues that Faulkner's style does, too, in a different way. See his *Pen of Iron: American Prose and the King James Bible* (Princeton, NJ: Princeton University Press, 2010), chs. 3 and 5. In this volume, Alter notes that one of the differences between the two writers in relation to the KJB is Faulkner's echoing the KJB's incantatory style (see ch. 2).

35 See Alister McGrath, *In the Beginning: The Story of the King James Bible and How It Changed a Nation, a Language, and a Culture* (New York: Anchor Books, 2001), 262–76.

36 See McGrath, 262–5, regarding once unfamiliar Hebrew idioms made familiar by the KJB, such as "the skin of my teeth," "to stand in awe," "to put words in his mouth," "rise and shine," and "a fly in the ointment."

37 Gregory Machacek, "Allusion," *PMLA* 122.2 (2007): 522–36; 528.

38 *Ibid.*, 534. Of course, recognizing such an echo at any time also depends on a given reader's familiarity with the KJB.

39 Glenn A. Meeter, "Beyond Lexicon: Biblical 'Allusion' in Faulkner," *Mississippi Quarterly* 49.3 (1996): 595–602.

40 Alter, *Pen of Iron*, 85–6.

41 Maxine Rose, "Echoes of the King James Bible in the Prose Style of *Absalom, Absalom!*" *Arizona Quarterly* 37.2 (1981): 137–48; 139.

42 *Ibid.*, 140–3. Rose further contends that the rhythms of biblical poetry, specifically the regular patterns of Hebrew accentual units, are also characteristic of *Absalom* (143–7).

43 *Ibid.*, 147.

44 *Ibid.*, 147.

45 For an extended discussion of the relationship between the law and the Bible in *Absalom*, see Jones, *Gay and Lesbian Historical Fiction*, 64–8.

46 See James Phelan's discussion of the variable significance of Beloved in *Narrative as Rhetoric: Technique, Audiences, Ethics, Ideology* (Columbus: Ohio State University Press, 1996), 175–9.

47 Emily Griesinger, "Why Baby Suggs, Holy, Quit Preaching the Word: Redemption and Holiness in Toni Morrison's *Beloved*," *Christianity and Literature* 50.4 (2001): 689–702; 693.

48 Nancy Berkowitz Bate, "Toni Morrison's *Beloved*: Psalm and Sacrament," in *Toni Morrison and the Bible: Contested Intertexualities*, ed. Shirley A. Stave (New York: Peter Lang, 2006), 26–70; 56.

49 See Katherine Bassard's discussion in this volume of the role of the Song of Sol. in Morrison's work more broadly (ch. 14).

14 | The King James Bible and African American literature

KATHERINE CLAY BASSARD

Prophetic as she was known to be, one wonders if former slave and abolitionist Sojourner Truth would have foreseen such a moment: Barack Obama taking the oath of office with his hand on the Lincoln Bible as he became the first African American president of the United States. In 1864, her own visit with President Abraham Lincoln at the "Executive Mansion" (or White House) was captured in a portrait as iconic in the nineteenth century as is the image of Obama's inauguration in the twenty-first (see Illustration 6). Truth's presence with Lincoln at the White House in 1864 represents a transgression of racial and gendered norms of mid-nineteenth-century America. In the portrait, she is gazing out at the viewer while Lincoln's gaze is focused on the open Bible, his left hand appearing to have just turned the page. Truth, who could not read or write, does not look at the text, but gestures to it with her right hand. The triangle formed by the three subjects of the portrait – Lincoln, Truth, the King James Bible – suggests the desire for the Bible to serve as a text of national unity. This is the reason President Obama chose this Bible specifically for his historic inauguration.

Of course the small, red-leather-bound volume upon which Obama's left hand rested on January 20, 2009 is not the same as the imposing volume in the portrait of Lincoln and Truth. In a letter dated November 17, 1864 from Freedman's Village, Virginia where she was working with a refugee camp of freedpeople, Truth wrote (with the aid of an amanuensis):

He then showed me the Bible presented to him by the colored people of Baltimore, of which you have no doubt seen a description. I have seen it for myself, and it is beautiful beyond description. After I had looked it over, I said to him, This is beautiful indeed; the colored people have given this to the head of the government, and that government once sanctioned laws that would not permit its people to learn enough to enable them to read this book. (178–9)

Illustration 6 "A. Lincoln showing Sojourner Truth the Bible presented by colored people of Baltimore, Executive Mansion, Washington, D.C., Oct. 29, 1864." Courtesy of the Library of Congress, LC-USZ62–16225.

She goes on to describe the ornate book in great detail:

The colored population of Baltimore have procured the most beautiful Bible ever manufactured in this country, to be presented to the President of the United States. The cover bears a large plate of gold, representing a slave with his shackles falling from him in a cotton field, stretching out his hands in gratitude to President Lincoln for the freedom of the slave. At the feet of the freedom there is a scroll bearing upon its face the word "Emancipation," in large letters. On the reverse cover is another gold plate containing the following inscription: "To Abraham Lincoln, President of the United States, the friend of universal freedom, by the loyal colored people of Baltimore, as a token of respect and gratitude. Baltimore, July 4th, 1864." The book is enclosed in a walnut silvermounted box. The entire affair cost $5,800.

The figure of the slave "with his shackles falling from him ... stretching out his hands in gratitude" is the famous anti-slavery emblem of the abolition-ist movement – usually captioned "Am I not a Man and a Brother?" – trans-posed to position Lincoln as the addressee of its utterance. Embedding the anti-slavery emblem onto the cover stamps the Bible, literally, with a plea for freedom and equality. Ironically, the chief justice who administered Lincoln's oath was none other than Roger Taney who issued the infam-ous decision in the Dred Scott case that "the black man has not rights that the white man is bound to respect." The 1864 inscription from the free Baltimoreans labeling Lincoln "the friend of universal freedom" is a delib-erate attempt to rewrite the long history of the King James Bible (KJB) as a text of oppression, often appropriated in pro-slavery ideology as the rationale for African enslavement.

Although the images – Truth with Lincoln at the White House and Obama being sworn in on the steps of the Capitol – span nearly a century and a half, they represent an historic meeting between past and present, symbolized by the King James Bible. That both images invoke Abraham Lincoln suggests that the Bible has meaning for Truth and Obama to the extent that it is allied with the cause of liberation and emancipation. Truth, a former slave who could neither read nor write, and Obama, the first black president, demonstrate that the influence of the Bible in African American history and culture crosses lines of gender, class, education, and historical period.[1] This essay will trace, briefly, some of the literary uses of the Bible by African American writers from the earliest beginnings of the literary tradition to Toni Morrison and Edward P. Jones in this millennium. My argument is that the African American writers' approach to the KJB within literature is based on a dual perception of the Bible as a book of both "signs and wonders." In other words African Americans were drawn to the Bible both as a field of signification – for language, words, phrases, and linguistic structures in the construction of self identity and culture as scholars such as Theophus Smith have argued[2] – and as a field for the miraculous and supernatural, the promise of radical individual and social change. "Signs and wonders" thus represents, in dialectical form, the fascination with the language of the KJB as the vehicle for social power and an acknowledgment of the spiritual authority bestowed upon the Bible as a sacred text within African American religious culture.

Between these two poles, moreover, we can trace the complex intertextuality of African American literature as writers of various genders, genres, literary periods, and religious and political persuasions interact with the KJB which, itself, consists of a dynamic and active representational field. The centrality of the Bible within the field of Western cultural production has shaped concepts of identity (including who is or is not "human") and has been used to legitimate and naturalize social relations of power. Thus, no other single text in the Western tradition can serve the function of delineating intertextual relationships within the often fragmented tradition of African American literature.

Beginnings: the eighteenth century

African American literature begins in the eighteenth century with what Henry Louis Gates refers to as the "classic slave narratives." Indeed, Equiano's *Interesting Narrative of Olaudah Equiano or Gustavas Vassa, the African* (1789) features one of the most famous examples of early African American portraiture, a stately Equiano, in Western dress, holding a Bible opened to Acts 4:12. As Lynn A. Casmier-Paz notes in "Slave Narratives and the Rhetoric of Author Portraiture," "In the likeness of a slave who writes, frontispiece portraits present the initial 'threshold' through which the overarching irony of the writing slave is readable."[3] Casmier-Paz observes that due to the power of the KJB, which "formed the fundamental and multiple ideologies of racist Europe," the presence of the Bible in Equiano's portrait served an overdetermined role in communicating his complex and ambivalent identity: "even more persuasive than his likeness, his British costume or powdered wig is the assertive iconography of his adopted text."[4]

In another famous frontispiece portrait, this one engraved by an African captive named Scipio Moorehead, a young Phillis Wheatley sits poised at a desk with a pen in her hand, an inkwell and paper (with a few indiscernible scribbles on its surface) and, at her elbow, a small book that might well be a Bible. Although the book is not identified as such, in his prefatory introduction to *Poems on Various Subjects Religious and Moral* (1773), John Wheatley, her master, notes with a degree of pride that Wheatley is capable of reading the "most difficult Parts of the Sacred Writings." For pre-Emancipation African Americans, knowledge of books, and of the Bible in particular, was seen as a hallmark of African humanity and assimilation into Western culture.

Indeed, not only does the Bible frame the "threshold" of the reader's entry into Equiano's *Interesting Narrative*, but it structures much of his text. Equiano's relationships with books and reading may be understood through what Gates has dubbed "the trope of the talking book."[5] Equiano narrates his desire to read as follows:

I had often seen my master and Dick employed in reading; and I had a great curiosity to talk to the books, as I thought they did; and so to learn how all things had a beginning. For that purpose I have often taken up a book, and talked to it, and then put my ears to it when alone, in hopes it would answer me; and I have been very much concerned when I found it remaining silent.[6]

Equiano succeeds in learning to read, and during a trip to St. Kitt's much later in the narrative he uses "eleven bits" borrowed from his captain and "bought a Bible" (86). The Bible now becomes a part of the economics of exchange within a text that will base its anti-slavery argument, true to its time, on economic rationale. After Equiano converts to Christianity, he references the scripture that appears on the cover portrait: "Thus I was, by the teaching of that all-glorious Deity, the great One in Three and Three in One, confirmed in the truths of the Bible, those oracles of everlasting truth, on which every soul living must stand or fall eternally, agreeably to Acts iv. 12" (144). Not only has Equiano employed the Bible for its linguistic constructs in forming an identity, he also attributes to it the power to transform him from sinner to saint through the "name ... whereby we must be saved" (Acts 4:12).

As Casmier-Paz notes, "in the nineteenth century, the Bible disappears from slave narrative frontispiece portraiture, and it loses its ability to clearly identify the African as a human being."[7] Between these two eighteenth-century writers and those of the nineteenth century, however, the Bible itself comes under scrutiny as ideas about its supernatural authority are questioned. Yet even as the Bible comes under critique for its claim to supernatural "wonders," African Americans continue to embrace its dialectical nature.

Challenges: the nineteenth century

"I think de people dat made de Bible was great fools," said Ned.

"Why?" asked Uncle Simon.

"'Cause dey made such a great big book and put nuttin' in it, but servants obey yer masters."

WILLIAM WELLS BROWN, *CLOTEL* (1853)

It is through the development and dissemination of the pro-slavery hermeneutic that we locate African Americans as Bible readers in the nineteenth century. As Dwight Callahan notes in *The Talking Book*, "the Bible ... is the book of slavery's children" and "has been available to African Americans as no other literature."[8] Mark Noll remarks in *America's God* that the debate over the Bible and slavery "was more than an exegetical debate ... it was always a question of who had the power to dictate how the Bible should be interpreted and who had no voice in shaping the accepted canons of interpretation. The issue from first to last was an issue of cultural hermeneutics as well as biblical exegesis."[9] The institution responsible for the dissemination of the pro-slavery biblical interpretation to enslaved men, women, and children was the slave missions movement which began in South Carolina in the 1820s and 1830s.[10] While black attendance at missionary churches and gatherings was voluntary, white "missionaries" – most of whom were slave holders themselves – were employed to reach out to the slave population with the gospel, embodying a contradiction of "evangelical belief and self-interested materialism."[11]

In an ironic twist, Nat Turner's revolutionary ideas, like those of Denmark Vesey and David Walker before him, attributed biblical texts as, in part, a source for black radicalism.[12] These Bible-sanctioned slave revolts stood in direct opposition to compromising reformers who insisted that "the Bible was a guarantor of peace, order, and stability on the plantation."[13] Vesey, Walker, and Turner internalized the strategy of biblical interpretation promoted by slave masters and reinvested the Bible as a text of black agency and revolution. The attempt to dismantle the master's house using the master's tools, to paraphrase Audre Lorde, had serious consequences for African Americans, especially for their religious practices. Not only were black perpetrators of conspiracies executed, but widespread and random white retaliatory violence ensued throughout black enslaved and free communities. Since both Vesey and especially Turner referred to the Bible in their expressions of the justice of their actions, African American Christianity became "black religion under white protection" as African Americans, slave and free, could not assemble even for religious purposes without the presence of a white overseer.[14] This unfree worship gave rise to hush harbors and an underground black Christianity.[15]

Most scholars assume a largely oral transmission of biblical texts among nineteenth-century African Americans because of laws prohibiting slaves from being taught to read or write. From the perspective of African Americans under slavery, the desire to read permeates slave narratives, and the link between literacy and freedom has been well documented.[16] In *When I Can Read My Title Clear*, Janet Cornelius demonstrates the almost inextricable link between literacy and religion; the desire to read was, more often than not, a desire to read not just any book, but the KJB.[17]

A notable case of the desire for biblical literacy is none other than Frederick Douglass, whose relationship to the Bible over his lifetime was at times ambivalent and contradictory. While much has been made of the revisions between his three autobiographies, no one has commented on the changing representations of Douglass's view of the Scriptures. In his 1881 autobiography, *Life and Times of Frederick Douglass*, he notes that his desire to read was specifically fueled by a desire to read the Bible: "The frequent hearing of my mistress reading the Bible aloud ... awakened my curiosity in respect to this *mystery* of reading, and roused in me the desire to learn."[18] When Master Auld comes in and puts a stop to the reading lessons, Douglass quotes him in *Life and Times* as saying, "If he learns to read the Bible it will forever unfit him to be a slave."[19] This is in stark contrast to the famous literacy scene of his 1845 *Narrative* where there is no specific mention of the Bible, noting simply that Mrs. Auld "commenced to teach me the A, B, C." The Bible is also taken out of Mr. Auld's speech: "If you teach that nigger (speaking of myself) to read, there would be no keeping him. He would become unmanageable, and of no value to his master."[20]

Why was any mention of the Bible as both the impetus for Douglass's desire for literacy and the slave master's fear excised from the 1845 text? I believe it is because the subject of African Americans and the Bible, highly contentious in 1845 when Douglass published his slave narrative, had ceased to be an issue in 1881 when he wrote *Life and Times*. Douglass's deliberate steering away from any mention of the Bible (and displaced mention of Nat Turner), although possibly motivated by abolitionist/mentor William Lloyd Garrison whose own views about the Bible and Christianity were ambivalent at best, reflects the embattled climate over biblical hermeneutics and interpretation as well as the role the Bible should play in anti-slavery arguments.[21]

While we might see this yearning for specifically biblical literacy as a desire for power – the need to appropriate the cultural authority and social cache invested in the Bible in nineteenth-century America – the sense of urgency in slaves' desire for Bibles seems to overreach such an explanation. As Cornelius summarizes, "Black Christians believed the Bible spoke to them in a special way, and they resented the slaveholders' abuse of God's word. Therefore, it was crucial that some people in the slave community gain reading skills, to 'take the Bible back,' to read what it really said."[22] Thus, in addition to seeing the Bible as a tool for liberation, slaves saw themselves as agents for liberating the Bible from oppressive, racially motivated hermeneutics. In order for the Bible to *be* the Bible, for most slaves, it must first be freed from its associations as the foundation and legitimation of the institution of slavery. By and large, African American hermeneutics in the nineteenth century was not motivated by a desire to de-authorize the Bible or question the Bible's claim to be the word of God, although such a de-mystifying discourse was available through both liberal northern abolitionists and southern ethnologists. Rather, they sought to de-authorize the master's unauthorized reading of the Bible as a racialized pro-slavery text.

To this end, African Americans became armed with Bibles through the efforts of the American Bible Society (ABS) organized in 1816, the same year of the incorporation of the African Methodist Episcopal Church as the first black denomination in the United States.[23] The mission of the ABS was to distribute as widely as possible "the Holy Scriptures without note or comment"[24]; thus, ABS Bibles contained neither notes nor pictures. In *America's Bible*, Paul Gutjahr describes the Bibles issued by ABS as

small, about six by three and one-half inches, printed in a two-column style with chapters preceded by a short heading and a handful of short tables of information. The pages were almost completely devoid of margins, a sign of paper conservation. Finally, the Society bound these bibles in low-cost leather without elaborate spine or cover ornamentation. This small, sturdy bible edition was designed for function; a modest product inexpensively produced.[25]

The "Bibles for Slaves" campaign, however, was not without contention. While one might imagine opposition within pro-slavery circles, there was also conflict over the policy in anti-slavery camps. In 1848, the "Bibles for Slaves" campaign of the American Missionary Association enlisted the services of fugitive slave Henry Bibb in its cause. The goal was "to give a Bible or Testament to every slave who could read";[26] however, Bibb and the campaign of the AMA soon found themselves attacked by other black abolitionists, primarily the preeminent figure of Frederick Douglass.

Douglass's opposition to the American Missionary Association and Henry Bibb derived from two sources. First, Bible Society reports that slaves were being taught to read blunted Douglass's insistence on the cruelty and deprivation of the system of chattel slavery. Although he himself had been taught to read while a slave, Douglass flat-out denied the Tract Society's report of slaves being taught by colporteurs who had become "permanent missionaries" on some plantations. Douglass viewed the Bibles for Slaves campaign as "a sham, a delusion, and a snare."[27] On closer inspection, Douglass did not object to the Bible per se, but to its connection to slavery: "The Bible is peculiarly the companion of liberty," he wrote; "It belongs to a new order of things – slavery is of the old – and will only be made worse by an attempt to mend it with the Bible." Seen in the light of a rationalist, northern liberalism, Douglass goes on to say that to give slaves Bibles constituted a perverse form of cruelty:

Away with all trifling with the man in fetters! Give a hungry man a stone, and tell what beautiful houses are made of it, – give ice to a freezing man and tell him of its good properties in hot weather, – throw a drowning man a dollar, as a mark of your good will, – but do not mock the bondman in his misery, by giving him a Bible when he cannot read it.[28]

Obviously Douglass's comments are predicated on the need for literacy, without which, as he suggests, the Bible is about as useful as a "stone." Here Douglass deliberately echoes the words of Jesus in Luke 11:11: "if a son shall ask bread of any of you that is a father, will he give him a stone?" Douglass uses the same rhetorical strategy of Jesus in this parable of an absurd example designed to provoke a powerful response in the hearer. Douglass was also, as Callahan points out, concerned that given the climate of the Bible defense of slavery, Bibles would be used for pro-slavery propaganda: "The master, holding the Bible and the whip, would now wield each in the service of the other."[29] In contrast, Henry Bibb agreed with the philosophy of the Bibles for Slaves proponents that the Bible could be understood by even semi- or functionally literate slaves and ex-slaves. As Cornelius explains, slaves were "bringing meaning to the text," combining "the knowledge they carried inside them with the letters on the printed page."[30] Many accounts of literacy included the commonly held belief that God himself would teach slaves to read; if they could just get their hands on a Bible, God would provide the literacy, supernaturally if necessary.

Thomas Lewis Johnson recounts his experience with literacy in his slave narrative, *Twenty-Eight Years a Slave*, in 1836:

There was a box of old books stored away in a lumber room, and amongst these books was a large Bible. I took this Bible to my room, and day after day, when I had finished my work in the house, and had a little time to spare, I would go to my room, lock myself in, and try to read the Bible, commencing at Genesis and calling over the letters of each word I could not understand as follows: – "In the b-e-g-i-n-n-i-n-g God c-r-e-a-t-e-d the heaven and the earth"; and thus I struggled on from day to day.[31]

This account of the painstaking acquisition of literacy did not deter slaves from reading and interpreting the Bible for themselves in an act of defiance of the pro-slavery hermeneutic.

Though the Bibles for Slaves campaign offered no immediate political relief for African Americans, most slaves valued the presentation of the Bible as worthy in and of itself. Thus slaves often shared the same understanding of Scripture as the ABS. In a popular pamphlet widely distributed by the American Tract Society, a slave named William reported:

God teach me to read ... God give me desire to read, and that make reading easy. Master give me a Bible, and one sailor show me the letters, and so me learn to read by myself, with God's goot [*sic*] help … Me read all about Jesus Christ, and how he loved sinners, and wicked men kill him, and he died, and came again from the grave, and all this for poor Negro.[32]

In sum, the nineteenth century is a time of contestations over hermeneutics and interpretation, naturalist and theological readings of the Bible and, for African Americans, the quandary of how to respond to arguments such as that put forth by Josiah Priest in his 1852 *Bible Defence of Slavery*.[33] These conflicts resulted in a division between African Americans who treated the Bible as more symbolic, appropriating its linguistic properties in order to make the argument for abolition, and those who continued to perceive it as a book imbued with supernatural power and authority. In short, within African American culture a division began to develop between treating the Bible merely as a book of elaborate signs, and retaining the sense of it as a text of supernatural wonders.

Recontextualizations: black postmodernisms

By the mid twentieth century, this shift from the Bible as a book of wonders to the Bible as a book of signs is reflected in modern and postmodern writers' deconstruction of the text as an emblem of religious authority and, instead, their individual and collective interrogation of its role in American racial power relations. In *Canon and Creativity*, Robert Alter writes of the tension in modern writing between creativity as a modernist value and canon as a sign of scriptural authority:

The engagement of modern writers with the Bible … cuts sharply two ways. They frequently translate biblical motifs and themes into radically redefining new contexts … At the same time, the Bible remains for them a value-laden, imaginatively energizing body of texts, helping make possible the novels and poems they write through the powers of expression and vision that inhere in it.[34]

Zora Neale Hurston notes in the introduction to her 1935 book of folklore, *Mules and Men*, that for African Americans "even the Bible was made over to suit our vivid imagination."[35] Toni Morrison, who describes the Bible not as part of her reading but as "part of my life," writes of her choice of biblical names as the "gesture of getting something holy."[36] At the opening of her 1993 Nobel Prize Lecture, Morrison relates a folktale about a blind seer whom she reads as "the daughter of slaves, black, American" in an effort to comment on the nexus between language and power. That oppressive uses of language are efficacious to the point of *becoming* what they enact is central to Morrison's thinking:

Oppressive language does more than represent violence; it is violence; does more than represent the limits of knowledge; it limits knowledge. Whether it is obscuring state language or the faux-language of mindless media; whether it is the proud but calcified language of the academy, or the commodity driven language of science; whether it is the malign language of law-without-ethics, or language designed for the estrangement of minorities, hiding its racist plunder in its literary cheek – it must be rejected, altered, exposed.[37]

Morrison's move beyond representation to embodiment also works, in her view, to reconceptualize the possibility of a non-oppressive, creative use of language. "Narrative," she writes, "is radical, creating us at the very moment it is being created."[38] The power of (re)creation that resides in story can undo the damaging effects of oppression by meeting the language of those structures on its own terms.

As I have argued elsewhere, one of the foundational tropes for black women writers from the nineteenth century forward was the Shulamite woman ("I am black but comely") of the biblical Song of Solomon.[39] Although subsequent translations revise the phrase, black women were keenly aware of the King James translation "black *but* comely," with its overtones of rendering black women as inferior and undesirable, and consistently represented its opposition: "I am black *and* beautiful."

In Sherley Anne Williams's 1986 novel, *Dessa Rose*, a pregnant slave is sold south for her violent retaliation of her husband/lover Kaine's death. Dessa then escapes with other slaves from the coffle, only to be caught and imprisoned again, this time sentenced to death by hanging upon the birth of her baby. While in prison, she is interrogated by Adam Nehemiah, a white ethnographer with dreams of a bestseller who attempts to extract her story for his own gain. With the help of a network of slaves, Dessa escapes again, ending up at the plantation of Miss Rufel, a southern white mistress who harbors runaways. After the birth of her baby, Dessa and other fugitives from Miss Rufel's plantation plan an elaborate escape to the West, in search of a space of unqualified freedom in the tradition of the great

American novel. In her Author's Note, Williams lays out her artistic vision for the novel:

Afro-Americans, having survived by word of mouth – and made of that process a high art – remain at the mercy of literature and writing; often these have betrayed us … This novel, then, is fiction … And what is here is as true as if I myself had lived it. Maybe it is only a metaphor, but I now own a summer in the 19th century.[40]

Here Williams insists on an alternative representation of the "curse" of the dehumanization of slavery: "I now know," she writes, "that slavery eliminated neither heroism nor love; it provided occasions for their expressions" (x). The novel traces Dessa's liberation from a series of misnamings signified by the subtitles that frame each section of the novel: "Darky," "Wench," "Negress." These phrases are prevalent in the written discourse of the ethnographer, Adam Nehemiah, and constitute the curse on African American women's subjectivity that will be dismantled by Dessa's own storytelling at the novel's end.[41]

Her choice for such a resistant sexuality is the biblical prototype of the Song of Solomon. The opening Prologue to *Dessa Rose* is almost a fictional account of the central theme of the Song of Solomon pronounced at the poem's end: "love is strong as death" (8:6), as Williams portrays the agency to choose one's love object, to be desired and desiring, as the very sign of freedom. In this sense, consensual heterosexuality[42] under slavery is represented as the "antidote," in Kristeva's language,[43] to the death-dealing power of the slavocracy:

He [Kaine] ran the tip of his tongue down the side of her neck. "Ain't no wine they got up to the House good as this" – fingers caught in her kinky hair, palms resting gently on her cheeks. "Ain't no way I'm ever going to let you get away from me, girl. Where else I going to find eyes like these?" He kissed her closed lids. "Or a nose?" He pecked playfully at the bridge, the tip. "Mouth" … Talk as beautiful as his touch. (4)

In this passage, the erotic language transgresses the cramped space of the slave quarters where the scene takes place. More importantly, it resonates with several passages from the Song of Solomon where the lovers describe one another's bodies in elaborate conceits:

Let him kiss me with the kisses of his mouth: for thy love is better than wine. (1:2)

Thou hast ravished my heart, my sister, my spouse; thou hast ravished my heart with one of thine eyes, with one chain of thy neck. How fair is thy love, my sister, my spouse! How much better is thy love than wine! (4:9–10)

In the Song of Solomon, the Shulamite is depicted as equally desiring of her Beloved and catalogues his attributes in 5:10–16. Similarly, Dessa insists on both Kaine's desire for her (a redirection of the circuit of desire under the Genesis "curse") and her own sexual desire and pleasure as signs of agency and autonomy. In the Prologue, Carrie Mae, one of the slave women, opens up the subject of slave breeding which forms the backdrop against which to view the relationship between Dessa and Kaine: "Massa done sent his butt down here to get it out of trouble: taking care that breeding business" (3). In this climate of regulated and controlled sexuality, Dessa emphasizes the importance of free choice. "He chosed me," she tells Nehemiah, "Massa ain't had nothin' to do wid it. It Kaine what pick me out and ask me for his woman. Massa say you lay wid this'n or that'n and that be the one you lay wid" (11).

Kaine (whose name, spelled with a K, signifies on the mark of Cain referenced in the Hamitic theology)[44] is both a gardener and musician, and it is his love-talk that marks Dessa's memory in ways that elude Nehemiah's attempts to "capture" her story in written discourse. His loving words – blessings, if you will – are the catalyst to Dessa's determination for resistance and ultimately freedom. That Kaine's discourse comes in the form of love song resonates strongly with the biblical prototype. One of Kaine's songs that Dessa recalls in captivity is itself a biblical intertext, alluding to the Noah story *before* the "curse of Ham" pericope:

> Lawd, give me wings like Noah's dove
> Lawd, give me wings like Noah's dove
> I'd fly cross these fields to the one I love
> Say, hello, darling; say how you be.   (31)

The power of this rewriting, the image of taking flight just before the "fateful" pronouncement of Noah's curse, is not lost on Dessa. After singing this verse, she remarks, "Kaine just laught when Mamma Hattie say that playing with God, putting yourself on the same level His peoples is on" (32).

Dessa's allusion to the revisionary power of African American spirituals arises again during a session with Adam Nehemiah, whose name signifies both the Adamic "everyman" and the prophet Nehemiah who is marked by his obsession with racial/ethnic purity in the Old Testament book that bears his name.[45] It is through Adam Nehemiah that Williams parodies the betrayals/cursings of written texts. In his journal entry of June 29, 1847, for example, Nehemiah has written, "As today is Sunday, I held no formal session with Odessa. But in order to further cultivate the rapport thus far achieved, I read and interpreted for her selected Bible verses." Later in that same entry, however, Nehemiah, whose whiteness rather than piety seems to qualify him to pray "briefly for the deliverance of [Dessa's] soul" mis-hears that biblical revision encoded in African American spirituals. Initially annoyed by what he calls Dessa's "humming" he asks her to sing the spiritual:

> Gonna march away in the gold band
> In the army by and by
> Gonna march away in the gold band
> In the army by and by
> Sinner, what you going do that day?
> Sinner, what you going do that day?
> When the fires arolling behind you
> In the army by and by?

Completely missing Dessa's reversal of the hierarchy of sinner and saint that places Nehemiah and his ilk in the "flames," he comments, "It is, of course, only a quaint piece of doggerel which the darkies cunningly adapted from the scraps of Scripture they are taught." Taking the "scraps of Scripture" – even those historically sent to "curse" black and female subjectivities – and adapting them to suit not only their present condition but to open up a discursive space for re-imagining the future is the heart of black women's turning the curse to a blessing.

Few writers have made such lavish and complex use of the Bible as Nobel Prize winner Toni Morrison. From the names of her characters – Pilate, First Corinthians, Shaddrach, Ruth, Hagar – to the inscription at the beginning of *Beloved* from Hosea and Romans, Morrison's novels are laden with biblical tropes, phrasing, and intonations. As the title to Shirley A. Stave's edited volume suggests, the relationship of Morrison to the Bible is one of "contested intertextualities."[46] As one writer remarked, "those who know their Bible well will have special access" to Toni Morrison's canon.[47] While Williams's use of the Shulamite trope works to dismantle the dominant discourse's restriction of black women's sexuality and desire, Toni Morrison's novels push the boundaries of the trope into the realm of community.

In "Through a Glass Darkly," Judy Pocock reads Morrison's 1977 novel, *Song of Solomon*, in light of its biblical predecessor, especially through Morrison's use of biblical names and typology. I would like to extend Pocock's reading to suggest that the Song of Solomon is possibly the biblical Ur-text for much of Morrison's novelistic and discursive project as elements of its poetics appear in several works. Not only does she exploit the subversive power of black female erotics in novels like *The Bluest Eye*, *Sula*, *Song of Solomon*, *Tar Baby*, and *Beloved*, but she explores and "demetaphorizes"[48] the allegorical interpretative tradition by insisting on the body as the site of narrative.

Two of Morrison's novels, *The Bluest Eye* (1970) and *Tar Baby* (1981) address the issues of female desire and desirability that reenact the but/and contradiction of the King James translation of the Song of Solomon 1:5. In her first novel, *The Bluest Eye*, Morrison relates the story of a little girl whose desire for blue eyes, the sign of normative white beauty standards, drives her to despair and insanity. In the Afterword to the Plume edition of the novel (1994), Morrison reflects on Pecola's predicament:

The assertion of racial beauty was not a reaction to the self-mocking, humorous critique of cultural/racial foibles common in all groups, but against the damaging internalization of assumptions of immutable inferiority originating in an outside gaze. I focused, therefore, on how something as grotesque as the demonization of an entire race could take root inside the most delicate member of society: a child; the most vulnerable member: a female. In trying to dramatize the devastation that even casual racial contempt can cause, I chose a unique situation, not a representative one.[49]

Based on a childhood memory of a very dark-skinned girl who wanted blue eyes, Morrison writes that "implicit in her desire was racial self-loathing."

Similarly, in *Tar Baby* we are introduced to Jadine, the exotic "copper Venus" who is caught between cultures as an elite fashion model. Yet it is the image of the Woman in Yellow in the novel that represents a counter-discourse of "transcendent beauty" that proves devastating to Jadine:

The vision itself was a woman much too tall. Under her long canary yellow dress Jadine knew there was too much hip, too much bust. The agency would laugh her out of the lobby, so why was she and everybody else in the store transfixed? The height? The skin like tar against the canary yellow dress? ... She looked up then and they saw something in her eyes so powerful it had burnt away the lashes.[50]

If Pecola's desire enacts the "but" in "I am black but comely," the woman in yellow is emblematic of the alternative translation: "I am black and beautiful." Her very presence is a direct refusal of the destructive version of racialized beauty and has the power to destabilize Jadine's entire sense of her self and world. That she is described as "unphotographable" suggests that she breaks the field of vision that tropes blackness as unbeautiful.

Recalling Kristeva's themes from the Song of Solomon, other Morrison novels reverberate with different aspects of the poem. The thematic "love is strong as death" figures in Morrison's *Song of Solomon* as Milkman and Guitar end in a deadly embrace, and Morrison's *Beloved* where Sethe's "too thick" love results in the death of her baby daughter.[51] Love as unacknowledged lament, where the lovers are "in love with each other's absence" could apply to Sula and Nel in *Sula*, and to Son and Jadine in *Tar Baby* who, in the relatively isolated space of Eloe, read "the sexy parts of the Bible" to each other. *Beloved* is almost entirely about absence and lamentation as it dramatizes the pain of family separation that was a hallmark of American chattel slavery. While in Williams's *Dessa Rose* the erotics of consensual intimacy is fully realized (albeit short-lived) in the relationship between Dessa and Kaine, in Morrison's works, it seems always to be deferred, just out of reach of the characters.

Continuing Williams's and Morrison's legacy, Edward P. Jones deconstructs the Bible as a text of racial exclusion and oppression in his 2003 Pulitzer Prize-winning novel *The Known World*. Taking on the taboo subject of free black slave owners in fictional Manchester County, Virginia, Jones approaches slavery from an entirely different angle of vision, one not so easily mapped onto coordinates of black/white, slave/free, or even female/male. To this end, he uses the figure of a white male character, Sheriff Skiffington, to illuminate the contradictions behind the

Bible defense of slavery. Skiffington is privately opposed to slavery but publicly charged with upholding the institution because of his position in law enforcement; he is determined to stay in power by representing to the slaveholding community "the good face of the law."[52] Throughout the novel, he is associated with two texts that represent the problem of slavery in antebellum America: a map titled "The Known World" hanging on his office wall and a Bible that is his constant companion at home. What Jones does with these emblems of authority in Skiffington's world is to blur the boundary between private/public, home/office, individual/social that Skiffington tries to construct to justify his passivity in opposing slavery (indeed, his active engagement in maintaining slavery). For Jones, this dichotomy between individual private conscience and collective public ill-will allowed whites to remain anti-slavery in the private sphere (home, faith, conscience) while continuing to support it publicly (marketplace, law, social structures). Moreover, Jones maintains that the Bible was the primary text used to support this: "Despite vowing to never own a slave Skiffington had no trouble doing his job to keep the institution of slavery going, an institution even God himself had sanctioned throughout the Bible" (43). Skiffington's prior commitment to the Bible defense of slavery even outweighed what the third-person narrator suggests was a series of prophetic dreams: "Wash your hands of all that slavery business, God had said in his dreams" (33).

At home, particularly at his bedside, Skiffington is constantly shown reading his Bible, yet he lacks any hermeneutic other than the Bible defense of slavery to give the text meaning:

He went back to the parlor and picked up the Bible where he had left off. But that chapter was not what he felt he needed right then so he flipped through the book and settled on Job ... (154)

Skiffington flipped through the pages of the Bible, wanting something to companion his mood. He came to the place in Genesis where two angels disguised as strangers are guests in Lot's house ... It was one of the more disturbing passages in the Bible for Skiffington and he was tempted to pass on, to find his way to Psalms and Revelation or to Matthew, but he knew that Lot and the daughters and the angels posing as strangers were all part of God's plan ... So he read through the passage, and not for the second time, and not for the third, and not for the fourth. Then he moved on to Psalms ... (162)

The Bible is reduced to a book Skiffington "flip[s] through" looking for meaning, guidance, consolation that will not come because the text remains at least partially closed to him. The failure to interpret the plight of African American slaves through the lens of Job the innocent sufferer or the residents of Sodom and Gomorrah renders the Bible as silent to Skiffington as was the book that failed to talk to Equiano in 1789. Skiffington's worldview depends on being guided by a book that he cannot, in the final analysis, either hear or understand. In this sense, he fulfills the prophetic injunction spelled out in the book of Isaiah: "Hear ye indeed, but understand not; and see ye indeed, but perceive not" (6:9).

The inability to read the Bible renders Skiffington unable to make a clear moral choice with respect to slavery. At the end when he is shot attempting to apprehend Moses, a runaway slave, the moment of his death is described as a metaphorical transition to a different afterlife than he imagined:

Skiffington was entering the house he had taken his bride to. He ran up the stairs because he felt there was something important he had to do. He found himself in a very long hall and he ran down the hall, looking in all the open rooms and wanting to stop but knowing he did not have time … At the very end of the hall there was a Bible, tilting forward, a Bible some three feet taller than he was. He got to it in time to keep it from falling over, his hands reaching to prop it up, his open left hand on the *O* in *Holy* and his open right on the second *B* in *Bible*. (369)

Skiffington is crushed by the text he "upheld," a text which, in his view, upheld the institution of slavery.

Similarly, Henry Townsend, the main character of *The Known World*, is a free black man who owns slaves of his own. The Bible for Henry is not a religious text as much as it is part of the western literary tradition from which he forms his identity as a slave owner. Henry is "mentored" as a slave owner by his former master William Robbins even as he draws his identity from the great texts of western culture: Shakespeare, Thomas Gray, John Milton, and the KJB. Henry is (mis)educated by Fern Elston, a free black woman (who refuses to pass as a white woman though light enough to do so) who teaches him to worship the superiority of western culture. Fern says of Henry, who admires the Devil's speech from Milton's *Paradise Lost*, "He thought only a man who knew himself well could say such a thing, could turn his back on God with just finality. I tried to make him see what a horrible choice that was, but Henry had made up his mind about that and I could not turn him back. He loved Milton and he loved Thomas Gray" (134–5). Thomas Gray is recalled at the moment of Henry's death when he has an afterlife experience similar to Skiffington's:

His wife and Fern were discussing a Thomas Gray poem. He thought he knew the one they were talking about but as he formed some words to join the conversation, death stepped into the room and came to him: Henry walked up the steps and into the tiniest of houses, knowing with each step that he did not own it, that he was only renting. He was ever so disappointed … Whoever was renting the house to him had promised a thousand rooms, but as he traveled through the house he found less than four rooms, and all the rooms were identical and his head touched their ceilings. "This will not do," Henry kept saying to himself, and he turned to share that thought with his wife, to say, "Wife, wife, look what they have done," and God told him right then, "Not a wife, Henry, but a widow." (10–11)

Henry did not own western culture but was, metaphorically, only "renting" it.

In contrast to Henry and Skiffington, Alice Night, thought to be insane from being kicked in the head by a mule, turns out to be the character who embodies transcendental knowledge and artistic vision. The multi-media installation she creates becomes a sort of Bible that restores the community's vision and hope:

an enormous wall hanging, a grand piece of art that is part tapestry, part painting, and part clay structure – all in one exquisite Creation, hanging silent and yet songful on the Eastern wall. It is … a kind of map of life of the County of Manchester, Virginia, but a "map" is such a poor word for such a wondrous thing … It is what God sees when He looks down on Manchester. (384)

Not only does Alice survive and escape from slavery, her art also survives as a new text that overwrites the social, legal, and literary discourse that upheld slavery, including the KJB. The question posed by postmodern black writers thus appears to be: if the Bible can no longer function as a text of supernatural wonders, what, then, might be its fate as a book of signs as well?

NOTES

1 For a comprehensive study of the Bible in African American culture, see the essays in Vincent L. Wimbush's exhaustive edited collection, *African Americans and the Bible: Sacred Texts and Social Textures* (New York: Continuum, 2000).

2 See Theophus H. Smith, *Conjuring Culture: Biblical Formations of Black America* (New York: Oxford University Press, 1994). Smith reads African American encounters with the Bible during slavery as a source of cultural formation, similar to a "conjure book" in African American folk religion. See also Wimbush's *African Americans and the Bible* and his more recent *Theorizing Scriptures: New Critical Orientations to a Cultural Phenomenon* (New Brunswick, NJ: Rutgers University Press, 2008); Mark A. Noll's *America's God: From Jonathan Edwards to Abraham Lincoln* (New York: Oxford University Press, 2002) has a detailed section on the crisis of American Bible interpretation, including the argument over the Bible and slavery. Most recently, Allen Dwight Callahan in *The Talking Book: African Americans and the Bible* (New Haven, CT: Yale University Press, 2006) documents the tensions and contradictions in African Americans' exposure to and embracing of the English Bible. For a black feminist treatment, see Katherine Clay Bassard, *Transforming Scriptures: African American Women Writers and the Bible* (Athens, GA: University of Georgia Press, 2010).

3 Lynn A. Casmier-Paz, "Slave Narratives and the Rhetoric of Author Portraiture," *New Literary History* 34 (2003): 91–116; 92.

4 *Ibid.*, 97.

5 Henry Louis Gates, Jr., *The Signifying Monkey: A Theory of Afro-American Literary Criticism* (New York: Oxford University Press, 1988), Ch. 4.

6 Olaudah Equiano, *The Interesting Narrative of Olaudah Equiano or Gustavas Vassa, the African*, in *The Classic Slave Narratives*, ed. Henry Louis Gates, Jr. (New York: New American Library, 1987), 1–182; 43–4. Further citations appear in the body of the text.

7 Casmier-Paz, "Slave Narratives and the Rhetoric of Author Portraiture," 98.

8 Callahan, *The Talking Book*, xi, xii.

9 Noll, *America's God*, 395.

10 I am indebted for most of the information on the slave missions system to Janet Duitsman Cornelius's excellent study, *Slave Missions and the Black Church in the Antebellum South* (Columbia, SC: University of South Carolina Press, 1999).

11 *Ibid.*, 74.

12 See William L. Andrews's provocative article, "*The Confessions of Nat Turner*: Memoir of a Martyr or Testament of a Terrorist?" in Wimbush, ed., *Theorizing Scriptures*, 79–87.

13 Cornelius, *Slave Missions*, 90.

14 *Ibid.*

15 See Albert J. Raboteau's definitive study, *Slave Religion: The "Invisible Institution" in the Antebellum South* (New York: Oxford University Press, 1978).

16 See Gates, *The Classic Slave Narratives*.

17 Janet Duitsman Cornelius, *When I Can Read My Title Clear: Literacy, Slavery, and Religion in the Antebellum South* (Columbia, SC: University of South Carolina Press, 1991).

18 Frederick Douglass, *Life and Times of Frederick Douglass* (Mineola, NY: Dover, 2003), 49.

19 *Ibid.*, 49.

20 Douglass, *Narrative of the Life of Frederick Douglass, An American Slave*, in *The Classic Slave Narratives*, ed. Gates, 243–331; 274.

21 See Sterling Stuckey, "'My Burden Lifted': Frederick Douglass, the Bible, and Slave Culture" in Wimbush, *African Americans and the Bible*, 251–65. See also Callahan, *The Talking Book*, 21–5. On the changing hermeneutical climate, see Hans W. Frei's *The Eclipse of Biblical Narrative: A Study in Eighteenth and Nineteenth Century Hermeneutics*, (New Haven, CT: Yale University Press, 1980).

22 Cornelius, *Slave Missions*, 86.

23 On the establishment and activities of the American Bible Society see Paul Gutjahr, *An American Bible: A History of the Good Book in the United States, 1777–1880*, (Stanford, CA: Stanford University Press, 1999).

24 Quoted in Gutjahr, *An American Bible*, 30.

25 *Ibid.*, 31.

26 *Ibid.*, 131.

27 Quoted in Cornelius, *Slave Missions*, 131.

28 Quoted in *ibid.*, 132.

29 Callahan, *The Talking Book*, 24.

30 Cornelius, *Slave Missions*, 94.

31 Thomas Lewis Johnson, *Twenty-Eight Years a Slave; or, the Story of My Life in Three Continents* (Bournemouth: W. Mate & Co., 1909), 18.

32 Quoted in Cornelius, *Slave Missions*, 112.

33 Josiah Priest, *The Bible Defence of Slavery: and Origins, Fortunes, and History of the Negro Race* (Glasgow, KY: W. S. Brown, 1852).

34 Robert Alter, *Canon and Creativity: Modern Writing and the Authority of Scripture* (New Haven, CT and London: Yale University Press, 2000), 8.

35 Zora Neale Hurston, *Mules and Men* (New York: Harper and Row), 3.

36 Danille Taylor-Guthrie, ed., *Conversations with Toni Morrison* (Jackson, MS: University Press of Mississippi, 1994), 97, 80.

37 Toni Morrison, *Lecture and Speech of Acceptance, Upon the Award of the Nobel Prize for Literature, Delivered in Stockholm on the Seventh of December, Nineteen Hundred and Ninety-Three* (New York: Knopf, 1994). Also available at http://nobelprize.org/nobel-prizes/literature/bureates/1993/morrison-lecture.html

38 *Ibid.*

39 See Bassard, *Transforming Scriptures.*

40 Sherley Anne Williams, *Dessa Rose* (New York: HarperCollins, 1999), ix–x. All further citations appear in the body of the text.

41 On Dessa's utterance, see Mae G. Henderson's seminal piece, "Speaking in Tongues: Dialogues, Dialectics, and the Black Woman Writer's Literary Tradition," in *Changing Our Own Words: Essays on Criticism, Theory, and Writing by Black Women*, ed. Cheryl A. Wall (New Brunswick, NJ: Rutgers University Press, 1989), 16–37.

42 I use this phrase in the sense of Ann duCille's term "coupling convention" to denote heterosexual unions that do not reinscribe heterosexism, but form part of black resistance to dominant cultural notions of marriage. See Ann duCille, *The Coupling Convention: Sex, Text, and Tradition in Black Women's Fiction* (New York: Oxford University Press, 1993).

43 Julia Kristeva, *Tales of Love*, trans. Leon S. Roudiez (New York: Columbia University Press,1987).

44 Kaine's name is also an allusion to sugar cane, the cash-crop of the Caribbean. Dessa describes him as: "the color of cane syrup" in the novel (58).

45 Adam Nehemiah is also a figure who signifies on the historical personage of Nehemiah Adams, author of the notorious *South-side View of Slavery*. See my "Crossing Over: Free Space, Sacred Place and Intertextual Geographies in Peter Randolph's *Sketches of Slave Life*," *Religion and Literature* 35.2–3 (2003): 113–41.

46 Shirley A. Stave, ed., *Toni Morrison and the Bible: Contested Intertexualities* (New York: Peter Lang, 2006).

47 Judy Pocock, "'Through a Glass Darkly': Typology in Toni Morrison's Song of Solomon," *Canadian Review of American Studies* 35.3 (2005): 281–98; 281.

48 André LaCocque, *Ruth: A Continental Commentary*, trans. K. C. Hanson (Minneapolis: Fortress Press, 2004), 96.

49 Toni Morrison, *The Bluest Eye* (New York: Plume, 1994), 210.

50 Toni Morrison, *Tar Baby* (New York: Vintage Books, 2004), 46, 45.

51 Toni Morrison, *Beloved* (New York: Vintage Books, 2004). Similar ideas about love and the death of children appear in Gwendolyn Brooks's poem "The Mother" and Lucille Clifton's "the lost baby poem." The representation of

black motherhood and infanticide I regard as a metaphor for the law of *partus sequitur ventrem* as the mother is deemed responsible for the slave status (and consequent "social death" *à la* Orlando Patterson) of her offspring.

52 Edward P. Jones, *The Known World* (New York: HarperCollins, 2003), 147. All further citations appear in the body of the text.

15 | Jean Rhys, Elizabeth Smart, and the "gifts" of the King James Bible

HEATHER WALTON

The girl's Bible

My cousin showed me the Bible she had been given for Christmas. It came in its own little box – hinged and clasped like a jewellery casket. The small book was bound in white leather embossed with stars. The pages were tissue-thin, and every one was edged with gold. It was very beautiful and I wanted one for myself.

The week before my birthday I went with my mother to the "Scripture Union" shop. There were shelves full of Bibles but they were: "new," "revised," "common," for the "plain man." Their covers were made of card and paper. The pages seemed thick and ordinary. I wanted a "girl's Bible" gleaming white and gold with transparent pages. At last we found one. It was entirely perfect from the white ribbons attached to the spine for bookmarks to the deep pink inside page upon which my mother wrote my name, my age, and all her love.

Such a lovely thing and so useful. I had always been afraid of the dark, but now each night I placed the sacred casket under my pillow and slept protected from all harm. If the darkness was particularly terrible I would hold the Bible to me and curl around it as its warmth spread out through every narrow vein.

● ● ●

For much of my adult life I have been engaged with the problems the Bible poses for women. My academic engagement with the Bible has been informed by feminist biblical criticism, and my research into the interdisciplinary encounters between literature and theology has addressed feminist literary revisionings of biblical texts. Revisioning, after Adrienne Rich,[1] has been framed as an act of cultural resistance: a return to tradition in order to "know it differently ... to break its hold over us."[2] But whilst all feminist revisionists have sought freedom from bondage to the text, not all have sought to break its hold entirely. Many have emphasized the continuing umbilical links between their personal identity and the Bible. Alicia Ostriker writes, "Layers of biblical textuality come into play with layers of my own identity and family history ... We intermingle and bleed into each other."[3] Michele Roberts speaks of the personal trauma caused by her efforts to "excise ... the past, my unconscious and the system of images which had formed me"[4] and describes her return to biblical figures in fiction as a political and personal quest both for restitution and wellbeing.

Whilst I remain fascinated by the energy and creativity women writers like Ostriker and Roberts have brought to refashioning biblical narratives, I have become increasingly aware that this work has problematic aspects – particularly for those of us who admit to being still intimately associated with the Bible. We are aware that engaging with a dominant tradition, even to renew it, inevitably reinscribes its power. We observe that the process of abstracting fragments of narratives and biblical characters from their textual context can facilitate their unwelcome transformation into archetypes which reinforce traditional binary understandings of masculine and feminine qualities.[5] We may also experience a sense of loss as the literary form and language of the Bible are emptied of significance and the "story" of the silenced woman assumes center stage. Even the most positive advocates of revisioning tend to describe it as a struggle to achieve a blessing or a pleasure that would otherwise be denied to women. The Bible, we thus imply, pronounces curses upon women and must be forced to yield its gifts.

But this was not my first experience of the Bible. To me it was beautiful and beneficent, and this impression did not change even when I eventually began to read it![6] I found it deeply boring – but in an unyielding and satisfying way that was proof of my powers of endurance. However, it was not only dry and difficult. It was also funny. Men appeared as strange creatures who "pisseth against the wall."[7] It was sexy: "My beloved put in his hand by the hole of the door."[8] It was sunny and fresh as Jesus walked by the lakeside, and it thrilled my rebel heart as the hypocrites were damned and the publicans and prostitutes jostled into the kingdom. What seemed its central message, "Thou shalt love the Lord thy God with all thy heart and with all thy soul ... Thou shalt love thy neighbour as thyself,"[9] was all the law and the prophets a young girl needed.

Of course I did notice some problems: "In sorrow thou shalt bring forth children,"[10] "Wives, submit,"[11] "Let your women keep silence ..."[12] However, the fact that my Bible was the King James Bible (KJB), this gold and white totemic object which was never intended as a book for reading – hence the archaic translation – meant that the (very) unpleasant aspects of the holy book were experienced at some remove. It did not occur to me to imagine that the strange words I was digesting could be directly traced back to historical events or straightforwardly applied to real life.

This experience of reading the Bible belonged to an age of *naïveté* before a hermeneutics of suspicion intervened and resulted in an appropriately adult relationship with the text. However, recalling it in the context of this book encourages me to explore the *gifts* the Bible has given to women writing in the twentieth century who encountered the KJB as a text offering important personal and literary resources. I have chosen to focus upon Jean Rhys and Elizabeth Smart as these women were both familiar with, and fascinated by, the KJB. Although they experienced the Bible as a text "set apart" because of its religious and cultural positioning, they do not associate its power with social convention. It is first of all a book and, as such, belongs to the realm of imagination which is, in some respects at least, opposed to the world of law and regulation. As might be expected, much of their attention is focused on the elemental dramas the text describes and the license these dramas afford them to engage directly with issues relating to female sexuality.[13] The Bible offered them dramatic personas and literary contexts of apocalyptic significance – far more artistically productive than those culturally ascribed to women. Above all, the form, style, and language of the KJB are persistent markers throughout their work.

Jean Rhys: the Bible is modern

Jean Rhys was born in Roseau, Dominica in 1890[14] into a small community riven by old conflicts. Amongst the white inhabitants a shameful awareness of the ills of slavery (including the illicit sexual liaisons that the system produced) was concealed beneath a rigid colonial social code and civic discourses of civilization and progress. As a child Rhys developed an uncomfortable awareness of the existence of opposing realities, each unable to accommodate the other and placed in irreconcilable opposition. This perception, deepened by family tensions and personal trauma,[15] coalesced into a binary vision of existence in which twinned powers (e.g., purity/sexuality, whites/blacks, England/Caribbean, clichés/imagination, wealth/dependency) eternally confront each other. This schema, which is inscribed throughout her writing, gradually developed and became more complex.[16] As this process unfolded the Bible came to be associated not with the forces of domination but with the vital, exhilarating, and yet tragic aspects of existence – always standing against "the huge machine of order, law and respectability"[17] whose cold white power bled life from its victims.

In an arresting passage from her autobiography, *Smile Please*, Jean Rhys describes her earliest perceptions of God: "I imagined God, this strange thing or person, I heard about, was a book. Sometimes it was a large book standing upright or half open and I could see the print inside but it made no sense to me. Other times the book was smaller and inside were sharp flashing things."[18] On the same page she makes reference to the Bible as amongst those books in a glass-fronted bookcase from which she eagerly learned to read. Whilst psychoanalytical analyses of this strange fragment have been offered,[19] I read it as indicative of an early association Rhys formed between an inscrutable and sometimes dangerous divinity and the world of books, including the Bible, which offered perplexing glimpses of an alternative world unrestrained by the restrictive codes of her colonial girlhood.

Another early association was made by Rhys between the intoxicating beauty of her environment, with its many casual threats to human life, and the biblical drama. She had the palpable sense that deadly struggles between good and evil were being fought out in her own island paradise:

It's strange growing up in a very beautiful place. It was alive I was sure of it. Behind the bright colours the softness, the hills like clouds and the clouds like fantastic hills. There was something austere, sad, lost, all these things …

I was aware of the existence of death, misfortune, poverty, disease. I finally arrived at the conclusion the devil was as powerful as God … It was a fight between the two.[20]

The sense of dwelling in an environment infused by potent religious symbols pressed upon her from all sides. Colonial settlers had themselves labeled the wild island with its sulphur springs and impenetrable forests in biblical terms. Dominica had its own Valley of Desolation in the center of which was the Abomination of Desolation, the huge crater of a semi-active volcano. The language of the Bible (particularly its apocalyptic imagery) was repeated in the everyday speech of black Dominicans – giving it a potency that in Rhys's fiction contrasts sharply with the too-anaemic discourses of white society.[21] In *Wide Sargasso Sea*[22] the sense of dwelling in Eden, but Eden after the fall, is compressed into this memorable description of an old colonial plantation:

Our garden was large and beautiful as the garden in the Bible – the tree of life grew there. But it had gone wild. The paths were overgrown and a smell of dead flowers mixed with the fresh living smell. Underneath the tree ferns, tall as forest ferns, the light was green. Orchids flourished out of reach or for some reason not to be touched. One was snaky looking. (17)

The Caribbean generated Rhys's first intimations of being drawn into a larger cosmic conflict the consequences of which were painfully evident in the natural environment and social relationships. Innocence was always already lost, and even children could recognize that hatred intruded into apparently harmonious relations[23] and that loveliness kept company with cruelty, guilt, and desire.[24] Whilst this situation was undeniably tragic it could also be exhilarating. There was no point, Rhys concluded, in seeking refuge; one might as well accept the adventure and intoxication of the fallen state. In a short story based upon Rhys's girlhood experience of engrossing but abusive conversational encounters with an older man, she reflects upon the loss of innocence: "She was not a good girl – who would object – but a wicked one … The prospect before her might be difficult and uncertain but it was … exciting."[25] Rhys's palpable sense of being one of those who had gained knowledge at the price of innocence came to be interpreted by her as revolt against those in control of society. Those in power, she believed, were active in maintaining the illusion that nothing terrible had happened. There had never been a serpent (or indeed God or nakedness) in the garden. The sense of suppressed horror Rhys experienced at the heart of things[26] was everywhere denied.

Although her writing frequently contrasts the passion, heat, and beauty Rhys experienced in her childhood with the coldness of Europe, apart from some short stories and *Wide Sargasso Sea*, the major body of Rhys's work is not set in the "extreme green"[27] of the Caribbean. In the harsh stone cities of Paris and London a range of female characters, all of whom are lost, move through a series of dreary hotel rooms. But in these urban environments the same fundamental dramas are re-enacted. The wallpaper in a cheap hotel recalls the "tree of life gone wild":

A large bird sitting on the branch of a tree, faced, with open beak, a strange wingless creature, half-bird, half lizard, which also had its beak open and its neck stretched in a belligerent attitude. The branch on which they were perched sprouted fungus and queerly shaped leaves and fruit.[28]

These grotesque images are signs of a fantastical reality breaking through the walls of the everyday world (dramatic moments are often symbolized through trees in Rhys's fiction), but its existence continues to be denied by the hypocrites who have refused the knowledge of good and evil. They dwell in "the heaven of those who cannot think, avoid thought, and have no imagination," which is the hell of those who "seek, strive, rebel."[29]

Although Rhys uses religious symbolism to describe the powers that sustain the status quo, she also names these directly in material terms as sex, money, and power. All Rhys's main female characters survive by trading on the sexual market – as did Rhys herself for a number of years. Through them she presents a penetrating fictional analysis of the interlinking powers that damn the weak and powerless whilst showering the wealthy and the fortunate with blessings. In the passage below from *After Leaving Mr. Mackenzie*, Julia attempts to confront her rich former lover with the realities of her existence:

"When you've had a baby and it dies for the simple reason that you don't have enough money to keep it alive, it leaves you with a sort of hunger … And then of course you're indifferent because the whole thing is too stupid to be anything other than indifferent about …"

"Look here, I don't believe that; you're making it up."

All right, don't believe it then.

And there was Neil James puckering his forehead and trying to be so kind. So kind, so cautious, so perfectly sure that all is for the best and no mistakes are ever made …

How rum if after all these years I hated him – not for any reason than that he's so damned respectable and secure sitting there so smugly …

Because he has money he is a kind of god. Because I have none I'm a kind of worm. (80–1)

The smug optimism of the damned respectable is sustained not by silence but rather by clichés and trivialities:

They think in terms of a sentimental ballad and that is what is terrifying about them. It isn't their cruelty … it's their extraordinary naivety. Everything within their whole bloody world is a cliché. Everything is born out of a cliché, rests on a cliché, survives by a cliché. And they believe in the clichés – there's no hope.[30]

In contrast the Bible does not deal in clichés or shy away from the "facts of life" and so must be studiously misread. Rhys humorously records this conversation with her aunt:

One afternoon while we were sipping tea she asked me, "Have you ever read the Song of Songs?"

I said, "You mean in the Bible? Yes I have read it."

"I hope," she said rather severely, "that you don't imagine it's about a woman, or a man's feelings about a woman."[31]

Amongst her unpublished papers we find a more sustained reflection on the differences between the Bible and the clichés of the hypocrites.

The typewritten draft of an article entitled "The Bible is Modern"[32] brings together some of the themes already discussed but takes us further by offering new insights into Rhys's own understanding of her writing style. The draft begins with a reflection upon the famous phrase from Genesis 1:3, "Let there be light …": Rhys argues that "There is something short, snappy and utterly modern about this sentence," fitting it for a place in the "newest starkest novel."[33] The English (who here stand for the bland hypocrites inhabiting this cold environment) would prefer a more ornate and fantastic description of God's work of creation and are disappointed about the way "this marvellous book" distils its content into "stories expressed in this stark, modern, manner" (1). What particularly upsets them is the fact that the Bible depends for its effect upon an intensity of feeling that is characteristic of "primitive" and "Oriental people" (1). Rhys argues that this excessive sensitivity is deeply repugnant to those shaped by the English social system where intense feelings are "forbidden." Intense feelings are "a quality of the subject peoples," and if the English began to have them, "the ruling classes in England could not continue to exist" (2). The final paragraph of the article reveals the close association Rhys perceives between the Bible and her own writing:

The idea that books written in short, simple sentences, depending for their effectiveness upon the intensity of feeling of the author, are inferior books, follows automatically, because of the whole solidarity of the English social system … [they] must not think very much … and as for expressing their feelings … Never. When you think of the mentality of the average Englishman, all this is understandable. But then what is difficult for us black people [sic] to understand is the ingenious way they set about making money out of "God said 'Let there be Light.'" (2)

As well as repeating the binary schema referred to previously (interestingly both the Bible and Rhys herself are here identified with black, primitive, and subject people who commit the transgressive act of seeing and feeling intensely), Rhys is offering here an implicit defense of her own brief books written in short simple sentences using direct language – she described *Voyage in the Dark* as written in words of one syllable, "like a kitten mewing."[34]

Elaine Savory has argued that Rhys's fiction with its recurring themes and characters can be read as "a series of long poems" each different but linked to the rest by powerful resonances and textual associations.[35] Savory might have added that these linked novels function very much like books in the Bible. They return over and over again to the same major themes which are explored in "biblical" prose that is never ornamental and rarely subjective but relies for its impact upon polyvalent symbols repeated to increasing effect. A passage from *Good Morning Midnight* describing the death of the narrator's child illustrates the intensity this technique achieves for Rhys. Particularly "biblical" is the heartbreaking lament constructed out of parallel phrasing – and once again the trees stand out as potent images of a cursed Eden:

The sage femme has very white hands and clear slanting eyes and when she looks at you the world stops rocking about …
  And there's always the tisane of orange flower water.
  But my heart, heavy as lead, heavy as a stone.
  He has a ticket tied around his wrist because he died. Lying so cold and still with a ticket around his wrist because he died.

Not to think. Only to watch the branches of that tree and the pattern they make standing out against a cold sky. Above all not to think … (116–17)

I have briefly described how the Bible, the "marvellous" book, provides literary resources which Rhys energetically utilized throughout her fiction and which she relies upon to justify her choice of defiance and the rebel's part. However, because she always takes the side of the lost, the dead, and the damned and dares to name the horror at the heart of existence, Rhys does not employ the Bible to transpose the ghostly trace of a redemptive schema into her narratives.[36] Indeed, she offers a bitterly humorous response to Joyce's optimistic ending in Ulysses. In the closing pages of Good Morning Midnight the aging and despairing Sasha clasps to herself the ghoulish form of damned humanity. Her "Yes, yes, yes" may betoken compassion for "another poor devil of a human being" but is very different from the cry of Molly Bloom which opens space for regeneration (159). There is no chance of regaining paradise. Rhys always remains firmly located within the dangerous garden of a world gone wild amongst its frightening creatures and strange fruits.

Towards the end of her life she composed a "calypso" which records a personal vigil in the garden experienced in the haunted dreams of her own "long night/lost night." This time the garden is Gethsemane where forever Judas kisses and Jesus weeps – while the tree stands witness:

> Oh I dreamt about Jesus and I dreamt about Judas
> And I dreamt about trees
> Watching
> I dreamt about Jesus and I dreamt about Judas
> Weeping[37]

Love is strong as death: the work of Elizabeth Smart

Elizabeth Smart was born in Ottawa in 1913, into a wealthy and socially well-connected family. Like Rhys she was deeply influenced by the wild beauty of her native land but struggled to feel at home in a context which she felt was far removed from emerging centers of artistic creativity and offered few opportunities for female self-expression. Smart greatly admired Rhys's work,[38] and there are many fascinating correspondences between the style and outlook of the two women.[39] Of most interest in the context of this volume, however, is the way both used the Bible in constructing works that represented a searing challenge to the social and sexual values of their times.

There are many references in Smart's autobiographical writings to reading the Bible as a girl and young woman. She read to alleviate the boredom and frustration she encountered in her Anglican girls' school where petty regulation passed for true religion:

You had to tie a pillow on your head before you went to chapel … but this was not religion. One simply laughed at it. Meanwhile there were those five minute waits while you assembled in the assembly room … so I read the Bible … The King James's version of course.[40]

She read when she quarreled with her mother or was scared of the dark:

I got scared. I said, " 'Though the mountains be carried off in the midst of the Sea'[41] – I think I will read the New Testament."[42]

She read when disappointed in the lukewarm embraces of a man she had thought herself in love with:

I sat in the sun and read bits of "The Song of Solomon." I thought … what lovers they could be and aren't these men who think they are lovers. They have no overriding passions. He did not adore my whole body.[43]

Although her upbringing was only conventionally religious, Smart was deeply interested in the ancient call of religion and the wayward movements of the Spirit. The Bible was Smart's familiar companion, but there were aspects of her reading that assumed particular significance as she began to develop a distinctive literary voice. From an early age Smart was convinced of her vocation to be a writer. She understood this as a sacred calling not merely to produce prose and verse but to express the infinite in finite form:

I know I've *heard* the poem. I've felt the WORD.

And above all I am aware of the inconvenient gift trapped in my lap. NOT to be ignored. A sacred duty is not too strong a way to put it.[44]

This calling was not easy to fulfill, however, particularly for a sensual young woman inconveniently burdened by her parents' social aspirations. Her early work testifies to a deep anxiety that she might fail her divine commission. In this context she was obsessively challenged by the parable of the talents (sometimes conflated with the parable of the sower, "how many seeds lie on the wet ground?")[45] and comforted and sustained by the parable of the seed that eventually bore much fruit.[46] When she was nineteen years old she pinned up a copy of "A Seed Growing Secretly" by Henry Vaughan to the wall of her cabin retreat:[47]

> Then bless thy secret growth, nor catch
> At noise, but thrive unseen and dumb;
> Keep clean, be as fruit, earn life, and watch
> Till the white-wing'd reapers come!

What marks Smart's wrestling with her calling is not only the sense of responsibility she felt towards her vocation – "I must not forget. IT is my heavenly key – my work, my purpose"[48] – but the way she came to understand, after many conflicts, that the vocation to write was deeply complicit with sexual desire and the overwhelming compulsions of maternity. Smart was not a reclusive author nurturing her spiritual insights apart from her other passions. All of these, she believed, shared the same fundamental characteristics of being responses to irresistible divine forces given shape through the body of the "writer" who enters "daily and nightly into the body of God."[49] Smart was developing a powerfully sensuous mysticism fed by her readings in the Bible and the poetic meditations of Thomas Traherne, Henry Vaughan, George Herbert, and other mystical writers.[50] It is this distinctive mystical awareness that animates her journals, prose books, and poetry. However, it was difficult for Smart to find the means to express her idiosyncratic spiritual vision in the cultural environment she sought out as a young woman (a milieu of modernist poetry, classical and jazz music, psychoanalysis, surrealism, and left-wing politics). She struggled with this challenge in many anxious passages and experimental pieces written in her journal notebooks.

Critics are agreed[51] that Smart's journals played an extremely important role in her writing life, and all her prose work is developed out of original entries in the notebooks. What is striking is the increasing use Smart makes of dramatic biblical imagery to transcribe everyday events. The use of such images lends an import to her writing enabling her to transcend the commonplace and, ironically, employing these ancient resources achieves a modern and surreal effect. Like the KJB translation of the Psalms and prophetic books, the entries are frequently interspersed with exclamative "O"s. This is typical: "From the beating of the heart O! like a pulse from the sea, uncontrollable, for a vision upward through the thorns."[52] Accounts of dinner parties, sea voyages, artistic encounters, and love affairs are presented in prophetic and apocalyptic images; for example,

God come down out of the eucalyptus tree and tell me who will drown in so much blood ... I pray god to understand my corrupt language and step down for a moment to sit on my broken bench. Will there be a birth from all this blood?[53]

In the journals Smart also repeatedly employs resonant words from the KJB such as blood, heart, flesh, bone, seed, fruit, and rock.[54] These simple words fuse together metaphorical and material references. As David Norton has argued, the presence of strong signifiers which carry symbolic weight whilst still connecting immediately to sense experience generates immense literary power.[55] Smart came to recognize the strength biblical language and imagery provided in her efforts to construct her own distinctive literary abode. It is a poignant indication of this identification with the Bible that when Smart withdrew alone to the remote outpost of Pender Island to conceal her first pregnancy, she papered the walls and even the windows (!) of her small cottage with quotations from the Bible – quite literally inhabiting the biblical text at this key period in her life.[56]

Whilst her journals constitute the fabric of all Smart's "prose works,"[57] her books are not constructed as a simple compilation of journal extracts. The need to discover an appropriate *form* for her writing preoccupied Smart, who found the conventional structure of even the most "modern" novel inappropriate:

I am irritated with the devious method and hidden indirectness of the novel ... when I think of what I want to say, I cannot think of that way of saying it. The fierce impart things, drawn over this huge irrelevant skeleton. But what form?[58]

The advice received from friends and publishers was imperiously rejected:

It is false and ridiculous to listen to fools advising me to think of other people and their positions, to invent characters ... and situations for them. I don't want the scope of the world laid out like the largest newspaper, no, but squeezed dry and compressed and reduced to its minimum but most potent.[59]

Having rejected a huge skeleton in favor of a more potent form, Smart worked obsessively at creating small, compressed pieces of writing which possess an energy born of extreme pressure (she used the metaphor of the black hole towards the end of her life to describe the nature of creative energy[60]). What is evident, once again, is that a biblical quality structures these tightly controlled pieces whose effect is generated by potency of language and constraint of form rather than the development of character or plot. Brigid Brophy argues that Smart's distinctive poetic prose "belongs to the tradition of the Authorized translation"[61] and succeeds because beyond it echoes the "sentence to sentence texture" of the Bible. The very form of her work is infused with referential power borrowed from the biblical books she employs "to such piercing purpose. Its insistent rhythm, like theirs, is the rhythm of a throb."[62]

Brophy's comments could be applied to all Smart's published work, but they were occasioned by her reading of the most famous and most misunderstood: *By Grand Central Station I Sat Down and Wept*. Smart planned and wrote this book in the years leading up to and during the Second World War. In this period she had significant relationships with two men in particular: Jean Varda and the poet George Barker. Smart had overcome her fear that the "compelling monster sex"[63] would distract her from writing and had come to believe that her body was a channel of revelation: "when virginity is lost the world becomes your lover."[64] In a situation of political threat and danger, "the seed" divinely entrusted to the writer assumes a new significance. It is still the WORD mysteriously producing its secret fruit, but now it also describes a fragile divine essence in danger of being obliterated in the conflict. Sexual associations are also brought into play: the seed is the fruit of love conceived by the woman lover but not cherished by her male partner. In this passage from her journal, which was later incorporated into the novel, Smart employs the metaphor of pregnancy to refer to this sacred charge. It is important to note that the passage was written many months before Smart conceived her first child:

I insist on looking the other way, like the last pregnant woman in a desolated world. It is the vital thing to keep your eyes on the sun … to hang on to that hope, to cherish with every ounce of love to be squeezed from the universe, the *seed*, the frail seed … (Cradle the seed, cradle the seed, even in the volcano's mouth.)[65]

Smart's developing use of a biblical symbol which already had great significance for her reflects the new concerns that dominate *By Grand Central Station*. She had already decided that the book was to be about love; "But love is so large and formless."[66] The question was how to approach this huge topic. For Smart, love would always be powerfully sexual, and sex in the work is not an allegorical pointer to something beyond itself but the very pathway love takes in human life. That love is sexual does not mean it is not cosmic or divine, however. The challenge was to unite these aspects of love in a compelling vision of a power as "strong as death,"[67] which would be her prophetic message to her generation.

The resources to do so came from an inspirational marriage between personal experience and the Bible – augmented by references to her favorite poets and writers. There are many biblical allusions: to the death of Absalom, to Lot's wife, and to the tree of knowledge, for example.[68] Sometimes these references are humorous: "I have done this twice today, he said as we lay in the orchard, once with her, once with you and once with the jaw-bone of an ass"[69] – but usually they are dramatic. Although the gospel and epistles of John are not quoted directly, they are frequently echoed, and "St. John" is acknowledged by Smart in "Note to Readers."[70] As the title indicates, psalms of lament haunt the text, and there are several "mini apocalypses" in which the author describes the awful consequences which follow the denial of love. The Song of Solomon is widely referenced throughout, and Smart employs it as a means of contrasting the ways of love with the powers of this world. This famous passage intertwines biblical verses with a narrative concerning her arrest in Arizona, on charges of immorality, whilst traveling with Barker:

How long have you known him? (I am my beloved's and my beloved is mine: he feedeth among the lilies.)
    Did you sleep in the same room? (Behold thou art fair my love, behold thou art fair: thou hast dove's eyes.)
    In the same bed? (Behold thou art fair, my beloved, yea pleasant, also our bed is green.)
    Did intercourse take place? (I sat down under his shadow with great delight and his fruit was sweet to my taste.)[71]

Smart was a very beautiful woman, and as I have argued elsewhere,[72] her reputation has suffered because she was seen as the "dumb blonde" of the literary world. *By Grand Central Station* has mostly been interpreted as a simple and immediate account of her love affair with George Barker, but as I have shown, the work is in fact a carefully crafted literary creation in which we can observe quite clearly the gifts the KJB has bestowed upon Smart's writing. The work itself is the fruit of a seed growing secretly for many years that produced a startlingly abundant literary harvest.

A lost garden?

It has been both challenging and restorative for me to turn my attention to the productive and creative engagement between twentieth-century women writers and the Bible. However, as I conclude this chapter I am left with a disturbing sense that the fruits both women were able to pluck from the text may now be unavailable to contemporary women writers. Both Rhys and Smart read the Bible in a translation that preserved a creative distance between themselves and the book. Ironically, this enhanced its potential for adoption as a literary resource and was particularly useful, as Rhys grasped, for women we might loosely describe as modernist[73] writers seeking to develop a distinctive voice and style.

Contemporary female authors are unlikely to have a similar relationship with the Bible. They are likely to encounter it either through dominant cultural myths and symbols (mainly unfriendly to women) or in the context of a religious environment in which modern translations are regularly used. A different dynamic of engagement and resistance will be brought into play in these contexts, and the freedom Rhys and Smart brought to their unorthodox but generative couplings with the Bible are unlikely to take place. This is not to say that there will not be other fruits to harvest, but perhaps something has been lost.

NOTES

1 Rich's generative essay, "When We Dead Awaken: Writing as Revision," in Adrienne Rich, *On Lies, Secrets and Silences: Selected Prose 1966–1978* (New York: W. W. Norton, 1978) has functioned as a manifesto for feminist literary revisioning.

2 *Ibid.*, 35.

3 Alicia Ostriker, *Feminist Revisioning and the Bible* (Oxford: Blackwell, 1993), 112.

4 Michele Roberts, "The Woman Who Wanted to Be a Hero," in *Walking on the Water: Women Talk About Spirituality*. ed. J. Garcia and S. Maitland (London: Virago, 1983), 50–65; 58.

5 See Maggie Humm, *A Reader's Guide to Contemporary Literary Criticism*, (London: Harvester Wheatsheaf, 1994), 55. Humm argues that when women attempt to engage with female figures in mythology they are in danger of reinforcing stereotypes rather than reclaiming archetypes. Both Ostriker and Roberts can be accused of offering readers images of female spirituality that are erotic, fleshly, earth related, and ecstatic – as opposed to the rational, ethical, and transcendent sacred traditions of men.

6 I read a chapter a night, completing the process on the eve of my sixteenth birthday.

7 For example, 1 Kings 21:21.

8 Song of Sol. 5:4.

9 Mark 12:30–1.

10 Gen. 3:16.

11 Eph. 5:22.

12 1 Cor. 14:34.

13 Both Rhys and Smart survived as moral outsiders in a context in which women's lives were bounded by respectability.

14 The date is uncertain due to Rhys's efforts to conceal it.

15 Rhys was conceived to replace a child who died. As a child she experienced an abusive relationship with an older man. See Elaine Savory, *The Cambridge Introduction to Jean Rhys* (Cambridge: Cambridge University Press, 2009), 4.

16 This aspect of her work has been of particular interest to postcolonial critics. See, for example, Helen Carr, *Jean Rhys* (Plymouth: Northcote House, 1996), 11–21.

17 Jean Rhys, "Vienne," in *Tigers are Better Looking* (London: Andre Deutsch, 1968), 226.

18 Jean Rhys, *Smile Please: An Unfinished Autobiography* (London: Andre Deutsch, 1979), 27.

19 See Anne Simpson, *Territories of the Psyche: The Fiction of Jean Rhys* (Basingstoke: Macmillan, 2005), 3. Rhys herself speculates that the sharp book might be associated with the needle case (and the needle sharpness) of her mother.

20 Rhys, *Smile Please*, 81–2.

21 See, for example, Rhys, *Wide Sargasso Sea* (London: Penguin, 1968), 16.

22 Set in Jamaica, not Dominica.

23 See Rhys, *Smile Please*, 49.

24 The character identified with Rochester in *Wide Sargasso Sea* states of the Caribbean: "I hated the mountains and the hills, the rivers and the rain, I hated

the sunsets of whatever colour. I hated its beauty and its indifference and the cruelty that was part of its loveliness" (147).

25 Jean Rhys, "Good-bye Marcus, Good-bye Rose," in *Sleep It Off Lady* (London: Penguin, 1979), 23–30; 30.

26 "But it was always the most ordinary things that suddenly turned round and showed you another face, a terrifying face. That was the hidden horror, the horror everyone pretended did not exist, the horror that was responsible for all the other horrors." Jean Rhys, "The Insect World," in *Sleep It Off Lady*, 123–36; 127.

27 Rhys, *Wide Sargasso Sea*, 58.

28 Rhys, *After Leaving Mr. Mackenzie* (London: Penguin, 1988), 7–8.

29 Rhys, *Smile Please*, 172.

30 Rhys, *Good Morning Midnight* (London: Penguin, 1975), 36.

31 Rhys, *Smile Please*, 70.

32 This work is undated, but there are indications it may have been composed in response to some new biblical translation.

33 Rhys, "The Bible is Modern." Unpublished and undated article, Jean Rhys Archives, University of Tulsa; 1.

34 *Jean Rhys Letters: 1931–1966*, ed. F. Wyndham and D. Melly (London: Andre Deutsch, 1984), 24.

35 Savory, *The Cambridge Introduction to Jean Rhys*, 63.

36 For a discussion of the biblical topography of desolation and fertility in Joyce see Robert Alter, *Canon and Creativity* (New Haven, CT: Yale University Press, 2000), 181.

37 *Jean Rhys Letters*, 282

38 She enthusiastically reviewed *Wide Sargasso Sea* and thought Rhys "ahead of her time both in style and mood" (see Rosemary Sullivan, *By Heart: Elizabeth Smart, a Life* [New York: Viking, 1991], 293).

39 Jill Neville makes links between the two authors in her introduction to Smart's book, *A Bonus* (London: Polytantric Press, 1977), 7–8; 8.

40 Sullivan, *By Heart*, 42.

41 A quote from Ps. 46 which begins, "God is our refuge and strength."

42 Sullivan, *By Heart*, 60.

43 Elizabeth Smart, *Necessary Secrets*, ed. Alice Van Wart, (London: Paladin, 1992), 73.

44 Elizabeth Smart, *On the Side of the Angels*, ed. Alice Van Wart (London: HarperCollins, 1994), 107–8.

45 Smart, *Necessary Secrets*, 183.

46 Mark 4:26–9.

47 Smart named her cabin "The Pulley" after the poem by George Herbert.

48 Smart, *Necessary Secrets*, 256.

49 *Ibid.*, 187.

50 Interestingly this list of respectable mystics was later expanded to include the work of the "hysteric" Margery Kempe. Smart writes, "An excessive lady … / Far too fond of love … / A lovely terrible person" (*A Bonus*, 42).

51 See Dee Horne, "Elizabeth Smart's Novel-Journal," in *Studies in Canadian Literature* 16.2 (1991): 128–46; and Nancy Wright, "The Proper Lady and the Second World War in Elizabeth Smart's Narratives," in *Essays on Canadian Writing* 48 (1992/3): 1–19.

52 Smart, *Necessary Secrets*, 187.

53 *Ibid.*, 64.

54 Robert Alter has argued that these words borrowed by Faulkner from the KJB and employed in *Absalom, Absalom!* give the author a biblicizing relation to historical reality (*Canon and Creativity*, ii).

55 David Norton, *A History of the English Bible as Literature* (Cambridge: Cambridge University Press, 2000), 421.

56 Sullivan, *By Heart*, 179.

57 She preferred this description to "novel."

58 Smart, *Necessary Secrets*, 217.

59 Sullivan, *By Heart*, 330.

60 Smart, *In the Meantime* (Ottawa: Deneau Publishers, 1984), 140.

61 Brigid Brophy, "Foreward," in Elizabeth Smart, *By Grand Central Station I Sat Down and Wept*, (London: Flamingo, 1992), 7–13; 9.

62 *Ibid.*, 9.

63 Smart, *Necessary Secrets*, 62.

64 *Ibid.*, 212.

65 *Ibid.*, 214–51.

66 *Ibid.*, 213.

67 Song of Sol. 8:6.

68 Smart recorded her reliance on these sources and was disappointed that her publishers refused to include them in the published text. Her extensive hand-written notes, entitled "References," are in the Canadian national archives.

69 Smart, *By Grand Central Station*, 75.

70 "Notes to Readers" is unpublished but now available online: www.collections-canada.gc.ca/obj/027005/f1/nlc008469.U7-v6.jpg (accessed February 20, 2010).

71 Smart, *By Grand Central Station*, 47.

72 Heather Walton, "Extreme Faith in the Work of Elizabeth Smart and Luce Irigaray," *Literature and Theology* 16.1 (2002): 40–50.

73 Especially in the sense of modernism's having a strong, if romantic, attachment to the primitive.

Chronology of major English Bible translations to 1957

Wyclif Bible, 1382–4. The first complete English Bible in manuscript form in two versions (early and late), translated by John **Wyclif** and his associates, including John Purvey and Nicholas of Hereford.

Tyndale's Translation, 1526 and 1530–1, 1534. The first complete English New Testament in printed form, translated by William Tyndale, 1526; Tyndale then published his translation of the Pentateuch (1530) and Jonah (1531). His revised New Testment appeared in 1534, partly in response to George Joye's unauthorized revision of Tyndale's New Testament. Tyndale was executed before he could complete his translation of the entire Bible.

Coverdale Bible, 1535. The first complete English Bible in printed form, translated by Miles Coverdale, a former assistant of Tyndale's.

Matthew Bible, 1537. The first complete English Bible in printed form that could be sold legally in England, it was an amalgam of the Tyndale translation and the Coverdale Bible, undertaken by John Rogers under the pseudonym Thomas Matthew.

Great Bible, 1539. A revision of the Matthew Bible directed by Miles Coverdale, printed by Edward Whitchurch by order of Henry VIII. The first official English Bible and the only one ever "authorized." Last edition 1569.

Taverner Bible, 1539. Richard Taverner's revision of the Matthew Bible, based on the Vulgate and Pagninus's Latin translation (OT) and the original Greek (NT).

Geneva Bible, 1560. The most popular and influential English Bible during most of the hundred years or so after it was published; many editions included extensive interpretive notes. It was translated by English Calvinists living in exile in Geneva. Major new editions were published in 1576 (the New Testament revised by Laurence Tomson based on Theodore Beza's 1565 Latin edition, with new NT notes) and 1599 (new notes on Revelation based on the 1596 commentary of Franciscus Junius).

Bishops' Bible, 1568. The official Bible of the Church of England under Elizabeth I, it was translated by a group composed largely of bishops and led by Matthew Parker, the Archbishop of Canterbury. Last edition 1602.

Douai–Rheims Bible, 1582 and 1609–10. Translated by English Catholics living on the Continent, first the New Testament (in Rheims) and later the Old Testament (in Douai).

King James Bible, 1611. Translated by six companies of scholars – "the best-learned in both universities" (Oxford and Cambridge) – by order of James I. Most modern editions are based on the 1769 Oxford Standard Edition by Benjamin Blayney. The first American printing of the KJB was in 1782 (printed by Robert Aitken by Act of Congress).

English Revised Version, 1885. The first major revision of the King James Bible.

James Moffatt, 1901, 1913, 1924. Moffatt's Historical New Testament (1901) was a milestone of biblical scholarship, informing his later English translations of the New (1913) and Old (1924) Testaments. Moffatt's complete Bible was published in 1926.

American Standard Version, 1901. An American revision of the King James Bible.

Revised Standard Version, 1952. A revision of the King James Bible that included updating archaic expressions.

Chronology of English Bible translations since 1957

PAUL C. GUTJAHR

The following chronology pertains especially to chapter 7 but also, in a more general way, to all of the chapters that address the reception history of the KJB since the middle of the twentieth century: this more recent reception history has been substantially shaped by the large and growing number of competing English Bible translations. By contrast, the KJB stood largely undisputed as the dominant English translation throughout the eighteenth, nineteenth, and early twentieth centuries (though it was revised during that time). In this regard, the current relationship of the KJB to other English translations bears some similarities now, as it enters its fifth century, to when it was just in its first century and was merely one of several widely read translations.

For information on English Bible Translations available in the United States before 1957, the standard works are: Margaret T. Hills, ed., *The English Bible in America* (New York: American Bible Society, 1962) and Edward O'Callaghan, *A List of Editions of the Holy Scriptures and Parts Thereof* (Albany, NY: Munsell & Rowland, 1861). What follows is a list of the English Bible translations to appear after 1957, in chronological order.

The New Testament in Modern English. J. B. Phillips. London: G. Bles, 1958.

The Holy Bible, The Berkeley Version in Modern English. Gerrit Verkuyl *et al.* Grand Rapids, MI: Zondervan, 1959.

The New English Bible. New Testament. Oxford and Cambridge: Oxford University Press and Cambridge University Press, 1961.

The New World Translations of the Holy Scriptures. Brooklyn: Watchtower Bible and Tract Society of New York, 1961.

The New Testament: An Expanded Translation. Kenneth S. Wuest. Grand Rapids, MI: Eerdmans, 1961.

The New Testament of Our Lord and Savior Jesus Christ. Fan S. Noli. Boston, MA: Albanian Orthodox Church in America, 1961.

The Children's King James Bible. Jay P. Green. New York: McGraw-Hill, 1962.

The New Testament in the Language of Today. William F. Beck. Saint Louis, MO: Concordia Publishing House, 1963.

The Amplified Bible. Frances E. Siewert. Grand Rapids, MI: Zondervan, 1965.

The Letters of Paul: An Expanded Paraphrase. Frederick F. Bruce, ed. Exeter, UK: Paternoster Press, 1965.

Good News for Modern Man: The New Testament in Today's English. Robert G. Bratcher. New York: American Bible Society, 1966.

The Jerusalem Bible. Alexander Jones, ed. New York: Doubleday, 1966.

Cotton Patch Version of Paul's Epistles. Clarence Jordan. West Sussex, UK: New Wine Publications, 1968. Jordan published further translations of the New Testament: Matthew and John (1970), Hebrews and the General Epistles (1973), Luke and Acts (1973), and the Sermon on the Mount (1980).

The New Testament: A New Translation. William Barclay. London and New York: Collins, 1969.

The New American Bible. Louis F. Hartman and Myles M. Bourke, eds. Paterson, NJ: St. Anthony Guild Press, 1970.

The New English Bible. C. H. Dodd, ed. Oxford and Cambridge: Oxford University Press and Cambridge University Press, 1970.

The Restoration of Original Sacred Name Bible. Buena Park, CA: Missionary Dispensary Bible Research, 1970.

The Living Bible, Kenneth N. Taylor *et al*. Wheaton, IL: Tyndale House Publishers, 1971.

New American Standard Bible. Reuben Olson, ed. La Habra, CA: Foundation Press Publications, 1971.

The Bible in Living English. Steven T. Byington. New York: Watchtower Bible and Tract Society, 1972.

Today's English New Testament. Don J. Klingensmith. New York: Vantage Press, 1972.

The Holy Bible: New International Version New Testament. Edwin H. Palmer, ed. Grand Rapids, MI: Zondervan, 1973.

Good News Bible: The Bible in Today's English Version. New York: American Bible Society, 1976.

The Holy Bible in the Language of Today: An American Translation. New Haven, MO: Leader Publishing Co., 1976.

The Christian Counselor's New Testament: A New Translation in Everyday English. Jay E. Adams. Grand Rapids, MI: Baker Book House, 1977.

The Holy Bible: New International Version, Containing the Old Testament and the New Testament. Grand Rapids, MI: Zondervan, 1978.

Holy Bible: The New King James Version, Containing the Old and New Testaments. Arthur Farstad, ed. Nashville, TN: Thomas Nelson, 1982.

Messianic Edition of the Living Bible. David Bronstein. Wheaton, IL: Tyndale House Publishers, 1982.

The New Jerusalem Bible. Henry Wansbrough, ed. New York: Doubleday, 1985.

The New Testament: Recovery Version. John C. Ingalls *et al.* Anaheim, CA: Living Stream Ministry, 1985.

Tanakh: A New Translation of the Holy Scriptures According to the Traditional Hebrew Text. Philadelphia, PA: The Jewish Publication Society of America, 1985.

The Holy Bible: New Century Version. Ft. Worth, TX: Worthy Publishing, 1987.

God's Word to the Nations: New Testament. Phillip B. Giessler, ed. Fairview Park, OH: Biblion Publishing, 1988.

McCord's New Testament Translation of the Everlasting Gospel. Hugo McCord. Henderson, TN: Free-Hardeman College, 1988.

God's New Covenant: A New Testament Translation. Heinz W. Cassirer. Grand Rapids, MI: Eerdmans, 1989.

Jewish New Testament: A Translation of the New Testament that Expresses Its Jewishness. David H. Stern. Jerusalem: Jewish New Testament Publications, 1989.

The Revised English Bible with Apocrypha. W. D. McHardy, ed. Oxford and Cambridge: Oxford University Press and Cambridge University Press, 1989.

The New Revised Standard Version. Bruce M. Metzger, ed. New York: Oxford University Press, 1990.

The Unvarnished New Testament. Andy Gaus. Grand Rapids, MI: Phane Press, 1991.

The Five Gospels: The Search for the Authentic Words of Jesus. Robert W. Funk, Roy W. Hoover, and the Jesus Seminar. New York: Macmillan, 1993.

The Message: The New Testament in Contemporary English. Eugene H. Peterson. Colorado Springs, CO: NavPress, 1993.

The Holy Bible: 21st Century King James Version. William D. Prindle, ed. Gary, SD: KJ21 Bible Publishers, 1994.

The Inclusive New Testament. Craig R. Smith, ed. Brentwood, MD: Priests of Equality, 1994.

The Five Books of Moses: A New Translation. Everett Fox. New York: Schocken, 1995.

God's Word. Eugene W. Bunkowske, ed. Iowa Falls, IA: World Bible Publishers, 1995.

Holy Bible: Contemporary English Version. Barclay M. Newman, ed. New York: American Bible Society, 1995.

The New Testament: An Understandable Version. William E. Paul. Seattle, WA: Impact Publications, 1995.

New Testament and Psalms: An Inclusive Version. Victor R. Gold, ed. New York and Oxford: Oxford University Press, 1995.

The Holy Bible: New International Version, Inclusive Language Edition. London: Hodder & Stoughton, 1996.

Holy Bible: New Living Translation. Wheaton, IL: Tyndale House, 1996.

The New Testament. Richard A. Lattimore. New York: Farrar Strauss Giroux, 1996.

The Holy Bible, English Standard Version. J. I. Packer, ed. Wheaton, IL: Crossway Bibles, 2001.

The Message: The Bible in Contemporary Language. Eugene H. Peterson. Colorado Springs, CO: NavPress, 2002.

The New Testament: Today's New International Version. John H. Stek *et al*. Grand Rapids, MI: Zondervan, 2002.

The Five Books of Moses: A Translation with Commentary. Robert Alter. New York: W. W. Norton & Company, 2004.

Good as New: A Radical Retelling of the Scriptures. John Henson. New Alresford, UK: O Books, 2004.

Holy Bible: Holman Christian Standard Bible. Edwin Blum, ed. Nashville, TN: Broadman & Holman, 2004.

New Living Translation, 2nd edn. Mark R. Norton, ed. Wheaton, IL: Tyndale House, 2004.

The Holy Bible: The NET Bible. W. Hall Harris, ed. Dallas, TX: Biblical Studies Press, 2005.

Today's New International Version. John H. Stek *et al*. Grand Rapids, MI: Zondervan, 2005.

Select bibliography on the King James Bible

The bibliography on the Bible, even in only its English translations, is vast; even more vast is the bibliography on the influence of the Bible on literature and other cultural forms in English. As a result, we have not attempted a comprehensive bibliography in either area. We have tried to include all books specifically on the King James Bible (KJB), with the exception of some of the more eccentric publications in the American "King James Only" movement. Our coverage of books on the general history of the English Bible, including the KJB, is extensive if not exhaustive; it includes the most important books on the English Bible before 1611. Books on the later reception of the KJB are also included, especially in the United Kingdom and the United States, though studies specifically of later translations of the Bible into English are not as extensively represented.

For the Bible's influence on literatures in English, the bibliography can be only representative, though every effort has been made to include major publications on major authors, as well as more general and theoretical studies. The focus remains on the KJB, however, rather than biblical influence more broadly.

Select articles have been included when they seemed important or interesting, but no attempt has been made to include even a representative sampling.

I The King James Bible: its background, history, and reception

Allen, Ward, ed. *Translating for King James: Notes Made By a Translator of King James's Bible*. Nashville, TN: Vanderbilt University Press, 1969.

Translating the New Testament Epistles, 1604–1611: A Manuscript from King James's Westminster Company. Nashville, TN: Vanderbilt University Press, 1977.

Allen, Ward and Edward C. Jacobus. *The Coming of the King James Gospels: A Collation of the Translators' Work-in-Progress*. Fayetteville: University of Arkansas Press, 1995.

Anderson, Christopher and Samuel Irenaeus Prime. *Annals of the English Bible*. 2 vols. New York: Robert Carter, 1852.

Backus, Irena Dorota. *The Reformed Roots of the English New Testament: The Influence of Theodore Beza on the English New Testament*. Pittsburgh: Pickwick Press, 1980.

Baikie, James. *The English Bible and Its Story: Its Growth, Its Translators and Their Adventures*. Philadelphia: Lippincott, 1928.

Barker, Henry. *English Bible Versions: A Tercentenary Memorial of the King James Version*. New York: New York Bible and Common Prayer Book Society, 1911.

Bobrick, Benson. *Wide as the Waters: The Story of the English Bible and the Revolution It Inspired*. New York: Penguin Books, 2002.

Bridges, Ronald F. and Luther Allan Weigle. *The King James Bible Word Book: A Contemporary Dictionary of Curious and Archaic Words Found in the King James Version of the Bible*. Nashville, TN: Nelson, 1994.

Brown, John. *The History of the English Bible*. Cambridge: Cambridge University Press, 1911.

Bruce, Frederick Fyvie. *The English Bible: A History of Translations from the Earliest English Versions to the New English Bible*. New York: Oxford University Press, 1970.

Burke, David G., ed. *Translation that Openeth the Window: Reflections on the History and Legacy of the King James Bible*. Atlanta, GA: Society of Biblical Literature, 2009.

Butterworth, Charles C. *The Literary Lineage of the King James Bible, 1340–1611*. Philadelphia: University of Pennsylvania Press, 1941.

Carleton, James G. *The Part of the Rheims in the Making of the English Bible*. Oxford: Clarendon Press, 1902.

Chamberlin, William J. *Catalogue of English Bible Translations; A Classified Bibliography of Versions and Editions, Including Books, Parts, and Old and New Testament Apocrypha and Apocryphal Books*. Westport, CT: Greenwood Press, 1991.

Conant, Hannah Chaplin. *The English Bible: History of the Translation of the Holy Scriptures into the English Tongue: With Specimens of the Old English Versions*. New York: Sheldon, Blakeman, 1856. Revised edn. ed. Thomas Jefferson Conant, *The Popular History of the Translation of the Holy Scriptures into the English Tongue*. New York: I. K. Funk, 1881.

Condit, Blackford. *The History of the English Bible: Extending from the Earliest Saxon Translations to the Present Anglo-American Revision*. New York: A. S. Barnes, 1882.

Cook, Albert S. *The Authorized Version and Its Influence*. Folcroft, PA: Folcroft Library Editions, 1976.

Corzine, Phyllis. *The King James Bible: Christianity's Definitive Text*. Lucent Books, 2000.

Cotton, Henry. *A List of Editions of the Bible and Parts Thereof in English, from the Year MDV. to MDCCCXX: with an appendix containing specimens of translations, and bibliographical descriptions*. 2nd edn. enlarged. Oxford: Oxford University Press, 1852.

Coxe, Arthur C. *An Apology for the Common English Bible*. Baltimore: Joseph Robinson, 1857.

Daiches, David. *The King James Version of the English Bible: An Account of the Development and Sources of the English Bible of 1611 with Special Reference to the Hebrew Tradition*. Chicago: University of Chicago Press, 1941. (Reprinted 1968 by Archon Books.)

Daniell, David. *The Bible in English: Its History and Influence*. New Haven, CT: Yale University Press, 2003.

Darlow, Thomas H. and Horace F. Moule. *Historical Catalogue of Printed Editions of Holy Scripture in the Library of the British and Foreign Bible Society*. 2 vols. 1903. New York: Kraus Reprint Corp. 1963. [Supplanted by Herbert edn., 1968.]

De Hamel, Christopher. *The Book: A History of the Bible*. London: Phaidon, 2001.

Dore, John R. *Old Bibles*. 2nd edn. London: Eyre & Spottiswoode, 1888.

Eadie, John. *The English Bible: An External and Critical History of the Various English Translations of Scripture*. London: Macmillan, 1876.

Edgar, Andrew. *The Bibles of England*. London: Alexander Gardner, Paisley and Paternoster Row, 1889.

Elliott, Melvin E. *The Language of the King James Bible: A Glossary Explaining Its Words and Expressions*. Garden City, NY: Doubleday, 1967.

Ferrell, Lori Anne. *The Bible and the People*. New Haven, CT and London: Yale University Press, 2008.

Fox, John. "The Influence of the English Bible on English Literature". *The Princeton Theological Review* 9.3 (1911): 387–401.

Freeman, James M. *A Short History of the English Bible*. New York: Phillips and Hunt, 1879.

Frerichs, Ernest S., ed. *The Bible and Bibles in America*. Atlanta, GA: Georgia Scholars Press, 1988.

Fry, Francis. *A description of the Great Bible, 1539, and the six editions of Cranmer's Bible, 1540 and 1541, printed by Grafton and Whitchurch : also of the editions, in large folio, of the Authorized Version of the Holy Scriptures, printed in the years 1611, 1613, 1617, 1634, 1640*. London: Willis and Sotheran; Bristol: Lasbury, 1865.

Gaebelein, Frank E. *Down Through the Ages: The Story of the King James Bible*. New York: Macmillan, 1924.

Gardiner, John Hays. *The Bible as English Literature*. New York: Charles Scribner, 1906.

Gell, Robert. *An Essay toward the Amendment of the Last English Translation of the Bible*. London: R. Norton for Andrew Crook, 1659.

Goodspeed, Edgar J. *The Making of the English New Testament*. Chicago: University of Chicago Press, 1925.

ed. *Translators to the Reader; Preface to the King James Version, 1611.* Chicago: University of Chicago Press, 1935.

Greenslade, S. L., ed. *The Cambridge History of the Bible,* vol. 3: *The West from the Reformation to the Present Day.* Cambridge: Cambridge University Press, 1963.

Gutjahr, Paul C. *An American Bible: a History of the Good Book in the United States, 1777–1880.* Stanford, CA: Stanford University Press; Cambridge: Cambridge University Press, 1999.

Hamilton-Hoare, Henry William. *The Evolution of the English Bible: A Historical Sketch of the Successive Versions from 1382 to 1885.* London: John Murray, 1901.

Our English Bible: The Story of Its Origin and Growth. Rev. edn. New York: Dutton, 1925.

Hammond, Gerald. *The Making of the English Bible.* Manchester: Carcanet New Press, 1982.

Hatch, Nathan O. and Mark A. Noll, eds. *The Bible in America: Essays in Cultural History.* New York and Oxford: Oxford University Press, 1982.

Herbert, Arthur Sumner. *Historical Catalogue of Printed Editions of the English Bible 1525–1961*; revised and expanded from the edition of T. H. Darlow and H. F. Moule, 1903. New York: The American Bible Society, 1968.

Hills, Margaret Thorndike, ed. *The English Bible in America: A Bibliography of Editions of the Bible and the New Testament Published in America, 1777–1957.* New York: American Bible Society, 1961.

Jasper, David and Stephen Prickett, eds. *The Bible and Literature: A Reader.* Oxford and Malden, MA: Blackwell, 1999.

Johnson, Anthony. *An Historical Account of the Several English Translations of the Bible, and the Opposition They Met with from the Church of Rome.* Printed for C. Rivington, sold by J. Roe in Derby and S. Lobb in Bath, London, 1730.

Kerr, John S. *Ancient Texts Alive Today: The Story of the English Bible.* New York: American Bible Society, 1999.

Kilburne, William. *Dangerous Errors in Several Late Printed Bibles: To the Great Scandal and Corruption of Sound and True Religion, Discovered by Wm. Kilburne.* Finsbury [London], 1659.

Knox, Ronald A. *On Englishing the Bible.* London: Burns & Oates, 1949.

Lampe, G. W., ed. *The Cambridge History of the Bible:* vol. 2, *The West from the Fathers to the Reformation.* Cambridge: Cambridge University Press, 1969.

Lemon, Rebecca, Emma Mason, Jonathan Roberts, and Christopher Rowland, eds. *The Blackwell Companion to the Bible in English Literature.* Chichester and Malden, MA: Wiley-Blackwell, 2009.

Lewis, John. *A Complete History of the Several Translations of the Holy Bible and New Testament into English.* 3rd edn. London: W. Baynes, 1818.

Loftie, William J. *A Century of Bibles*. London, 1872.

Long, Lynne. *Translating the Bible: From the 7th to the 17th Century*. Aldershot: Ashgate, 2001.

Malless, Stanley and Jeffrey McQuain. *Coined By God: Words and Phrases That First Appear in English Translations of the Bible*. New York: W. W. Norton & Co., 2003.

McAfee, Cleland Boyd. *The Greatest English Classic: A Study of the King James Version of the Bible and Its Influence on Life and Literature*. New York: Harper, 1912.

McClure, Alexander. *The Translators Revived*. New York: Charles Scribner, 1853.

McComb, Samuel. *The Making of the English Bible, with an Introductory Essay on the Influence of the English Bible on English Literature*. New York: Moffat, Yard and Company, 1909.

McGrath, Alister. *In the Beginning: The Story of the King James Bible and How It Changed a Nation, a Language and a Culture*. New York: Doubleday, 2000.

Moulton, William F. *The History of the English Bible*. 2nd edn. New York: Cassell Petter & Galpin, 1878.

Nicolson, Adam. *God's Secretaries: The Making of the King James Bible*. New York: HarperCollins, 2003. UK version published as *Power and Glory: Jacobean England and the Making of the King James Bible*.

Norton, David. *A History of the Bible as Literature*. 2 vols. Cambridge: Cambridge University Press, 1993.

  A History of the English Bible as English Literature. Cambridge: Cambridge University Press, 2000.

  A Textual History of the King James Bible. New York: Cambridge University Press, 2005.

O'Callaghan, Edmund B. *A List of Editions of the Holy Scriptures and Parts Thereof Printed in America Previous to 1860*. Detroit: Gale Research Company, 1966 [1861].

Opfell, Olga S. *The King James Bible Translators*. Jefferson, NC: McFarland, 1982.

Orlinsky, Harry M. and Robert G. Bratcher. *A History of Bible Translation and the North American Contribution*. Society of Biblical Literature. Atlanta, GA: Scholars Press, 1991.

Paine, Gustavus S. *The Men Behind the King James Bible*. Grand Rapids, MI: Baker Book House, 1988. Originally published as *The Learned Men* (New York: Thomas Y. Crowell Co., 1959).

Pattison, T. Harwood. *The History of the English Bible*. Philadelphia: American Baptist Publication Society, 1894.

Payne, Julius D. *The English Bible: An Historical Survey*. London: Wells Gardner Darton, 1911.

Pelikan, Jaroslav. *The Reformation of the Bible/The Bible of the Reformation*. New Haven, CT: Yale University Press, 1996.

Pollard, Alfred W. *Records of the English Bible: The Documents Relating to the Translation and Publication of the Bible in English, 1525–1611*. London: Oxford University Press, 1911.

Pope, Hugh. *English Versions of the Bible*. St. Louis: Herder, 1952.

Price, David and Charles C. Ryrie. *Let It Go Among Our People: An Illustrated History of the English Bible from John Wyclif to the King James Version*. Cambridge: Lutterworth Press, 2004.

Price, Ira Maurice. *The Ancestry of Our English Bible: An Account of Manuscripts, Texts, and Versions of the Bible*. Philadelphia: The Sunday School Times Company, 1907.

Rhodes, Erroll F. and Liana Lupas, eds. *The Translators to the Reader: The Original Preface of the King James Version of 1611 Revisited*. New York: American Bible Society, 1997.

Robinson, H. Wheeler. *The Bible in Its Ancient and English Versions*. Oxford: Clarendon Press, 1940. Rpt. with appendix, Oxford: Oxford University Press, 1954.

Rosenau, William. *Hebraisms in the Authorized Version of the Bible*. Baltimore: Lord Baltimore Press, 1902.

Scrivener, F. H. A., ed. *The Cambridge Paragraph Bible of the Authorized English Version, with the text revised by a collation of its early and other principal editions, the use of the italic type made uniform, the marginal references remodelled, and a critical introduction prefixed*. Cambridge: Cambridge University Press, 1873.

  The Authorized Edition of the English Bible (1611). Cambridge: Cambridge University Press, 1884.

Sims, Marion P. *The Bible in America: Versions That Have Played Their Part in the Making of the Republic*. New York: Wilson-Erickson, 1936.

Smith, Walter E. *The Great "She" Bible*. Pensacola, FL: Vance, n.d. (orig. pub. in *The Library* 2 [1890]: 144–52).

Stevens, Henry. *The Bibles in the Caxton Exhibition MDCCCLXXVII, or, A bibliographical description of nearly one thousand representative Bibles in various languages chronologically arranged from the first Bible printed by Gutenberg in 1450–1456 to the last Bible printed at the Oxford University Press the 30th June 1877: with an introduction on the history of printing as illustrated by the printed Bible from 1450 to 1877 in which is told for the first time the true history and mystery of the Coverdale Bible of 1535: together with bibliographical notes and collations of many rare Bibles in various languages and divers versions printed during the last four centuries*.

London: Henry Stevens IV; New York: Scribner Welford & Armstrong, 1878.

Stoughton, John. *Our English Bible: Its Translations and Translators*. London: Religious Tract Society, 1878.

300 Years of Printing the Authorized Version of the Holy Bible at Cambridge 1629–1929. Cambridge: Cambridge University Press, 1929.

Weigle, Luther A. *The English New Testament from Tyndale to the Revised Standard Version*. New York: Abingdon-Cokesbury, 1949.

Westcott, Brooke F. *A General View of the History of the English Bible*. London: Macmillan, 1868. 3rd edn. revised by William Aldis Wright, 1905.

Whitley, William Thomas. *The English Bible Under the Tudor Sovereigns*. London: Marshall Morgan & Scott, 1937.

Wild, Laura H. *The Romance of the English Bible: A History of the Translation of the Bible into English from Wyclif to the Present Day*. Garden City, NY: Doubleday Doran, 1929.

Willoughby, Edwin E. *The Making of the King James Bible: A Monograph with Comparisons from the Bishops Bible and the Manuscript Annotations of 1602, with an Original Leaf from the Great "She" Bible of 1611*. Los Angeles: The Plantin Press, 1964

Wilson, Derek A. *The People and the Book: The Revolutionary Impact of the English Bible, 1380–1611*. London: Barrie and Jenkins, 1976.

Wilson, Lea. *Bibles, Testaments, Psalms and other Books of the Holy Scriptures in English, in the Collection of Lea Wilson*. London, 1845.

Wimbush, Vincent L., ed. *African Americans and the Bible: Sacred Texts and Social Textures*. New York: Continuum, 2000.

The Bible and African Americans: A Brief History. Minneapolis: Fortress Press, 2003.

II The literary–cultural influence of the King James Bible

Alter, Robert. *Canon and Creativity: Modern Writing and the Authority of Scripture*. New Haven, CT and London: Yale University Press, 2000.

Pen of Iron: American Prose and the King James Bible. Princeton: Princeton University Press, 2010.

apRoberts, Ruth. *The Biblical Web*. Ann Arbor: University of Michigan Press, 1994.

Balsamo, Gian. *Scriptural Poetics in Joyce's* Finnegan's Wake. Lewiston, NY: Edwin Mellen Press, 2002.

Bartell, Roland, with James S. Ackerman and Thayer S. Warshaw. *Biblical Images in Literature*. Nashville, TN: Abingdon Press, 1975.

Bassard, Katherine Clay. *Transforming Scriptures: African American Women Writers and the Bible*. Athens, GA: University of Georgia Press, 2010.

Bauman, Michael. *A Scripture Index to John Milton's* De doctrina Christiana. Binghamton, NY: Medieval & Renaissance Texts & Studies, 1989.

Bennett, Fordyce R. *A Reference Guide to the Bible in Emily Dickinson's Poetry.* Lanham, MD: Scarecrow Press, 1997.

Berkner, Will. *The Great Mural: The World of Biblical Novels.* Lima, OH: Fairway Press, 1994.

Bevan, David, ed. *Literature and the Bible.* Amsterdam and Atlanta, GA: Rodopi, 1993.

Bloch, Chana. *Spelling the Word: George Herbert and the Bible.* Berkeley: University of California Press, 1985.

Blumenthal, Friedrich von. *Lord Byron's Mystery "Cain" and its Relation to Milton's* Paradise Lost *and Gessner's* Death of Abel. Philadelphia: R. West, 1976.

Boer, Roland. *Last Stop Before Antarctica: The Bible and Postcolonialism in Australia.* 2nd edn. Leiden and Boston, MA: Brill, 2008.

Boitani, Piero. *The Bible and Its Rewritings.* Oxford and New York: Oxford University Press, 1999.

Bradford, Ernest M. "Biblical Metaphors of Bondage and Liberation in Black Writing: A Study of the Evolution of Black Liberation as Mediated in Writing Based on the Bible." Ph. D. diss., University of Nebraska at Lincoln, 1976.

Brown, Amy Benson. *Rewriting the Word: American Women Writers and the Bible.* Westport, CT: Greenwood Press, 1999.

Buell, Lawrence. "Literature and Scripture in New England Between the Revolution and the Civil War." *Notre Dame English Journal* 15.2 (1983): 1–29.

Burrell, Harry. *Narrative Design in* Finnegan's Wake: *The Wake Lock Picked.* Gainesville: University Press of Florida, 1996.

Callahan, Allen Dwight. *The Talking Book: African Americans and the Bible.* New Haven, CT and London: Yale University Press, 2006.

Caron, Timothy Paul. *Struggles Over the Word: Race and Religion in O'Connor, Faulkner, Hurston, and Wright.* Macon, GA: Mercer University Press, 2000.

Chevalier, Jacques M. *Semiotics, Romanticism, and the Scriptures.* Berlin and New York: Mouton de Gruyter, 1990.

Clark, Ira. *Christ Revealed: The History of the Neotypological Lyric in the English Renaissance.* Gainesville: University Presses of Florida, 1982.

Coffee, Jessie McGuire. *Faulkner's Un-Christlike Christians: Biblical Allusions in the Novels.* Ann Arbor, MI: UMI Research Press, 1983.

Coleman, Edward Davidson. *The Bible in English Drama: An Annotated List of Plays Including Translations from Other Languages.* New York: The New York Public Library, 1931.

Cook, Eleanor. "Wallace Stevens and the King James Bible." *Essays in Criticism* 41.3 (1991): 240–52.

Crook, Margaret Brackenbury, ed. *The Bible and Its Literary Associations*. New York, Cincinnati: Abingdon Press, 1937.

Daw, Charles P. "Swift's Favorite Books of the Bible." *The Huntington Library Quarterly* 43.3 (1980): 201–12.

Deena, Frank H. and Karoline Szatek, eds. *From Around the Globe: Secular Authors and Biblical Perspectives*. Lanham, MD: University Press of America, 2007.

Downey, Katherine Brown. *Perverse Midrash: Oscar Wilde, André Gide, and the Censorship of Biblical Drama*. New York: Continuum, 2004.

Erdman, David V., ed. *Blake and His Bibles*. West Cornwall, CT: Locust Hill Press, 1990.

Evans, J. Martin. Paradise Lost *and the Genesis Tradition*. Oxford: Clarendon Press, 1968.

Exum, J. Cheryl, ed. *The Bible in Film – The Bible and Film*. Leiden and Boston, MA: Brill, 2006.

   Retellings: The Bible in Literature, Music, Art and Film. Leiden and Boston, MA: Brill, 2007.

Fairman, Marion. *Biblical Patterns in Modern Literature*. Cleveland, OH: Dillon/ Liederbach, 1972.

Finley, C. Stephen. *Nature's Covenant: Figures of Landscape in Ruskin*. University Park: Pennsylvania State University Press, 1992.

Fisch, Harold. *The Biblical Presence in Shakespeare, Milton, and Blake: A Comparative Study*. Oxford: Clarendon Press; New York: Oxford University Press, 1999.

   Jerusalem and Albion: The Hebraic Factor in Seventeenth-Century Literature. New York: Schocken Books, 1964.

   New Stories for Old: Biblical Patterns in the Novel. Basingstoke: Macmillan Press; New York: St. Martin's Press, 1998.

Fletcher, Harris Francis. *The Use of the Bible in Milton's Prose, with an Index of the Biblical Quotations and Citations Arranged in the Chronological Order of the Prose Works; Another Index of All Quotations and Citations in the Order of the Books of the Bible; and an Index of the Quotations and Citations in the De Doctrina*. New York: Haskell House, 1970.

Flinker, Noam. *The Song of Songs in English Renaissance Literature: Kisses of their Mouths*. Cambridge, UK and Rochester, NY: D. S. Brewer, 2000.

Frontain, Raymond-Jean, ed. *Reclaiming the Sacred: The Bible in Gay and Lesbian Literature*. New York: Harrington Park Press, 2003.

Frontain, Raymond-Jean and Jan Wojcik, eds. *Old Testament Women in Western Literature*. Conway, AR: UCA Press, 1991.

Froula, Christine. "Rewriting Genesis: Gender and Culture in Twentieth-Century Texts." *Tulsa Studies in Women's Literature* 7.2 (1988): 197–220.

Fulghum, Walter B. *A Dictionary of Biblical Allusions in English Literature.* New York: Holt, Rinehart and Winston, 1965.

Gay, David. *The Endless Kingdom: Milton's Scriptural Society.* Newark, NJ: University of Delaware Press; London, Cranbury, NJ: Associated University Presses, 2002.

Gibbs, Mary and Ellen Gibbs. *The Bible References in John Ruskin.* New York: Oxford University Press, 1898.

Gilmour, Michael J. *Tangled Up in the Bible: Bob Dylan & Scripture.* New York: Continuum, 2004.

Glover, Willis B. *Biblical Origins of Modern Secular Culture: An Essay in the Interpretation of Western History.* Macon, GA: Mercer, 1984.

Goldsmith, Steven. *Unbuilding Jerusalem: Apocalypse and Romantic Representation.* Ithaca, NY: Cornell University Press, 1993.

Gunn, Giles, ed. *The Bible and American Arts and Letters.* Philadelphia: Fortress Press; Chico, CA: Scholars Press, 1983.

Haskin, Dayton. *Milton's Burden of Interpretation.* Philadelphia: University of Pennsylvania Press, 1994.

Henderson, Heather. *The Victorian Self: Autobiography and Biblical Narrative.* Ithaca, NY: Cornell University Press, 1989.

Hirsch, David H. and Nehama Aschkenasy, eds. *Biblical Patterns in Modern Literature.* Chico, CA: Scholars Press, 1984.

Hirst, Wolf Z. *Byron, the Bible, and Religion: Essays from the Twelfth International Byron Seminar.* Newark, NJ: University of Delaware Press; London and Cranbury, NJ: Associated University Presses, 1991.

Hyde, Virginia. *The Risen Adam: D. H. Lawrence's Revisionist Typology.* University Park: Pennsylvania State University Press, 1992.

Jasper, David. *Readings in the Canon of Scripture: Written for Our Learning.* New York: St. Martin's Press, 1995.

The Sacred and Secular Canon in Romanticism: Preserving the Sacred Truths. New York: St. Martin's Press, 1999.

Jasper, David and Stephen Prickett, eds. *The Bible and Literature: A Reader.* Oxford and Malden, MA: Blackwell, 1999.

Jeffrey, David Lyle. *A Dictionary of Biblical Tradition in English Literature.* Grand Rapids, MI: Eerdmans, 1992.

Jiménez, Nilda. *The Bible and the Poetry of Christina Rossetti: A Concordance.* Westport, CT: Greenwood Press, 1979.

Joseph, Oscar Loos. *The Influence of the English Bible upon the English Language and upon English and American Literature.* 1935. Reprint, Folcroft, PA: Folcroft Library Editions, 1976.

Katz, David S. *God's Last Words: Reading the English Bible from the Reformation to Fundamentalism*. New Haven, CT and London: Yale University Press, 2004.

Kelley, Mark R. and Joseph Wittreich, eds. *Altering Eyes: New Perspectives on Samson Agonistes*. Newark, NJ: University of Delaware Press; London and Cranbury, NJ: Associated University Presses, 2002.

King, Jeannette. *Women and the Word: Contemporary Women Novelists and the Bible*. New York: St. Martin's Press, 2000.

Knight, Mark, ed. *Biblical Religion and the Novel, 1700–2000*. Aldershot and Burlington, VT: Ashgate, 2006.

Kreitzer, Larry J. *Biblical Images in Fiction and Film: On Reversing the Hermeneutic Flow*. Sheffield: Sheffield Academic, 1999.

Kurth, Burton O. *Milton and Christian Heroism: Biblical Epic Themes and Forms in Seventeenth-Century England*. Berkeley: University of California Press, 1959.

Larson, Janet L. *Dickens and the Broken Scripture*. Athens: University of Georgia Press, 1985.

Law-Viljoen, Bronwyn. "Midrash, Myth, and Prophecy: George Eliot's Reinterpretation of Biblical Stories." *Literature & Theology* 11.1 (1997): 80–92.

Lemon, Rebecca, Emma Mason, Jonathan Roberts, and Christopher Rowland, eds. *The Blackwell Companion to the Bible in English Literature*. Chichester and Malden, MA: Wiley-Blackwell, 2009.

Lester, George. *Lord Tennyson and the Bible*. London: Howe, [189?].

Lewis, C. S. "The Literary Impact of the Authorized Version," in *They Asked for a Paper: Papers and Addresses*. London: Geoffrey Bles, 1962. 26–50.

Lim, Walter S. H. *John Milton, Radical Politics, and Biblical Republicanism*. Newark, NJ: University of Delaware Press, 2006.

Long, Larry R. "The Bible and the Composition of *Walden*." *Studies in the American Renaissance* (1979): 309–53.

Looper, Travis. *Byron and the Bible: A Compendium of Biblical Usage in the Poetry of Lord Byron*. Metuchen, NJ: Scarecrow Press, 1978.

Machen, Minnie Gresham. *The Bible in Browning, with Particular Reference to The Ring and the Book*. New York: Macmillan, 1903.

Morrissey, L. J. *Gulliver's Progress*. Hamden, CT: Archon Books, 1978.

Moseley, Virginia Douglas. *Joyce and the Bible*. De Kalb: Northern Illinois University Press, 1967.

Mueller, William Randolph. *The Prophetic Voice in Modern Fiction*. New York: Association Press, 1959.

Nagashima, Daisuke. "The Biblical Quotations in Johnson's Dictionary." *The Age of Johnson* 10 (1999): 89–126.

Nelson, Laurence E. *Our Roving Bible: Tracking its Influence through English and American Life*. New York: Abingdon Press, 1945.

Oberhaus, Dorothy Huff. *Emily Dickinson's Fascicles: Method and Meaning*. University Park: Pennsylvania State University Press, 1995.

O'Neale, Sondra A. *Jupiter Hammon and the Biblical Beginnings of African-American Literature*. Metuchen, NJ: Scarecrow Press; [Philadelphia]: American Theological Library Association, 1993.

Osborn, Eric and Lawrence McIntosh, eds. *The Bible and European Literature: History and Hermeneutics: Proceedings of a Conference Held at Queen's College, University of Melbourne*. Melbourne: Academia Press, 1987.

Ostriker, Alicia S. *Feminist Revision and the Bible*. Oxford and Cambridge, MA: Blackwell Publishers, 1993.

Pardes, Ilana. *Melville's Bibles*. Berkeley: University of California Press, 2008.

Parkin, Rebecca Price. "Some Rhetorical Aspects of Dryden's Biblical Allusions." *Eighteenth-Century Studies* 2.4 (1969): 341–69.

Phy, Allene Stuart, ed. *The Bible and Popular Culture in America*. Philadelphia: Fortress Press; Chico, CA: Scholars Press, 1985.

Piper, Herbert W. *The Singing of Mount Abora: Coleridge's Use of Biblical Imagery and Natural Symbolism in Poetry and Philosophy*. Rutherford, NJ: Fairleigh Dickinson University Press, 1987.

Price, Victoria H. *Christian Allusions in the Novels of Thomas Pynchon*. New York: P. Lang, 1989.

Prickett, Stephen. *Origins of Narrative: Romantic Appropriations of the Bible*. Cambridge: Cambridge University Press, 1996.

Prochaska, Bernadette. *The Myth of the Fall and Walker Percy's Last Gentleman*. New York: P. Lang, 1992.

Purdy, Dwight H. *Biblical Echo and Allusion in the Poetry of W. B. Yeats: Poetics and the Art of God*. Lewisburg: Bucknell University Press; London and Cranbury, NJ: Associated University Presses, 1994.

Joseph Conrad's Bible. Norman: University of Oklahoma Press, 1984.

Radzinowicz, Mary Ann. *Milton's Epics and the Book of Psalms*. Princeton: Princeton University Press, 1989.

Reichert, John. *Milton's Wisdom: Nature and Scripture in Paradise Lost*. Ann Arbor: University of Michigan Press, 1992.

Robinson, Edna Moore. *Tennyson's Use of the Bible*. Göttingen: Vandenhoeck & Ruprecht; Baltimore: The Johns Hopkins Press, 1917.

Rogal, Samuel J. *An Index to the Biblical References, Parallels, and Allusions in the Poetry and Prose of John Milton*. Lewiston, NY: Mellen Biblical Press, 1994.

Rosenblatt, Jason P. *Torah and Law in* Paradise Lost. Princeton: Princeton University Press, 1994.

Roston, Murray. *Biblical Drama in England: From the Middle Ages to the Present Day*. Evanston, IL: Northwestern University Press, 1968.

Prophet and Poet: The Bible and the Growth of Romanticism. Evanston, IL: Northwestern University Press, 1965.

Rowland, Christopher. *"Wheels within Wheels": William Blake and the Ezekial's Merkabah in Text and Image*. Milwaukee: Marquette University Press, 2007.

Schneidau, Herbert N. *Sacred Discontent: The Bible and Western Tradition*. Berkeley: University of California Press, 1976.

Schwartz, Regina M. *Remembering and Repeating: Biblical Creation in* Paradise Lost. Cambridge and New York: Cambridge University Press, 1988.

Shelley, Bryan. *Shelley and Scripture: The Interpreting Angel*. Oxford: Clarendon Press; Oxford and New York: Oxford University Press, 1994.

Shepherd, David, ed. *Images of the Word: Hollywood's Bible and Beyond*. Leiden and Boston, MA: Brill, 2008.

Sims, James H. *The Bible in Milton's Epics*. Gainesville: University of Florida Press, 1962.

Sims, James H. and Leland Ryken, eds. *Milton and Scriptural Tradition: The Bible into Poetry*. Columbia: University of Missouri Press, 1984.

Smith, Theophus H. *Conjuring Culture: Biblical Formations of Black America*. New York: Oxford University Press, 1994.

Stave, Shirley A., ed. *Toni Morrison and the Bible: Contested Intertextualities*. New York: P. Lang, 2006.

Steadman, John M. *Milton's Biblical and Classical Imagery*. Pittsburgh: Duquesne University Press, 1984.

Stevens, James Stacy. *Whittier's Use of the Bible*. Orono, ME: University Press, 1930.

Sugirtharajah, R. S. *The Bible and Empire: Postcolonial Explorations*. Cambridge and New York: Cambridge University Press, 2005.

The Bible and the Third World: Precolonial, Colonial, and Postcolonial Encounters. Cambridge and New York: Cambridge University Press, 2001.

Troublesome Texts: the Bible in Colonial and Contemporary Culture. Sheffield: Sheffield Phoenix Press, 2008.

Tannenbaum, Leslie. *Biblical Tradition in Blake's Early Prophecies: The Great Code of Art*. Princeton: Princeton University Press, 1982.

Tate, William Carroll. *Solomonic Iconography in Early Stuart England: Solomon's Wisdom, Solomon's Folly*. Lewiston, NY: Edwin Mellen Press, 2001.

Tichy, Henrietta J. *Biblical Influences in English Literature: A Survey of Studies*. Ann Arbor, MI: Edwards Bros., 1953.

Tkacz, Catherine Brown. "The Bible in *Jane Eyre*." *Christianity and Literature* 44.1 (1994): 3–27.

Turner, James Grantham. *One Flesh: Paradisal Marriage and Sexual Relations in the Age of Milton*. Oxford: Clarendon Press; Oxford and New York: Oxford University Press, 1987.

Valkeakari, Tuire. *Religious Idiom and the African American Novel, 1952–1998*. Gainesville: University Press of Florida, 2007.

Walker, Jeanne Murray. "'Jubilate Agno' as Psalm." *Studies in English Literature* 20.3 (1980): 449–59.

Weaver, Bennett. *Toward the Understanding of Shelley*. Ann Arbor: University of Michigan Press, 1932.

Werman, Golda. *Milton and Midrash*. Washington, DC: Catholic University of America Press, 1995.

West, Philip G. *Henry Vaughan's Silex Scintillans: Scripture Uses*. Oxford and New York: Oxford University Press, 2001.

Westbrook, Deeanne. *Wordsworth's Biblical Ghosts*. New York: Palgrave, 2001.

Wheeler, Michael. *The Art of Allusion in Victorian Fiction*. London: Methuen, 1979.

Wimbush, Vincent L., ed. *The Bible and the American Myth: A Symposium on the Bible and Constructions of Meaning*. Macon, GA: Mercer University Press, 1999.

ed. *Theorizing Scriptures: New Critical Orientations to a Cultural Phenomenon*. New Brunswick, NJ: Rutgers University Press, 2008.

Wittreich, Joseph. *Shifting Contexts: Reinterpreting Samson Agonistes*. Pittsburgh: Duquesne University Press, 2002.

Wright, Terence R. *D.H. Lawrence and the Bible*. Cambridge and New York: Cambridge University Press, 2000.

Zemka, Sue. *Victorian Testaments: The Bible, Christology, and Literary Authority in Early-Nineteenth-Century British Culture*. Stanford, CA: Stanford University Press, 1997.

Zink, Harriet Rodgers. *Emerson's Use of the Bible*. Folcroft, PA: Folcroft Library Editions, 1977.

Zwicker, Stephen N. *Dryden's Political Poetry: The Typology of King and Nation*. Providence, RI: Brown University Press, 1972.

Index of Bible quotations

General index